The Princeton Review®

AP® HUMAN GEOGRAPHY
PREMIUM PREP

2023 Edition

The Staff of The Princeton Review

PrincetonReview.com

Penguin Random House

The Princeton Review
110 East 42nd St, 7th Floor
New York, NY 10017

Copyright © 2022 by TPR Education IP Holdings, LLC. All rights reserved.

Published in the United States by Penguin Random House, LLC, New York.

Terms of Service: The Princeton Review Online Companion Tools ("Student Tools") for retail books are available for only the two most recent editions of that book. Student Tools may be activated only once per eligible book purchased for a total of 24 months of access. Activation of Student Tools more than once per book is in direct violation of these Terms of Service and may result in discontinuation of access to Student Tools Services.

ISBN: 978-0-593-45081-9
eBook ISBN: 978-0-593-45125-0
ISSN: 2690-5531

AP is a trademark registered and owned by the College Board, which is not affiliated with, and does not endorse, this product.

The Princeton Review is not affiliated with Princeton University.

The material in this book is up-to-date at the time of publication. However, changes may have been instituted by the testing body in the test after this book was published.

If there are any important late-breaking developments, changes, or corrections to the materials in this book, we will post that information online in the Student Tools. Register your book and check your Student Tools to see if there are any updates posted there.

Editor: Meave Shelton
Production Artist: Jason Ullmeyer
Production Editor: Sarah Litt and Nina Mozes
Content Contributor: Jason Morgan

Printed in the United States of America.

10 9 8 7 6 5 4 3 2 1

2023 Edition

The Princeton Review Publishing Team
Rob Franek, Editor-in-Chief
David Soto, Senior Director, Data Operations
Stephen Koch, Senior Manager, Data Operations
Deborah Weber, Director of Production
Jason Ullmeyer, Production Design Manager
Jennifer Chapman, Senior Production Artist
Selena Coppock, Director of Editorial
Aaron Riccio, Senior Editor
Meave Shelton, Senior Editor
Chris Chimera, Editor
Orion McBean, Editor
Patricia Murphy, Editor
Laura Rose, Editor
Alexa Schmitt Bugler, Editorial Assistant

Penguin Random House Publishing Team
Tom Russell, VP, Publisher
Alison Stoltzfus, Senior Director, Publishing
Brett Wright, Senior Editor
Emily Hoffman, Assistant Managing Editor
Ellen Reed, Production Manager
Suzanne Lee, Designer
Eugenia Lo, Publishing Assistant

For customer service, please contact **editorialsupport@review.com**, and be sure to include:

- full title of the book

- ISBN

- page number

Acknowledgments

The Princeton Review would like to thank Jason Morgan for his valuable contributions to the 2023 edition of this book.

We are also very grateful to Jason Ullmeyer, Sarah Litt, and Nina Mozes for their time and attention to each page.

Contents

Get More (Free) Content
at PrincetonReview.com/prep

As easy as 1·2·3

1 Go to PrincetonReview.com/prep or scan the **QR code** and enter the following ISBN for your book: **9780593450819**

2 Answer a few simple questions to set up an exclusive Princeton Review account. *(If you already have one, you can just log in.)*

3 Enjoy access to your **FREE** content!

Once you've registered, you can...

- Get our take on any recent or pending updates to the AP Human Geography Exam

- Access your 4th, 5th, and 6th AP Human Geography practice tests (there are 3 right here in your book and 3 online), plus answer keys and complete answers and explanations

- Take a full-length practice SAT and ACT

- Get valuable advice about the college application process, including tips for writing a great essay and where to apply for financial aid

- If you're still choosing between colleges, use our searchable rankings of *The Best 388 Colleges* to find out more information about your dream school

- Access comprehensive study guides and a variety of printable resources, including content supplements and bubble sheets for the practice tests in the book

- Check to see if there have been any corrections or updates to this edition

Need to report a potential **content** issue?

Contact **EditorialSupport@review.com** and include:
- full title of the book
- ISBN
- page number

Need to report a **technical** issue?

Contact **TPRStudentTech@review.com** and provide:
- your full name
- email address used to register the book
- full book title and ISBN
- Operating system (Mac/PC) and browser (Chrome, Firefox, Safari, etc.)

Look For These Icons Throughout The Book

 ONLINE ARTICLES

 ONLINE PRACTICE TESTS

 PROVEN TECHNIQUES

 APPLIED STRATEGIES

 OTHER REFERENCES

 STUDY BREAK

 ONLINE VIDEO TUTORIAL

Part I
Using This Book to Improve Your AP Score

- Preview: Your Knowledge, Your Expectations
- Your Guide to Using This Book
- How to Begin

PREVIEW: YOUR KNOWLEDGE, YOUR EXPECTATIONS

Your route to a high score on the AP Human Geography Exam depends a lot on how you plan to use this book. Respond to the following questions.

1. Rate your level of confidence about your knowledge of the content tested by the AP Human Geography Exam:
    A. Very confident—I know it all
    B. I'm pretty confident, but there are topics for which I could use help
    C. Not confident—I need quite a bit of support
    D. I'm not sure

2. If you have a goal score in mind, circle your goal score for the AP Human Geography Exam:

    5   4   3   2   1   I'm not sure yet

3. What do you expect to learn from this book? Circle all that apply to you.
    A. A general overview of the test and what to expect
    B. Strategies for how to approach the test
    C. The content tested by this exam
    D. I'm not sure yet

YOUR GUIDE TO USING THIS BOOK

This book is organized to provide as much—or as little—support as you need, so you can use this book in whatever way will be most helpful to improving your score on the AP Human Geography Exam.

- The remainder of **Part I** will provide guidance on how to use this book and help you determine your strengths and weaknesses.

- **Part II** of this book contains Practice Test 1 and its Diagnostic Answer Key, answers and explanations, and scoring guide. (Bubble sheets can be found in the very back of the book for easy tear-out.) We strongly recommend that you take this test before going any further, in order to realistically determine:
    o your starting point right now
    o which question types you're ready for and which you might need to practice
    o which content topics you are familiar with and which you will want to carefully review

Once you have nailed down your strengths and weaknesses with regard to this exam, you can focus your test preparation, build a study plan, and be efficient with your time. Our Diagnostic Answer Key will assist you with this process.

- **Part III** of this book will:
  - ○ provide information about the structure, scoring, and content of the AP Human Geography Exam
  - ○ help you to make a study plan
  - ○ point you toward additional resources

- **Part IV** of this book will explore various strategies, such as:
  - ○ how to attack multiple-choice questions
  - ○ how to write high-scoring free-response answers
  - ○ how to manage your time to maximize the number of points available to you

- **Part V** of this book covers the content you need for the AP Human Geography Exam.

- **Part VI** of this book contains Practice Tests 2 and 3, along with their answers and explanations. (Bubble sheets can be found in the very back of the book for easy tear-out.) If you skipped Practice Test 1, we recommend that you take both Practice Tests 1 and 2 (with at least a day or two between them) so that you can compare your progress between the two. Additionally, this will help to identify any external issues. If you get a certain type of question wrong both times, you probably need to review it. If you get it wrong only once, you may have run out of time or been distracted by something. In either case, this will allow you to focus on the factors that caused the discrepancy in scores and to be as prepared as possible on the day of the test.

You may choose to use some parts of this book over others, or you may work through the entire book. This will depend on your needs and how much time you have. Let's now look at how to make this determination.

Don't Forget Practice Tests A, B, and C Online!
Access your three free Premium practice tests by registering your book online at PrincetonReview.com/prep. These tests are available as PDFs for you to download and print. See pages vi–vii for details.

HOW TO BEGIN

1. Take a Test

Before you can decide how to use this book, you need to take a practice test. Doing so will give you insight into your strengths and weaknesses, and the test will also help you make an effective study plan. If you're feeling test-phobic, remind yourself that a practice test is a tool for diagnosing yourself—it's not how well you do that matters but how you use information gleaned from your performance to guide your preparation.

So, before you read further, take **Practice Test 1** starting at page 9 of this book. Be sure to do so in one sitting, following the instructions that appear before the test.

2. **Check Your Answers**

    Using the Diagnostic Answer Key on page 30, follow our three-step process to identify your strengths and weaknesses with regard to the tested topics. This will help you determine which content review chapters to prioritize when studying this book. Don't worry about the explanations for now, and don't worry about why you missed questions. We'll get to that soon.

3. **Reflect on the Test**

    After you take your first test, respond to the following questions:

    *   How much time did you spend on the multiple-choice questions?

    *   How much time did you spend on each free-response question?

    *   How many multiple-choice questions did you miss?

    *   Do you feel you had the knowledge to address the subject matter of the free-response questions?

    *   Do you feel you wrote well-organized, thoughtful free responses?

4. **Read Part III of this Book and Complete the Self-Evaluation**

    As noted in the Guide section beginning on page 2, Part III will provide information on how the test is structured and scored. It will also explain the areas of content that are tested.

    As you read Part III, re-evaluate your answers to the questions above. At the end of Part III, you will revisit and refine the questions you answered above. You will then be able to make a study plan, based on your needs and time available, that will allow you to use this book most effectively.

5. **Engage with Parts IV and V as Needed**

    Notice the word *engage*. You'll get more out of this book if you use it intentionally than if you read it passively, hoping for an improved score through osmosis.

    Strategy chapters in Part IV will help you think about your approach to the question types on this exam. This part opens with a reminder to think about how you approach questions now and then closes with a reflection section asking you to think about how/whether you will change your approach in the future.

    Content chapters in Part V are designed to provide a review of the content tested on the AP Human Geography Exam, including the level of detail you need to know and how the content is tested. You can review key terms at the end of each chapter.

6. **Take Practice Tests 2 and 3, and Assess Your Performance**

Once you feel you have developed the strategies you need and gained the knowledge you lacked, you should take Practice Test 2, which starts on page 409 of this book. You should do so in one sitting, following the instructions at the beginning of the test.

When you are done, check your answers to the multiple-choice questions beginning on page 427. See if a teacher will read your free responses and provide feedback.

Once you have taken the test, reflect on what areas you still need to work on, and revisit the chapters in this book that address those deficiencies. Repeat this process with Practice Test 3. Download Practice Tests A, B, and C from your Student Tools, and repeat as needed. Through this type of reflection and engagement, you will continue to improve.

7. **Keep Working**

As discussed in Part III, there are other resources available to you, including a wealth of information at the AP Students website. You can continue to explore areas that can stand improvement and engage in those areas right up to the day of the test.

Bonus Tips and Tricks
Check us out on YouTube for additional test taking tips and must-know strategies at www.youtube.com/ThePrincetonReview

Part II
Practice Test 1

Practice Test 1

AP® Human Geography Exam

SECTION I: Multiple-Choice Questions

DO NOT OPEN THIS BOOKLET UNTIL YOU ARE TOLD TO DO SO.

At a Glance

Total Time
60 minutes
Number of Questions
60
Percent of Total Grade
50%
Writing Instrument
Pencil required

Instructions

Section I of this exam contains 60 multiple-choice questions. Fill in only the ovals for numbers 1 through 60 on your answer sheet.

Indicate all of your answers to the multiple-choice questions on the answer sheet. No credit will be given for anything written in this exam booklet, but you may use the booklet for notes or scratch work. After you have decided which of the suggested answers is best, completely fill in the corresponding oval on the answer sheet. Give only one answer to each question. If you change an answer, be sure that the previous mark is erased completely. Here is a sample question and answer.

Sample Questions

Sample Answers

The first president of the United States was
(A) Millard Fillmore
(B) George Washington
(C) Benjamin Franklin
(D) Andrew Jackson
(E) Harry Truman

Use your time effectively, working as quickly as you can without losing accuracy. Do not spend too much time on any one question. Go on to other questions and come back to the ones you have not answered if you have time. It is not expected that everyone will know the answers to all the multiple-choice questions.

About Guessing

Many candidates wonder whether or not to guess the answers to questions about which they are not certain. Multiple-choice scores are based on the number of questions answered correctly. Points are not deducted for incorrect answers, and no points are awarded for unanswered questions. Because points are not deducted for incorrect answers, you are encouraged to answer all multiple-choice questions. On any questions you do not know the answer to, you should eliminate as many choices as you can, and then select the best answer among the remaining choices.

GO ON TO THE NEXT PAGE.

This page intentionally left blank.

HUMAN GEOGRAPHY
SECTION I
Time—60 minutes
60 Questions

Directions: Each of the questions or incomplete statements below is followed by five suggested answers or completions. Select the one that best answers the question or completes the statement.

1. The reasons for massive influx of foreign manufacturing to China in the 1990s and 2000s include all of the following EXCEPT

    (A) low-cost Chinese labor
    (B) internal Chinese political reforms
    (C) establishment of SEZs (special economic zones) in Chinese coastal cities
    (D) more efficient shipping of goods back from China
    (E) competition from domestic Chinese companies

2. The quaternary sector of the economy includes

    (A) copper mining
    (B) guitar manufacturing
    (C) chemical waste disposal
    (D) financial analysis
    (E) tour guide

3. As a percentage of total national power, alternative forms of energy are being used with the most success in which of the following nations?

    (A) Denmark (solar); France (wind); Morocco (nuclear)
    (B) France (solar); Germany (wind); Ecuador (nuclear)
    (C) Germany (solar); Spain (wind); France (nuclear)
    (D) Morocco (solar); Mexico (wind); Denmark (nuclear)
    (E) Mexico (solar); South Korea (wind); Germany (nuclear)

4. Which of the following is NOT a common criticism of Rostow's theory of the stages of growth?

    (A) A traditional society is not necessary for growth.
    (B) The preconditions for takeoff do not need to exist prior to takeoff.
    (C) Not all societies have a comparative advantage in international trade.
    (D) There is considerable overlap between the stages.
    (E) The takeoff implies an end to historical change.

5. A developing country is experiencing a shortage of socks. Instead of purchasing socks that were manufactured in a developed country, this developing country could best help itself accumulate capital by

    (A) using tax breaks to lure foreign manufacturers to open a sock factory within its borders
    (B) building a locally owned factory to manufacture its own socks
    (C) boycotting the purchase of all foreign socks
    (D) lifting requirements that foreign companies deposit all profits from sock manufacturing in local banks of the developing country
    (E) nationalizing all related textile industries and converting them to sock manufacturing

6. Tourism plays the most vital role in the economy of which of the following regions?

    (A) Central Asia
    (B) The Middle East
    (C) Sub-Saharan Africa
    (D) Scandinavia
    (E) The Caribbean

GO ON TO THE NEXT PAGE.

Questions 7–9 refer to the following graphs.

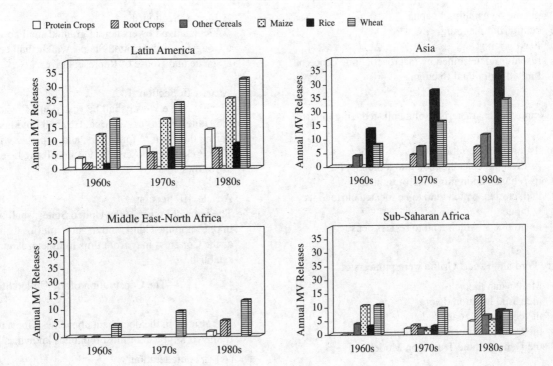

7. The graphs above illustrate the consequences of which of the following events in agricultural history?

   (A) Scientific plant breeding
   (B) The invention of the moldboard plow
   (C) The Industrial Revolution
   (D) The Green Revolution
   (E) The invention of the combine harvester

8. Which of the following statements can be best concluded from the graphs?

   (A) Latin America currently leads Asia in the production of wheat.
   (B) Latin America is the most productive agricultural region in the world.
   (C) Asia consistently produces more wheat than Sub-Saharan Africa.
   (D) Asia saw growth in every type of crop during this time period.
   (E) It is difficult for the geography of the Middle East and northern Africa to support the cultivation of rice.

9. The sharp increase in the rate of wheat production in most parts of the developing world can be attributed primarily to the efforts of which of the following people?

   (A) Norman Borlaug
   (B) Eli Whitney
   (C) Louis Pasteur
   (D) Johann Von Thünen
   (E) Mahatma Gandhi

GO ON TO THE NEXT PAGE.

10. A command economy is marked by all of the following EXCEPT

    (A) private ownership of capital
    (B) centralized planning
    (C) fixed pricing
    (D) resources determined by macroeconomic concerns
    (E) limited individual freedom

11. One important characteristic of a bulk-reducing industry is

    (A) its low transportation costs
    (B) its eventual consolidation into a monopoly
    (C) its reliance upon minerals for inputs
    (D) its factories, which tend to be located close to its inputs
    (E) its products, which tend to be less dense

12. Larry Ford and Ernest Griffin were pioneers of

    (A) Malthusian theory
    (B) industrial location theory
    (C) the concentric zone model
    (D) the Latin American city model
    (E) the Demographic Transition Model

13. The process of adjusting the legislative representation of a county after it loses population is called

    (A) gerrymandering
    (B) devolution
    (C) reapportionment
    (D) splitting
    (E) sovereignty

14. Nazi Germany's claim on Sudetenland of Czechoslovakia is an example of

    (A) diaspora
    (B) deterritorialization
    (C) socialism
    (D) irredentism
    (E) ethnonationalism

Questions 15–16 refer to the document below.

Article. I. Section. 1.
All legislative Powers herein granted shall be vested in a Congress of the United States, which shall consist of a Senate and House of Representatives.

Article. II. Section. 1.
The executive Power shall be vested in a President of the United States of America. He shall hold his Office during the Term of four Years, and, together with the Vice President, chosen for the same Term, be elected, as follows…

Article. III. Section. 1.
The judicial Power of the United States, shall be vested in one supreme Court, and in such inferior Courts as the Congress may from time to time ordain and establish.

—The Constitution of the United States (1787)

15. The articles in the document above describe a political framework typical of most republics known as

    (A) a confederation
    (B) separation of powers
    (C) Bill of Rights
    (D) democracy
    (E) amendments

16. In 2005, a constitution with similar provisions failed to be ratified by which of the following groups?

    (A) The North Atlantic Treaty Organization
    (B) The republic of South Sudan
    (C) The European Union
    (D) Yugoslavia
    (E) The International Monetary Fund

GO ON TO THE NEXT PAGE.

17. To calculate the rate of natural increase (RNI), the difference between what two factors should be divided by ten?

    (A) The obesity rate and the death rate
    (B) The birth rate and the densification rate
    (C) The densification rate and the death rate
    (D) The death rate and the birth rate
    (E) The birth rate and the obesity rate

18. North Carolina's Research Triangle consists of three major scientific research universities and is home to numerous high-tech companies. This region is known as a

    (A) superimposed boundary
    (B) contemporary cultural hearth
    (C) buffer state
    (D) growth pole
    (E) technopole

19. According to the rank-size rule, in a country whose largest city contains 800,000 people, its fourth-largest city contains

    (A) 1,600,000 people
    (B) 800,000 people
    (C) 400,000 people
    (D) 200,000 people
    (E) 100,000 people

20. A negative rate of natural increase can often be seen in societies that

    (A) have banned or greatly restricted immigration
    (B) do not take censuses
    (C) are developing nations and do not recognize modern methods of measurement
    (D) feature an aging population
    (E) have suffered a devastating war

21. All of the following are reasons for American suburbanization in the 1950s EXCEPT

    (A) increased use of freight trains for industrial transportation
    (B) new federal home loan programs
    (C) assembly line method of home construction
    (D) increased family incomes
    (E) an expanding network of roads and freeways

22. An example of a fuzzy cultural border would be

    (A) where Dixie ends and the American Northeast or Midwest begins
    (B) between the epicenter of Jainist belief and the region where African Voodoun is mainstream
    (C) where the Wailing Wall ends and the Temple of Solomon begins
    (D) the transition from modern to contemporary architecture
    (E) between the Kurgan hearth and the Anatolian hearth

GO ON TO THE NEXT PAGE.

Questions 23–24 refer to the following photo.

A woman wearing a *niqāb* in Yemen, 2005

23. The headwear portrayed in the photo is best interpreted as

   (A) an instance of Islamic diffusion
   (B) a key example of mainstream Arabic clothing customs
   (C) an outdated regional clothing preference
   (D) symbolic belief in the innate corruption of humans
   (E) a strict interpretation of cultural rules governing modest dress

24. The prohibition of the *niqāb* by France is an example of

   (A) an instance of cultural superiority
   (B) a denial of cultural diffusion
   (C) the reluctant rejection of globalization
   (D) a shift in cultural hearth
   (E) the role of trade in human migration

25. All of the following are policies or programs that attempt to increase capital accumulation within Third World economies EXCEPT

   (A) internalization of economic capital
   (B) nationalization of natural resource-based industries
   (C) technology development programs
   (D) export substitution
   (E) profit-sharing agreements

26. Which of the following is a monotheistic religion?

   (A) Hinduism
   (B) Islam
   (C) Buddhism
   (D) Voodoo
   (E) Animism

27. A primary problem with a communist system of agriculture, as compared to the capitalist system, is that

   (A) there is no incentive to produce over a quota
   (B) the demand for products is never high enough to generate income
   (C) individuals produce far more product than necessary and demand lowers
   (D) there is a decentralized agricultural network that leads to high transportation costs
   (E) the reward for producing excess crop is limited to the social elite

28. Stage 4 of the Demographic Transition Model is characterized by

   (A) a pre-agricultural economy
   (B) an agricultural economy
   (C) a manufacturing economy
   (D) a service-based economy
   (E) an evolving economy

29. All of the following are considered examples of a life-course change EXCEPT

   (A) going away to college
   (B) accepting a job in a different city
   (C) going on vacation to Florida
   (D) retiring to Arizona
   (E) moving to the suburbs to raise children

30. The language with the greatest number of native speakers in the world is

   (A) Spanish
   (B) English
   (C) Hindi
   (D) Mandarin
   (E) Arabic

GO ON TO THE NEXT PAGE.

Questions 31–32 refer to the following graph.

Average Carbon Emissions by Transport Mode Broken Down by Category
(in gram per PKM)

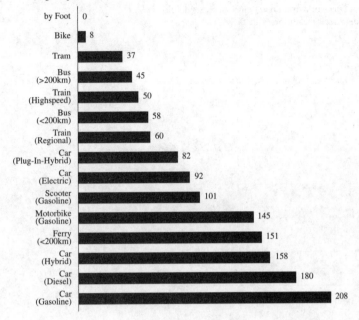

31. It can be most logically concluded from the graph that

    (A) when compared with the amount of emissions from buses and trains, there is no substantial difference between the amount of emissions from hybrid, diesel, or gasoline automobiles

    (B) private, individual forms of transportation emit less than public, shared forms of transportation

    (C) nations with public transportation systems will emit less carbon dioxide than nations without public transportation

    (D) it is always recommended to take a tram over a motorbike

    (E) the operation of all forms of transportation causes emissions

32. An increase in transportation emissions is most closely correlated with

    (A) a decrease in food production

    (B) a decrease in total population

    (C) an increase in population density

    (D) an increase in per capita income

    (E) a decrease in per capita income

33. Which of the following is NOT an example of a universalizing religion?

    (A) Baha'i

    (B) Christianity

    (C) Buddhism

    (D) Islam

    (E) Hinduism

34. There have been three major periods of immigration to the United States: 1840-1850, 1880-1924, and 1965-present. Which of the following, arranged in chronological order, represents the primary immigrant groups of each period?

    (A) Mexicans and Irish; Eastern and Southern Europeans; Jews, Muslims, and Latinos

    (B) English and Irish; Irish and Germans; Eastern Europeans and Mexicans

    (C) Eastern and Southern Europeans; Irish and Germans; Africans and Latinos

    (D) Irish and Germans; Eastern and Southern Europeans; Chinese, Indians, and Mexicans

    (E) French, Dutch, and English; Italians and Scandinavians; Arabs and Chinese

35. The Know-Nothing party is an example of what common political reaction to large-scale immigration?

    (A) A multiethnic state

    (B) Expansion of civil rights

    (C) Nativism

    (D) Conservatism

    (E) Populism

36. Within the Demographic Transition Model, the difference between migration in stage 2 societies and migration in stage 4 societies is that

    (A) stage 2 migrants tend to be male, whereas stage 4 migrants tend to be both male and female

    (B) stage 2 migrants tend to seek political freedom, whereas stage 4 migrants tend to seek education

    (C) stage 2 migrants tend to migrate internationally to developed countries, whereas stage 4 migrants tend to migrate internally

    (D) stage 2 migrants tend to migrate towards rural areas, whereas stage 4 migrants tend to migrate towards urban areas

    (E) stage 2 migrants tend to migrate for economic reasons, whereas stage 4 migrants tend migrate for religious reasons

37. The North and South Poles are

    (A) 0° latitude

    (B) 0° longitude

    (C) 90° latitude

    (D) 90° longitude

    (E) 180° longitude

GO ON TO THE NEXT PAGE.

Questions 38–40 refer to the following graph.

Numbers of autocracies and democracies

Shown is the number of a given political regime of the world over time. Democracies are defined as the combination of both liberal and elected democracies; autocracies are the sum of closed and elected autocracies.

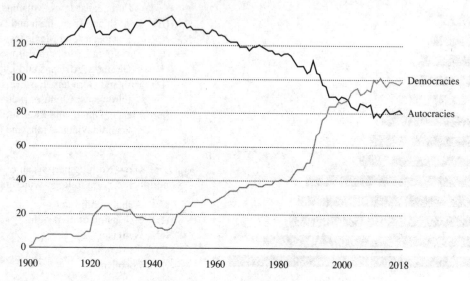

38. The trend depicted in the graph has been challenged in recent years by

    (A) the Arab Spring
    (B) the global takeover of reactionary politics
    (C) a sudden uptick in the number of countries embracing autocracy
    (D) a series of democratic revolutions
    (E) the spread of globalized culture

39. Which of the following has NOT been suggested as a cause of the rise of democracy in the twentieth and twenty-first centuries?

    (A) Economic development
    (B) Industrialization
    (C) Globalization
    (D) Wealth from petroleum
    (E) Mixed geographic constituencies

40. The Arab Spring of 2011

    (A) undermines the depicted trend, because it roughly suppressed democratic uprisings
    (B) supports the depicted trend, because it represented the outbreak of the demand for democratic rights in an autocratic region
    (C) neither challenges nor supports the depicted trend, because it was unrelated to politics
    (D) continues to be felt in religious communities around the world
    (E) changed the direction of the depicted trend

GO ON TO THE NEXT PAGE.

41. The workers who survived the Black Plague, which killed nearly a third of the European population, ironically saw their wages rise in later years. This phenomenon is best explained by

    (A) natural resource depletion
    (B) national choice theory
    (C) Marx's theory of surplus value
    (D) Keynesian economics
    (E) the iron law of wages

42. When the largest city in a country has at least twice the population of the country's next largest city, it can be designated as a(n)

    (A) megacity
    (B) world city
    (C) megalopolis
    (D) entrepôt
    (E) primate city

43. Which of the following best illustrates the difference between pop culture and folk culture?

    (A) High-rise polyester blend jeans and Levi's 501 original denim jeans
    (B) A 2003 Coldplay pop song and a 1903 Scott Joplin ragtime song
    (C) The *Harry Potter* series and *Beowulf*
    (D) Roy Lichtenstein and Leonardo da Vinci
    (E) Daft Punk and Bob Dylan

44. The United Nations developed a metric by which the health of a nation can be judged. It measures standard of living, longevity, and access to education. The name of this metric is

    (A) the Global Peace Index
    (B) the Human Development Index
    (C) the Genuine Progress Indicator
    (D) the Social Progress Index
    (E) the Gross National Happiness Index

45. Geographers define *place* as

    (A) the geometric surface of the earth
    (B) an area wherein activity occurs on a daily basis
    (C) the relationship between an object to the earth as a whole
    (D) an area of bounded space of some human importance
    (E) the ratio of distance on a map to distance in the real world

46. Compared with the Indo-Iranian language family branch, the Romance language family branch is

    (A) more complicated
    (B) older
    (C) less numerous
    (D) less diffused throughout the world
    (E) more enjoyable to speak

GO ON TO THE NEXT PAGE.

Questions 47–49 refer to the following graphs.

The 38 Megacities (2019)
Urban areas with population of more than 10 million

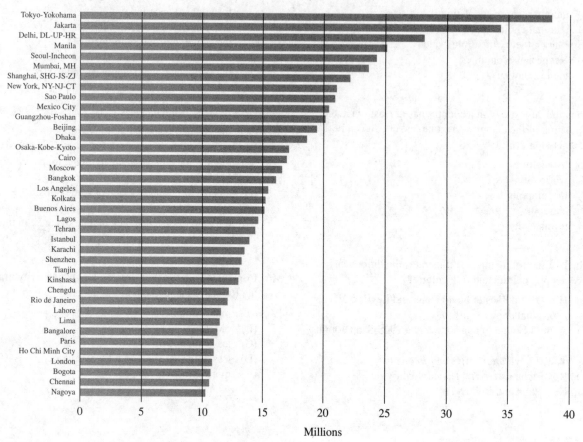

Figure 1: 38 Megacities (counts cities with 10 million+)

World Population Distribution: 2019
Urban (by population) & Rural

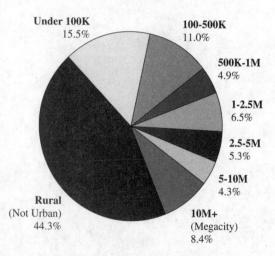

Figure 2: Population Distribution

GO ON TO THE NEXT PAGE.

47. According to Figure 2, the majority of the world's population is

    (A) living in rural areas
    (B) living in urban areas of any size
    (C) living in urban areas of 100,000 or more people
    (D) living in urban areas of 500,000 or more people
    (E) living in megacities

48. Which of the following conclusions can be drawn from Figure 1?

    (A) Nations with more megacities generate more waste per capita than nations with smaller cities.
    (B) No megacities existed until the first half of the twentieth century.
    (C) All of the megacities on the list are still growing.
    (D) Most of the biggest megacities in the world are found in Asia.
    (E) The future of the human race lies in urban environments.

49. The contradiction that can be best drawn from both Figures 1 and 2 is that

    (A) population density does not correlate with overall population
    (B) Asia is viewed by the rest of the world as largely rural
    (C) excessive urbanization is mostly a Western phenomenon
    (D) the rate of natural increase is greater in Asia than it is in other continents
    (E) while megacities account for the largest individual urban populations, the number of people living in megacities is actually less than the number of people living in smaller categories of cities

50. From a linguistic perspective, the birth of modern English is typically dated to which year?

    (A) 711 C.E.
    (B) 814 C.E.
    (C) 1066 C.E.
    (D) 1492 C.E.
    (E) 1588 C.E.

51. According to the Demographic Transition Model, which of the following is NOT a cause of the decreased death rate in stage 2 societies?

    (A) increased sanitation
    (B) increased factory production
    (C) increased physical labor
    (D) increased access to education
    (E) increased access to food markets

52. Which of the following is an example of agricultural biotechnology?

    (A) fertility sensors for cattle
    (B) genetically modified soybean oil
    (C) controlled fire management
    (D) a strain of wheat that is naturally resistant to pests
    (E) a pesticide made from inorganic chemicals

53. From a production perspective, the biggest challenge to modern popular consumer culture is

    (A) boredom resulting from too many entertainment choices
    (B) income inequality, leading to economic crashes
    (C) animal rights activists protesting the global spread of meat consumption
    (D) finding sources of the raw materials needed for production
    (E) the amount of waste that it generates

54. India has an RNI (rate of natural increase) of 1.09 percent. This results in a population doubling time of approximately

    (A) 36 years
    (B) 64 years
    (C) 69 years
    (D) 76 years
    (E) 140 years

GO ON TO THE NEXT PAGE.

Questions 55–57 refer to the following passage.

Most students of modern Cuba have observed at least three major phases in the revolutionary process during its first fifteen years... The political revolution—the successful convergence of the anti-Batista forces and the assumption of power by Castro and his colleagues—was followed by a few years in which the political support of the lower classes was consolidated through demand satisfaction. The old ruling elite and their foreign investor allies were displaced, and the material base that had sustained them was distributed in the form of services and consumer goods among the formerly deprived groups, particularly the peasants....

By the mid-1960s, however, the strategy of government by inventiveness and euphoria had run its course.... The upper and middle sectors, who had been billed for the impressive initial advances in health care, housing, education, and other services, had emigrated en masse to the United States. The hardships imposed by the international economic boycott and the costs of further development could only be borne by supporters and previous beneficiaries of the Revolution....

Full employment had been a fundamental goal and major achievement of the Revolution. Employment was more than a right, however; it was also an obligation. It was intended to underwrite not only adequate standards of living for every family in the short run but also productivity levels required for sustained growth.

—*Area Handbook for Cuba*, Jan Knippers Black, 1976

55. It can be concluded that the behavior of "the upper and middle sectors" alluded to in the passage was most affected by which of the following?

    (A) The rate of natural increase
    (B) The demographic transition model
    (C) Advances in biotechnology
    (D) Irredentism
    (E) Push and pull factors

56. Which of the following is NOT a typical consequence of "impressive initial advances in health care" such as the ones seen in Cuba?

    (A) Lower infant mortality rate
    (B) A reduced fertility rate
    (C) A reduced rate of disease
    (D) Higher health care costs
    (E) Increased longevity

57. The "productivity levels required for sustained growth" in the final paragraph implies that

    (A) according to the Demographic Transition Model, Cuba was attempting to move from a stage 2 to a stage 3 society
    (B) a society's standard of living is determined entirely by the work ethic of that society
    (C) it is possible for a society to reach full employment
    (D) economic growth cannot be achieved by a communist society
    (E) the revolution was a mistake and that foreign investors should have been invited to return

58. One problem with conformal projection maps of the earth, such as the Mercator, is that they distort

    (A) the topography of the land masses
    (B) the size of the continents, particularly as the longitude increases
    (C) the actual shape of polygons
    (D) the relative area of one part of the map to another
    (E) both the actual shape of the polygons and the relative area

59. In the last five hundred years, the island of Taiwan has received various waves of invasive settlements, from the Dutch to the Spanish to the Han Chinese to the Japanese. This phenomenon is collectively known as

    (A) agglomeration
    (B) uniformity
    (C) sequent occupancy
    (D) central place theory
    (E) concentric zoning

60. All of the following are examples of formal regions EXCEPT

    (A) an area whose inhabitants are clustered around the same central business district
    (B) an area whose inhabitants speak the same language
    (C) an area whose inhabitants play the same traditional sport
    (D) an area whose inhabitants eat the same traditional food on the same day of the week
    (E) an area whose inhabitants construct the same three-story buildings

END OF SECTION I

This page intentionally left blank.

HUMAN GEOGRAPHY
SECTION II
Time—1 hour and 15 minutes
3 Questions

Directions: You have <u>1 hour and 15</u> minutes to answer all three of the following questions. It is recommended that you spend approximately one-third of your time (25 minutes) on each question. It is suggested that you take up to 5 minutes of this time to plan and outline each answer. You may use the unlined space below each question for notes. For this practice test, write your answers on lined notebook paper.

Question 1

1. Remote-sensing technology has a long history, beginning with the French balloonist who made the first aerial photographs of Paris in 1858. Today, this technology has become an essential part of the field of human geography.

   A. Define remote-sensing technology.

   B. Describe TWO types of data analyzed by remote-sensing technology.

   C. Explain ONE commercial application of remote-sensing technology.

   D. Explain ONE agricultural application of remote-sensing technology.

   E. Describe ONE advantage of remote-sensing technology over on-site observation.

   F. Describe ONE disadvantage of remote-sensing technology compared with on-site observation.

   G. Explain why a government might invest in remote-sensing technology.

GO ON TO THE NEXT PAGE.

Question 2

THE PORT OF ROTTERDAM, NETHERLANDS, 1400 c.e. TO THE PRESENT

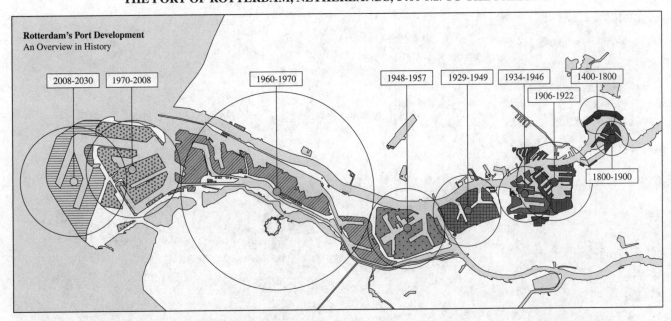

2. The following questions are based on the map shown above.

A. Discuss ONE reason why human civilizations traditionally develop alongside rivers.

B. Analyze ONE reason for the founding of a port in this location, given the Netherlands' location as a below-sea-level nation.

C. Analyze ONE reason for the founding of the port in this location, given industrial location theory.

D. Describe ONE obstacle that a traditional medieval port such as Rotterdam would have in adapting to the twentieth century.

E. Describe the effect of globalization upon the shipping industry.

F. Explain shipping's position in the modern global freight transportation system.

G. Discuss ONE technique that a below-sea-level nation such as The Netherlands uses to manage itself.

GO ON TO THE NEXT PAGE.

Question 3

THE COFFEE BELT

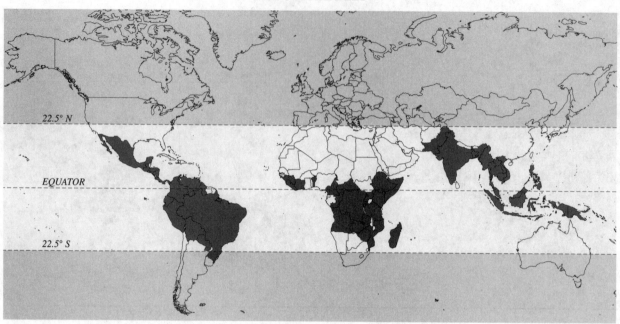

Source: German Coffee Association, Hamburg

MAIN WINE-PRODUCING COUNTRIES IN THE WORLD

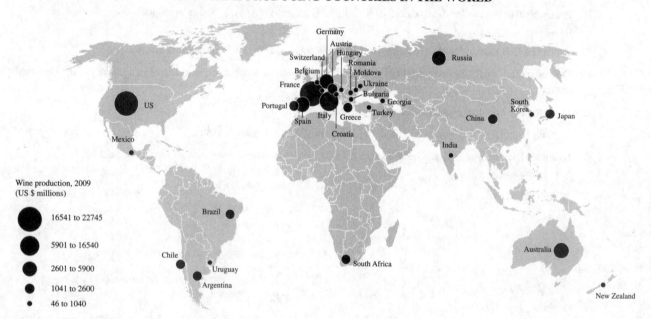

Wine production, 2009
(US $ millions)

- 16541 to 22745
- 5901 to 16540
- 2601 to 5900
- 1041 to 2600
- 46 to 1040

GO ON TO THE NEXT PAGE.

3. The following questions are based on the maps shown to the left.

    A. Describe ONE reason for the geographic distribution of the production of coffee.

    B. Describe ONE reason for the geographic distribution of the production of wine.

    C. From plant to consumable liquid, the production of both beverages is a long process. Briefly explain the FOUR stages of any commodity chain.

    D. Analyze ONE potential obstacle in the coffee industry's commodity chain.

    E. Analyze ONE potential obstacle in the wine industry's commodity chain.

    F. Explain one economic difference between coffee-growing regions and wine-growing regions.

    G. Describe ONE challenge faced by either industry, given the quickly growing global market for both beverages.

STOP

END OF EXAM

Practice Test 1:
Diagnostic
Answer Key and
Explanations

PRACTICE TEST 1: DIAGNOSTIC ANSWER KEY

Let's take a look at how you did on Practice Test 1. Follow the three-step process in the diagnostic answer key below and go read the explanations for any questions you got wrong or you struggled with but got correct. Once you finish working through the answer key and the explanations, go to the next chapter to make your study plan.

STEP 1 » Check your answers and mark any correct answers with a ✔ in the appropriate column.

Section 1—Multiple Choice							
Q #	Ans.	✔	Chapter #, Title	Q #	Ans.	✔	Chapter #, Title
1	E		9, Industrial and Economic Development Patterns and Processes	19	D		8, Cities and Urban Land-Use Patterns and Processes
2	D		9, Industrial and Economic Development Patterns and Processes	20	E		4, Population and Migration Patterns and Processes
3	C		9, Industrial and Economic Development Patterns and Processes	21	A		8, Cities and Urban Land-Use Patterns and Processes
4	C		9, Industrial and Economic Development Patterns and Processes	22	A		5, Cultural Patterns and Processes
5	B		9, Industrial and Economic Development Patterns and Processes	23	E		5, Cultural Patterns and Processes
6	E		9, Industrial and Economic Development Patterns and Processes	24	B		5, Cultural Patterns and Processes
7	D		7, Agriculture and Rural Land-Use Patterns and Processes	25	D		9, Industrial and Economic Development Patterns and Processes
8	E		7, Agriculture and Rural Land-Use Patterns and Processes	26	B		5, Cultural Patterns and Processes
9	A		7, Agriculture and Rural Land-Use Patterns and Processes	27	A		7, Agriculture and Rural Land-Use Patterns and Processes
10	A		9, Industrial and Economic Development Patterns and Processes	28	D		4, Population and Migration Patterns and Processes
11	D		9, Industrial and Economic Development Patterns and Processes	29	C		4, Population and Migration Patterns and Processes
12	D		9, Industrial and Economic Development Patterns and Processes	30	D		5, Cultural Patterns and Processes
13	C		6, Political Patterns and Processes	31	A		8, Cities and Urban Land-Use Patterns and Processes
14	D		6, Political Patterns and Processes	32	D		8, Cities and Urban Land-Use Patterns and Processes
15	B		6, Political Patterns and Processes	33	E		5, Cultural Patterns and Processes
16	C		6, Political Patterns and Processes	34	D		4, Population and Migration Patterns and Processes
17	D		6, Population and Migration Patterns and Processes	35	C		6, Political Patterns and Processes
18	E		8, Cities and Urban Land-Use Patterns and Processes	36	C		4, Population and Migration Patterns and Processes

Section 1—Multiple Choice, Continued

Q #	Ans.	✔	Chapter #, Title	Q #	Ans.	✔	Chapter #, Title
37	C		**3,** Thinking Geographically	49	E		**8,** Cities and Urban Land-Use Patterns and Processes
38	C		**6,** Political Patterns and Processes	50	C		**5,** Cultural Patterns and Processes
39	D		**6,** Political Patterns and Processes	51	C		**4,** Population and Migration Patterns and Processes
40	B		**6,** Political Patterns and Processes	52	B		**7,** Agriculture and Rural Land-Use Patterns and Processes
41	E		**9,** Industrial and Economic Development Patterns and Processes	53	E		**9,** Industrial and Economic Development Patterns and Processes
42	E		**8,** Cities and Urban Land-Use Patterns and Processes	54	B		**4,** Population and Migration Patterns and Processes
43	C		**5,** Cultural Patterns and Processes	55	E		**4,** Population and Migration Patterns and Processes
44	B		**9,** Industrial and Economic Development Patterns and Processes	56	D		**4,** Population and Migration Patterns and Processes
45	D		**6,** Thinking Geographically	57	A		**4,** Population and Migration Patterns and Processes
46	C		**5,** Cultural Patterns and Processes	58	D		**3,** Thinking Geographically
47	B		**8,** Cities and Urban Land-Use Patterns and Processes	59	C		**6,** Population and Migration Patterns and Processes
48	D		**8,** Cities and Urban Land-Use Patterns and Processes	60	A		**3,** Thinking Geographically

Section 2—Free Response

Q #	Ans.	✔	Chapter #, Title
1	See Explanation		**3,** Thinking Geographically
2	See Explanation		**9,** Industrial and Economic Development Patterns and Processes
3	See Explanation		**9,** Industrial and Economic Development Patterns and Processes

 **STEP 2** ≫ Tally your correct answers from Step 1 by chapter. For each chapter, write the number of correct answers in the appropriate box. Then, divide your correct answers by the number of total questions (which we've provided) to get your percent correct.

CHAPTER 3 TEST SELF-EVALUATION

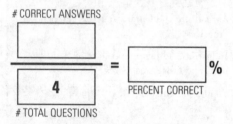

CORRECT ANSWERS

= ___ % PERCENT CORRECT

4

TOTAL QUESTIONS

CHAPTER 4 TEST SELF-EVALUATION

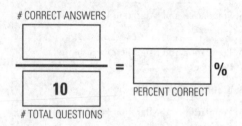

CORRECT ANSWERS

= ___ % PERCENT CORRECT

10

TOTAL QUESTIONS

CHAPTER 5 TEST SELF-EVALUATION

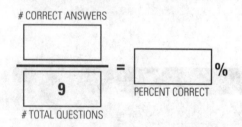

CORRECT ANSWERS

= ___ % PERCENT CORRECT

9

TOTAL QUESTIONS

CHAPTER 6 TEST SELF-EVALUATION

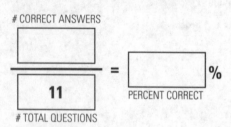

CORRECT ANSWERS

= ___ % PERCENT CORRECT

11

TOTAL QUESTIONS

CHAPTER 7 TEST SELF-EVALUATION

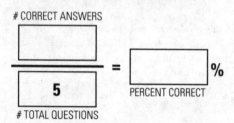

CORRECT ANSWERS

= ___ % PERCENT CORRECT

5

TOTAL QUESTIONS

CHAPTER 8 TEST SELF-EVALUATION

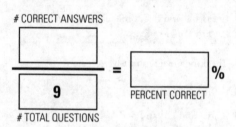

CORRECT ANSWERS

= ___ % PERCENT CORRECT

9

TOTAL QUESTIONS

CHAPTER 9 TEST SELF-EVALUATION

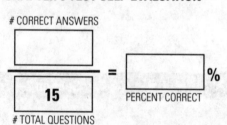

CORRECT ANSWERS

= ___ % PERCENT CORRECT

15

TOTAL QUESTIONS

STEP 3 ≫ Use the results above to customize your study plan. You may want to start with, or give more attention to, the chapters with the lowest percents correct.

PRACTICE TEST 1: ANSWERS AND EXPLANATIONS

Multiple-Choice Questions

1. **E** The global economic story of the century is the rise of China, which has attracted a massive influx of foreign manufacturing companies. Those foreign companies are attracted by the low-cost, non-unionized Chinese workforce, so eliminate (A). Internal political reforms in the 1980s, which steered the country away from a Soviet-style command economy and towards a free-market model, set the stage for this phenomenon, so eliminate (B). The special economic zones along the coast of the country, (C), as well as improved shipping around the world, (D), are other reasons for its great success. But competition from local companies are starting to drive out this foreign investment, so much so that Chinese President Xi made a speech in 2017 to the World Economic Forum in Davos promising to maintain open doors to foreign companies.

2. **D** The five answer choices correspond directly and in order with the five sectors of the economy. Choice (A), copper mining, is part of primary production, which includes obtaining raw materials. Choice (B), guitar manufacturing, represents the secondary sector. Choice (C), chemical waste disposal, is one of the many services that make up the tertiary, or third, sector. Choice (D), financial analysis, is part of the quaternary sector, which is defined as the knowledge-based part of the economy. And (E), tour guide, is a part of the quinary sector, which is entirely consumer services. You may have noticed that the third, fourth, and fifth sectors are all services. In the past, they were lumped into a single category, but in recent years they have been separated into business services (tertiary), knowledge services (quaternary), and consumer services (quinary).

3. **C** Use a combination of Process of Elimination and common sense. Remember that Europe and East Asia are on the forefront of renewable energy, but none of the answers are from East Asia. In solar energy, Germany is the leader of the Western world—only China and Japan get a greater percentage of their total energy from solar, and neither is listed in the answers. Germany is also the European leader in wind power, as a percentage of its total power, but Spain is in second place—together they make up 48% of Europe's total wind power capacity. Regarding nuclear energy, the United States is the world leader in production, but France is very close behind. Trap answers include (A) and (B), because neither Morocco nor Ecuador have significant nuclear energy. Morocco does have enormous amounts of sun, (D), but it has only just begun to add solar installations. In (E), Germany is actually reducing its nuclear energy as the share of other renewables increases; it plans to completely eliminate all nuclear power plants by 2022.

4. **C** *Comparative advantage* is an economic term that refers to a society's ability to produce goods or services at a lower opportunity cost, not necessarily at a greater volume or quality. It's fair to say that even the poorest, most distressed society—one that has no resources to offer, no ease of transportation, etc.—still can offer cheap labor to the international market. That is conceivably enough to give them a leg up on some of their competition. In other words, there is no society that does not possess at least one positive characteristic that might attract the international market.

5. **B** Increased domestic manufacturing is a common goal of many societies, especially since it has been shown that a favorable balance of trade includes slightly more exports than imports. Constructing a sock factory of its own would help the developing country by guaranteeing that all profits from the domestically produced socks stay within the country. Several of the answer choices mention foreign companies, but foreign countries are not necessarily going to plow their profits back into the local host country. In fact, in practice, they often take their profits elsewhere.

6. **E** Some questions are going to be easier than others, and this is one of them. Yes, the Caribbean is highly dependent on tourism. In fact, of the fifteen countries with the highest percentage of GDP attributed to tourism, six are in the Caribbean. (Many others are in the South Pacific.) The truth is that most nations that rely heavily on tourism are small islands with tropical climates. Being located geographically close to a gigantic economy, such as the United States, also helps create a heavily touristic economy. Breaking news: people like to sit in the sun on tropical beaches.

7. **D** The figure represents the growth of agriculture in developing regions of the world from the 1960s to the 1980s. While it's true that scientific plant breeding, (A), and the brand-new combine harvester (E), were two major changes in agriculture at that time, both elements were part of a larger movement known as the Green Revolution, which introduced plant breeding and fertilizer to what used to be known as Third World countries. The invention of the moldboard plow, (B), occurred in the 18th century, as did the Industrial Revolution, (C), and are irrelevant.

8. **E** The graphs are current only until the 1980s. Without up-to-date data, it's impossible to say which region leads which region in the present-day, so eliminate (A). While Latin America is the most productive of the four regions listed, it is not necessarily the most productive in the world; eliminate (B). In the 1960s, sub-Saharan Africa produced more rice than Asia; eliminate (C). Asia didn't see any growth in protein crops or maize during this period, so eliminate (D). However, rice is a water-intensive crop, and the terrain of northern Africa and the Middle East are largely desert; many countries in those regions suffer water shortages and are therefore unable to grow rice.

9. **A** The Green Revolution can be traced back almost entirely to the efforts of Norman Borlaug. This American agronomist labored for years to develop a strain of wheat that resisted disease, adapted to different growing conditions across different latitudes, and featured very high yield. Beginning in Mexico, his new breed of wheat was then imported to Asia and other parts of the developing world. A winner of the Nobel Peace Prize, Borlaug has been credited with saving more lives than any other human has ever done.

10. **A** Under a command economy, a centralized government controls every aspect of business—it owns the machines and the businesses, it sets the prices, it decides upon production quotas, it determines the distribution. The needs of individuals are rarely consulted and almost never fulfilled. However, most of the world follows a market economy structure instead, so there are very few examples of command economies. Cuba, North Korea, and even China (to a much lesser extent) are among the few remaining ones.

11. **D** Under a bulk-reducing industry, heavy inputs are reduced during the manufacturing process to a product that is less heavy than those inputs. One example would be the production of copper, which is extracted from the considerably larger and heavier copper ore. As a result, it is much more efficient to locate factories close to the source of the heavier inputs. The opposite is true of bulk-increasing industry, such as baking—the inputs are lighter than the product.

12. **D** The Latin American city model demonstrated that traditional elements of Latin American urban design were blending with elements of modern design to create a unique cityscape. Specifically, Ford and Griffin noted that cities were built around a CBD (Central Business District), out of which comes a commercial spine that is surrounded closely by expensive upper-class housing. Then, surrounding that spine, are concentric circles of housing that gradually decrease in quality as one moves further from the center. (The North American model, by contrast, often looks quite the opposite, with expensive housing the furthest away from the CBD—though there is evidence that this model is changing.) Ford and Griffin formed the Latin American city model in the early 1980s.

13. **C** While all these terms relate to the division of voting districts, only *reapportionment* describes the question stem exactly. Gerrymandering, (A), is the way of redistricting solely for political advantage, while devolution, (B) describes the process by which regions within a state demand and get political power at the expense of the central government. Splitting, (D), refers to majority and minority populations spread evenly across the districts. Sovereignty, (E), refers to the power of legitimate rulers of independent states.

14. **D** Hitler and the Nazi party claimed the Sudetenland because of the large number of ethnic Germans living there. This is *irredentism*, or the movement to unite a nation's homeland when part of it is contained in another state. Choice (E), ethnonationalism, is the trap answer—it refers to the *feeling* of patriotism experienced in the hearts of those living outside their homeland in such circumstances. However, the question asks about the movement to reclaim these people, not about their feelings.

15. **B** The U.S. Constitution, in the first three articles, explicitly spells out the separation of powers. First invented by Montesquieu, this framework makes sure that different groups of people are controlling the three different branches of government. This reduces the potential for corruption, since the three branches can act as checks upon one another. At the same time, it can make government less efficient and responsive, so it's a double-edged sword.

16. **C** The European Union still doesn't have a working constitution, nearly two decades after it was formed, because it was never ratified by all 25 members. France and the Netherlands rejected the constitution, sending it back to the drawing board. The issue has never been resolved.

17. **D** The rate of natural increase (RNI) is defined as the difference between the birth rate and the death rate, then divided by ten. For example, a nation with a birth rate of 25 and a death rate of 11 would have an RNI of 1.4, since $25 - 11 = 14$, and 14 divided by 10 equals 1.4. The obesity rate and densification rate (which is a physics term, not an AP Human Geography term) are irrelevant.

18. **E** A technopole is a node of scientific research, innovation, and activity. Often, a high-technology zone grows up around that node. In the case of the Research Triangle, there were originally three nodes—North Carolina State University, Duke University, and University of North Carolina at Chapel Hill. Other examples of technopoles include Silicon Valley (in California), Route 128 (in Massachusetts), Praetoria (in South Africa), and Hyderabad (in India).

19. **D** The rank-size rule states that the *n*th largest city is 1/*n* the size of the country's largest city. Therefore, in a country whose largest city contains 800,000 people, the second largest city contains one-half of 800,000, which is 400,000. The third largest city contains one-third of 800,000, which is approximately 267,000 people. The fourth largest city contains one-fourth of 800,000, which is 200,000 people.

20. **E** The rate of natural increase is typically positive, since world population has been generally increasing, at least for the last several hundred centuries. However, at times, the overall population can decrease as a result of the death rate exceeding the birth rate. This typically happens in times of war, either external or civil. Other situations can include pandemics that wipe out a large portion of the population, such as the Black Plague, but unfortunately that wasn't offered as a choice.

21. **A** The 1950s saw the opposite happen—a *decreased* use of freight trains for industrial transportation. In their place, trucking arose as a preferred method of shipment. Freed from the bond of inflexible railroad routes, companies began to slowly relocate their warehouses and industrial properties not in the cities, but in the suburbs. The other four answers are hallmarks of the suburbanization movement.

22. **A** A fuzzy cultural border is one that cannot be defined by any concrete boundaries, such as the location where Dixie ends and the American Northeast or Midwest begins. While some attempt to apply a political boundary like the Mason-Dixon line, this line actually runs south and west of Delaware and north of Maryland; thus, there is no place one could physically place a sign that says, "Welcome to Dixie!" Furthermore, the characteristics that define that culture, such as country music appreciation, cannot be used to determine Dixie's regional boundary due to inconsistency along its edges. The epicenter of Jainism was in Western India at approximately 2,900 years B.C.E., while Voodoun has been practiced in western Africa since pre-historic times; eliminate (B), as the border is clearly defined both temporally and geographically. The Wailing Wall and the western wall of the Temple of Solomon are the same physical locations; eliminate (C). Choice (D) can be eliminated because the transition from modern to contemporary architecture is not a cultural border, but a difference in architectural form. Eliminate (E), as both the Kurgan and Anatolian hearths represent possible locations regarding the origins of European language.

23. **E** The *niqāb* is worn in non-Arabic regions of the world by immigrants; it has almost never been adopted by other cultures, and is even prohibited in many countries. Therefore, it hasn't diffused. Eliminate (A). Likewise, the *niqāb* is viewed as a fringe practice even by the people of Saudi Arabia and close neighbors, its native cultural region; eliminate (B). You may have been tempted by (C), but the *niqāb* is not outdated, since millions of women still wear them in Saudi Arabia, Yemen, Oman, and UAE (United Arab Emirates). Lastly, it is not symbolic of anything, but is instead a long-standing cultural custom that predates Islam.

24. **B** The French are famous for protecting their culture, going to lengths that are unheard of in other societies. (For example, the Académie Française keeps a list of prohibited crossover words from English.) In 2011, France banned the *niqāb* in public except when worshiping in a religious place or when traveling in private vehicles. This is not an instance of cultural superiority—it is an attempt to protect native culture—and neither is it a wholesale rejection of globalization; both are exaggerated answers. Eliminate (A) and (C). The Arabic cultural hearth is not shifting, so eliminate (D), and trade is not necessarily driving the ban on the *niqāb* either; many Muslims arrive in France for education or to escape political violence. Eliminate (E).

25. **D** Internalization of economic capital, nationalization of natural resource-based industries, technology development programs, and profit-sharing agreements are all policies and programs that attempt to increase capital accumulation within Third-World economies; eliminate (A), (B), (C), and (E). However, export-substitution is not a policy that is implemented by Third-World economies to increase capital accumulation. Rather, import-substitution, which calls for producing simple goods within the country and reinvesting profits locally, is the actual policy implemented by Third-World economies to increase capital accumulation.

26. **B** Islam is a monotheistic belief system with a singular supreme being; i.e., God or Allah. Hinduism and Buddhism are both polytheistic denominations that had spread throughout Asia by the 1200s BCE; eliminate (A) and (C). Voodoo is a system based upon multiple deities that control different parts of the inhabited world; eliminate (D). Finally, (E) can be eliminated because animism comprises various ethnic, tribal, or naturalistic religious traditions that espouse the belief that items in nature have spiritual being.

27. **A** The primary problem with a communist system of agriculture, as compared to the capitalist system, is that there is no incentive to produce over a quota or products outside the mandated crop. In a communist system of agriculture, demand far exceeds supply; eliminate both (B) and (C). Furthermore, there is no evidence that a communist system of agriculture either has a decentralized transportation network or provides rewards to the social elite; (D) and (E) can be eliminated.

28. **D** Stage 4 of the Demographic Transition Model is characterized by a service-based economy. Stages 1 through 3 of the Demographic Transition Model are characterized by a pre-agricultural economy, an agricultural economy, and a manufacturing economy, respectively; eliminate (A), (B), and (C). Eliminate (E) as there is no economic stage of the Demographic Transition Model deemed *evolving*.

29. **C** A simple vacation doesn't count as a life-course change. A life-course change occurs when a person's needs or resources change, which necessitates moving one's home. This is also known as a form of internal migration, and it is more common among younger people than older people, though both do it. For the last century or so, life-course changes tended to move outwards from city centers—the process of suburbanization—but that trend seems to have slowed recently as a result of growing gentrification of our cities.

30. **D** Surprise! Mandarin has the greatest number of native speakers, nearly 1.3 billion. However, they're mostly concentrated in one country—China—as well as Malaysia, Taiwan, etc. Spanish is second with 400 million, and English is third with 360 million. However, English is the most widely spoken language in the world.

31. **A** This question is full of trap answers. Choice (B), for example, ignores the fact that walking and bicycling is an individual, private method transportation; eliminate it. Same goes for (C)—just because a nation has poor or nonexistent public transportation does not mean that that nation relies heavily upon automobiles, or is a large emitter. Extremely undeveloped nations, such as Chad or Burundi, emit almost nothing because they have little transportation of any type other than bicycles or walking. Choice (E) discusses the operation of all forms of transportation—but the operation of a bicycle is almost emissions free. Eliminate (E).

32. **D**   Transportation emissions usually increase when a nation's trade and commerce increase; when trade and commerce increase, so does the per capita income. (This correlation may be weakening in the future, as zero-emissions transportation becomes more common.) The other answer choices are either not correlated or only weakly correlated with a rise in transportation emissions.

33. **E**   A universalizing religion is one that attempts to be global, and to appeal to all people, no matter where they may be living. Choices (B), (C), and (D) can be easily identified as universalizing religions, because Christianity, Buddhism, and Islam (three of the five major world religions) have clearly spread to various nations and cultures around the globe. Baha'i, while having far fewer adherents (only 7 million), was founded in Iran in the 19th century with the belief that there should be no class distinctions. This message has spread quickly to small communities around the world. Eliminate (A). Interestingly, though Hinduism is one of the five major world religions, it has retained its identity as an ethnic religion, practiced primarily by a single group of people in India.

34. **D**   The first large wave of immigrants, from 1840 to 1850, was overwhelmingly Irish and German. The second wave of immigrants, from 1880 to 1925, was mostly immigrants from Italy, Poland, Russia, and other parts of southern and eastern Europe. The recent wave of immigration, which began in 1965, has been from developing nations all around the world and is too varied to characterize. Topping that list has been China, India, Mexico, and lately, Central American republics.

35. **C**   Nativism is the policy of protecting the interests of the native-born population over the interests of the arriving immigrants. The Know-Nothing party was the political expression of this impulse. In the 1840s, in reaction to the arrival of many Irish and Germans—there were riots attacking German immigrants—this political party was born. It never achieved high office, but its members did hold lower offices. It was opposed to not only immigrants but also specifically Catholics.

36. **C**   Migrants from stage 2 societies often decide to leave their own society and head toward the developed nations. There are many contemporary examples of developed countries accepting migrants from developing countries; in fact, it's a highly contentious issue, particularly among right-wing conservatives. There are many reasons for this phenomenon, including the fact that many of the migrants are leaving urban slums and shantytowns that have sprung up on the outskirts of their own major cities (another sign of a stage 2 society). Stage 4 societies, by contrast, feature higher standards of living, and any migration that occurs tends to be within the country.

37. **C**   The North and South Poles are 90° latitude. The equator is 0° latitude and the Prime Meridian is 0° longitude; eliminate both (A) and (B). Eliminate (D) because 90° longitude is a line of longitude 90° west of Greenwich. The anti-meridian, which is the basis for the International Date Line, is located at 180° longitude; eliminate (E).

38. **C**   The Arab Spring was an expression of rising democracy, so eliminate (A). While reactionary politics has made a comeback recently, it hasn't been a *global takeover*—avoid extreme answers—so eliminate (B). Choices (D) and (E) both support the idea of a globalized democracy, so eliminate those. Only (C) describes the quick spurt of reactionary politics that has erupted in countries such as Brazil, the Philippines, Austria, Syria, the U.K., the U.S., and elsewhere.

39. **D**   You can arrive at this answer using common sense. The Middle East contains some of the most closed, autocratic nations in the world—Saudi Arabia, Yemen, etc.—as well as a majority of the world's oil reserves. Interestingly, this correlation is a real thing. Michael Ross has written about it, and a 2014 study has supported it. The other four answers have all been proven, at one time or another, to correlate with democracy.

40. **B**   The Arab Spring was an outbreak of democratic revolt in one of the most autocratic areas of the globe, the Middle East. Originating in Tunisia and spurred by social media, the revolts spread like wildfire and toppled four of the most long-standing autocrats in the world. Choice (D), while attractive, mentions religious communities, which is out of scope.

41. **E**   The iron law of wages, voiced by David Ricardo, states that real wages always trend towards the minimum required to sustain the life of the workers. It also states that as the pool of workers widens, the amount paid to each person decreases, but as the pool of workers narrows, the amount paid to each person increases. The only other choice that should've possibly tempted you was (C), Marx's theory of surplus value, but that's only distantly related. It describes the difference between the amount of money raised by the sale of a good and the amount of money it cost the owner to produce that good. Wages are only a small part of this theory.

42. **E**   When the largest city in a country has at least twice the population of the country's next largest city, it can be designated as a primate city. A megacity is a metropolitan area with more than 10 million people, while a world city is used to designate a metropolitan area as a global center for finance, trade, and commerce; eliminate both (A) and (B). Choices (C) and (D) can be eliminated because a megalopolis is the merging of the urbanized areas of two or more cities, while an entrepôt is a port city in which goods are exported at a higher rate than imported.

43. **C**   The difference between pop culture and folk culture is important to know. Folk culture is made by homogeneous, isolated groups, and the names of their creators are never recorded. In other words, all folk culture is anonymous. That alone should help you discard (B), (D), and (E), because Scott Joplin, Leonardo da Vinci, and Bob Dylan are all individuals, and clearly not anonymous. The remaining wrong answer, (A), can be eliminated because we know a lot about Levi's 501 denim jeans; they were sold to miners all over the American West during the Gold Rush, by two individuals named Levi and Strauss. But *Beowulf* is a textbook definition of folk literature, since the story was part of an oral tradition passed along by unknown, isolated northern European tribes at unknown dates during the Dark Ages.

44. **B**   The Human Development Index grew out of the Human Development Reports that the United Nations Development Program was commissioning in the 1990s. The purpose of the Index was to shift the focus of conversation away from national income—which often fails to measure the distribution of national income, meaning the gap between rich and poor—and towards more people-oriented measurements of success. Currently, Norway, Switzerland, and Australia sit in the top three places on this index, as they have for the last several years.

45. **D**   Geographers define *place* as an area of bounded space of some human importance. The geometric surface of the earth is defined as *space;* eliminate (A). An area wherein activity occurs on a daily basis is known as an *activity space*; eliminate (B). Choice (C) can be eliminated because the relationship between an object to the earth as a whole is the definition of *scale*. Choice (E) can be eliminated because the ratio of distance on a map to distance in the real world is the definition of *map scale*.

46. **C**   The number of major Romance languages sits at five: Spanish, Portuguese, French, Italian, and Romanian. (There are a few minor ones as well.) However, the number of Indo-Iranian languages sits at well over 100, including Hindi, Urdu, Bengali, Farsi, Pashto, and Kurdish. Both families are diffused across great areas of land, with Romance languages found on four different continents. The Indo-Iranian languages sit primarily in central Asia.

47. **B**   Remember that a majority means 50% or more, and pie charts make it easy to judge this at a glance. What segments of this chart add up to more than 50% of the circle's total area? Since the rural piece of the chart accounts for 44.3%, then the rest of the pieces account for 55.7%, which is a majority. Those include all urban-dwelling humans, in cities of any size—even the portion marked "under 100,000". Select (B).

48. **D**   The only statement that can be safely deduced from this particular graph is (D). It's clear that 7 of the 10 largest megacities in the world are located in Asia. The four other choices are unsupported, even the ones that may be true, such as (B)—New York indeed became the world's first megacity in 1930, when it crossed the 10 million threshold.

49. **E**   The interesting thing about Figure 2, the pie chart, is that there are two other categories of cities (under 100,000, and 100,000–500,000) that each contain a greater percentage of the world's population than do the megacities. This indicates that while megacities may hog the spotlight for their bloated individual sizes, far more people in the world choose to live in smaller, more manageable cities. The other answer choices are out of scope.

50. **C**   The Battle of Hastings occurred in 1066, when William the Conqueror sailed across the English Channel to take the tribes of the British Isles by force. Prior to that, these inhabitants spoke a mostly monosyllabic Germanic dialect known as Anglo-Saxon, aka Old English. However, when William arrived, he displaced the entire Anglo-Saxon ruling classes (many of whom fled to Scotland, Wales, Ireland, and even Turkey) and instead placed his Norman supporters in positions of power. The Normans spoke a polysyllabic, complex, Latin-influenced language known today as Old French—after all, they were from modern-day France! As a result, for the next 300 years, the rulers spoke in their complex Romance language, while the ruled spoke in their simpler Anglo-Saxon. The gradual blending of the two created Middle English—the language of Chaucer—which is still understandable to speakers of modern English today.

51. **C**   As societies arrive at stage 2 of the Demographic Transition Model, they often experience increased access to education, health care, and sanitation—all the things that result in extended lifespans. They begin building more factories; the population grows more urbanized. All of this, particularly the shift away from subsistence farming, means less physical labor, not more.

52. **B**   Biotechnology is defined as the broad area of biology in which living systems and organisms are used to develop products. In this case, agricultural products. Choice (A) is incorrect because the sensors are not necessarily made of organic materials. Choice (C) is incorrect because setting fire to a piece of land is not producing anything. Choice (D) is incorrect because a strain of wheat that is *naturally* resistant to pests is the product of *natural selection*, not biotechnology. Choice (E) is incorrect because a chemical pesticide is the opposite of biotechnology, which uses naturally occurring materials to make products.

53. **E** The key here is the phrase *from a production perspective*. While there are several challenges presented to the survival of popular culture, including boredom, the biggest challenge in the physical production of popular culture is the enormous amount of packaging and waste that is generated. Choice (D) is a trap; there is no shortage of raw materials. Choice (C) is also a trap; while the consumption of meat presents a growing challenge to our agriculture systems, the animal activists themselves are irrelevant.

54. **B** The doubling time of a population can be easily calculated: 70 ÷ the RNI (rate of natural increase). Since India's RNI is 1.09, either do the math exactly, or estimate it: 70 ÷ 1.09 = 64.22 years. Keep in mind, however, that this doesn't take any outside factors into account, such as migration, wars, or epidemics.

55. **E** The passage notes that the upper and middle sectors "had emigrated en masse to the United States." The only answer choice directly related to emigration is (E). Push factors are those characteristics of a homeland that "push" its citizens to emigrate, and pull factors are those characteristics of another country that "pull" citizens from other countries to immigrate. The other four answers are out of scope.

56. **D** While it's possible that health care costs could increase as the quality of care increases, it's not necessarily true. Cuba itself stands as an example of the opposite being true—the passage states that "services and consumer goods among the formerly deprived groups, particularly the peasants" had been redistributed. In other words, the wealthy people were taxed heavily to pay for an improved standard of living for the lower classes. The other four choices are all heavily correlated with improved access to health care.

57. **A** In the Demographic Transition Model, stage 3 is where most manufacturing-based or industrialized countries find themselves. Cuba was attempting, via the changes described above, to move out of stage 2 by squeezing more productivity from its workers. One could argue, however, that guaranteeing full employment is not necessarily going to result in more industrial productivity. This sort of centralized economy could—and did—create a society devoid of incentives to actually produce.

58. **D** A conformal map, such as a Mercator projection, tries to keep the shape of the polygons accurate. However, on a two-dimensional surface, this means distorting the size of the polygons themselves. The trap answer is (B), since the size of the continents are distorted in this type of map—but as a function of *latitude*, not longitude. Antarctica, for example, is much more distorted than land masses near the equator.

59. **C** Sequent occupancy is the notion that successive societies each leave their cultural imprints upon a place, thus contributing to the cultural landscape. Some places in the world, such as Egypt or Jerusalem or China, have seen multiple civilizations—two, three, even four—on the same land. This is what has happened (on a smaller scale) to Taiwan.

60. **A** These five answers may seem so close that they are virtually indistinguishable, but the central business district is not a characteristic of a formal region. In fact, a central commercial node is the definition of a functional region. Also, according to this definition, the influence of that central node decreases as the distance from the center increases. The third type of region is a vernacular region, which is based largely on perceived culture.

Free-Response Questions

Don't look at the following section until you've completed the free-response questions in Practice Test 1.

For each of the questions, we have provided a rubric that will give you a decent sense of what information your responses should have mentioned. Each of the questions comprises seven parts (A–G), each of which is worth one point. That point is awarded for addressing any of the possible ideas listed under that part.

Keep in mind that these rubrics are by no means exhaustive. We recommend asking your AP Human Geography teacher to check your responses, particularly if they mention other details not listed here.

Scoring Rubrics for Free-Response Questions

---

1. Remote-sensing technology has a long history, beginning with the French balloonist who made the first aerial photographs of Paris in 1858. Today, this technology has become an essential part of the field of human geography.

   A. Define remote-sensing technology.

   B. Describe TWO types of data analyzed by remote-sensing technology.

   C. Explain ONE commercial application of remote-sensing technology.

   D. Explain ONE agricultural application of remote-sensing technology.

   E. Describe ONE advantage of remote-sensing technology over on-site observation.

   F. Describe ONE disadvantage of remote-sensing technology compared with on-site observation.

   G. Explain why a government might invest in remote-sensing technology.

Rubric—1 + 1 + 1 + 1 + 1 + 1 + 1 = 7 pts

A. Definition
   a. Remote-sensing technology is the acquisition of information about an object or a phenomenon without physical contact with the object or phenomenon.

B. Two types of data analyzed
   a. Visual light wavelengths
   b. Infrared data
   c. Radar data—aerial traffic control and meteorology
   d. Acoustic data—includes sonar, seismograms, ultrasound
   e. Geodetic data—includes all data mapping Earth's true geometric shape, including motion of the plates, curvature of the Earth, etc.

C. Commercial application
   a. Weather data is sold to media companies
   b. Agricultural data is sold to farmers
   c. Mineral data is sold to mining companies

D. Agricultural application
   a. To assess the health of agricultural fields and other vegetation, thereby accurately predicting harvests
   b. To monitor environmental degradation after disasters
   c. Tracking livestock via drone

E. Advantages of remote-sensing technology

    a. It reduces the number of human survey teams that have to be sent out to remote (or not-so-remote) places, so it's more cost-effective

    b. It reduces damage done on the ground in sensitive habitats

    c. It allows repetitive data to be measured in real time, which helps analyze dynamic things such as water levels

    d. Fast processing through computers

    e. Large area coverage for relatively small amounts of time/effort

F. Disadvantages of remote-sensing technology

    a. Digital data can be tampered with or lost more easily than larger, more physical methods of storage

    b. It can be fairly expensive, especially when measuring smaller areas

    c. Radars that emote their own electromagnetic radiation can affect the phenomenon being measured

G. Government's interest in investing in remote-sensing technology

    a. Military purposes—to know the terrain of one's own nation as well as the terrain of foreign enemies

    b. Highway system—this can be improved using up-to-the-minute data

    c. Fast decision-making for response to landslides, flood zones, etc.

    d. Law enforcement uses it to search for hidden operations, such as drug traffickers

    e. To record property data for tax assessments

2. The following questions are based on the map shown above.

   A. Discuss ONE reason why human civilizations traditionally develop alongside rivers.

   B. Analyze ONE reason for the founding of a port in this location, given the Netherlands' location as a below-sea-level nation.

   C. Analyze ONE reason for the founding of the port in this location, given industrial location theory.

   D. Describe ONE obstacle that a traditional medieval port such as Rotterdam would have in adapting to the twentieth century.

   E. Describe the effect of globalization upon the shipping industry.

   F. Explain shipping's position in the modern global freight transportation system.

   G. Discuss ONE technique that a below-sea-level nation such as The Netherlands uses to manage itself.

Rubric—1 + 1 + 1 + 1 + 1 + 1 + 1 = 7 pts

A. Why human civilizations develop alongside rivers
   a. Prior to the invention of the steam engine, rivers made easy transportation for trade of goods.
   b. Prior to modern methods of communication, rivers made communication easier.
   c. The soil alongside rivers was often more fertile, which meant more consistent food production.
   d. Water from the river was (obviously) available for drinking, but it may not have been as easy to find further inland.

B. Why Rotterdam became a port (the Netherlands' location as a below-sea-level nation)
   a. In 1400, the country's extremely low elevation meant that the coastal regions of the Netherlands were affected by highly damaging storms, so setting the port far inland reduced the possibility of both flooding and destruction.
   b. Setting the port inland made it easier to transport goods from the city and the interior of the country to the port, and vice versa.

C. Why Rotterdam became a port (industrial location theory)
   a. Alfred Weber invented the term in his book *Theory of Industrial Location.*
   b. Weight-losing manufacturing (close proximity of resources to manufacturing) v. weight-gaining manufacturing (close proximity of finished goods to consumers)

D. One obstacle that a traditional medieval port such as Rotterdam would have in twentieth-century shipping.
   a. Difficult to accommodate the width of supersized cargo ships
   b. Increased traffic means that the narrow channel can no longer accommodate all the ships that wanted to use it
   c. Shallow waterways—many were dredged to accommodate the other side
   d. Outmoded quays and other equipment

E. Effect of globalization on shipping industry
   a. Globalization has occurred *because of* maritime shipping—the trade of goods between nations. It's a symbiotic relationship.
   b. Increased shipping of not only legal goods but also illegal goods, such as weapons, drugs, and trafficked humans
   c. The formation of the European Union in the early 21st century accelerated commerce, since it removed the barriers to trade within Europe.

F. Shipping's place in the modern global freight transportation system
   a. Unlike the medieval era—when maritime shipping was the only way to move goods—the twentieth century has seen many other advances in transportation options.
      i.   Airplanes
      ii.   Railways
      iii. Inland waterways
      iv.   Roads
   b. International maritime shipping often works in conjunction with these other new options.
   c. Maritime shipping is low-cost, high-time-consuming method of shipping non-perishable items, whereas airplanes serve as high-cost, low-time-consuming methods of shipping perishable items.
   d. Maritime shipping continues to transport more goods by volume than any other transportation option.

G. One technique a below-sea-level nation uses to maintain itself
   a. A system of dykes
   b. Canal systems—to redistribute water when it arrives
   c. Water gates—they swing shut when storms arrive
   d. Sea walls—to block storm surges
   e. Dams
   f. Ditches—to contain the sudden floodwaters
   g. Windmills—to pump out flooded lands

3. The following questions are based on the maps shown to the left.

    A. Describe ONE reason for the geographic distribution of the production of coffee.

    B. Describe ONE reason for the geographic distribution of the production of wine.

    C. From plant to consumable liquid, the production of both beverages is a long process. Briefly explain the FOUR stages of any commodity chain.

    D. Analyze ONE potential obstacle in the coffee industry's commodity chain.

    E. Analyze ONE potential obstacle in the wine industry's commodity chain.

    F. Explain ONE economic difference between coffee-growing regions and wine-growing regions.

    G. Describe ONE challenge faced by either industry, given the quickly growing global market for both beverages.

Rubric—1 + 1 + 1 + 1 + 1 + 1 + 1 = 7 pts

A. Reasons for geographic distribution of coffee production
    a. Distance from the equator—it grows from the equator to the 23rd parallel, in both the northern and southern hemispheres.
    b. Altitude—coffee grows between 1000 to 2000 m altitude, just below the frost line.
    c. Temperature—coffee needs consistent warmth.
    d. Rainfall—coffee needs moist terrain.
    e. Rich soil—coffee needs a lot of nutrients.

B. Reasons for geographic distribution of wine production
    a. Distance from the equator—grapes grow from the 30th to 50th parallel, in both the northern and southern hemispheres.
    b. Altitude—certain grapes only thrive at a certain altitude, while others grow well at sea level.
    c. Temperature—all grapes need warmer temperatures.
    d. Sunshine—most varieties of grapes need a lot of sunshine.

C. Four stages of the commodity chain
    a. Growth or excavation of raw materials
    b. Manufacture, assembly, and/or processing of raw materials
    c. Distribution of final goods
    d. Retail sales at markets

D. One potential obstacle in the coffee industry's chain of commodity
    a. Unreliable rainfall or sunshine impedes growth
    b. Strikes by laborers
    c. Lack of infrastructure in developing world inhibits distribution

E. One potential obstacle in the wine industry's chain of commodity
    a. Unseasonable temperatures or excessive rain can destroy the entire crop.
    b. Lack of skill in manufacturing the wine from the grapes
    c. Transportation can be sensitive given both the weight and the fragile nature of wine bottles.

F. One economic difference between coffee-growing regions and wine-growing regions
   a. Coffee-growing regions are located mostly in developing nations, while wine-growing regions are located mostly in developed nations.
   b. There is a long tradition of appellations in Europe, which allows those countries to charge more for their products. Developing countries until recently have not enjoyed the same advantage.

G. Challenge to large-scale production
   a. The growing middle class in China (and elsewhere) has created a skyrocketing demand for nonessential beverages such as coffee and wine, which has created a host of problems for both industries.
      i.   Need for increased use of chemical fertilizers
      ii. Need to create a sustainable yield—the amount of crops that can be raised without endangering local resources
      iii. Potential aquifer depletion
      iv. Potential loss of subsistence farming as farmers choose to grow these cash crops instead

HOW TO SCORE PRACTICE TEST 1

Section I: Multiple Choice

_____	× 1.25 =	_____
Number Correct (out of 60)		Weighted Section I Score (Do not round)

Section II: Free Response

Question 1:

_____ × 3.5714 = _____
(out of 7)   (Do not round)

Question 2:

_____ × 3.5714 = _____
(out of 7)   (Do not round)

Question 3:

_____ × 3.5714 = _____
(out of 7)   (Do not round)

AP Score Conversion Chart Human Geography	
Composite Score Range	AP Score
107–150	5
90–106	4
73–89	3
56–72	2
0–55	1

Sum = _____
Weighted Section II Score (Do not round)

Composite Score

_____	+	_____	=	_____
Weighted Section I Score		Weighted Section II Score		Composite Score (Round to nearest whole number)

Part III
About the
AP Human
Geography Exam

- The Structure of the AP Human Geography Exam
- Overview of Content Topics
- How the AP Human Geography Exam Is Scored
- How AP Exams Are Used
- Other Resources
- Designing Your Study Plan

THE STRUCTURE OF THE AP HUMAN GEOGRAPHY EXAM

The AP Human Geography Exam is divided into two sections: multiple-choice questions and free-response questions. Section I of the test consists of 60 multiple-choice questions to be answered in 60 minutes. There is a 10-minute break following Section I. Section II of the test contains three free-response questions (FRQs) that are all to be completed within a 75-minute period.

OVERVIEW OF CONTENT TOPICS

The AP Human Geography Exam is based upon seven knowledge areas. The material draws examples from all over the world, and there is a limited historical timeframe with which you must be familiar. On the multiple-choice section, the distribution of questions is as follows:

Multiple-Choice Question Distribution (Approximation)

Question Types	Percent of Test	Number of Questions on Test
Thinking Geographically	8–10%	4–6
Population and Migration Patterns and Processes	12–17%	7–10
Cultural Patterns and Processes	12–17%	7–10
Political Patterns and Processes	12–17%	7–10
Agricultural and Rural Land-Use Patterns and Processes	12–17%	7–10
Cities and Urban Land-Use Patterns and Processes	12–17%	7–10
Industrial and Economic Development Patterns and Processes	12–17%	7–10

Keep in mind that geography is an academic field, and these knowledge areas overlap quite often. Still, as you can see from the table, the six major subject areas are each about one-sixth of the test and the general geographic foundations questions are scattered throughout the test. So don't spend too much study time on the foundations section versus the other six subject areas.

Free-Response Questions

Section II of the AP Human Geography Exam is the free-response section. While there is no requirement that any particular subject area be covered, there are some things you can expect in the free-response questions (FRQs):

- Each of the three free-response questions will assess at least two areas of human geography. For example, one question may ask you to explain political effects of migration, while another may involve both agricultural and economic geography.

- All three questions will present you with a real, specific geographic scenario. At least two of them will ask you to describe and discuss spatial relationships.

- The first question will be a freestanding question with no visual element such as a map or chart. The second question will involve one visual stimulus. The final question will have two stimuli, like a map and a data table, and may ask you to both analyze and explain them separately and make connections between them.

- One common task on the free-response section is the process question, for which you have to describe the details of a geographic theory, principle, or issue. In other words, explain how and why something works in a particular order—which factors, for example, affect people and cause them to migrate to place Z.

- Other things you may be asked to do on the FRQs include comparing concepts or specific situations, providing precise definitions or information, identifying cause/effect relationships, and describing potential solutions involved in a certain scenario.

Be Ready for Anything

The questions do not come in any particular order on the multiple-choice section, so be ready to jump from subject to subject throughout the exam. For example, when you take the multiple-choice portion of the exam, there may be a population question, then a city model question, and then a question on religions. Plus, we never know from year to year exactly which subjects will fall into the free-response section. This is why practice tests are so important. Your mind has to shift gears many times in the course of the exam. Think about it: your teacher has presented your AP class in an ordered manner, subject by subject. Yet you are going to be tested in a disorganized manner. Thus, you need to be mentally prepared to link subjects and jump around in order to do well.

This book will help you. If you know how the test works, then there will be far less of a chance that the randomness of the subject matter will be a problem.

Stay Up to Date!
For late-breaking information about test dates, exam formats, and any other changes pertaining to AP Human Geography, make sure to check the College Board's website at https://apstudents.collegeboard.org/courses/ap-human-geography/assessment

How Should I Study?

To figure out what to study, you need to know what is on the test and what the test-writers are looking for. We recommend you take a look at the AP Human Geography Course Description on the College Board's AP Students website. This is a great resource for studying the course topics and understanding how they will be tested on the exam.

What Do They Want From Me?

What is the AP Human Geography Exam really testing? In a nutshell, they want to know if you can use the different models, theories, principles, and issues in human geography to explain how we organize the inhabited surface of the Earth.

The AP Human Geography course is meant to help you see the world around you in a new way. For example, you shouldn't just see a city with streets and buildings. Instead, by using urban models, you can divide cities into their component parts: a central business district (CBD), industrial land use, and housing zones differentiated by income, ethnicity, age, or architecture. And you need to know how cities became that way. What are the forces that shape the theoretical place? How do principles such as site and situation matter? Are contemporary issues, such as urban sprawl, a problem for expanding cities? These are the types of questions you should ask yourself as you walk around each day to prepare for the test.

Here's Your Game Plan

To show what you know about human geography, keep the categories of models, theories, principles, and issues in mind as you study and prepare for the exam. Also, be ready to produce real-world examples to explain how something works, or even to explain why a theory may not be correct. To help you do this, here are a few overall strategies to prepare for the exam:

- Always look for linkages between the seven subject areas. If you can build associations in your mind between what may seem at first to be unrelated subjects (for example, population and economy), then you will remember it far better than if you studied those areas separately.
- Know only the relevant history required for the test (the Industrial Revolution is important, the French Revolution is not). Start approximately at 1800 C.E. and go all the way to the present.
- Ask yourself what innovative theories were developed by geographers and related scientists. Who were these people and why were their ideas important?
- Examine the component parts of models and know the details about those parts. Consider why a model is organized in a particular way. How and why do parts of different models change over time?

- Keep a personal glossary of key principles in addition to the lists we provide you with in this book. The glossary should include general terms like *space* and *place*, and specific ones like the *Zone of Peripheral Squatter Settlements*. Knowing your vocabulary and the names of important concepts helps in the multiple-choice section. Using these terms will earn you many points in the free-response section.

HOW THE AP HUMAN GEOGRAPHY EXAM IS SCORED

The scores that you receive for the AP Human Geography Exam are very different from the grades that you get in school. The report that you receive sometime around early July will give you a 1- to 5-point score rating your performance. Here is the distribution of scores among test-takers for the 2021 exam administrations.

Score	Percentage 2021	Credit Recommendation	College Grade Equivalent
5	14.4%	Extremely Well Qualified	A
4	19.7%	Well Qualified	A–, B+, B
3	18.3%	Qualified	B–, C+, C
2	15.1%	Possibly Qualified	–
1	32.4%	No Recommendation	–

Scores from the May 2021 test administration. Data taken from the College Board website.

These qualifications are the recommendation to colleges and universities as to whether you should receive credit for the course. Although these scores are associated with certain levels of grade performance by college students, you should not attach an A, B, C, D, or F grade to these scores. Why? It's a difficult standardized test—good students can do poorly, and mediocre students can achieve a high score if they are good at this type of exam. Nonetheless, **your goal is a score of 4 or 5**. A score of 3 sounds okay, but it probably won't earn you college credit. Each year somewhere between 25 percent and 27 percent of students will earn a 4 or 5. Be in the top 75 percent or above and you've achieved the goal.

How Do They Decide on the Scores?

AP scoring is a highly regulated and statistics-driven process. The overall exam score is divided evenly between the two sections:

Section Number	Section Name	Percent of Score
Section I	Multiple Choice	50%
Section II	Free Response	50%

That seems simple enough, but it's important to realize that in Section I there are 60 questions and that you write three free responses in Section II. Likewise, the way points are accumulated in each section is very different. In the following sections and in Part IV of this guide, you'll get the details of how scores are earned in each section and how you can use an AP Human Geography-specific test-taking strategy to maximize your score.

Multiple-Choice Section Scoring

As in other standardized tests, answers to the multiple-choice section are filled out by the student on a bubble sheet. Scores from these sheets are tabulated by scanning machines.

In the end, a raw score is tabulated and then compared to the performance of all the other students who took the exam. This comparison may result in a scaled score that will then be combined, at equal weight (fifty-fifty), with the score on the free-response section. How points are scaled may seem like magic, but scaling scores are done under traditional rules set by statisticians using a normalized distribution, or "bell curve."

What's a Good Multiple-Choice Score?

Depending upon how scaled scores are divided by statisticians, the number of correct answers needed to get a 4 or 5 score can vary from year to year. Set yourself a target of at least 40 correct questions out of 60 on the multiple-choice section to increase your chances of a 4 or 5 score for the exam.

Free-Response Section Scoring

You must attempt to answer each of the three free-response questions on the exam. Leaving a free-response question, or FRQ, blank will make it nearly impossible to get a 4 or 5 on the AP Human Geography Exam. What to do if you are stumped by a FRQ is covered in Chapter 2 of this guide.

The three FRQs are scored by "readers" who are experienced AP Human Geography high school teachers and university-level geography instructors or professors. Readers are organized into three teams that each focus on reading only one of the questions. All of the readers on a team are trained simultaneously to score their FRQs, and they all use the same training materials. This is done to maintain consistency in the scoring process. In addition, each reader uses a scoring "rubric," or table, that divides up the possible number of points from each section of the FRQ and indicates how points are given. Readers must follow the rubric on each and every FRQ. This is good news for AP students. There are clear and standardized ways to score points no matter who reads your responses.

Readers do not give your responses an A, B, C, D, or F grade. Instead, each FRQ score begins with 0 points, and you earn points along the way as you construct your answer and provide the correct information. You are not penalized if you write incorrect information. Each FRQ is worth 7 points, one for each task you are asked to complete.

What's a Good Free-Response Score?

Like the multiple-choice scaled score, how the free-response section is scored varies each year depending on overall student performance. To ensure a 4 or 5 exam score, set the goal of averaging at least 60 percent of the available points on the three FRQs, or about 4 points per FRQ. Be sure to score at minimum two points on your lowest-scoring response.

HOW AP EXAMS ARE USED

At the several hundred institutions of higher education that accept AP results, your score of 4 or 5 will earn you semester credit hours for a number of introductory geography classes or fulfill a general education requirement (and possibly both). These equivalent classes fall under several names at different universities, and the number of credits you earn will depend on your college's policy. You can look online or in the college's official course catalogue for class names or titles similar to the following:

- Introduction to Geography
- Introduction to Human Geography, Principles of Human Geography
- World Regional Geography, Survey of World Regions, The World Around Us
- (The Geography of) Peoples and Places (of the World)

More Great Books
For more information on colleges, you might want to check out some of our guide books, which include *The Best 388 Colleges, The Complete Guide to College Essays, Paying for College*, and many more!

Look at the general education requirements (aka liberal arts or distribution requirements) of the university to see if the class for which you receive credit also fulfills a requisite in an area such as social science, cultural diversity, or global education. At some universities, an introductory geography or world geography class can fulfill two of these general education requirements simultaneously—known as "double-dipping."

Make sure to speak to an academic advisor at the colleges or universities to which you are applying or have been accepted about how they issue credit for the 4 or 5 AP score. If they don't know or if the college does not have a policy concerning credit for the AP Human Geography Exam, there are a number of resources you can contact to help make sure that you are rewarded for your work. To resolve AP Human Geography Exam credit issues, you or your high school AP teacher should contact:

- the geography department or a geography faculty member at the university
- the dean's office of the university's school or college where the geography department is housed
- the Geographic Alliance office for the state where you are enrolled in college
- the Association of American Geographers in Washington, D.C.: www.aag.org
- the College Board: apstudents@info.collegeboard.org

Any 4s and 5s earned before you have applied to college are great to highlight on your college applications. By maximizing your score on this test in ninth, tenth, or eleventh grade, you can increase your chances of being accepted at a more prestigious institution.

Looking for More Help with Your APs?
We now offer specialized AP tutoring and course packages that guarantee a 4 or 5 on the AP. To see which courses are offered and available, and to learn more about the guarantee, visit PrincetonReview.com/college/ap-test-prep.

OTHER RESOURCES

There are many resources available to help you improve your score on the AP Human Geography Exam, not the least of which are your **teachers**. If you are taking an AP class, you may be able to get extra attention from your teacher, such as obtaining feedback on your free responses. If you are not in an AP course, reach out to someone who teaches AP Human Geography and ask if they will review your free responses or otherwise help you with content.

Another wonderful resource is **AP Students**, the official site of the AP Exams for students. The information on this site is quite broad and includes the following:

- the course description, which provides details on what content is covered and sample questions
- free-response question prompts from previous AP Human Geography Exams, along with scoring guidelines
- access to AP Classroom if you are enrolled in a course (teacher assistance required)
- exam practice tips

The AP Students home page address is: https://apstudents.collegeboard.org.

Finally, **The Princeton Review** offers tutoring and small-group instruction. Our expert instructors can help you refine your strategic approach and add to your content knowledge. For more information, call 1-800-2REVIEW.

DESIGNING YOUR STUDY PLAN

In Part I, you identified some areas of potential improvement. Let's now delve further into your performance on Practice Test 1, with the goal of developing a study plan appropriate to your needs and time commitment.

Read the answers and explanations associated with the multiple-choice questions (starting at page 33). After you have done so, respond to the following questions:

- Review your results from Step 2 of the Diagnostic Answer Key on page 32, and make a list of the chapter topics (these can be found in Step 1 as well as in the handy topic chart on page 50). Next to each chapter topic, indicate your rank of the topic as follows: "1" means "I need a lot of work on this," "2" means "I need to beef up my knowledge," and "3" means "I know this topic well."

- How many days/weeks/months away is your exam?

- What time of day is your best, most focused study time?

- How much time per day/week/month will you devote to preparing for your exam?

- When will you do this preparation? (Be as specific as possible: Mondays and Wednesdays from 3:00 to 4:00 P.M., for example.)

- Based on the answers above, will you focus on strategy (Part IV) or content (Part V) or both?

- What are your overall goals in using this book?

Need some help devising a plan of action for your studying? Check out our free AP Human Geography Exam study guide in your Student Tools. Register your book at Princeton-Review.com/prep for access.

Part IV
Test-Taking Strategies for the AP Human Geography Exam

PREVIEW

Review your Practice Test 1 results and then respond to the following questions:

- How many multiple-choice questions did you miss even though you knew the answers?
- On how many multiple-choice questions did you guess randomly?
- How many multiple-choice questions did you miss after eliminating some answers and guessing based on the remaining answers?
- Did you find any of the free-response questions easier or harder than the others—and, if so, why?

HOW TO USE THE CHAPTERS IN THIS PART

For the following Strategy chapters, think about what you are doing now before you read the chapters. As you read and engage in the directed practice, be sure to think critically about the ways in which you can change your approach.

Chapter 1
How to Approach
Multiple-Choice
Questions

WHAT YOU NEED TO KNOW

Before you begin to prepare for the multiple-choice questions, let's review the critical information about the section that we covered in the introduction.

SECTION I: MULTIPLE-CHOICE QUESTIONS

Number of Questions: 60
Time Allowed: 60 minutes
Writing Instrument: No. 2 pencil
Needed for a 4 or 5: Minimum 40 correct answers

Now that you have that in mind, to do well on this part of the AP Human Geography Exam you need to know your human geography and how to answer multiple-choice AP questions. You may know the material from class and your textbook very well, but if you don't know *how to take the test,* then you won't get the credit you deserve.

Let's consider two possible scenarios:

> Josh is a student getting good grades in high school AP Human Geography all year and then gets a low score on the AP exam because he's not ready for these types of questions. On the other end of the spectrum, Jessica is a student who is not very comfortable with all the various topics in the AP Human Geography course. However, because she knows how to effectively answer the multiple-choice questions, she winds up getting a 4 on the exam—much to the chagrin of Josh.

You may be wondering, "How can I do well on the exam and not end up like Josh?" *You need a strategy.* The key is to get inside the head of the people testing you. In this section we will show you how the College Board and their test-writers put you under pressure, and how they write the questions to trick you into choosing the wrong answer. Along the way, we will give you several strategies and practice opportunities to crack the multiple-choice section.

MULTIPLE-CHOICE STRATEGY

In this section, we'll go over the rules of effective multiple-choice test-taking, discuss time management, and teach you how to use Process of Elimination. Combined, these strategies will improve your AP multiple-choice test-taking skills and score.

RULES OF EFFECTIVE AP TEST-TAKING

To score your best on the multiple-choice section of this test, you will first need to remember the following rules:

- Finishing is not the real goal; accuracy is.
- Keep in mind you have limited time.
- Four out of every five answer choices are wrong.

Pacing

Guessing also raises your score because it saves you time. Wasted time is your enemy. Sixty questions in 60 minutes is a lot. In practical terms, it's about one minute per question. How can you possibly answer all the questions in such a short time period? Two ways: Guess and Go, or Don't.

Guess and Go

Consider the thought process of two AP Human Geography test-takers as it relates to the following question:

The international treaty that laid the interior political boundaries of sub-Saharan Africa was

(A) Treaty of Ghent
(B) Potsdam Agreement
(C) Camp David Accords
(D) Treaty of Versailles
(E) Berlin Conference

Josh

The political boundaries of Africa—I know this was decided by European colonial powers, and not Africans. It was in the late 1800s or early 1900s, so that eliminates (A). Potsdam was at the end of World War II, and Camp David was much more recent. So that gets rid of (B) and (C). Now, what were the other two? Versailles was the home of the French kings. But, they were gone at the end of the French Revolution, in the late 1700s. Berlin is near Potsdam. Here it's a "conference" and not a "treaty" like in (D)...Hmmm...Both sound possible. Was it in France? The French had a lot of colonies in Africa. I think the Germans had colonies in Africa too, but I'm not sure how many or where. Which country would be most likely to host such an international treaty? The Germans were really powerful in the early twentieth century and defeated France a few times. But the French were the larger colonial power around the world. Hmmm...Which one is more likely to be the location of this treaty? Well, (D) sounds great but so does (E). I put (D) for the last answer so maybe this one should be (E), or maybe that last one was wrong. Maybe I should read and rephrase the question again...

Jessica

The political boundaries of Africa—these were divided by European colonial powers around the late 1800s. Africa was the last part of the world to become colonized by Europeans. And the last part of the world to gain independence. Ghent was part of American history, so cross off (A). Potsdam and Camp David were about World War II and Israel, respectively, so cross off (B) and (C). Versailles is in France and Berlin is in Germany. So it's either (D) or (E). Versailles was the home of Louis XV, who lived in the 1700s. And it's a museum today. Thus, (D) doesn't sound right. I'll *guess* (E).

Next question.

The central business district within that concentric zone model is found...

In the scenario above, Josh continues to deliberate between (D) and (E) while Jessica goes on to the next question. What's the difference? Jessica did all the work she could considering the remaining options, took a smart guess, and then moved on. Josh did all the work he could, but he got stuck trying to make a decision between the two remaining options. As the test goes on, Josh will lag further and further behind Jessica, not because he knows less human geography, but because he is less willing to take that guess and move onward, and *save time*. To do well on the AP Human Geography Exam, you'll need to do what you can, be willing to *take your best guess, and then move on* to the next question.

...OR DON'T

This is not to suggest that speeding through the test is your goal. In fact, focusing on finishing the section is the wrong goal altogether. You should work accurately and efficiently on the questions you *can* answer correctly so that you earn a solid raw score. To do so, you might not even attempt some of the questions. If you truly cannot eliminate even one answer choice, then you're better off randomly guessing, which costs you nothing. Or, if you prefer to save the question for later, put a circle around the number of the question you're skipping in the test booklet—not on the answer sheet! This way you know to skip bubbling in an answer for that question. Additionally, you'll be able to take another look at those questions if you have time after you answer all the ones that are easier for you.

Rushing to finish the test only to misread questions or make a bunch of careless mistakes won't get you a good score. Likewise, avoid wasting extra time with a question once you've done all that you can to solve it. Instead, as you practice for the exam, find the pace at which you can work efficiently and effectively without sacrificing accuracy.

YOU SET THE PACE

After you study your geography notes, textbook, and the content-review chapters of this book, practice your multiple-choice strategy by using the full-length practice tests in this book to determine your optimal pace. Can you answer 60 questions in 60 minutes and get most of them right? If so, you can very well receive 48 or more raw score points, and likely score a 4 or above depending on your free responses. Are you able to answer only about 48–50 questions and maintain accuracy? If so, you can still get nearly 48 raw score points by being accurate. In the end, being accurate can be far more important than finishing.

PROCESS OF ELIMINATION

Every time you read a multiple-choice question, remember that four of the five answer choices are wrong. Use the Process of Elimination (POE) method to get rid of what you know is wrong as you go through the answer choices (use a diagonal slash through the letter—(E̸)—in the question booklet, *not on the bubble sheet!*) Then deal with any answer choices that remain.

For most questions, you'll be able to eliminate two or three answer choices relatively quickly. That leaves you with two choices to consider. Don't forget about the guessing reward. We'll talk more about POE throughout the rest of this chapter. Just remember that all the answer choices are "wrong until proven right," and you'll be on your way to showing what you know on the multiple-choice part of the test.

What If I Can't Eliminate ANYTHING?

If you can't eliminate any answers, it's best to pick a "Letter of the Day" (or LOTD, as we call it) and move on. There is no penalty for incorrect answers; your score is based on the number of questions you answer correctly, so you have nothing to lose by guessing. Always keep in mind that the multiple-choice section is difficult if not impossible for most students to finish on time. Your goal is to end up with a minimum of 40 correct answers. If you did that on a regular test at school that had 60 questions, you'd see a score of 66 percent and most likely have a "D" next to your name. Fortunately, that's not how the AP exam works. As long as you do reasonably well on the free-response section, you'll have a chance to earn that 4 or 5 that you are working to achieve.

"EXCEPT" Questions

Occasionally, the multiple-choice question is inverted. When you see a question with the word "EXCEPT" or "NOT" in it, then you know four out of five answers are correct. Your job is to uncover the wrong one. Often these are comparison questions where the two things being compared have a lot in common. In the question booklet, put a check mark next to each answer that is true, or not an exception. Then use Process of Elimination (POE) to work through the other possibilities and find the one that doesn't fit.

POE = BFF

Process of Elimination can make all the difference when it comes to multiple-choice question strategy. Instead of trying to pinpoint the correct answer, focus on getting rid of the wrong ones!

Guessing and Your LOTD

Since this test does not have a guessing penalty (in other words, you don't lose points for wrong answers), you should ALWAYS guess on questions you don't know. Pick a Letter of the Day (LOTD) and bubble in that letter on questions where you can't eliminate any answer choices.

THE STEPS TO CRACKING A QUESTION

Now we'll show you a step-by-step method to solving multiple-choice questions. The best way to learn this process is to practice on an AP Human Geography Exam question.

5. The purpose of the European Coal and Steel Community and the European Economic Community (Common Market), which later led to the European Union, was to form supranational organizations based upon the concept of

    (A)   open border policies
    (B)   a single European currency, or Euro
    (C)   nuclear disarmament
    (D)   military cooperation with the United States and Canada
    (E)   free-trade policies

Step 1: Read and Rephrase the Question

First you must make sure that you understand what the question is asking. Rephrase the question so that it is clear to you. Read the sample question again; what is it really asking?

What was the purpose of the organizations that preceded the European Union?

Step 2: When? Who and Where? What?

Before you read the answer choices, you must get an idea of the historical period or the political or economic context you are in (the when), who is involved and where, and what the question is asking you. Answer these questions in your mind or even in the question booklet before you read the answer choices. For example, in the above question about European supranationalism, you can answer in the following way:

When? Post-World War II Europe
Who and Where? The original members of the European Union, Western Europe
What? Supranational organizations

Once you've answered these questions, take a moment to call up the relevant economic geography that you know. If it's a topic you know, it should be easy to find the correct answer. If not, you can still use what you know to get rid of the wrong answer choices using Process of Elimination.

Step 3: Process of Elimination

Even if you don't exactly know the history of the formation of the European Union, you can still use strategy to eliminate wrong answer choices. Remember to read each answer choice with a critical eye, looking for what makes it wrong. Cross off the choices that you know are wrong; leave ones that you are uncertain about or those you think may be correct.

Let's review what we know so far about the question:

When? After World War II
Who and Where? Western European countries
What? Supranational organizations

Ask yourself what you know about the European Union and its predecessors. You probably know that it's mainly an organization based upon economic policy, unlike NATO, which has a military-strategic purpose. Armed with this information, let's take a look at the answer choices.

Learn more about the EU in Chapter 6.

5. The purpose of the European Coal and Steel Community and the European Economic Community (Common Market), which later led to the European Union, was to form supranational organizations based upon the concept of

   (A) open border policies

   (B) a single European currency, or Euro

   (C) nuclear disarmament

   (D) military cooperation with the United States and Canada

   (E) free-trade policies

Take a look at (C). Do coal and steel have anything to do with nuclear arms? No. Cross off (C). How about (D)? Again, none of the names of these groups imply anything to do with the military. However, many of the countries that we're talking about, but not all, were members of the North Atlantic Treaty Organization (NATO). NATO and the EU are two different types of the same thing. So scratch off (D). You may not be sure about (A), (B), or (E). All of these are major functions of the European Union today. Thus, you have to ask which of these was the *purpose* of these precursor organizations. You may know that the Euro was only recently introduced, in the year 2000. Therefore, you should feel confident in scratching off (B).

If you're stuck between (A) and (E), what should you do? Take a guess.

Step 4: Guess and Go

Once you've narrowed down the choices as much as you can, take a guess. As you learned, the *guessing reward* benefits students who are willing to take smart guesses throughout the test. Using Process of Elimination (POE) to get rid of choices that you know are wrong, and then taking a smart guess from among the remaining choices, can help you score a personal best on this test.

After using POE, you have a fifty-fifty shot of guessing the right answer on our sample question, so just pick one if you can't get any further.

Let's look at (A). Open-border policies are something that Europeans enjoy, because they no longer have to stop at the border for customs or immigration officers. This does not seem directly linked to coal and steel or larger markets. And coal and steel are commodities that are directly *traded* between countries. Thus, (A) is not likely the answer, and (E) is the correct answer.

> The European Coal and Steel Community and the Common Market were established as free-trade zones that removed tariffs on goods moving across international borders between member states. This reduced production costs and made European steel and other products cheaper on international markets. This was an attempt to create a comparative advantage for European Steel companies.

Can you see how taking a moment to frame the question can help you find the right answer quickly and easily? Knowing just some of the information can be enough to make a smart guess. This does not mean that you should not learn as much of the material on supranational organizations as possible. The more you know, the easier it will be to eliminate wrong answer choices and zero in on the correct answer. However, using the steps and POE will help you get the right answer quickly by making the most of the information you know.

Step by Step by Step by Step

Let's go through the four steps again by working on another AP Human Geography multiple-choice question.

19. The population statistic that uses the difference between crude birth rates and crude death rates, and estimates the annual percentage growth rate of a country's population, is known as the

(A) total fertility rate (TFR)

(B) replacement rate

(C) rate of natural increase (RNI)

(D) doubling time

(E) total life expectancy

Step 1: Read and Rephrase the Question

What statistic is used to measure a country's population growth?

Step 2: When? Who and Where? What?

When? This is not a question that requires a historical, political, or economic context. However, there is an important context clue in the word "annual." The question is asking about a statistic that is calculated each and every year.

Who and Where? The whole country's population. Nothing in the question tells us that we're dealing with a specific group or place.

What? A population statistic that measures "annual" growth.

Step 3: Process of Elimination

You know that both doubling time (D) and total life expectancy (E) are statistics that are measured over a long period of time. So cross them off. You know that the replacement rate is a TFR of 2.1. So cross off (B). However, you are not sure how the TFR is calculated, so leave (A).

Step 4: Guess and Go

Now you have (A) and (C) left. Guess and go or reason it out a little more. You think fertility has something to do with births, but not deaths. So cross off (A). And (C) is your answer. Move on to the next question.

PRACTICE THE STEPS

Now it's your turn. Use the four steps to solve the following multiple-choice question by filling in the blanks on page 72.

14. Which of the following countries is the best example of a current theocracy?

   (A)   China
   (B)   Greece
   (C)   Great Britain
   (D)   Iran
   (E)   Turkey

Step 1: Read and rephrase the question.

_____

_____

_____

Step 2: When? Who and Where? What?

When? _____

Who and Where? _____

What? _____

Step 3: Process of Elimination

_____

_____

_____

_____

Step 4: Guess and Go

_____

_____

_____

Step 1: Read and Rephrase the Question

First, take a moment to identify the word *theocracy*. If you can't think of it off the top of your head, try to think of a country that might be a theocracy, like Saudi Arabia. This should help you to ask, "Which country is ruled by religion?"

Step 2: When? Who and Where? What?

Remember that these questions are meant to narrow down and eliminate choices.

When? Unless otherwise indicated, a question is generally asking about present conditions.

Who and Where? In this instance, the two are the same: we're looking for an entire country.

What? More specifically, we're looking for a country ruled by religion.

Step 3: Process of Elimination

Choice (A), China, can be crossed off immediately, as a formal religion rarely exists under Communism. Choice (B), Greece, may be a possibility. *Theocracy* is a Greek word, but the Greeks have a long tradition of democracy. So cross off this answer. Choice (C), Great Britain, is also a possibility. The monarch of Great Britain is also the head of the Church of England. Before you decide on this answer, take a look at the other answers to see if there is a better one—remember the word *best* in the question. Choice (D), Iran, is a strong possibility. The country has been ruled by ayatollahs, which are Muslim clerics who have ruled the country since the fall of the Shah. Choice (E), Turkey, is a possible choice. Turkey is mostly Muslim; however, the nation is applying to become part of the European Union. Keep this point in mind: a theocracy like the one in Saudi Arabia would not be what Europeans had in mind for the EU. Thus, Turkey must not be a theocracy.

Step 4: Guess and Go

Now you have to guess between Great Britain and Iran. The monarch in Great Britain (currently Queen Elizabeth II) is the head of the Church of England. But, in Britain, people seem to have a lot of religious freedom. However, in Iran, there is not much religious freedom at all. Therefore, Iran, (D), is the best answer (and is correct).

MAP QUESTIONS

There are going to be a number of questions on the multiple-choice section that require you to identify a region, read the pattern on a map, or analyze a graph or table of data.

For the map questions, you'll need to be able to identify the places and examples that you have learned in class. One way to test yourself is to get blank maps and fill in the locations of regions, migration patterns, and example countries and cities as you study your class notes.

You might be saying to yourself, "My teacher said there isn't a map quiz on the exam!" On the AP Human Geography Exam, there aren't any map questions that ask you to simply identify a point or a country. Nor would you be asked to name the capital of a country. These questions are too simple. It is assumed that you have learned where most places are on the map as part of the course. However, you are expected to answer map questions that involve geographic principles and theories. Often these questions ask you to identify examples of the concepts you have learned, and for that you'll need the background knowledge and map practice.

Many map questions are like simple definition questions. Either you know where something is or you don't. However, as we just learned with the definition and definition-example questions, there are ways to eliminate some of the possible answers and increase your chances of guessing correctly even when you don't have the concrete knowledge.

Let's work through a map question together.

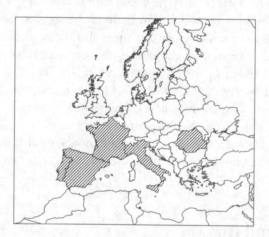

32. The shaded area on the map depicts areas in Europe where

(A) Roman Catholicism is the most popular religion
(B) Romance languages are the dominant linguistic group
(C) the Euro is the only accepted currency
(D) agriculture represents more than 50 percent of the economy
(E) constitutional monarchy is the form of government

Step 1: Read and Rephrase the Question

Read the map to rephrase the question:

What do southwestern Europe and Romania have in common?

Step 2: When? Who and Where? What?

When? Recognize that the map is of contemporary Europe.

Who and Where? The two areas, which include Portugal, Spain, France, Italy, and Romania, but also southern Belgium and parts of Switzerland. Also notice the parts of Europe not included in the two areas.

What? A common regional characteristic or trait common to both areas.

Step 3: Process of Elimination

With little to go on from the printed question, let's go through the answers one by one. All of the areas in the western area appear to be Catholic-dominated. Is Romania? No. But if you weren't sure, ask yourself if there are other Catholic-dominated areas in Europe. One in particular should stick out, Ireland—it's not shaded. Therefore, (A) is probably not the answer.

Choice (B), Romance languages include Portuguese, Spanish, French, Italian, and (as you might guess from the name) Romanian. But what about Belgium and Switzerland? So far, (B) looks like a good answer, but we should go through the rest to make sure it's the *best* answer. The Euro, (C), is not accepted in Great Britain, true. But it is the only currency in Germany, Denmark, Austria, Sweden, and Finland. So (C) is not likely. Choice (D) is very unlikely, because even in the peripheral regions of Europe (e.g., Portugal and Romania), services and manufacturing dominate economic productivity. Choice (E) is like (D) and (A). There are constitutional monarchies outside of the shaded area (e.g., Great Britain, the Netherlands, Denmark, and Sweden). Also, consider that in France and Italy, monarchy has long since vanished. Cross that one off, too.

Step 4: Guess and Go

No need to guess here; (B) is the only answer that fits. Here are the details. The southern half of Belgium, referred to as Wallonia, is French-speaking. Likewise, French and Italian are two of the four regional languages within Switzerland (along with German and Romansch).

QUESTIONS WITH GRAPHS AND TABLES

Another common type of question involves reading graphs or tables. In the AP Human Geography course, you are expected to be able to read and analyze numerical data—what geographers refer to as "quantitative" data. Why? A lot of geographical analysis work involves number crunching. Being able to read the numerical results of analysis is a necessary skill.

What Do They Ask?

Most of the numerical data in the exam is drawn from the *population* and *economic* geography sections of the course. As will be discussed in Part V of this book, knowing what is a **high**, **low**, and **normal** or **stable rate** (like RNI, or rate of natural increase), **indicator** (like GNP, or gross national product), or **index** (like HDI, or human development index) score is important to your ability to answer such questions correctly. A graph will often show you two types of data and ask about the relationship between them. For example, a population pyramid shows the total population by gender and age cohort—the bottom bar shows the number of males age 0 to 4 on the left and females age 0 to 4 on the right, and then moves up in age from there—5 to 9, 10 to 14, and so on. A table shows you groupings of data, often in rows and columns. The categories of data will be across the top and the place-names will be the first column on the left, like in the example in the following table:

Name	Population	RNI	Total Life Expectancy
Country X	10,000,000	1.2%	64
Country Y	40,000,000	−0.2%	78
Country Z	50,000,000	2.3%	53

You are then going to be asked one or more questions about what you see in the data. Sometimes not all of the data is relevant, but it's likely that you are going to have to read the entire table to get the gist of the question.

Furthermore, *if you know the theory or principle behind the question, the actual numbers may be irrelevant.* You will need to be able to identify one example as being in a specific category versus another example being in a separate category. For example, in the table above, Country Z is likely a Third-World agricultural-based economy, versus Country Y, which is a First-World nation in Europe. How do you know? The numbers are indicative of these categories and places. A negative RNI (shrinking population) with a high life expectancy is a combination found only in highly developed nations with service-based economies and good social services. A high RNI (strong population growth) and low life expectancy is expected only in agriculturally based Third-World regions.

Mastering the basic skills of numerical analysis is not only possible for every student, but is a necessity for the AP Human Geography Exam. These tables are essentially puzzles with basic rules required to solve them. The rules are determined by the theories and principles behind the data. *Know the theories and principles, and you will know the rules.*

Let's look at a graph question to apply the principles we know to answer the puzzle.

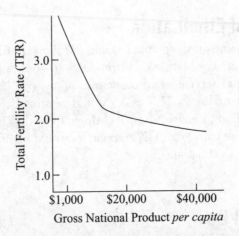

18. Using the graph above, what would be the expected total fertility rate (TFR) of a Third-World, agriculture-based country?

(A) 1.8
(B) 2.0
(C) 2.4
(D) 3.2
(E) 6.0

Now let's practice those steps again.

Step 1: Read and Rephrase the Question

What is a TFR that would be found in your average Third-World agricultural country?

Step 2: When? Who and Where? What?

When? This is not a question that requires a historical or political context.

Who and Where? The economic context of "Third-World" and "agricultural" is critical here. The question is *not* asking you about newly industrialized countries (NICs). Instead, think about poor Third-World countries where agriculture is the primary source of economic production.

What? Fertility in poor countries, which we expect to be high, just as fertility in wealthier countries tends to be low.

Step 3: Process of Elimination

Reading the curved trend line on the graph, (A) and (B) show TFRs that are too low, as they represent GNP *per capita* at very high levels of production—per capita dollar amounts found only in manufacturing- and service-based economies. Cross out (A) and (B). Choice (C) is unlikely because on the trend line, a TFR of 2.4 would be around $6,000 to $8,000 per year, which is what you would find in many NICs. To help you visualize it, use the straight edge on the side of your pencil to measure what GNP *per capita* would be for a particular TFR. Cross out (C). Now you're left with (D) and (E).

Step 4: Guess and Go

Note that the question says "Using the graph above"; 6.0 does not appear on the graph, even though the trend line could, in theory, reach that level. Choice (D) is your best choice since a TFR of 3.2 is around $1,000 in GNP *per capita*, which is representative of the economic productivity of agriculture-based economies.

THEORY QUESTIONS

So far, so good! However, not all questions are going to be factual (such as names of treaties), historical (such as the history of European free-trade), definitional (such as fertility rates), or definition-example (such as theocracy in Iran). Some questions are going to require you to *interpret* theories that you have learned in your AP course. When theory questions come up, you have to make sure that you understand the question. This step becomes even more critical, as we will see in the example below.

33. The relationship between Thomas Malthus's theory of population and the Green Revolution is best historically characterized by which of the following?

    (A) Green Revolution agricultural technologies have increased food production, thus extending global carrying capacity and decreasing the overpopulation predicted by Malthus.

    (B) Green Revolution theorists ideologically rejected Malthus's theory, and his ideas were not accepted until the late twentieth century by neo-Malthusian scholars.

    (C) As part of the Green Revolution, Malthus predicted many of the environmental problems that emerged in the twentieth century, such as famine and global warming.

    (D) Malthus predicted the coming of the Green Revolution, where new agricultural technologies, such as pesticides, hybrids, fertilizers, and mechanization, would play an important role in increasing agricultural production.

    (E) Malthus invented several Green Revolution technologies, such as chemical fertilizers and pesticides. He predicted that his inventions would allow for a larger global population.

Step 1: Read and Rephrase the Question

Your first inclination is to ask, "What's the link between Malthus and the Green Revolution?" However, you should step back and ask yourself what you know about these two bodies of theory. Malthus makes a warning against overpopulation, and the Green Revolution feeds more people. The two theories are, in a way, contradictory. Therefore, you should ask, "How might the Green Revolution contradict Malthus, or vice versa?"

Step 2: When? Who and Where? What?

This step is still important for the theory question. Divide up these questions and ask yourself what you know about each theory.

When? Malthus was in the early 1800s. The Green Revolution was in the 20th century.

Who and Where? Malthus was concerned that the world would become overpopulated and not be able to feed itself. The Green Revolution benefited farmers in the Third World.

What? Malthus used mathematics to model population growth and food production. The Green Revolution was a collection of agricultural technologies that made for large increases in global farm production.

> Malthusian theory is discussed in Chapter 4, and the Green Revolution is explained in Chapter 7.

Step 3: Process of Elimination

From your answers in Step 2, you can automatically eliminate some of the multiple-choice answers. Choices (B), (C), and (E) should be obvious eliminations based on what you know about the two theories. They are factually wrong. This leaves you with (A) and (D). Both list the Green Revolution and Malthus's theory in the correct chronological order.

Step 4: Guess and Go

What was Malthus's prediction? Did he just worry about too many people and not enough food, or did he also predict the solution? Go back to your reformulation of the question. Malthus (and later neo-Malthusians) *warned* about the dangers of overpopulation. He predicted gloom and doom, not the bounty of new farming technologies. Thus, (A) is the best answer.

COMPARISON QUESTIONS

In addition to being a theory question, the last example was also a comparison question. Comparison questions ask you to examine the relationships between two concepts or phenomena. Let's look at another comparison question for which there may be two answers to each of the when, who, where, and what in Step 2.

21. In an examination of the Burgess concentric zone model of the Anglo-American city and the Ford Griffin Model of the Latin American city, what differences are found in the location of poor residential areas?

   (A) In the concentric zone model, the poor are in the CBD, and in the Latin American city model, the poor are in the Zone of Maturity.

   (B) In the concentric zone model, the poor are in the periphery, and in the Latin American city model, the poor are in the inner city.

   (C) In the concentric zone model, the poor are in the periphery, and in the Latin American city model, the poor are in Zones of Disamenity.

   (D) In the concentric zone model, the poor are in the CBD, and in the Latin American city model, the poor are in the Zone of *in situ* Accretion.

   (E) In the concentric zone model, the poor are in the inner city, and in the Latin American city model, the poor are in the periphery.

Step 1: Read and Rephrase the Question

Again, we have two theories being compared. You might first be inclined to ask, "How are the two urban models different in structure and where are poor residential areas found in each?" However, a more basic question can be asked: "Where do poor people live in U.S. cities versus those in Latin American cities?" Remember that urban models try to generalize the average city in a region. In relative terms, locations should be roughly the same in most cities.

Step 2: When? Who and Where? What?

Divide up these questions to ask yourself what you know, basically, about each region and theory.

When? In the models, concentric zones are from the 1920s; the Latin American city model is contemporary and updated.

Who and Where? Poor in cities. In Anglo-America (the United States and Canada), they have been there for a while. In Latin America, many are recent migrants from the rural areas.

What? Residential space (homes) of the poor in cities.

Step 3: Process of Elimination

The concentric zone model doesn't necessarily say where the poor live. Yet, you do know that many poor people in the United States and Canada live in the inner city. The Latin American city model says that there are peripheral squatter settlements. Squatters are typically poor and cannot afford to buy land. Having said this, we can eliminate (A), (B), and (C). Choice (A) is wrong since in the Latin American city model, the poor aren't in the Zone of Maturity. Choice (B) is wrong because of the first part of the answer, and (C) is wrong because both parts of the answer are wrong. You're left with (D) and (E).

Step 4: Guess and Go

Looking at (D), you may think the poor in the United States and Canada could be in the CBD (central business district), and you may not be sure what *in situ* accretion means. Choice (E) seems to fit better with "inner city" and the poor being located in peripheral squatter settlements. We'll go with (E), even though (D) appears to be a parallel answer ((E) is correct). For what it's worth, *in situ* accretion is a less affluent area where homes and businesses are in a continual state of construction and renovation.

This question required you to visualize two graphical models. Knowing the models is very important in the AP Human Geography Exam, as sometimes the questions will show you the models, and sometimes they won't—you need to be able to visualize them in your head. Therefore, we advise you to pay close attention to the Know the Models sections of the content-review chapters in Part V of this book.

Okay! That was a lot of practice. Now you'll do some problems on your own, score yourself, review, and then move on to the next chapter and learn about the free-response questions.

PRACTICE QUESTIONS

Now that you have the basic tools to crack the multiple-choice section, use what you have learned on the following set of 10 questions. Use a watch to time how long it takes you to answer the questions accurately. Answers and explanations follow the quiz. Following the explanations, we will show you what your time and score mean and how you should adjust your pacing and strategy.

1. A port where goods are imported from other parts of the world and then re-exported for profit to foreign locations is known as a(n)

   (A) exclusive economic zone
   (B) break-in-bulk point
   (C) resource node
   (D) entrepôt
   (E) commodity chain

2. What type of economic production contributes to the majority of the GDP in the United States and Great Britain?

   (A) Agriculture
   (B) Real estate
   (C) Manufacturing
   (D) Services
   (E) Construction

3. The concept in which all things in geographic space are related, but closer things are more related than others, is the basis of

   (A) environmental determinism
   (B) spatial analysis
   (C) spatial statistics
   (D) contagious diffusion
   (E) Tobler's law

4. Which of following would be a negative social effect of gentrification in cities?

   (A) Old homes would be converted with updated materials and fixtures.
   (B) Older residents would receive new homes in suburban areas.
   (C) Increased real estate prices and rents would force out poor residents.
   (D) Construction companies would have projects in areas of existing housing.
   (E) Older architecture would be preserved instead of building new structures.

5. In von Thünen's model of the Isolated State, the main factor in the cost-to-distance relationship of agricultural patterns and land rent is the

   (A) degree to which land use is labor-intensive
   (B) cost of energy, particularly fuel wood
   (C) cost of livestock and feed
   (D) volume of sales in the market center
   (E) distance from transport lines, mainly rivers and roads

6. Communities of Pakistani citizens who today live in Birmingham, England, yet who retain many of their unique Pakistani cultural markers, would be an example of

   (A) colonies
   (B) exclaves
   (C) enclaves
   (D) culture hearths
   (E) special economic zones

7. What is the major limitation of solar panel electricity production, in comparison to other "renewables"?

   (A) They can be used only during the summer.
   (B) The process requires large amounts of water.
   (C) Solar panels have to be imported from foreign manufacturers.
   (D) On average, electricity can be produced for only half of the day.
   (E) The panel reflectance contributes to the greenhouse effect.

8. The origin of San Francisco, California, as a human settlement is based upon the site characteristic of its

   (A) relative position halfway between New York and Hawaii
   (B) location as a transport node at the intersection of the Pacific Ocean and the inland waterways of San Francisco Bay
   (C) relative position halfway between Europe and Asia
   (D) relative position halfway up the coast of California
   (E) location as a resource node within the California gold-mining region

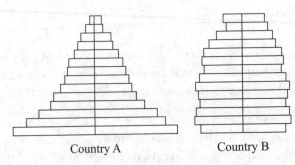

Country A   Country B

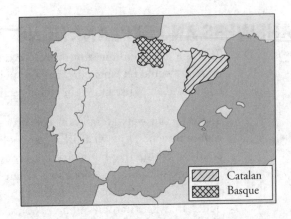

Catalan
Basque

9. From the two population pyramids above, what can we deduce about these countries?

(A) Country A is slow-growing, and Country B is growing quickly.

(B) Country A is likely in the Third World, and Country B is in the First World.

(C) Country A has a low percentage dependent population, and Country B has almost no dependents.

(D) Country A is a First-World country, and Country B is likely in the Third World.

(E) Country A is a shrinking population, and Country B has stable population growth.

10. These two areas within Spain have the following in common EXCEPT

(A) both nations have primary languages other than Spanish

(B) both areas have status as autonomous regions with limited self-government

(C) both nations have a strong French cultural influence

(D) both are areas of irredentism

(E) both are distinct culture regions separate from the main Spanish culture

ANSWERS AND EXPLANATIONS

1. **D**   This is a definition question from the economic geography section of the course. An example of an entrepôt would be Singapore, a major port where manufactured goods are shipped in from the rest of Asia and then redistributed in global retail networks to consumers around the world.

   The other answers are all concepts from the economic geography section of the course. Exclusive economic zones, known as EEZs, are political boundaries that lie 200 nautical miles off the coast of a country. Within that boundary, countries control the economic resources of that sea or ocean territory. Break-in-bulk points are locations where goods are off-loaded from one form of transportation onto another form of transportation, thus breaking up goods into smaller units to be distributed. Resource nodes are where natural resources connect to lines of transportation. Commodity chains are the production linkages from resources to suppliers and then assemblage networks.

2. **D**   The United States and Great Britain are First-World economies where the majority of the GDP is derived from services. Although both the United States and United Kingdom are often referred to as "industrialized" countries, the percent of GDP gained from manufacturing has been in decline since the 1960s. Services such as finance, insurance, and real estate along with health care and entertainment create much of the wealth and employment for these countries. Remember that GDP is the total volume of economic production.

   Use POE to eliminate (A), agriculture, right away on this question. Real estate and construction, (B) and (E) respectively, are each too narrow of a category of economic sectors to be a "majority" of the GDP. This leaves manufacturing, (C), and services, (D), as your two choices. Knowing that manufacturing is in decline in the United States and Britain would give you the perfect guess-and-go answer. If you didn't know this, another thing to think about is the dollar value of services compared to manufacturing. Think of buying a new car. The sticker price may be $15,000. However, when you use a financial service to get a loan to pay for it, with interest you will wind up paying much more. Likewise, imagine that you just paid $100,000 for a dump truck. However, the insurance policy (a service) for all of a company's dump trucks combined with the value of the construction contracts (services) where these trucks will be used will be in the millions of dollars.

3. **E**   Waldo Tobler was a geographer who specialized in spatial analysis. His idea about relationships in geographic space is one of the few "laws" in geographic science. Choice (A), environmental determinism, is the scientific ideology that the physical world shapes culture and society. As major subfields in geography, (B) and (C) are concepts that are too broad to be the answer for what is a specific definition question. Contagious diffusion, (D), is a process in which an idea or technology moves across physical space, from location to location, in a contiguous pattern, where the idea or technology moves between locations that touch each other on the map.

4. **C**   In this theory question, similar to the "EXCEPT" questions, four out of five answers are likely to be things that may sound like positive social effects of gentrification. Your job is to pick out the negative one. Increased real estate prices as a result of gentrification often create a real estate market in which poor residents cannot afford increased rents or to buy a home in their neighborhood.

   Choice (A) is the answer for a definition question on gentrification. Choice (B) is not always true, but can be a possibility for those who still own older homes and use the proceeds to buy elsewhere. In (D), the term "construction" exists to distract you. Is construction bad? Many people complain about dust, equipment, or road construction. Or is it good? It doesn't matter. Choice (E) is often seen as a positive to those people who are concerned about historical preservation.

5. **A** This is a theoretical model question that does not tell you the model. It is asking you about the principles behind the geography of the model. Von Thünen was not designing an agricultural landscape. He was observing common patterns in the landscape and asking why these patterns existed. At the center of this model were the most labor-intensive activities: dairying, vegetable farming, and woodcutting for lumber and energy. At the outer edge of the model were activities such as animal grazing and the raising of grain crops, which required little tending. Land rents that farmers would pay were scaled upon the type of agriculture and intensity of the labor performed. Know your models!

6. **C** An enclave exists where a minority ethnic group is concentrated within a country. The UK has a long history of accepting immigrants from Pakistan, particularly to neighborhoods in Birmingham, where Pakistani language, food, music, and cultural practices are often retained and celebrated. Choice (A) can be eliminated, as the concept of the "colony" in political terms went out of use in the 1970s when the last European colonies in Africa gained independence. Choice (B), exclaves, refers to a situation in which part of the political state is separated by land from the main body of the state. Russia, Armenia, Azerbaijan, and Oman all have exclaves. Even Alaska can be considered an exclave of the United States. Culture hearths, (D), can be eliminated, as they refer to areas where ancient civilizations began. Likewise, (E) can be eliminated as special economic zones refer to export processing areas in China.

7. **D** Here is a difficult comparison question from the resources category. Solar electricity has a number of technical development issues, as well as production costs. But there is one practical issue that may escape analytical comparison with other forms of renewable energy such as geothermal power or hydropower—that is, the sun shines for half a day, on average. In fact, none of the other answers are true. Here the distraction is caused by making you contemplate these wide-ranging possibilities.

8. **B** San Francisco, although it is associated with the gold rush of 1849, was inhabited before Europeans arrived and was utilized as a transportation intersection between two major bodies of water. This is a definition-example question, in which the term "transport node" is buried in one of the answers. You must extract the "San Francisco" example from the question. The trick here is not to be distracted by the concept of relative position. Choices (A), (C), and (D) are all relatively true, but none are meaningful in determining the origins of human settlement in this place.

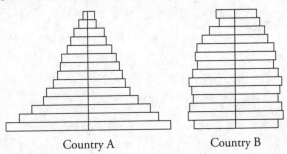

Country A   Country B

9. **B** Here's your graph question. You need to be able to interpret the shape of the population pyramids. Notice the question does not give you age cohorts or population sizes. Country A with its broad base and narrow top shows the typical equilateral pyramid shape of Third-World countries. Here there are many children being born (a large youth-dependent population), but very few old people. This large number of children indicates high fertility rates, typical of the Third World. Country B has the columnar shape typical of First-World countries, where the narrow bottom shows a limited number of children in the total population, and thus low fertility rates and high survival rates.

Use POE to eliminate (A), (D), and (E) as a result. The issue of dependent populations in (C) is indeterminate. In each country, if you added up the young people and the old people, the total of the dependent population could turn out to be about the same. The thing to watch out for here is the second part of (C), which says that country B has almost no dependents. This cannot be true for any country.

10.   **C**   Here is an example of both a map question and an "EXCEPT" question. Despite both of these areas being on Spain's northern border with France, neither the Basques nor the Catalan derived much, if any, of their culture from the French. Remember that four out of the five answers are correct. Both Catalan and Basque are minority groups in Spain, which have their own languages; in recent decades, they have gained limited autonomy, though some in their community still yearn for political independence; and they have well-defined culture regions surrounding the centers of Barcelona and Bilbao.

HOW DID I DO? HOW CAN I DO BETTER?

Remember, your goal on Section I of the exam is to answer at least 40 of the 60 questions correctly. Therefore, you need to get two out of every three right. With just ten questions, that means that you need to get seven out of ten correct to support the score that you hope to receive after completing the free-response section.

If you got six or fewer questions correct, see if you can identify what problems you are having and how you might use the rest of the book to solve them.

If you said,

> I didn't know what the question was asking!

skip it and move on. This strategy saves you the critical time that you need to answer the other questions *correctly*.

If several of these questions were mysterious to you, then you need to review the material from those sections of the course. First, determine what kind of geography the question is drawn from (see Part V of this book). Then determine what kind of question it was (definition, definition-example, comparison, theory, models, maps, graphs, or tables). Once you have figured out that, for instance, you did not know the definition of an enclave or could not name a single example, then you need to revisit that section on political geography and make sure that you know all the key terms and examples of them.

At the end of each of the review chapters in Part V of this book, there will be a list of key terms. Make sure that you know these and other terms that your teacher or textbook has highlighted.

If you said,

> There's so much different stuff to know; I can't keep a grip on so many different things!

don't despair. All of the material in the course is somehow interrelated. The key to knowing the material well is understanding the links between the subjects. Part V of this book will focus on linkages to help you remember the material better.

If you looked at your watch at the end and said,

> That took forever!

then you need to think about the four-step process and what we said about time at the beginning of this chapter. Remember: once you've eliminated the incorrect answers, you'll need to quickly guess from your remaining choices and move on.

Time and the 10 Questions

The optimal time for 10 questions is 9 minutes, 10 seconds. Arrive at this number by using the ratio 60 questions to 60 minutes. Then subtract a little additional time so that you have a few minutes at the end of the exam to go back and answer the questions you circled as "uncertain."

Using this 9:10 pace for 10 questions would leave you just over 5 minutes at the end of the 60-question exam period to handle any "unfinished" business, such as questions you wanted to revisit.

Of course, you probably didn't meet that goal time for this practice set and that is fine! Go through the four-step process and learn your strategies well; you'll get quicker with more practice. (You'll get plenty of practice in the chapters to come.)

LET'S REVIEW

Here are your essential four steps to answer any multiple-choice question:

1. Read and Rephrase the Question
2. When? Who and Where? What?
3. Process of Elimination
4. Guess and Go

If you can't eliminate even one of the possibilities, or if you just don't know the subject matter of the question, *don't spend too much time contemplating*. There's no penalty for skipping. If you're deciding between the last two or three answers, you've already done your job by eliminating some bad answers. You HAVE to guess here, but don't take too long deciding. Relax. When you're down to two choices, your odds are pretty good, so you should always guess! Make sure to leave a few minutes before the end of the 60-minute period to go back and re-check the questions that you circled to review. Keep an eye on your watch.

In addition to the four-step process, we have also learned that there are different types of questions in the multiple-choice section of the test. The question types are as follows:

*   Definition
*   Definition-example
*   Theory questions, including models
*   Comparisons
*   Map questions
*   Graph and table questions

Be familiar with all of these types and be able to identify the type of question when you see it. Remember: some questions can be more than one type. Knowing the question type as you answer will help you reformulate the question when going through Step 1 and will make you feel more comfortable and confident as you go through the exam.

Now let's move on to free-response questions!

Chapter 2
How to Approach
Free-Response
Questions

WHAT YOU NEED TO KNOW ABOUT THE AP HUMAN GEOGRAPHY FRQS

After you finish the multiple-choice section, you will have a 10-minute break before you begin Section II: Free-Response Questions. In this part of the exam, you will be given a separate test booklet that contains the questions and lined paper to write your three responses. Let's review the basic facts of the FRQ section.

Number of Questions:	3
Time Allowed:	75 minutes
Writing Instrument:	Pen with blue or black ink
Goal:	12 of the 21 available points (60%) in the free-response section

Just like on the multiple-choice section, to do well on the FRQs you need to know your human geography *and* how to answer the AP Human Geography Exam free-response questions. You may know the material from class and may consider yourself a decent writer, but if you don't know how to write *this* kind of response, then you won't get the credit you deserve.

Even if you aren't totally comfortable with the material in the course and even if you don't consider yourself the best writer, you can learn to write an effective, point-winning AP Human Geography free-response. Data from previous years shows that the average AP Human Geography student earns only 35 percent of the available points on this section. We'll show you how to get all of those points that most students aren't earning.

How can you do this? You need strategies to earn the maximum number of points. In this section, we will give you tools to help score free-response points and get a 4 or 5 on the exam—even if you are worried that you don't write well. We'll go through the scoring system, the writing style, and the rules.

The Scoring System

Each response is scored by an individual reader—a real human being, who is either an AP Human Geography teacher or a geography professor. This person is part of a team of readers who are trained to read the same question and assign it a standard number of points.

Before the reading begins, each team establishes a scoring rubric. The rubric is a set of guidelines that tells the reader accepted responses for each part of the question. Each year in June, after school is out, the readers are retrained and the rubric is recalculated to maintain accurate scores.

No Grading, Just Points

When readers begin to look at each of your responses, they begin with a blank slate of zero points. As they go through your response, they will issue points when your writing matches the material on the scoring rubric. There are 7 points available for each FRQ. No half points are awarded.

Readers are not allowed to say, "That seemed like a nice response. I'll give it 6 out of 7 points." They also may not think to themselves, "That response would fail in my class. I'll give this student only 2 points." Instead they must use the rubric to score every response. Readers' scoring is constantly checked for accuracy.

How a Rubric Works

The rubric awards 1 point per lettered task on each of the FRQs. The reader cannot give you extra credit just because you wrote very well in Part B. The reader also can't transfer points within a response if you did better on one part than another. It's important to know that *there are no negative or penalty points in the FRQ section*. A reader cannot take points away that you've already earned just because you wrote something else incorrectly.

To get the maximum number of points, make sure that you cover all parts of the question in your response. *Most students lose points because they forget to answer part of the question.* An easy way to do this is to write a short response for each lettered task separately, but we'll also show you how to write a shorthand outline in case you prefer to write your response in essay form. Likewise, students lose points because they don't use the vocabulary from the course to explain what they know. Using keywords is another critical tool, which we will discuss. Before we do that, let's go over the kinds of questions you will see.

Types of Questions

As we said on page 53, there are no strict requirements that any particular subject be covered in the free-response section. We do know, however, that the first question will not include any visual elements, whereas the second and third questions will be based on one and two sources, respectively, of graphic information such as data, maps, and/or images.

There is no way of knowing what will show up as a FRQ topic. However, we can tell you what questions have been asked in the past. These past questions won't be asked again any time in the near future. In fact, the reuse of past questions is wholly unlikely, given the recent updates to the test and the large number of potential questions from the course.

Past AP Human Geography FRQ Subjects

2014
- Comparison and discussion of Rostow's model and Wallerstein's theory
- The lasting impact of colonial borders in Africa
- The effect of a global network of agricultural systems

2015
- The political phenomenon of redistricting in Maryland
- Globalization of the English language and *lingua franca*
- Increasing refugee population and their experience in Middle Eastern countries

2016
- Development results in a number of economic and social changes within a country
- Bilingualism and the nation-state concept as they apply to Canada
- Economic differences between and environmental impact of subsistence agriculture and commercial agriculture

2017
- New Urbanism movement, mixed-use development, and traditional zoning practices
- High population growth rates around the world, and related economic incentives and social policies
- Unitary states versus federal states

2018
- Women in the agricultural labor force in developing countries
- The impact of gentrification on urban neighborhoods
- Terms in popular culture: how they diffuse globally, and barriers to diffusion

2019
- Urban food deserts in developed countries
- Infant mortality rates in South Asia and Western Europe, economic factors, and the intended impact of sustainable development goals
- Devolutionary pressures related to cultural differences, and other contributing forces

2021—Set 1
- Dairy farming and changes in recent decades
- World cities and the global cities index
- Association of Southeast Asian Nations (ASEAN) and supranational organizations

2021—Set 2
- The concept of total fertility rate (TFR)
- English speakers in selected countries
- Selected specialized manufacturing clusters in Southern China

Remember!
You can find released past official FRQs and sample student responses on the College Board website. Go to apstudents. collegeboard.org/ courses/ap-human-geography and navigate to "About the Exam." Bear in mind, though, that some of these questions will not reflect the current FRQ format.

Great Expectations (for FRQs)

It's not that the College Board will never again include a free-response question on a particular topic. In fact, von Thünen's model was the focus of a question in 2007 and was half of a comparison question in 2008. Therefore, keep in mind that authors may use one of the topics again, but approach it from a different angle. For example, it's likely immigration to Europe will one day show up in a question asking about the relationship between low fertility rates and the need for guest workers (for example, Turkish *gastarbeiter* in Germany). Don't count out previous topics; just be prepared to approach them from a few different angles.

There are some general expectations about AP Human Geography FRQs that you should keep in mind as you prepare. Repeating what we covered in Part III, here is a list of the things you can expect in the free-response section:

- Each of the three FRQs will assess at least two areas of human geography. For example, one question may ask you to explain political effects of migration, while another may involve both agricultural and economic geography.
- All three questions will present you with a real, specific geographic scenario. At least two of them will ask you to describe and discuss spatial relationships.
- The first question will be a freestanding question with no visual element such as a map or chart. The second question will involve one visual stimulus. The final question will have two stimuli, like a map and a data table, and may ask you to both analyze and explain them separately and make connections between them.
- One common task on the free-response section is the process question, for which you have to describe the details of a geographic theory, principle, or issue. In other words, explain how and why something works in a particular order—which factors, for example, affect people and cause them to migrate to place Z.
- Other things you may be asked to do on the FRQs include comparing concepts or specific situations, providing precise definitions or information, identifying cause/effect relationships, and describing potential solutions involved in a certain scenario.

Expect the Unexpected

We're really not kidding when we suggest, to some degree, that you expect the unexpected. Think of how the students in 2004 must have felt when they were confronted with a question about the American poultry industry. "Poultry? You can't be serious! Neither my teacher nor the textbook ever mentioned chickens and turkeys!" To some degree, this is what the exam wants to test, which is why their topics keep shifting. For instance, even after studying, how much would you have known about 2010's ethanol manufacturing plants? The real question, so to speak, is how well can you use what you know about people, places, and time periods to fill in information about other subjects?

The point is that you should expect at least one question on the exam to touch on an unfamiliar subject. *The key is to not panic.* Approach the question like you would the other questions. Here, you must read behind the question and get into the writer's head.

Generally, these unexpected topics ask you to consider the theories and principles that you have learned and apply them to places or situations that you have not. For example, in 2006 students were shown a photograph of a small industrial park and asked about the factors behind the change in land use from manufacturing to a telephone call center in a small southern town in the United States. Think of the picture and reference to the American South as *distractors* to some degree. The distractors should help guide your answer to the question, not make you freak out because you don't know the details.

The question really asked about the shift from manufacturing to service industries in the American economy, often referred to in textbooks as "deindustrialization" of First-World economic restructuring. Regardless of where it is or what it looks like, the same principles apply. In today's economy, companies seek cheaper land, cheaper labor, and fewer regulations. The English language is necessary for call centers. That's why they are located in the less expensive and non-unionized southern states. Low-cost manufacturing, on the other hand, has moved to Third-World and newly industrialized locations, where language is not an issue.

Answer these unexpected questions as best as you can. Remember the rules and don't leave any question or part of a question blank. Make an outline and attempt each part of the question. You never know where you will pick up a point or two or four.

AP HUMAN GEOGRAPHY EXAM FRQ STRATEGY

In this section, we will explain the writing style for the FRQs, give you the rules for effective essay writing, show you the directions, and discuss time management. Combined, these strategies will improve your AP Human Geography Exam FRQ writing skills.

No Intro Needed
Your free-response answers should be concise and straightforward. Don't include an introduction or conclusion—just get right to the point.

Writing Style for the AP Human Geography Exam

Here's something most people don't expect. *There is no required writing style* on the AP Human Geography Exam. This differs significantly from the AP History tests, on which students are required to use a specific style that includes things such as thesis statements. On the new AP Human Geography Exam, the structure of the questions lends itself well to short-answer responses, though you may also address all of a question's tasks in a single essay if you prefer. However, unless the question specifically requires an introduction, *you should **not** write an introductory paragraph, and you should **not** write a thesis statement for your essay.* This fact may drive your AP U.S. History and English teachers nuts, but it is the truth. The rubric doesn't give points for it, so you don't need it.

Unless you have some additional information to write about, the same policy goes for concluding paragraphs. Do not just write a concluding paragraph to restate the exact same things that you wrote in the body of your essay. As we will show you later in this chapter, the only use for a concluding paragraph is to add points that you may have forgotten to cover earlier in your writing.

As a Matter of Facts

You've probably always been told to put introductory and concluding paragraphs in your essays at school, but the simple cold fact is that the readers don't care since they *just want to see your straightforward answer to the question*. You should not write anything that is not going to earn you points. Just as in the multiple-choice section, *you cannot waste time*. To focus on all of the essay questions within the 75-minute time period, you need all the extra time you can get. Sure, it's better to say more than to say less to pick up additional points. However, you have only 75 minutes in which to finish.

Now, you should feel somewhat relieved. Not having to write your responses so formally is one of the "easier" aspects of the AP Human Geography Exam. Nonetheless, you still need to approach the FRQ section with a plan for all contingencies. Before we get to the "what to do" parts of strategy, we are going to give you the "what *not* to do" rules.

The Rules for Effective Free-Response Writing

Here are a few rules to follow on the free-response section. Disregarding these rules can eliminate your possibility of earning a 4 or 5 on the exam. Included are instructions for what you can do to avoid losing points:

Rule #1: Don't Leave Anything Blank

If you write responses to two of the questions and leave a third one blank, it will be almost statistically impossible to score a 4 or 5 on the exam. If you are stumped on a question, you need to write brief responses to at least a couple of the lettered tasks of each question using what you know about the material or anything you think might be related. What's the difference between a blank sheet and a few sentences? It has to do with the type of score you'll be issued. A blank essay receives a "–" score, which will take you out of the running for that 4 or 5 score. A couple of lines of writing on the subject of the question will at least give you a "0" score, and if you use the right vocabulary, might even earn you a point or two. This approach will significantly increase the possibility of earning at least a score of 4. Think of the 0 as a low score and the – as a disqualification.

Likewise, if there is a part of the question that you don't know the answer to, you should still write something using the technical vocabulary from the course. Do this just in case you can pick up a point or two for identifying significant issues. Another approach to earning last-ditch points is to give a real-world example of something that you're not sure how to technically explain.

Rule #2: No Artwork, Please

Even if the question refers to a particular geographic model or place, do not draw your answer as a diagram or map. The reader will not be able to give you any points, even if what you're drawing is basically correct. Answers must be in written format, plain and simple. If you're visualizing a model or a map, write down what you see in your mind. Don't just describe the structure or places; discuss processes and explain why things are in a particular place or how they got to be there. Don't forget to use the technical vocabulary from that part of the course.

Rule #3: Editt Yoru Worrk!

As much as you think it might be fun to spend what time you have left over to draw pictures or write poems about population pyramids in the back of the test booklet, this is not a good idea. Use this time to edit. Editing helps prevent errors like those in the heading above. See page 114 for tips on editing.

What the Directions Say

The free-response instructions are straightforward, and they mean what they say. There's nothing hidden here.

Directions: You have <u>1 hour and 15 minutes</u> to answer all three of the following questions. It is recommended that you spend approximately one-third of your time (25 minutes) on each question. It is suggested that you take up to 5 minutes of this time to plan and outline each answer. You may plan your answers in this orange booklet, but no credit will be given for anything written in this booklet. **You will only earn credit for what you write in the separate Free Response booklet.**

Time Management

The most important thing in the directions is the advice on how to spend your time. What may sound confusing is the bit about "5 minutes." On average, here's how you would plan your time:

Question 1:	5 minutes to outline and 20 minutes to write
Question 2:	5 minutes to outline and 20 minutes to write
Question 3:	5 minutes to outline and 20 minutes to write
	for a total of 75 minutes

However, after the exam, you might find out that this would have been *a better schedule*:

Question 2:	4 minutes to outline, 14 minutes to write, and 2 minutes to edit
Question 3:	6 minutes to outline, 19 minutes to write, and 3 minutes to edit
Question 1:	5 minutes to outline, 21 minutes to write, and 1 minute to edit

Why? You are going to answer the question that you know best first. Moreover, you are likely to spend less time doing it because the responses flow easily. And you won't need as much time to edit, so you'll just do the *quick editing* that we'll show you in a few pages. The second question is one in which you also know the material, but it's trickier and you'll need more time to formulate and write your answer. The third question is the tough one, possibly even a "stumper" that you are just not ready to answer. You are just going to answer this one to pick up as many points as possible.

The point is to be flexible with your time within the 75-minute time frame. Try to target 20 total minutes for the first response you choose to write, 25 total minutes for the second response, and 30 total minutes for the last response. Within those totals, keep in mind that you need to outline, write, and edit your work.

A Few Other AP Free-Response-Writing Facts and Guidelines

- You may write your responses in any order in the answer booklet. For example, you can start with Question 3, then Question 1, and finish with Question 2. Don't forget to write the number of the question you are responding to in the box at the top of each page.

- When you begin the next response, start on a fresh page.

- With average-sized handwriting, most high-scoring responses use two to three pages of the answer booklet.

- If you choose to respond in an essay format, there's no need to give your essay a title. Focus on getting points.

- You may double-space your responses.

- Very small and poor handwriting will harm your score. If a reader can't decipher your writing, then he or she can't give you points. Write carefully and legibly.

- Readers do not grade for spelling or grammar. You don't get extra points for spelling Zimbabwe correctly, nor can a reader deduct points for your attempt to spell "the palace of Verseye" when you meant Versailles. They still have to give you credit. Yes, they understand you are under pressure.

Room to Write
On the actual test, you will be given a separate booklet to record your answers for each free-response question. For the practice tests in this book, you should use scrap paper. After you've gotten a hang of the timing, be aware of how much space each response is taking up, in case you need to write in smaller print or use fewer words on the test.

Also Keep in Mind…

It's important to recognize if the question specifies a certain place. If the question refers to, for instance, "European border policies' effect on free trade," then you must talk about Europe. If the question is more general, such as "Describe an example of a fuzzy border between two culture regions," then you can pick any example, such as the American "Dixie" border with the Northern United States.

Make sure to recognize any historical time frame. If the question says "since 1950," then make sure your descriptions and examples are not from a previous time period. Likewise, if the question specifies "geopolitics during the Cold War," then you should refer to events between 1946 and 1991.

HOW TO CRACK THE AP HUMAN GEOGRAPHY FREE-RESPONSE QUESTIONS

In this section, we will discuss outlining, keyword vocabulary, writing tools, and editing strategies. Keep in mind that you are not just writing; *you are constructing an answer.* Think about it: you could unknowingly write an answer that reads well but falls apart under the rubric. Or, using the following strategies, you can construct an answer that "reads to the rubric" and considerably raises your FRQ section score.

Data shows that the average student earns only one-third of the available points on the FRQ section. Why? In addition to the problems covered in the "rules" section above, students tend to have problems organizing their answers and using the intended vocabulary.

How to Make a Shorthand Outline

The key to writing an effective and organized response is to understand that the questions are written with a particular structure in mind. This question structure is how you should *construct your written answer. The basic way to outline your response is to outline the question.* One of the best things about the shorthand outline is that you answer each part of the question in the order asked. This is not required but it makes your response easier to follow, decreasing the chance a reader will miss potential points. Moreover, by checking off each part of the question that you complete, you will make sure that you answer all parts of the question, thus avoiding the trap that causes most students to lose points. This is why jotting down a quick outline can be helpful even if you plan to respond in a short-answer format.

Where to Write Your Outline

The answer booklet for the AP Human Geography FRQs contains many blank sheets of lined paper. In fact, there's far more paper than you actually need to write the three responses. You can write your outline in the booklet. Just label it as "outline" and the reader will go on to your full response. And no, you are not allowed to take scrap paper into the exam room.

There are two approaches you can take on where in the booklet to write your outline:

1. Before Your Response

Do this if you decide to approach and outline the questions one at a time for your full response. Open the booklet to the first two side-by-side blank pages. On the left-hand page, write the outline for the response to the question you have decided to answer first. On the right-hand page, begin writing the full-response. When you finish the first question, flip to the next two empty side-by-side pages and repeat for the second. Likewise for the third question. As we will show you later in this section, make sure to leave space next to the outline to insert keywords.

The advantage of this approach is that you have your outline right next to your full-response as you write it. This will allow you not only to remember the order in which you are writing, but also to check off each section as you complete it.

2. In the Front or Back of the Book

If you read all three questions and have ideas coming out of your head for all of them, it might be better to do all of your outlines first. In this case, turn to either the first or last sheet of lined paper in the booklet. Write all three outlines on this sheet, or use the first three or last three pages if you need more space. Do this so that when you are in the middle of writing out your response you can easily flip back to the outline. Again, make sure to leave space for your keyword list.

The advantage here is that you won't have to estimate the length of each response and possibly make a mistake by writing an outline on a page you'll need for a full answer.

Double-Check Your Work

No matter which method you use, you should check off each part of the outline as you complete that part of your response. Then move to the next part of the outline to consider the next point in your response. At the end of each response, go over the outline one last time to make sure you didn't forget to address a part of the question. Something else might pop into your head at this point and you can add it as a follow-up.

HOW TO CRACK A FRQ

Let's take a sample question and show how it's done:

1. Many economic factors have advanced suburbanization in the United States.

   (A) Explain the role that deindustrialization played in the growth of American suburbs in the 20th century.
   (B) Using service location theory, describe the effect that service industries have had on the expansion of suburbs since the 1960s.
   (C) Define suburban sprawl.
   (D) Discuss the negative aspects of suburban sprawl for **each** of the following service sectors:
           Education
           Transportation
   (E) Discuss the environmental impact of suburban sprawl.
   (F) Describe some political and economic responses to the effects of suburban sprawl.
   (G) Compare North American suburbs to peripheral areas elsewhere in the world.

A shorthand outline is just that—short. To save time outlining, use abbreviations for long terms that you know. Label each section to make sure you cover all parts of the question. Here's an example of what a shorthand outline would look like for this question.

Q1 outline:
- A.   Explain—Deind.
  - A1. Factories closed
  - A2. Workers left cities, to subs.
  - A3. Serv. providers/employers moved
- B.   Describe
  - B1. Serv. loc.: where workers are, where customers are
  - B2. Serv. jobs available in sub. CBDs
  - B3. Serv. consumers living in sub. areas
- C.   Define: exp. of housing, trans., dev. into undeveloped periphery
- D.   Discuss (2)
  - D1. Ed.
    - D1a. Schools are expensive. Taxes are high.
    - D2b. Growth = more school bldgs./land needed
  - D2. Trans.
    - D2a. Highways expensive
    - D2b. More roads, more problems
    - D2c. Commuting costs
- E.   Discuss
  - E1. More traffic causes pollution
  - E2. Change from nature to living space
  - E3. New homes eat up land
- F.   Describe
  - F1. Anti-growth movements, limit dev.
  - F2. Retrofit existing buildings, mixed-use dev.
- G.   Compare
  - G1. NA: mostly res. and serv., middle/upper class, white collar, single family
  - G2. Elsewhere: poor, squatter settlements, some industrial

Labeling Each Part

Notice how we have numbered the outline Q1 as this is for the question numbered in the test booklet as "1" (not the first question you choose to answer). A1 and A2, for example, refer to the points you want to address in section A. D1a through D2c refer to section D, which has two required example areas, and asks for aspects (plural), meaning you must discuss more than one aspect per example.

Abbreviate Even More

If you can, abbreviate terms in your outline even further than what we have done here. As long as you understand what you are writing, the more shorthand abbreviations you use, the more time you will save.

What to Do? Operator Terms

We need to consider what the question is asking you to do. Each question will direct you with an operator term that specifies what you are expected to do with the topic material.

To help guide your writing, put the operator term at the top of each section, as we have done in the outline above. These verbs include *describe, discuss, analyze, define, give an example, explain, compare, contrast,* and *assess.* In addition, a question may inquire *to what extent (or degree)* and ask *the limitations of* a particular principle or factor. What do these operators ask you to do?

- **Describe:** Write out the details or component parts of the concept or issue that the question addresses. Emphasize the most important elements and say why these are significant. The test-writer wants you to illustrate in your writing (but don't draw a picture).

- **Discuss:** Write about both sides of an issue or concept. State the positive and negative aspects. Explain who benefits and who loses in the process or situation. Or, explain the impacts of the issue or concept.

- **Analyze:** Write about the relationship between factors and their impacts. Look for cause-and-effect relationships. State why the process you describe is a problem or a benefit in the real world.

- **Define:** Write out the definition of a term or process. Say why the concept is significant to geographic thinking or why it matters in the real world. Some definitions are simple (like "place") and others can be complex (like "environmental determinism").

- **Example:** Write about a real-world place, process, or situation that captures the essence of the concept that the question addresses. Make sure that the example you give is the most topical. Don't just use one that you like. Some questions will give you the example and you will have to describe how and why that place fits the concept.

- **Explain:** Write about a process that is implied in the question. In conceptual terms: A happens, resulting in B, which then leads to C. Say why these things occur. State why the process you describe is a problem or a benefit in the real world.

- **Compare:** Take two or more concepts or examples and state their similarities (give more than one). If there are differences, list these as well. State why the similarities or differences are significant and say what impact they have.

- **Contrast:** Specifically describe the differences between two or more concepts or examples. Make sure to find at least two differences (unless the question says to give only one or the primary difference).

- **Assess:** Write about the importance, impact, or effectiveness of a concept or issue. You will need to determine the positives and negatives of the conceptual or real-world situation. It's okay if you state that positives and negatives balance out, or if the good outweighs the bad (or vice versa).

Some operators may ask you *to criticize a topic or issue*. Examples include the following:

- **To what extent (or degree):** Not all concepts or examples have the impact or effect they were supposed to. Sometimes intervening factors limit these impacts or effects. Your job is to illustrate these processes in your writing.

- **The limitations of:** In addition to intervening factors, conflicts and controversies can emerge that dampen the expected result of a concept or process.

In either case, the important thing to keep in mind is that you are expected to be critical. Say why there is a problem with the concept. Think of it this way. Someone had a good idea, but other things made it impossible or only partly useful; or some idea was good in theory but not in practice, and here is why. When applicable, identify who the winners and losers are, like you would in a "discuss" question.

Directions in the Question

Read questions carefully so that you know what and how much is being asked of you in each question, and so that you construct your outline correctly. The question format matters a lot. This is why you use your outline of the question as your outline for the answer. If a question asks for one example, that's all you have to give. If it says two, or if it asks for plural "examples," "descriptions," "countries," or "places," you must provide more than one in order to get that point from the rubric.

Should you give more than what is asked in the question? Or what if you are not sure of the answer but have several ideas? The value of providing several answer possibilities in excess of what is asked is debatable and, depending on the question, the rubric may not give you more points for this. In addition, including many ideas in a response may add little to your score and will waste valuable time that could be used earning points on the other responses.

Giving Examples

Should You Make a Laundry List?

Giving several more examples than what's requested is known as "laundry listing," and most readers will treat it as a futile attempt to see what sticks to the rubric. In this situation, a reader is likely to give you points only for the first examples you give. For instance, let's say a question asks for two countries as examples and you list six. The reader will look at only the first two, see if they score on the rubric, and move on. This will be the case even if the first four are wrong and the fifth and sixth are correct—no points.

What If You're Not Sure Which Examples to Give?

If you are unsure of your answer(s) and have more ideas than the number requested, *add only one additional example*. A forgiving reader will see this as you being thorough, and will be less likely to see you as a laundry-lister. Remember to use what you think are your best answers first, just in case the rubric or a reader rejects extra answers.

Should You Give Examples, Even If They Don't Ask?

Giving examples, even when they are not required, is a good strategy. This can help especially if you are not sure whether you have fully discussed or defined a topic. If you think your answer sounds weak, it probably is. Use an example to further illustrate your answer. Why? It can help add clarity and depth to your response. If you're able to provide an example, the reader may take that as a sign of your mastery of the topic and award you the point.

BE THE RUBRIC

Each question is worth 7 points, one for each lettered part. The rubric lists acceptable responses for each part. In the end, you want the reader to say (covering his mouth to make the Darth Vader voice), "The rubric is strong in this one." Well, not all the AP Human Geography readers are *Star Wars* fans, but you do want the reader to have that feeling that you have nailed down the rubric in your response, or as a Zen Buddhist might proclaim, "Be at one with the rubric." Your goal is to consider what the rubric might look like as you are writing your response. This is not a requirement, but it can help you better conceptualize the question and your response.

How to Crack It: Keyword Lists

We haven't quite finished our preparation for writing the response. Let's see how applying keywords can enrich our outline and make for a more complete response.

There is an extensive vocabulary list to know for the AP Human Geography Exam. A problem that many students have with the FRQ section is that they don't use the technical vocabulary and terms they learned in class. Doing so will earn additional points. Don't study vocabulary just in case you're asked a definition question on the multiple-choice section. *Study vocabulary so that you know what to say* in the FRQ section.

But It Sounds SO Forced!

If you feel uncomfortable talking in terms of "core-periphery relationships" and "diffusion processes," or if it feels silly to liken something to "economic restructuring," *get over it now!*

Remember where you are and what you're doing. You're taking the AP Human Geography Exam, not casually hanging out or composing an emoji-filled tweet. Your audience is made up of technical readers who will appreciate your use of these terms, just as your friends might enjoy an inside joke.

Keyword Lists

Now that we have that out of the way, how do you know where to insert the vocabulary in your essay? What if you forget?

Using a keyword list is a good way to make sure that you use technical vocabulary at the right point in your response. When you write your shorthand outline, leave room to the right of the outline to make a keyword list. Write down terms that you know are part of the material on the question topic. Try to write them alongside the part of the outline where they should fall in your response. For example, using your outline for the example question, add appropriate words for each point.

1. Many economic factors have advanced suburbanization in the United States.

    (A) Explain the role that deindustrialization played in the growth of American suburbs in the 20th century.
    (B) Using service location theory, describe the effect that service industries have had on the expansion of suburbs since the 1960s.
    (C) Define suburban sprawl.
    (D) Discuss the negative aspects of suburban sprawl for **each** of the following service sectors:
          Education
          Transportation
    (E) Discuss the environmental impact of suburban sprawl.
    (F) Describe some political and economic responses to the effects of suburban sprawl.
    (G) Compare North American suburbs to peripheral areas elsewhere in the world.

    Q1 outline:
    A.   Explain—Deind.
           A1. Factories closed (off-shore locations, investment value)
           A2. Workers left cities, to subs.
           A3. Serv. providers/employers moved (proximity, return on investment)
    B.   Describe
           B1. Serv. loc.: where workers are, where customers are (footloose)
           B2. Serv. jobs available in sub. CBDs (R&D, office parks, white collar)
           B3. Serv. consumers living in sub. areas (retail, professional services proximity)
    C.   Define: exp. of housing, trans., dev. into undeveloped periphery
    D.   Discuss (2)
           D1. Ed.
                 D1a. Schools are expensive. Taxes are high. (local tax revenue)
                 D2b. Growth = more school bldgs./land needed (facilities)
           D2. Trans.
                 D2a. Highways expensive (infrastructure)
                 D2b. More roads, more problems (congestion, commuter)
                 D2c. Cars favored over public transport (sustainability)
    E.   Discuss
           E1. More traffic causes pollution (smog, sustainability, climate change)
           E2. Change from nature to living space (population pressure)
           E3. New homes eat up land (farmland preservation)

F.   Describe
       F1. Anti-growth movements, limit dev. (growth boundaries, permits)
       F2. Retrofit existing buildings, mixed-use dev.
G.   Compare
       G1. NA: mostly res. and serv., middle/upper class, white collar, single family
       G2. Elsewhere: poor, squatter settlements, some industrial (Latin American city model)

Now you have a complete shorthand outline and are ready to write your answer.

As you write your response, cross off the keywords so that you don't forget to use them. Although we have not done it here, you should abbreviate keywords on your outline as well.

How Much Time to Outline?

Recall the time breakdowns from earlier in the chapter. Keep in mind that you need to complete the outline in *a target time of 5 minutes or less*. There's a lot to keep in mind just for the outline, but this will improve your score, so don't skip it. Don't spend a huge amount of time writing an elaborate outline or thinking about the rubric. Remember: the more shorthand you use, the better. To practice, use the free-response questions at the end of this chapter. Make sure to time yourself on both the outline and the response-writing, separately.

EXAMPLE RESPONSE

Using our completed shorthand outline, we've written an example of a response to the question that would get all 7 points. We repeat the question and the outline below for your convenience:

1. Many economic factors have advanced suburbanization in the United States.

    (A) Explain the role that deindustrialization played in the growth of American suburbs in the 20th century.
    (B) Using service location theory, describe the effect that service industries have had on the expansion of suburbs since the 1960s.
    (C) Define suburban sprawl.
    (D) Discuss the negative aspects of suburban sprawl for **each** of the following service sectors:
             Education
             Transportation
    (E) Discuss the environmental impact of suburban sprawl.
    (F) Describe some political and economic responses to the effects of suburban sprawl.
    (G) Compare North American suburbs to peripheral areas elsewhere in the world.

Q1 outline:
- A. Explain—Deind.
  - A1. Factories closed (off-shore locations, investment value)
  - A2. Workers left cities, to subs.
  - A3. Serv. providers/employers moved (proximity, return on investment)
- B. Describe
  - B1. Serv. loc.: where workers are, where customers are (footloose)
  - B2. Serv. jobs available in sub. CBDs (R&D, office parks, white collar)
  - B3. Serv. consumers living in sub. areas (retail, professional services proximity)
- C. Define: exp. of housing, trans., dev. into undeveloped periphery
- D. Discuss (2)
  - D1. Ed.
    - D1a. Schools are expensive. Taxes are high. (local tax revenue)
    - D2b. Growth = more school bldgs./land needed (facilities)
  - D2. Trans.
    - D2a. Highways expensive (infrastructure)
    - D2b. More roads, more problems (congestion, commuter)
    - D2c. Cars favored over public transport (sustainability)
- E. Discuss
  - E1. More traffic causes pollution (smog, sustainability, climate change)
  - E2. Change from nature to living space (population pressure)
  - E3. New homes eat up land (farmland preservation)
- F. Describe
  - F1. Anti-growth movements, limit dev. (growth boundaries, permits)
  - F2. Retrofit existing buildings, mixed-use dev.
- G. Compare
  - G1. NA: mostly res. and serv., middle/upper class, white collar, single family
  - G2. Elsewhere: poor, squatter settlements, some industrial (Latin American city model)

Question 1.

A.   Deindustrialization occurred when manufacturing companies in the U.S. closed their factories in American cities, choosing to relocate them to cheaper off-shore locations. Furthermore, services provide a higher return on investment and are therefore more profitable, so the economy shifted away from manufacturing toward service. Without urban manufacturing jobs, workers moved out of cities and into the suburbs in search of service jobs.

B.   Service location theory holds that some high-benefit service industries are considered "footloose" and are not tied to any particular location. However, there are a number of factors that corporations must consider when deciding where to locate offices, such as the proximity to consumers, the availability of a qualified workforce, and affordable real estate. Starting in the 1960s, many companies decided to locate in the suburbs because affordable land space was available to build office parks and research and development facilities. This led to the availability of service sector jobs in suburban CBDs and edge cities, and professionals settled in these areas due to the strong job market.

In turn, as more Americans moved to the suburbs, it created a larger consumer base in those areas. Rather than continuing to locate in traditional downtown CBDs, retailers and professional services chose locations in close proximity to their consumers. Thus, malls and both medical and office buildings have been a part of expanding suburban land space.

C.   Suburban sprawl is defined as the expansion of housing, transportation, and commercial development into previously undeveloped land on the periphery of an urban area.

D.   One negative result of suburban sprawl for the education sector has been the need for schools to continuously expand capacity to keep pace with growing populations. School construction and increasing teacher salaries require increased local taxes, which homeowners complain about. In addition, the limited space in suburbs may make it difficult to find places for new facilities.

Highways and public transportation are another increasing infrastructure expense for suburban public services. Soaring land prices and limited space can make building new roads a challenge. Some also argue that governments must spend more money on sustainable public transportation solutions, like rail and buses, to help relieve congestion caused by the increased number of cars on the road. However, the spread-out nature of suburban areas makes them difficult to navigate on foot and by mass transit, so many people prefer to drive their own cars.

E.   One environmental issue caused by suburban sprawl is the pollution caused by heavy traffic congestion. Commuter vehicles significantly contribute to smog and greenhouse gases in the atmosphere, which play a role in public health issues locally and climate change globally. Additionally, construction of new suburbs consumes existing natural areas and farmland, encroaching on natural habitats of native species. Population pressure on available resources can also become a problem.

F.   Numerous anti-growth political movements have formed in the United States and Canada in response to suburban sprawl, especially in areas near environmentally sensitive or historically significant places. Measures to counter excessive growth include growth boundaries that set minimum lot sizes for new construction (as in Loudoun County, Virginia) and stricter permitting regulations for new roads and both commercial and residential development. Economic responses can involve innovative forms of development, such as retrofitting existing buildings for new businesses or creating mixed-use developments in which businesses and residences are in close proximity to one another.

G.   The demographics of peripheral (suburban) areas in the United States and Canada are very different from those in many other parts of the world. North American suburbs are mostly middle-class, and sometimes upper-class, single-family homes interspersed with white-collar service firms. This is reflected in urban models like the galactic city, or peripheral, model. In other urban structures internationally, such as in Latin America, the periphery is home to large squatter settlements that house multiple families. The population in these settlements is poor, often rural-to-urban migrants who cannot afford land in the city. Living conditions generally become worse farther away from the city. In contrast to the service-based businesses of North American suburbs, commercial development in the periphery of Latin American and Southeast Asian cities is largely industrial.

The Labels

The labels help the reader figure out what part of the question you are answering. This is especially useful in questions with similar descriptions between two sections. Although it will help your writing and possibly your score to follow the structure of the question, you are not required to present the material in a particular order.

Another Way to Do It

If you prefer, you may write your response in an essay format:

Deindustrialization occurred when manufacturing companies in the U.S. closed their factories in American cities, choosing to relocate them to cheaper off-shore locations. Furthermore, services provide a higher return on investment and are therefore more profitable, so the economy shifted away from manufacturing toward service. Starting in the 1960s, many companies decided to locate in the suburbs because affordable land space was available to build office parks and research and development facilities. This led to the availability of service sector jobs in suburban CBDs and edge cities, and professionals settled in these areas due to the strong job market. Without urban manufacturing jobs, workers moved out of cities and into the suburbs in search of service jobs.

In turn, as more Americans moved to the suburbs, it created a larger consumer base in those areas. Rather than continuing to locate in traditional downtown CBDs, retailers and professional services chose locations in close proximity to their consumers. Thus, malls and both medical and office buildings have been a part of expanding suburban land space. The migration of business and people is in line with service location theory: some high-benefit service industries are considered "footloose" and are not tied to any particular location, but there are a number of factors that corporations must consider when deciding where to locate offices, such as the proximity to consumers, the availability of a qualified workforce, and affordable real estate.

The construction of new office and retail facilities is just one aspect of suburban sprawl, which is defined as the expansion of housing, transportation, and commercial development into previously undeveloped land on the periphery of an urban area. Suburban sprawl can have a negative impact on a number of services, such as education and transportation. Education has suffered from the need for schools to continuously expand capacity to keep pace with growing populations. School construction and increasing teacher salaries require increased local taxes, which homeowners complain about. In addition, the limited space in suburbs may make it difficult to find places for new facilities. Highways and public transportation are another increasing infrastructure expense for suburban public services. Soaring land prices and limited space can make building new roads a challenge. Some also argue that governments must spend more money on sustainable public transportation solutions, like rail and buses, to help relieve congestion caused by the increased number of cars on the road. However, the spread-out nature of suburban areas makes them difficult to navigate on foot and by mass transit, so many people prefer to drive their own cars.

Not only does increased traffic congestion from suburban sprawl inconvenience commuters, it also causes significant environmental problems like air pollution. Commuter vehicles significantly contribute to smog and greenhouse gases in the atmosphere, which play a role in public health issues locally and climate change globally. Additionally, construction of new suburbs consumes existing natural areas and farmland, encroaching on natural habitats of native species. Population pressure on available resources can also become a problem.

Numerous anti-growth political movements have formed in the United States and Canada in response to suburban sprawl, especially in areas near environmentally sensitive or historically significant places. Measures to counter excessive growth include growth boundaries that set minimum lot sizes for new construction (as in Loudoun County, Virginia) and stricter permitting regulations for new roads and both commercial and residential development. Economic responses can involve innovative forms of development, such as retrofitting existing buildings for new businesses or creating mixed-use developments in which businesses and residences are in close proximity to one another.

Suburban areas in the United States and Canada are demographically very different from peripheral areas in many other parts of the world. North American suburbs are mostly middle-class, and sometimes upper-class, single-family homes interspersed with white-collar service firms. This is reflected in urban models like the galactic city, or peripheral, model. In other urban structures internationally, such as in Latin America, the periphery is home to large squatter settlements that house multiple families. The population in these settlements is poor, often rural-to-urban migrants who cannot afford land in the city. Living conditions generally become worse farther away from the city. In contrast to the service-based businesses of North American suburbs, commercial development in the periphery of Latin American and Southeast Asian cities is largely industrial.

The Box

Note the box in the corner above the essay. You are instructed on the test to enter the number of the question to which you are responding in this box. Make sure you do it for every page on which you have written. As you do practice FRQs, get into the habit of writing the question number in a box on the corner of every page. On the exam these boxes are meant to keep a reader from accidentally missing all or part of your response.

The Rubric

As we mentioned before, each question is worth 7 points, one for each lettered part. On the next page is the rubric for the example question.

Scoring Guidelines for Question 1: No stimulus (7 points)

1 point

A. Explain the role that deindustrialization played in the growth of American suburbs in the 20th century.

Accept one of the following:

- The main source of economic activity shifted from manufacturing to services, which yield a higher return on investment.

- Factories in urban centers shut down, leaving workers in search of employment in new service sectors.

- Service providers located offices in suburban areas where they were in closer proximity to both consumers and available workforce.

1 point

B. Using service location theory, describe the effect that service industries have had on the expansion of suburbs since the 1960s.

Accept one of the following:

- Location theory studies the factors that influence where businesses choose to locate their facilities; such factors include available natural and human resources, accessibility, and proximity to consumers.

- Some high-benefit service industries are theoretically "footloose" and not tied to the proximity of resources or consumers, but studies have shown that even service firms must consider such factors as consumer base, available workforce, and cultural fit.

- Service firms relocated to the suburbs beginning in the 1960s to serve the growing residential population in those areas, as well as to attract the largely professional workforce that had settled there.

- As service firms moved out of CBDs and urban factories shut down following deindustrialization, urban workers also relocated to the suburbs in search of new employment opportunities in the service sector.

1 point

C. Define suburban sprawl.

- The expansion of residential and commercial development, along with supporting infrastructure, into previously undeveloped lands on the periphery of an urban area.

D. Discuss the negative aspects of suburban sprawl for **each** of the following service sectors:

1 point

Education

Transportation

Accept one of the following for **each** sector:

Education:

- Population growth and expansion require the construction of additional school facilities.

- Residents feel the financial burden of increased property taxes to support public school expansion.

- Potential shortages of existing available land on which to build new facilities may limit the ability of school systems to expand as desired and force them to build on undeveloped land, further contributing to sprawl.

Transportation:

- Suburban expansion requires new road construction, which is expensive and places a tax burden on current residents.

- Increased commuter traffic by residents and employees of area businesses creates road congestion.

- Typically, public transportation infrastructure that would help alleviate traffic problems is not widespread in suburban areas and can be costly and logistically challenging to implement.

- Residential areas are typically isolated from business and retail districts, creating a strong preference for cars over other means of transportation.

E. Discuss the environmental impact of suburban sprawl.

1 point

Accept one of the following:

- Emissions from commuter cars generate air pollution including greenhouse gases, contributing to smog and global climate change.

- New development fragments natural habitats and displaces populations of existing species, placing them at risk of habitat loss and increased road mortality.

- New construction can degrade environmentally sensitive areas (e.g., wetlands).

- Existing farmland is consumed by new construction, altering the landscape and permanently removing agricultural production from arable land.

1 point

F. Describe some political and economic responses to the effects of suburban sprawl.

Accept one of the following:

- Anti-growth movements have gained traction and advocate for increased regulation to slow development, especially in areas with historical significance or near environmentally sensitive habitats.

- Some local governments have set growth boundaries to limit the scope and amount of new construction.

- Some local governments have changed their policies regarding permitting new construction and development.

- Mixed-use development helps cut down on land use and traffic congestion by locating homes, businesses, and other facilities in close proximity to each other.

- Some development avoids new construction by retrofitting existing buildings for new commercial and residential space.

1 point

G. Compare North American suburbs to peripheral areas elsewhere in the world.

Accept one of the following:

- North American suburbs are predominantly middle-class to upper-class, whereas peripheries in other areas around the world are populated by poor squatters.

- Suburban residential areas in the United States and Canada primarily contain single-family homes, while peripheral squatter settlements elsewhere may house multiple families in a single makeshift camp.

- Squatter settlements are largely populated by rural-to-urban migrants who cannot afford to buy property in the city.

- On the periphery of cities in Latin America and other areas, living conditions degrade farther from the city, to the point that the farthest settlements may lack the most basic amenities. The opposite is frequently true in the United States, where the extreme periphery has traditionally been populated by the wealthy living on country estates.

- Commercial areas on the periphery of Latin American and Southeast Asian cities tend to be industrial, whereas in the United States and Canada they are largely composed of retail and white-collar professional service firms.

Editing: Do It and Earn Extra Points!

Plan to take any leftover time to reread your responses and edit them. Try to leave at least 3 minutes in each response for editing. When editing, you won't need to erase anything you've written. This is because readers cannot subtract points from the score that you've earned. If you think you have written something incorrectly, cross it out and write in the margin of the page next to where it should be. Or, in a concluding paragraph, you can add the correct information, parenthetically noting that you're correcting a statement from before. If you see a place where you forgot to include an important vocabulary word, insert it with an arrow connecting it to where the term should fall within the text.

A smart tactic that the author has seen is to double-space your responses—skipping every other line in the answer booklet while writing. This will give you extra space to add edits during a reread of your responses. This also makes the response easier to read (a good thing). Don't worry; there is plenty of space in the answer booklet.

What If You Forgot Something and Need to Go Back?

Instead of a concluding paragraph that sums up and earns no extra points, consider a "follow-up paragraph" to add any extra details or examples. To do this, begin your follow-up statements with something like the following:

In addition to my previous description of _____, I would like to add…

or

To further illustrate my discussion on _____, I can offer the example of…

Regardless of how you begin this type of follow-up statement, it is important to direct the reader back to where the added text should have been included.

Use the Time Wisely

If you have time left at the end of the exam, spend the extra time editing or writing follow-ups. We know you just want to give your cramped hand a break, or you may have the desire to run out of the room to finally relax. Remember: in general it's better to say more than to say less if you have the time.

But Don't Second-Guess Yourself

Unless you are absolutely sure that you've written something incorrectly, don't erase or scratch out anything you've written. Readers cannot deduct points for incorrect information.

What If You Didn't Meet the 60 Percent Goals?

If you thought you knew the answers but scored below 60 percent, go back through this chapter and see how you missed points. Did you violate any of the "rules"? Did you understand the question directions? Or were you not thorough enough in your answers?

Another thing to examine is how well your outlines mimic the rubric. Did you understand the requirements for plural descriptions or examples?

Repeat what you have learned in this chapter when you take the full practice exams in the back of this book. Practice might not make perfect, but at least you can meet the 60 percent goals and earn a 4 or 5 on the exam.

Part V
Content Review for the AP Human Geography Exam

HOW TO USE THE CHAPTERS IN THIS PART

The following chapters are a review of the basic content of the AP Human Geography Exam. Of course there is no way of knowing precisely what material will appear on the exam, nor how it will be asked. However, due to the broad nature of the test material, you can expect that much of what you read in this book will appear on the exam in some form or another.

After each chapter, reflect on the following questions to help you determine whether or not you have truly mastered the content of that chapter:

Take Time to Unwind

The chapters in this section are long and densely packed with information, so for the best results we recommend taking a break after every chapter you read. Giving your brain a rest every now and then makes your studying even more efficient—after a break, you'll be ready to dive right back in!

- For which content topics discussed in this chapter do you feel you have achieved sufficient mastery to answer multiple-choice questions correctly?
- For which content topics discussed in this chapter do you feel you have achieved sufficient mastery to discuss effectively in a free-response question?
- What parts of this chapter are you going to re-review?
- Will you seek further help outside of this book (such as a teacher, tutor, or AP Students) on any of the content in this chapter—and if so, on what content?

In addition, pay especially close attention to spatial models and theories in the review, as these are valued highly among question authors. Learn the shape and parts of each model. However, it's equally important to understand why the models are shaped in different ways and how they have changed over time.

Keep note of keywords and technical vocabulary to know for multiple-choice questions and to use in your free responses. In the following text, important keywords appear in **bold**; note their definitions and use them in your free responses to earn valuable points.

Finally, be aware that the subject matter in the following chapters has been written in the same style, length, and format in which you should write your free responses during the AP Human Geography Exam. It's important to train your mind to write with straightforward descriptions, keywords, and definitions, and to present detailed examples. The author has thrown in a few interesting stories along the way to keep you going as you prepare for the exam.

CED Alignment

Throughout Part V, you'll see sidebars indicating where to find each of the topics we discuss in the College Board's AP Human Geography Course and Exam Description (CED).

Chapter 3
Thinking Geographically

Are You a Visual Learner?

Check out *ASAP Human Geography*, our class notes-style guide packed with tons of visuals to help you understand key concepts and must-know info for the exam.

CHAPTER OVERVIEW

In this chapter we will review the central concepts and tools in human geography that may show up on the AP exam. The first part focuses on the central concepts that encompass all of the six areas (covered in Chapters 4–9) that you must know for the test. Then we'll review the necessary information regarding maps, map types, and map scale, as well as geographic technologies. There is also a list of several models that you are required to know for the exam, with information on where to find detailed explanations of them. Finally, we will provide a list of the names of important geographers along with their contributions, and then the key terms for the chapter.

KEY CONCEPTS

Space and Place

Of the general concepts in geography, *space* and *place* are the two terms that human geographers consider most important. Most other scientific fields do not consider the importance of space and place, or do so only slightly, as opposed to geographers, who consider them central concepts in research and theory.

Space

When geographers talk about **space**, they're not talking about "the final frontier" or anything outside of Earth's atmosphere. Instead, geographers are referring to the geometric surface of the Earth. It's best to think about geographic space as an abstract concept. Close your eyes and think of the global surface of the Earth as an empty slate. Imagine placing objects on the Earth's **spatial** surface that are defined by their location and are separated by some degree of distance from other things. These objects could be people, trees, buildings, or even whole cities—whatever you choose to visualize. So when geographers talk about **activity space,** they're referring to an area wherein activity occurs on a daily basis. Thinking spatially means understanding the pattern and distribution of objects and analyzing their relationships, connectedness, movement, growth, and change across space and over time.

Place

Well, that was deep! The concept of **place** is less abstract, but still important theoretically. It's important to have an open and broad concept of place. Think of place as an area of bounded space of some human importance. People don't have to live there for it to be a place. Instead, you can have a **sense of place** about somewhere, even in the midst of a desert or an ocean. When human importance is recognized, it is common to assign a place-name, or more technically a **toponym,** to that location. Place-names often reveal the historical interrelatedness of locations.

An area of bounded space could be somewhere small, such as a room, or as large as a continent. **Regions** are a type of place, and there are other categories of places, such as urban places, places of work, resource locations, and transportation nodes. When considering the importance of a location, region, town, or city, it is necessary to consider, why does this place matter?

The attributes of a place change over time. Over the long term, we can consider the concept of **sequent occupancy**: in other words, the succession of groups and cultural influences throughout a place's history. In many places we find that there are several different historical layers that contribute to a **place-specific** culture, society, local politics, and economy. For example, the place specificity of Santa Fe, New Mexico, is a complex mix of indigenous, Spanish colonial, and modern American influences based upon the sequence of past and current societal developments.

Scale

Scale is the relationship of an object or place to the Earth as a whole. In geography, scale can be thought about in two ways. There is **map scale**, which describes the ratio of distance on a map to distance in the real world in absolute terms (more on map scale later in the chapter). And there is **relative scale**, or what can also be referred to as the **scale of analysis**. This describes the **level of aggregation**, or in other words, the level at which you group things together for examination. Scales can range from the individual or the local, from city to county and state, from regional to national to continental, or to the international and global scales. Recently, some geographers and organizations have started to use the word "glocal" to express the importance of both local and global scales.

CED 1.6
Scales of Analysis

Scale modifiers are good to use in the free-response section of the exam. Specify whether a company is a transnational corporation or a local business or if you are discussing a local government, a federal regulation, or an international organization.

Relative scale is important to understand because it is erroneous to compare different scales of analysis or places at different scales. For example, it would be wrong to visit Atlanta and assume the rest of Georgia had the same characteristics. Likewise, if you examined economic data from Alabama and assumed the rest of the United States had the same median income, types of businesses, or unemployment rates, you would be incorrect.

Worth Its Weight In Points

Remember that free-response questions are carefully graded based on a metric. Specifying the scale of the items you're being asked about may earn you points for detail or example material.

Regions

Let's go over the three categories of regions: **formal, functional,** and **vernacular.** Keep in mind that there are many different types of regions, and a single place can exist in several regions simultaneously. For example, the Everglades in Florida exist within the Southern U.S. region and are also considered a wetland region. Regions exist at many different scales and can overlap. Keep an open mind about what can be considered a region.

CED 1.7
Regional Analysis

Formal Regions

As a type of place, the spatial definition of the **formal region** is an area of bounded space that possesses some **homogeneous characteristic** or **uniformity**. This means that, across the region, there is at least one thing that is the same everywhere within the regional boundary.

The defining homogeneous character can be as simple as a common language. In a **linguistic region,** everyone speaks the same language, but groups in that region can be very different culturally. For example, the United States and Australia are in the same linguistic region, but the two countries share little else in culture, economy, or landscape. Regional concepts can also be very complex. The American South, or "Dixie," is one such region; a multitude of factors define the region, such as dialect, vocabulary, food, architecture, climate, ethnicity, and religion. Because these defining characteristics are imprecise, people disagree over whether states like Virginia, West Virginia, and/or Maryland are parts of Dixie.

Regional boundaries differ based upon the type of region. **Culture regions** tend to have fuzzy borders. It's hard to tell where one region ends and the other begins, such as the border between Dixie and "the North" in the United States. Boundaries between **political regions** are finite and well-defined. Some political boundaries are porous, such as those between Canada and the United States, and other boundaries are protected, such as that between the United States and Mexico. **Environmental region** boundaries are transitional and measurable. The environmental transition zone between two **bioregions**, or **biomes**, is known as an **ecotone**. For example, the space between the Sahara Desert and the tropical savanna of Africa is a dry grassland region known as the Sahel.

Functional Regions

Functional regions, or **nodal regions,** are areas that have a **central place,** or **node,** that is a focus or point of origin that expresses some practical purpose. The influence of this point is strongest in the areas close to the center, and the strength of influence diminishes as distance increases from that point.

Make the Link:
See the concept of **distance decay** on page 125.

Market areas are a type of functional region. A professional sports team will have the strongest fan base and intensive media network coverage in areas close to the team's home city. There are fans and media viewing in the larger region around that city, but they diminish as you get farther and farther away. Eventually you reach a point where the fans transition to another team's functional region and the media networks are oriented in that direction.

An outlet mall can have a single market area effect on consumers. Shoppers will come mostly from the local area and neighboring cities. Because outlets are often placed far apart, there will also be a larger **area of influence** for the mall that will have shoppers traveling from longer distances but making fewer trips. Many outlet shoppers "just passing through" on the interstate see a very brief **intervening opportunity** to do some discount shopping. An intervening opportunity is an attraction at a shorter distance that takes precedence over an attraction that is farther away.

Vernacular Regions

The vernacular region is based upon the perception or collective **mental map** of the region's residents. The overall concept can vary within the region due to personal or group variations. Looking again at the American South, or "Dixie," some residents define it by the location of country music bands or fans, where others recognize the numbers of Southern Baptist church congregations or NASCAR races as the defining statistic. There are those who consider Dixieland only as the states of the Civil War-era Confederacy or the part of the country where it never (or almost never) snows. Some people think it's defined by the areas where people have Southern accents. No matter what is used to spatially define the regional concept, the reason tends to be a point of pride for residents.

Be careful in your vernacular definitions. There are country music radio stations in all 50 U.S. states and throughout Canada (remember Shania Twain). Some of NASCAR's events with the largest attendance are in decidedly un-Southern states like Wisconsin, California, and New Hampshire.

> **CED 1.4**
> Spatial Concepts

Location

The concept of location is similar to scale, and we can consider location in both relative and absolute terms. **Absolute location** defines a point or place on the map using coordinates such as latitude and longitude. **Relative location**, by contrast, refers to the location of a place compared to a known place or geographic feature.

Absolute Location

The most common way to fix a point on the Earth's surface is using **latitude** and **longitude** coordinates (there are other more technical coordinate systems used in geography, such as Universal Transverse Mercator, or UTM). Many students become confused and mix up the definitions of latitude and longitude. Here's an easy way to think about it:

> Lines of latitude measure distance, in degrees, north or south of the equator (latitude = ladder). Lines of longitude measure distance, in degrees, east or west of the Prime Meridian (longitude = how long the ladder is).

Some people remember the difference between the two as the lines of longitude being the longest lines on the globe, going all the way from pole to pole.

Notation is also important to keep in mind. Absolute location is given with latitude first and then longitude, each with a cardinal direction and separated by a comma. Degrees can be divided up into smaller minutes, and minutes can be divided up into seconds. For instance, the absolute location of the United States' Capitol building is

$$38° \ 53' \ 23.2980" \ N, \ 77° \ 0' \ 32.6016" \ W$$

meaning it lies at the point 38.889805 degrees north of the Equator and 77.009056 degrees west of the Prime Meridian. When decimals are used to divide partial degrees instead of minutes and seconds, the coordinate system used is known as **decimal degrees.**

The **equator** is 0° latitude. The **North** and **South Poles** are 90° latitude. The **Prime Meridian** is 0° longitude. On the opposite side of the Earth is the 180° line of longitude. Parts of this line compose the **International Date Line** that also meanders around a number of international boundaries.

What's Up with the Prime Meridian?

The Prime Meridian (0° longitude) runs through Great Britain because the means to accurately calculate longitude at sea was developed by the British Royal Navy. With the development of the chronometer, a gear-driven clock, by London jeweler John Harrison in 1785, British ships at sea could accurately determine their longitude. For practical purposes, 0° was fixed on the **Royal Naval Observatory** at Greenwich in London. This allowed ship captains to know how far they were east or west of their home country. The French, who were the other great naval power at the time, didn't mind so much because the line also runs directly through the center of France. Other nations soon accepted the standardized international system of longitude. The Prime Meridian was officially adopted as 0 degrees longitude at the 1884 International Meridian Conference.

Time Zones

Time zones are divided up in 15-degree-wide longitudinal zones around the world with some exceptions. This is because 360° divided by 24 hours a day equals 15°. One exception to this rule comes from China, where leaders established one time zone for the entire country. For practical purposes, dividing lines between time zones often follow political boundaries, sometimes even along local area divisions. Time zones were created relatively recently, in the era of transcontinental railways, to standardize time across long east-west train lines.

Relative Location

As mentioned before, relative location is based upon a place's relationship to other known geographic features or places. For instance, when someone from a metropolitan-area suburb is asked where they are from, the response is often relative and will refer to the larger city. A person from Arlington, Virginia, might say she is from Washington, D.C., and someone from Santa Monica, California, might say he is from Los Angeles, or simply L.A.

You might also put significant value on a place due to its relative location. In the early 1990s, Dublin, Ireland, became an important international business location due to its low-cost economy, English language skills, and close relative location to Great Britain, where the cost of doing business was extremely high (especially in London).

Site and Situation

Two locational concepts that work together are **site** and **situation.** Site refers to the physical characteristics of a place, such as the fact that New York City is located on a large, deep water harbor, next to the Atlantic Ocean. Situation refers to the place's **interrelatedness** with other places. How is a place related to other places?

In this case, New York City became the most prominent trade and finance center in the United States during the 1800s, due to its position as a terminal for trade goods on the ship-navigable Hudson River to and from the rest of New England, and as a major port-of-call on the Atlantic Circular Trade Route. As a result, New York City had much greater market potential than Boston, Massachusetts; Philadelphia, Pennsylvania; or Charleston, South Carolina; all of which did not have the benefit of the large inland waterway above the main port location.

Distance

Like scale and location, you should consider **distance** in both absolute and relative terms. Distance is measured absolutely, or it can be measured relatively in terms of the degree of interaction between places or in units of time traveled. Linear **absolute distance** is the distance between two places as measured in linear units such as miles or kilometers.

The effect of distance on relationships is important to understand, and geographers often utilize the concept of **distance decay** to explain **relative distance**. Distance decay (also known as gravity) means that the farther away different places are from a place of origin, the less likely interaction will be with the original place.

Relative distance is also expressed by the principle of **Tobler's law**, which states that all places are interrelated, but closer places are more related than farther ones. This law was developed by American-Swiss geographer and cartographer Waldo Tobler around 1970 and his exact phrasing was, "Everything is related to everything else, but near things are more related to each other." When the length of distance becomes a factor that inhibits the interaction between two points, this is known as the **friction of distance**. This can be seen when the combined time and cost of moving a product prevents it from being sold in far-off locations.

Space-Time Compression

Decreased time and relative distance between places is referred to as **space-time compression**. Technology can reduce the relative distance between places. **Modes of transportation** such as airplanes reduce travel time between two distant points, and as a result, increase interaction. Even the **Internet** can be used as an example of how a whole network of physically distant places can be brought virtually together and increase interaction significantly.

Human-Environmental Interaction

CED 1.5
Human-Environmental Interaction

The effect that humans have on their environment, and vice versa, is defined as **human-environmental interaction**. This concept will be explored in more depth in later chapters, but you should know that this broad area of study covers **environmental determinism**, **resource depletion**, **sustainability**, **conservation efforts**, various economic forces, and globalization.

SPATIAL INTERACTIONS

Central Places

Central places can be thought of as any node of human activity. However, they are most often the centers of economic exchange. Markets are often located at **transportation nodes**, which provide accessibility to and from these points; market centers tend to be centrally located within the larger economic region.

See Chapter 8 for more details on central place theory, market areas, and the range and threshold of the service.

Using this notion of centrality, the school of thought known as **central place theory** was developed in the 1930s by the German geographer Walter Christaller. He saw the economic world as an abstract spatial model. In the model, city location and the level of urban economic exchange could be analyzed using central places within hexagonal market areas, which overlapped each other at different scales. There's much more to this, as you have probably learned.

Core and Periphery

One thing that emerges from central place thinking is the idea of **core and periphery**. Many different regional, cultural, economic, political, and environmental phenomena and human activities display some sort of core and periphery relationship. Just as the **CBD** (central business district) is the core of the urban landscape, a country's capital is the core of its political landscape. Note that the core does not have to be exactly in the center of the peripheral region.

For example, in the Western United States, the core of the Mormon culture region is in the Salt Lake City-Provo-Ogden metropolitan area, also referred to as the Wasatch Front. This is where the highest concentration of members of the Church of Jesus Christ of Latter-Day Saints (LDS) is located. However, there is a significant LDS population throughout most of the rest of Utah, eastern Nevada, southwestern Wyoming, northern Arizona, southern Idaho, and eastern Oregon. These areas compose the combined **peripheral** Mormon culture region.

> **The Value of a Strong Relationship**
>
> When you analyze a map or a model for a FRQ on the exam, explaining the core-periphery relationships that you see as part of the larger question can earn you additional points.

Pattern

Geographers also use special terms to describe different types of spatial patterns. When things are grouped together on the Earth's surface, it is referred to as a **cluster**. When clustering occurs purposefully around a central point or an economic **growth pole**, it is referred to as **agglomeration**. When there is no rhyme or reason to the distribution of a spatial phenomenon, it is referred to as a **random pattern**. Objects that are normally ordered but appear dispersed can be referred to as **scattered**. If a pattern is in a straight line, it is **linear**, and if it's wavy, the pattern is **sinuous**—like the pattern of heartbeats on an EKG.

Land survey patterns have an effect on the property lines and political boundaries of states and provinces. East of central Ohio and Ontario, land surveys until the 1830s used natural landscape features to divide land on a system of **metes and bounds** (see below), which had been developed in Europe centuries earlier. After the 1830s, when new techniques to accurately determine longitude were transferred from sea navigation to land survey, surveyors in the United States and Canada used a rectilinear **township and range** survey system based upon lines of latitude and longitude. This produced the block-shaped property lines and more geometric shapes of many western states and provinces. Former French colonial areas such as Québec and Louisiana have **long-lot patterns**. These have a narrow frontage along a road or waterway with a very long lot shape behind.

Land Survey Patterns in North America

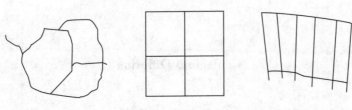

Metes and Bounds   Township and Range   Long Lots

Density

The concept of density is most often calculated as the number of things per square unit of distance. This is called **arithmetic density.** For instance, in New York City, which has the highest population density in the nation, there are six Starbucks per square mile.

Physiologic density measures the number of people per square unit of arable land, meaning land that either is actively farmed or has the potential to be. By contrast, **agricultural density** refers only to the number of farmers per square unit of arable land.

Diffusion Patterns

There are a number of different ways and patterns in which human phenomena **diffuse** spatially, or spread across the Earth's surface. Most often we examine how culture, ideas, or technology spread from a point of origin to other parts of the world. Sometimes that point of origin or place of innovation is called a **hearth**. Here's a quick rundown of the different types of diffusion. Hierarchical diffusion, contagious diffusion, and stimulus diffusion are types of expansion diffusion.

> For more details and examples of diffusion, see Chapter 5.

Expansion Diffusion

The **expansion diffusion** pattern originates in a central place and then expands outward in all directions to other locations. Note that the distance does not have to be equal in all directions.

Hierarchical Diffusion

> **CED 3.4**
> Types of Diffusion

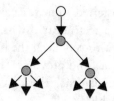

The pattern of **hierarchical diffusion** originates in a first-order location and then moves down to second-order locations and from each of these to subordinate locations at increasingly local scales.

Contagious Diffusion

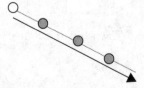

The pattern of **contagious diffusion** begins at a point of origin and then moves outward to nearby locations, especially those on adjoining transportation lines. This could be used to describe a disease but can also describe the movement of other things, such as the news in rural regions.

Stimulus Diffusion

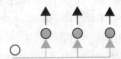

In the **stimulus diffusion** pattern, a general or underlying principle diffuses and then stimulates the creation of new products or ideas. For example, stimulus diffusion occurs when vegetarian eating habits (principle) influence restaurants to offer more vegetarian dishes (new products).

Relocation Diffusion

The **relocation diffusion** pattern begins at a point of origin and then crosses a significant physical barrier, such as an ocean, a mountain range, or a desert, and then relocates on the other side. Often the journey can influence and modify the items being diffused.

GEOGRAPHIC TOOLS

Maps and Mapping Concepts

For geographers, maps are important because they separate geographers from other social scientists, like sociologists or political scientists. Maps are not just a graphic art form; they are a science. Many scientific maps are the results of spatial analysis—the mathematical analysis of one or more quantitative geographic patterns.

Map Types

There are many map types, and there are a few specific ones that you should know for the AP Human Geography Exam.

CED 1.1
Introduction to Maps

Topographic maps show the contour lines of elevation, as well as the urban and vegetation surface with road, building, river, and other natural landscape features. These maps are highly accurate in terms of location and topography. They are used for engineering surveys and land navigation, especially in wilderness regions.

A number of different map types can be considered **thematic maps**. Remember that each one expresses a particular subject and does not show land forms for other features. The theme could be something like a dot density map showing the distribution or population within a country. It could also be very complex, showing multiple related subjects, such as a weather map that shows temperature **contour lines (isotherms)**, wind patterns, pressure zones, and areas of precipitation. Here are a few common types of thematic maps:

> The word "choropleth" is commonly misspelled as "chloropleth," so don't make that mistake on the test!

- **Choropleth maps** express the geographic variability of a particular theme using color variations. These variations can be expressed using colorized symbols, contour areas filled with different colors, or polygons denoting country boundaries filled with different colors to express the variability in the map data.

- **Isoline maps** calculate data values between points across a variable surface. Between point *A* (with a value of 5) and point *B* (with a value of 10), a series of contour lines can be drawn to show the change in data between the two points. If the value of each contour line is 1, then we would see six lines total labeled 5, 6, 7, 8, 9, and 10. Point *A* would sit inside of the contour line labeled 5, and point *B* would fall within the area for contour line labeled 10. Each point is then interpolated with the other nearby or neighboring points to create a continuous surface of isoline contours. Weather maps showing temperature contours (isotherms) are the most common isoline maps.

- **Dot density maps** use dots to express the volume and density of a particular geographic feature. The dots can represent the numbers of people in an area, or they can express the numbers of events or phenomena that occurred in an area. An example would be dots representing the numbers of people who suffer heart attacks on a state-by-state basis. Each state would have a number of dots inside its boundary polygon representing the number of heart attacks. Oftentimes, each dot represents a certain number of events; in our example, the map might read, "one dot equals 1,000 heart attacks."

- **Flow-line maps** use lines of varying thickness to show the direction and volume of a particular geographic movement pattern. An example would be a map of flow lines showing the total number of foreign immigrants in the United States. Each line would begin in the immigrants' country of origin and point to the United States, with a thickness based upon the total number of immigrants. In this example, a thin line would be drawn from Portugal to the United States and a much thicker line would be drawn from Ireland to the United States.

- **Cartograms** use simplified geometries to represent real-world places. Political boundaries become polygons, and linear features such as roads become lines with basic angles often at 90° and 135°. Cartograms are more about the data being expressed than they are about landscape. Linear cartograms are often used in subway systems and other transportation maps where the exact geography of the route is less important than the items along the way.

What Is a Mental Map?

Everyone has a **mental map.** It's the cognitive image of landscape in the human mind. What is common about each person's mental map is that we have very accurate geographies of the areas around our home, school, and workplace. We also have very good knowledge of the landscape along the transportation corridors that we commonly travel. Elsewhere, our mental maps tends to be pretty much blank.

By understanding the science behind location, distance, scale, and different map types, you can improve your mental map from the data that you read on both paper and computerized maps.

Map Scale

As we said earlier in the chapter, there are two different types of geographic scale: map scale and relative scale. Map scale is the "absolute" form of the scale concept. Map scales can be expressed in a couple of ways. A linear map scale expresses distance on the map surface. It can be found either in the legend or in a corner of the map, like so:

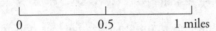

The ratio scale of the map will also be expressed on the map legend. This shows the mathematical relationship between the distance on the map compared to the real distance on the Earth's surface. It will appear as a 1 separated by a colon from a much larger number, like so:

$$1:24,000$$

In this case, 1 inch on the map equals 24,000 inches on the Earth's surface, or about two-thirds of a mile. This is the map scale used on topographic maps produced by the United States Geological Survey (USGS). This map scale can also be expressed as the mathematical ratio $\frac{1}{24,000}$.

A large-scale map is one with a ratio that is a comparatively large real number. A small-scale map is one with a ratio that is a comparatively very small real number. Consider the amount of area and level of detail expressed depending upon the type of map scale. Compare the following two map scales and ratios in terms of their size in real numbers to understand which one is the large-scale map and which one is the small-scale map, as well as what purpose each would serve:

Map Scale	1:50,000	1:1,000,000
Ratio	$\frac{1}{50,000}$	$\frac{1}{1,000,000}$
Scale Type	Large Scale	Small Scale
Area Covered	Small Area	Large Area
Level of Detail	High Detail	Low Detail
Purpose	City	State or Province

Although there is no agreed-upon convention as to a dividing line between large- and small-scale maps, think of 1:250,000 as the break point.

Projections

There probably won't be a question that asks you to differentiate between the projections on the AP Human Geography Exam, but they could ask you about the practical issues behind certain projections. Each given projection creates different levels of accuracy in terms of size and shape distortion for different parts of the Earth. A map projection's level of accuracy is based upon two concepts: area preservation and shape preservation.

Equal-area projections attempt to maintain the relative spatial science and the areas on the map. However, these can distort the actual shape of polygons, such as the **Lambert projection** bending and squishing the northern Canadian islands to keep them at the same map scale as southern Canada on a flat sheet of paper.

Conformal projections attempt to maintain the shape of polygons on the map. The downside is that conformal projections can cause **distortion** of the relative area from one part of the map to the other. For instance, in the commonly used **Mercator projection**, the shape of Greenland is preserved, but it appears to be much larger than South America, when in reality it is much smaller.

Some map projections try to balance area and form, sacrificing a bit of both to create a more visually practical representation of the Earth's surface. Examples would be the **Robinson projection** and the **Goode's homolosine projection**.

MODELS

What Are Models?

Unlike a map, a **model** is an abstract generalization of real-world geographies that share a common pattern. **Spatial models** attempt to show the commonalities in pattern among similar landscapes. For instance, **urban models** try to show how different cities have similar spatial relationships and economic or social structures. There are also some **non-spatial models**. The **demographic transition model**, for instance, uses population data to construct a general model of the dynamic growth in national scale populations without reference to space.

Why Do We Use Them?

Despite being abstract generalizations, models give us a way to picture geographical patterns that are not normally visible to the human eye. These patterns are rarely evident on topographic or road maps. Models also allow us to address certain theoretical questions. For instance, the **concentric zone model** can be modified to create a graph showing the cost-to-distance relationship in urban real estate prices. The resulting **bid-rent curve** explains why land prices are relatively low in suburban areas, but exponentially higher in the central business district (CBD). See Chapter 8 for a detailed explanation of the bid-rent curve.

Models to Know

Here is a list of where to find each of the major models and theories on the exam in this book:

Population Models: Chapter 4
Demographic transition model
Epidemiological transition model
Malthusian theory
Population pyramids

Agriculture Models: Chapter 7
Von Thünen's model of the Isolated State

Urban Models: Chapter 8
Central place theory
Concentric zone model
Sector model
Multiple-nuclei model
Galactic city model
Latin American city model

Not That Kind of Model

Be cautious: these models are reportedly one of the more difficult parts of the AP Human Geography Exam. You should make it a point to feel comfortable discussing these in detail. At the very least, make sure you know the name of the person who developed each model and what historical significance it represents, as these questions may lack context clues.

The Gravity Model: A Central Model in Geography

The **gravity model** is a mathematical model that is used in a number of different types of spatial analysis. Gravity models are used to calculate transportation flow between two points, determine the area of influence of a city's businesses, and estimate the flow of migrants to a particular place. To do this, a gravity model multiplies the quantitative size of two places and divides that by the distance between them, squared. Here's a brief Know the Math moment (more on this in Chapter 9) to show you the formulaic definition:

$$\frac{\text{Location}_1 \ \text{Population} \times \text{Location}_2 \ \text{Population}}{\text{Distance}^2}$$

The result gives you a relative score that rates the gravity, or in other words, the pull or strength of the relationship between two places. In the following basic example, we compare the potential business relationships of New York City (NYC) with London and Tokyo, which would estimate the comparative likelihood of business interactions:

NYC metro population:	19,120,000
London metro population:	14,372,596
Tokyo metro population:	37,468,000

NYC to London Distance:	3,470 miles	Squared: 12,040,900
NYC to Tokyo Distance:	6,760 miles	Squared: 45,697,600

Gravity of NYC and London: $\dfrac{19,120,000 \times 14,372,596}{12,040,900} = 22,822,549$

Gravity of NYC and Tokyo: $\dfrac{19,120,000 \times 37,468,000}{45,697,600} = 15,676,713$

Despite the vastly greater distance from NYC to Tokyo, the gravity model score of that relationship is not much smaller than the gravity model score of NYC and London. This can help explain, for example, why there are very close relationships between financial investors in NYC and Tokyo, as well as NYC and London, Frankfurt, and Zurich. Or this can help explain the higher-than-expected amount of air travel between Tokyo and NYC compared with that between NYC and London.

GEOGRAPHIC TECHNOLOGY

Geographic Information Systems (GIS)

Geographic Information Systems (GIS) became practical with the onset of the desktop computer in the 1970s. GIS incorporate one or more **data layers** in a computer program capable of spatial analysis and mapping. Data layers are numerical, coded, or textual data that is attributed to specific geographic coordinates or areas. As all data is geographically fixed to specific locations, data between layers can be analyzed spatially. Each layer can show a different type of geographic feature.

CED 1.2
Geographic Data

Examples of GIS Usage

The **spatial analysis** capabilities of GIS are shown in the following example. Utah Valley University students used GIS for a 2005 analysis of the relationship between personal wealth and earthquake danger in Provo, Utah. One data layer quantified housing values, while other layers were coded for variable degrees of earthquake hazards based upon ground shaking potential, landslide potential, and soil liquefaction potential (soil liquefaction is when sandy or sedimentary soils liquefy during a large earthquake). In these layers each part of the city was coded for low, moderate, or severe damage.

The analysis showed that the largest category of homes in the city were at risk for the most severe damage. These neighborhoods were almost all middle-class housing zones. Thus, the analysis showed that the city's average-wealth homeowners, as a group, were at greatest risk during a large earthquake.

Another important example of GIS's benefit to society is 911 emergency phone systems. When you call 911 from a land line, your phone number is checked in a GIS database to automatically bring up your address. If you call from a cell phone, your phone location can be triangulated using three or more cell towers.

Data about your home is also stored in the 911 database. If you call to report a house fire, data regarding the type of heating (gas, propane, heating oil, or electric) used in your home is available to first responders. Some cities keep data on the number of elderly, disabled, or persons requiring oxygen in a residence in the case of rescue emergencies. This GIS data can save the lives of firefighters and residents alike.

Mapping using GIS has made the art and science of hand-drawn cartography an endangered species of sorts. GIS is used in a multitude of paper, computerized, and online mapping systems. In-car navigation systems are one of the most popular uses of GIS combined with Global Positioning System (GPS) data.

Global Positioning System (GPS)

"Turn right in 500 feet" is a common phrase heard in American automobiles today. This is not coming from a person. Instead, this is a vocal cue from the in-car GPS system regarding the next turn toward your destination. In-car GPS systems are demonstrably popular around the world, and over two-thirds of smart phone users rely on mapping apps on a monthly basis.

> **CED 1.3**
> The Power of Geographic Data

The Global Positioning System (GPS) utilizes a worldwide network of satellites, which emit a measurable radio signal. When this signal is available from three or more **Navstar satellites**, a GPS receiver is able to triangulate a coordinate location and display map data for the user. In addition, there are handheld GPS units for outdoor sporting use, GPS units on delivery trucks and emergency vehicles that notify supervisors of their location, and units that land surveyors use to locate property lines, find buried utility lines, and accurately lay out new construction sites.

Remote Sensing

Aerial photography and **satellite-based remote sensing** make up a large amount of the geographic and GIS data used today. Aerial photographs have been used for mapping since the mid-1800s. Like GIS, space-borne remote-sensing satellites became available in the 1970s. The difference between aerial photographs and remotely sensed imagery is in the recording media. Aerial photographs are just that—images of the Earth from an aircraft, printed on film, but digital camera usage is on the increase. Instead of a camera, remote-sensing satellites use a computerized scanner to record data from the Earth's surface. This data includes not only visual light wavelengths, but also infrared and radar information.

Examples of Remote Sensing

Large-scale aerial photographs are commonly used by local governments to record property data and set tax assessments. Aerial photographs can also be used to revise topographic map data without having to send out a survey team to update old maps.

Remote sensing is currently used to monitor the loss of wetlands and barrier islands on the Gulf Coast of Louisiana. Each year, satellite data is collected and compared with GIS to show the areas and patterns of wetland and beach loss. This analysis is used by engineers and environmental planners to develop wetland and beach restoration projects.

Infrared satellite imagery is commonly used to determine the health of vegetation on the Earth's surface. This data can be analyzed in a GIS to create crop yield predictions of agricultural harvests. The results are then used by commodity traders to set prices for staple food crops such as corn, wheat, and soybeans. These predictions keep food prices relatively stable over the long term. Without satellite data, basic foodstuffs such as milk, bread, and cereal could be subject to wild price swings due to uncertainty in the national supply of cattle feed.

GEOGRAPHERS TO KNOW

In the remaining chapters of this book, we will mention a number of geographers and allied scientists who have contributed significant research over the last couple of centuries. There have been examples of questions on the AP Human Geography Exam where you must be able to associate a geographer with a particular concept, theory, or model. Here's a short list:

Name	Known For	Page
Ernest Burgess	Concentric zone model	326
Walter Christaller	Central place theory	322
William Denevan	Native American depopulation	231
Larry Ford and Ernst Griffin	Latin American city model	333
Homer Hoyt	Sector model	329
Thomas Malthus	Malthusian theory	166
Friedrich Ratzel	*Anthropogeographie*, father of human geography	225
Walt Rostow	Stages of growth	382
Carl Sauer	Possibilism, cultural landscape	226
Johann Heinrich von Thünen	Isolated State model	309
Immanuel Wallerstein	World systems theory	387
Alfred Weber	Industrial location theory	388

CHAPTER 3 KEY TERMS

space

activity space

spatial

place

sense of place

toponym

regions

sequent occupancy

place-specific

scale

map scale

relative scale (scale of analysis)

level of aggregation

formal region

functional region

vernacular region

homogeneous characteristic
  (uniformity)

linguistic region

regional boundaries

culture regions

political regions

environmental regions

bioregions (biomes)

ecotone

nodal regions

central place (node)

market area

area of influence

intervening opportunity

mental map

absolute location

relative location

latitude

longitude

notation

decimal degrees

equator

North Pole

South Pole

Prime Meridian

International Date Line

Royal Naval Observatory

site

situation

interrelatedness

time zones

distance

absolute distance

distance decay

relative distance

Tobler's law

friction of distance

space-time compression

modes of transportation

Internet

central places

transportation nodes

central place theory

core and periphery

central business district (CBD)

peripheral

cluster

growth pole

agglomeration

random pattern

scattered pattern

linear pattern

sinuous pattern

land survey patterns

metes and bounds

township and range

long-lot patterns

arithmetic density

agricultural density

physiologic density

diffuse

hearth

diffusion patterns

expansion diffusion

hierarchical diffusion

relocation diffusion

contagious diffusion

stimulus diffusion

topographic maps

thematic maps

contour lines (isotherms)

choropleth maps

isoline maps

dot density maps

flow-line maps

cartograms

mental map

projections

equal-area projections

Lambert projection

conformal projections

distortion

Mercator projection

Robinson projection

Goode's homolosine projection

model

spatial model

urban model

non-spatial model

demographic transition model

concentric zone model

bid-rent curve

gravity model

Geographic Information Systems (GIS)

data layers

spatial analysis

Global Positioning System (GPS)

Navstar satellites

aerial photography

satellite-based remote sensing

CHAPTER 3 DRILL

See the end of this chapter for answers and explanations.

1. A place defined on a map using coordinates such as latitude and longitude is referred to as a(n)

   (A) relative location
   (B) area of influence
   (C) absolute location
   (D) nodal region
   (E) formal region

2. The phenomenon that occurs when distance plays a role in obstructing interaction between two locations is known as

   (A) distance decay
   (B) friction of distance
   (C) relative distance
   (D) space-time compression
   (E) Tobler's law

3. If an individual were to find the number of items per square unit of distance, this individual has calculated

   (A) arithmetic density
   (B) dot density
   (C) agricultural density
   (D) energy density
   (E) physiological density

4. All of the following would be examples of places with sequent occupancy EXCEPT

   (A) New York City
   (B) Spain
   (C) Jerusalem
   (D) Sweden
   (E) New Zealand

5. The Mexican/U.S. border culture region is best defined as

   (A) a formal region
   (B) a functional region
   (C) a vernacular region
   (D) an absolute location
   (E) a relative location

6. An instance of contagious diffusion can be seen in the way that

   (A) the ancient Polynesians traveled to Hawaii in canoes
   (B) humanistic ideas spread through the Italian peninsula and eventually into northern Europe
   (C) the British brought soccer to rural Argentina through their railroad lines
   (D) a Cabinet secretary issues orders to his underlings, who then pass on the orders to their underlings
   (E) young city dwellers' desire to avoid vehicle ownership stimulated the creation of ride-sharing services

7. The type of map that would best describe the massive human migration that followed the partition of India in 1947 would be

   (A) a choropleth map
   (B) an isoline map
   (C) a dot density map
   (D) a flow-line map
   (E) a cartogram

8. One of the first uses of remote-sensing technology was to

   (A) determine soil moisture content to make crop yield predictions
   (B) unearth ancient archaeological sites in inaccessible jungles
   (C) monitor environmental degradation in wetland ecosystems
   (D) predict retail earnings and market share by counting cars in shopping mall parking lots
   (E) provide intelligence regarding Soviet arms during the Cold War

9. The gravity model of human geography estimates the strength of the relationship between two places. What is it that causes Rio de Janeiro, Brazil (population: 11 million) to have a greater gravity with Belo Horizonte, Brazil (2 million) than with New York City (20 million)?

   (A) Their shared language
   (B) Their transportation network
   (C) Their crime rates
   (D) Their governing philosophies
   (E) Their distance apart

10. Central place theory is most obviously expressed in

    (A) a pulpit facing a congregation in most synagogues
    (B) a city market's location at a transportation node
    (C) a ring freeway that encircles a metropolitan area
    (D) a school playground located adjacent to the structure
    (E) a police station's location closest to the sites of crime

11. On certain maps, the shape of Greenland is accurate, but the size of the island appears to be larger than South America. The name of this intentional distortion is called a(n)

    (A) equal-area projection
    (B) Lambert projection
    (C) Mercator projection
    (D) Robinson projection
    (E) Goode's homolosine projection

CHAPTER 3 DRILL: ANSWERS AND EXPLANATIONS

1. **C** This is a definition question that requires you to know that an absolute location, (C), is a place defined on a map by latitude and longitude, or some other form of precise coordinates. If you're not sure, you can also narrow down the choices by identifying the other answers. A relative location, (A), refers to the location of a place as compared to a known place or geographic feature. An area of influence, (B), can be thought of as a geographic area in which a business affects a consumer. A nodal region, (D), has a central place that is the focus and expresses some practical purpose. A formal region, (E), is an area of bounded space that possesses uniformity.

2. **B** The phenomenon that occurs when distance plays a role in obstructing interaction between two locations is known as friction of distance; (B) is therefore correct. The other choices can be eliminated by their definitions. Distance decay, (A), means that the farther away different places are from a place of origin, the less likely there will be interaction with the place of origin. Relative distance, (C), is a measure of distance that includes the costs of overcoming the friction of distance occurring between two places, and is often used to describe the cultural, economic, or social connectivity between such places. Space-time compression, (D), refers to the decreased time and relative distance between two places. Tobler's law, (E), states that all places are interrelated, but that closer places are more related than farther ones.

3. **A** Arithmetic density refers to the number of things per square unit of distance; thus, (A) is correct. Dot density, (B), is a type of thematic map that uses dots to express the volume and density of a particular geographic feature. Agricultural density, (C), refers to the number of farmers per square unit of arable land. Energy density, (D), is a physics term related to potential energy per unit volume or mass. Physiological density, (E), measures the number of people per square unit of arable land.

4. **D** Sequent occupancy is a term that refers to the succession of groups and cultural influences through a place's history. New York City has seen many waves of occupants, beginning with Indigenous Americans, then the Dutch, then Irish, Italians, Jews, and more recently Third-World groups. Spain has been inhabited by the Romans, Moors (North African Muslims), and finally Christian groups from the northern half of the peninsula. Just in the last few hundred years, Jerusalem has seen three groups—Ottomans, British, and now Israeli. New Zealand has seen first Maori and then British rule. Choose (D).

5. **A** As a region that possesses a singular homogeneous characteristic—the presence of Spanish as an unofficial second, and in many cases first language—the Mexican/U.S. border culture is a formal region. It doesn't have a central node, so eliminate (B). The overall concept of Spanish language doesn't vary within the region, so eliminate (C). Absolute location is latitude and longitude coordinates, so eliminate (D). No other region was mentioned, so eliminate (E). Choose (A).

6. **C** Contagious diffusion can be defined as a pattern of movement that originates at a single point and then travels in a line to outward locations, usually along lines of transportation. The Polynesians followed relocation diffusion, so eliminate (A). The Italian humanistic movement exhibited an expansion diffusion, so eliminate (B). Orders given from above are considered hierarchical diffusion, so eliminate (D). When an underlying desire or principle stimulates the creation of new services, you have yourself a stimulus diffusion, so eliminate (E). The correct answer is (C).

7. **D** A flow-line map uses lines of varying thickness to track the size and direction of a particular movement. The partition of India was the largest human migration in history; approximately 14 million people were forced to relocate owing to the creation of Bangladesh and Pakistan. Choose (D).

8. **E** While all the answers are uses of GIS technology—even the parking lot option—most heavy technology is developed by the military first, and therefore is applied to the military's needs. During the Cold War, the first reconnaissance satellites were launched with the intention of spying on Soviet missile sites. The correct answer is (E).

9. **E** The gravity model not only takes into account the populations of two cities, but also divides those multiplied populations by the squares of their distance apart. This means that despite the much greater population of New York City, its much greater distance from Rio de Janeiro reduces the gravitational pull. And Belo Horizonte, being only 200 miles from Rio, exerts a nonetheless stronger influence.

10. **B** Developed in the 1930s by a German geographer, Walter Christaller, the central place theory views the economic world solely in terms of physical spaces. He viewed all of human territory as a series of overlapping hexagons, and asserted that settlements were simply places where services could be offered to surrounding areas. A city market is the only answer that is related to economic transactions.

11. **C** The Mercator projection preserves the shapes of the polygons on the map, but it does so at the expense of distorted size. It can be compared to trying to peel an orange and flatten it on a rectangular piece of paper. You would need to expand certain parts of the peel to cover the entire space.

Summary

- Key foundational concepts of geography include space, place, location, scale of analysis, regionalization, and spatial patterns.

- Diffusion of culture, technology, or ideas may occur by relocation or expansion.

- Geographers use a variety of tools to understand spatial organization: maps, projections, spatial and mathematical models, and geographic technologies. Be sure you can explain and apply the major geographical models.

- The gravity model, which measures the strength of the relationship between two places, is used in a variety of spatial analyses:

$$\frac{\text{Location}_1 \text{ Population} \times \text{Location}_2 \text{ Population}}{\text{Distance}^2}$$

Chapter 4
Population and Migration Patterns and Processes

CHAPTER OVERVIEW

This chapter is intended to help you better understand the dynamics, growth, and change of populations. First, we'll go over some basic math tools to help you recall many of the complicated statistics and numerical indicators. After that, we'll apply these concepts to the significant models in population geography. Then we'll review several related concepts that show up frequently on the exam, and we'll finish up with key terms.

Know the Math

In this section, we're not going to drop a ton of math on you; instead, we'll give you a few helpful tips you need to know to understand how population changes occur. You can handle it.

BASIC POPULATION STATISTICS

Population growth is understood through the concepts of the **rate of natural increase (RNI)** and the **demographic equation**. The demographic equation uses **birth rates** and **death rates** along with **immigration** and **emigration statistics** to show **population growth** or change. Over the next few pages, we will walk you through the process of how population growth is calculated.

Birth Rate

Natality, which is the **crude birth rate (CBR)** or just the **birth rate**, as we will call it here, is an **annual statistic**. The total number of infants born living is counted for one calendar year and then calculated. This figure is then divided by the population multiplied by one thousand, or "every thousand members of the population," as it is often presented. Why? By standardizing the denominator (the lower number in the ratio), the resulting quotient will be a small integer number, such as 32 or 14. This makes the data much easier to work with.

CED 2.4

Population Dynamics

$$\text{CBR} = \frac{\text{Number of Live Births}}{\text{Total Population}} \times 1,000$$

Estimate and Simplify

So if you have a country with 100,000 live births in a year and a population of 5,000,000, the birth rate is 20: more precisely, 20 live births for every 1,000 members of the population. To make this easier, 5,000,000 divided by 1,000 is 5,000. Knock the three zeros off the end of 1,000 and the end of 5,000,000 and you have a simplified ratio of $\frac{5,000}{1}$, or just 5,000. Do the same with 100,000 over 5,000. Knock off the three zeros of each and you have $\frac{100}{5}$, or 20.

What Does the Birth Rate Tell You?

Birth rate is just one piece of the larger demographic picture. When you examine the section on demographic transition later in this chapter, you'll find that high birth rates (18 to 50) are found in mostly rural agricultural Third-World countries and that low birth rates (8 to 17) are more likely to be found in urbanized industrial and service-based economies. However, without knowing what's going on with mortality in that country (death rate), it's hard to know whether the population is growing and, if so, how quickly.

Death Rate

Okay, it sounds scary. Death is an emotional issue. What you need to do here is to think scientifically about these statistics. The **mortality rate**, also known as the **crude death rate (CDR)** or what we'll simply call the **death rate,** is an annual statistic calculated in the same way as the birth rate. The number of deaths are counted for the calendar year in a country and divided by every thousand members of the population.

$$CDR = \frac{\text{Number of Deaths}}{\text{Total Population}} \times 1,000$$

What Does the Death Rate Tell You?

Well, not much in today's world. High death rates usually indicate a country that is experiencing war, disease, or famine. Historically, higher death rates (20 to 50) were recorded in the poorest of Third-World countries where the combination of poverty, poor nutrition, epidemic disease, and a lack of medical care resulted in low **life expectancy**. However, as conditions have improved in the Third World through the **Green Revolution** (increased food and nutrition) and access to sanitation, education, and health care have increased, life expectancies have gone up, and the death rate has gone down. See more on mortality in the section on stage one, starting on page 156.

Rate of Natural Increase

By comparing the birth rate and death rate for a country, we can calculate the rate of natural increase (RNI), sometimes referred to as the **natural increase rate (NIR).** We'll call it the RNI from here on. Simply put, if you subtract the death rate from the birth rate, the difference is the amount of population change per thousand members of the population for that year. But you are not done yet. Divide the result by 10 and then you will have the RNI. The RNI is also the annual percentage of population growth of that country for that one-year period. Make sure to put a % sign after you get the answer to the equation.

$$RNI = \frac{\text{Birth Rate} - \text{Death Rate}}{10} \%$$

Simple Math

Let's look at an example. If a country has a birth rate of 27 and a death rate of 12, then the RNI equals 1.5 percent. If that country had 10,000,000 people the previous year, then the population this year would total 10,150,000. The added 150,000 people are 1.5 percent of the previous 10,000,000. We can check our work to see if the birth rate and death rate concur with the math. In this country, the birth rate would be calculated as follows: 270,000 infants born divided by $\frac{10,000,000}{1,000}$ or $\frac{270,000}{10,000}$ = 27; the death rate would be 120,000 deaths divided by $\frac{10,000,000}{1,000}$ or $\frac{120,000}{10,000}$ = 12. Think about it: 270,000 − 120,000 = 150,000 new people added to the country's population.

Negative RNI: Is It Possible?

In a couple of situations, it is possible to have a negative RNI. Mathematically, the death rate can be larger than the birth rate, resulting in a negative number that is divided by 10 to get the negative RNI. When the RNI is negative, it means the population has shrunk during the year the data was collected.

Shrinkage!?!

A negative RNI can be seen, for example, in First-World countries that are highly urbanized and where women in the country are taking on the roles of "mother" and "homemaker" less and less. In these places, the status of women in society has become *increasingly* equal to that of men (not quite there, yet). When the majority of women are heavily engaged in business, political activity, and urban social networks, they are far less likely to have children (reduced **fecundity**), and phenomena such as **double-income no-kid (DINK)** households and single-parent–single-child homes are far more common. They are also likely to benefit from better health care and more access to contraception, both of which lead to lower fertility rates. Higher rates of divorce are another sign.

CED 2.8
Women and Demographic Change

Germany is a prime example where the already low birth rates have dipped below death rates and, as a result, the RNI has ranged between −0.1 percent and −0.2 percent annually. For more examples, look at the stage one and stage four parts of the demographic transition model in this chapter.

Why "Natural" Increase?

An important thing to keep in mind regarding the rate of natural increase is that it does not account for immigration or emigration. A country with a high rate of natural increase can have an unexpectedly low long-term population prediction if there is a large amount of emigration. Conversely, a country with a low rate of natural increase can still grow significantly over time if the number of immigrants is high. Data shows that migrant populations also have much higher fertility rates than the general population in the country. Therefore, in places such as the United States, population growth is not necessarily from the immigrants themselves crossing the border, but the fact that they will have large numbers of children once they have settled.

Doubling Time

We can try to quickly estimate how long it would take for a country to double in size using this formula:

$$\text{Doubling Time} = \frac{70}{\text{Rate of Natural Increase}}$$

Using Bolivia as an example, its current RNI of 1.37 would result in a doubling time of over 51 years. That's fast, but unless something changes significantly in Bolivian society, we shouldn't expect the nearly 12 million people of today to grow to nearly 24 million by 2074. But it won't. Why not? There is negative net migration in Bolivia. Out-migration to other countries reduces the long-term prediction to around 18 million by 2063. This is why we call the RNI an estimate.

The more accurate way would be to estimate the RNI for each year in the future by examining a country's position on the demographic transition model. Then you would multiply each year's population by the RNI and add that to the next year's growth, and so on, and so on:

$$(\text{Pop.} \times \text{RNI}_1) + (\text{Pop.} \times \text{RNI}_2) + (\text{Pop.} \times \text{RNI}_3) \dots + (\text{Pop.} \times \text{RNI}_n) = \text{Future Population}$$

This is the same method used to estimate the value of a currency multiplied by annual inflation rates to find the real dollar value over time.

Add Migration and Voilà! The Demographic Equation

The last part of the demographic equation to calculate population growth is factoring in migration. Using annual birth rates and death rates to calculate the natural increase in overall population (note that we're not talking about the "rate" of natural increase here, just the total number of people), we can add the balance to the **net migration rate (NMR)**. This is the number of immigrants minus the number of emigrants for every thousand members of the population. Here is the formula used to calculate the net migration rate:

$$\text{NMR} = \frac{\text{Number of Immigrants } - \text{ Number of Emigrants}}{\text{Population} \div 1,000}$$

Take this and add it to the birth rate minus the death rate and you will have the total population growth per thousand members of the population. The demographic equation would look like this:

$$\text{Population Growth Percentage Rate} = \frac{(\text{Birth Rate} - \text{Death Rate}) + \text{Net Migration Rate}}{10}\%$$

Take the United States as an example. The United States has a birth rate of 13 and a death rate of 8. Add the difference to a net migration rate of 2.45 and we find that the United States adds about 7.5 people for every thousand in the population annually. Divide by 10 to find that the population growth rate (including immigration) is 0.75 percent annually.

Shrinkage, Again!?!

Net migration rates can be negative. Guyana in South America has net emigration to such a degree that the population is expected to fall over the long term. Currently, Guyana's birth rate is 16 and the death rate is 7. Adding to the net migration rate of −32 (that is, subtracting 32), we find that the population growth is negative 23 per thousand, or −2.3 percent.

Total Fertility Rate

By definition, the **total fertility rate (TFR)** is the estimated average number of children born to each female of birthing age (15 to 45).

We can still use a basic formulaic definition to help remember TFR:

$$\text{TFR} = \frac{\text{Number of Children Born}}{\text{Women Aged 15 to 45}}$$

However, the TFR *is not an annual statistic* like the RNI. It is more of an estimate, taken as a snapshot of fertility for birth over the prior 30 years. Thus, TFR and RNI are not comparable. They are two different things—apples and oranges. You cannot have a negative TFR, for one thing. TFR highlights the importance of replacement in the population.

Replacement Rate

By definition, the replacement rate is a TFR of 2.1. Think about this in basic biological terms. If a mating pair has two offspring, they have replaced themselves. What about the remaining 0.1, you ask? This is what would be referred to as an error factor. We have to estimate that some small portion of the population will die before they reach adulthood—diseases and accidents do happen.

Thus, to truly replace itself, a large population must have 2.1 children per female of birthing age.

How to Remember RNI

When a country hits a TFR of 2.1 (the replacement rate), you've hit the brakes on the car and the speed of population growth slows down. It's not until the RNI hits 0 that the car comes to a complete halt and population stops growing altogether. The RNI can go negative and the car rolls backward, shrinking the population as you fumble to find the emergency brake.

Dependency Ratio

It can also be helpful to know the number of people in a population supported by a single individual in the labor force. The **dependency ratio** provides the number of people too young or too old to work compared to the number of people in the work force. In a small population of dependents, there is less of a financial burden on those who work to provide financial support than exists in a large population of dependents.

CED 2.9
Aging Populations

KNOW THE MODELS

Demographic Transition Model

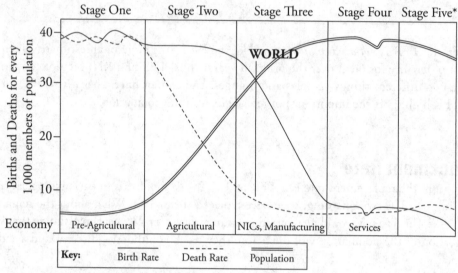

*Note that Stage Five is theoretical.

CED 2.5

The Demographic
Transition Model

The **demographic transition model (DTM)** has a number of uses. You should think of it as a central unifying concept in your understanding of the AP Human Geography course. Not only is it a theory of how population changes over time, but it also provides important insights into issues of migration, fertility, economic development, industrialization, urbanization, labor, politics, and the roles of women.

By placing a country on the model, you are defining the **population dynamics** and **economic context** of that country. Knowing where a country falls on the model lets you know what kind of economy the country has, whether or not there is significant migration going on, and, like economic indicators, this "picture" of a country's population can tell you much about its quality of life. These are theoretical estimates and averages, and not all countries fit the model perfectly. The lines shown are approximate and not always representative of every country's birth and death statistics. Closely linked to the DTM is the **epidemiological transition model (ETM)**, which specifically accounts for development due to the increasing population growth rates caused by medical advances. In the ETM, the phase of development is directly followed by a stabilization of population growth as the procreation rates decline.

The Crystal Ball

The ETM also has a **predictive capability**. If a country currently falls within stage two of the transition, we can use this model to predict how its population will change over time and speculate as to how much it can grow in size. Likewise, you can also look at the whole world, which falls into early stage three. Knowing this, we can estimate a **population projection** that the planet's population has reached only about two-thirds of its potential. If the planet is currently at about 7.9 billion people, then we can expect that once global populations level off in stage four, global population will be somewhere around 10 billion people. This may happen in your lifetime, sometime around 2060.

A Look into the Past

The DTM also provides insight into economic history. If we look at the United States, Canada, or Western Europe, we can apply dates to the bottom of the model to show how stage four countries have progressed through the system. Looking at the model below, we can see the beginning of the Renaissance in Western Europe; the **Industrial Revolution** in Western Europe and in the United States and Canada; and, likewise, the recent **deindustrialization** or shift to **service-based economies**.

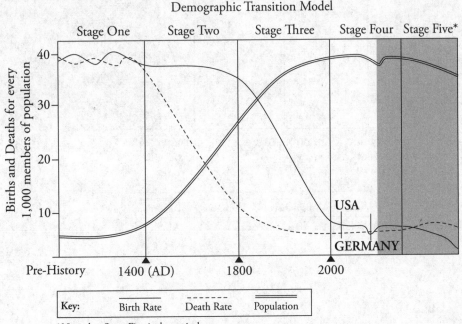

Demographic Transition Model

*Note that Stage Five is theoretical.

Pre-history goes all the way back to the origin of humanity. Around 1400, there was both a cultural and economic renaissance in Europe. The year 1800 represents the Industrial Revolution, when countries like the United States and Great Britain were **newly industrialized countries (NICs).** And 2000 represents a turning point of the rise of service-based economies of **more developed countries (MDCs).** The typical MDC has a birth rate of 11 and a death rate of 10, or very little growth.

The NICs

Countries that are not as demographically or economically advanced can also be placed on the model, but you have to change the dates as to when they reach the significant turning points in their history. If we look at newly industrialized countries (NICs) such as Brazil, Mexico, and India, we can see a much more recent turning point from the **agricultural economy** of stage two to the **manufacturing-based economy** of stage three. The NICs are shown in the model below.

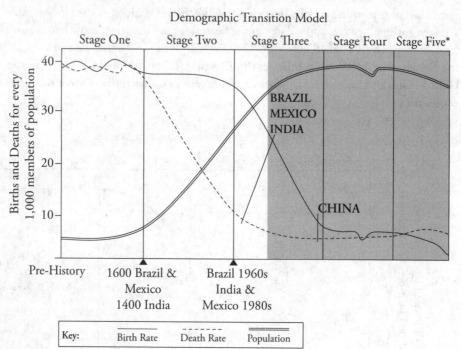

Demographic Transition Model

* Note that Stage Five is theoretical.

Even non-NIC stage two countries that are still agricultural-based economies can be outlined in the model. Let's take a look at Laos and Mozambique, as shown below.

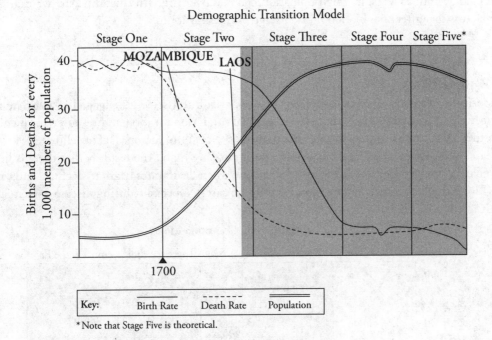

Demographic Transition Model

* Note that Stage Five is theoretical.

These stage two agricultural economies still have a lot of population growth ahead. Expect these countries to also have more rural-to-urban migration in the long term.

The S-Curve of Population

You've probably noticed that the population line in the model has a distinct shape to it until stage four. This is what demographers (population scientists) and population biologists call the **S-curve**. Humans are not the only ones whose population follows such a pattern. In fact, give any animal population a vast amount of food or remove predators from their habitat and you will see rapid population growth followed by a plateau or decline due to a population reaching or exceeding the area's **carrying capacity**. Globally, humans may be doing the same thing and, as we mentioned before, the human population may reach **equilibrium** in the global habitat. Find out more when we talk about carrying capacity in the Know the Concepts part of this chapter.

STAGE BY STAGE

The best way to learn the model is not to memorize it, but to know *why* the birth rate and death rate change and, as a result, why population changes over time. In this next part we examine the factors that affect population in each stage of the transition.

Stage One

Historically, stage one was characterized by pre-agricultural societies engaged in **subsistence farming** and **transhumance**, that is, the seasonal migration for food and resources or owning livestock. Birth rates and death rates fluctuate as the result of factors such as climate, warfare, disease, and ecological factors, but overall, both rates are high. The result is that there is little population growth until the later part of stage one when death rates begin to decline. Thus, the RNI is generally low (and can be negative in some cases), especially during disease epidemics.

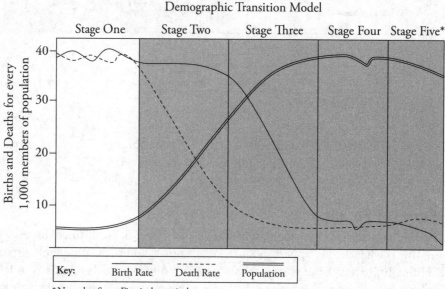

Demographic Transition Model

* Note that Stage Five is theoretical.

Lots of Life; Lots of Death, Too

Birth rates are high for a number of reasons. Children were an expression of a family's productivity and status. The more kids a family had, the more work that could be done raising crops, hunting, gathering, herding, or laboring in the **feudal political economy** as domestic servants or soldiers. **Child mortality** and **infant mortality** were also very high, which motivated parents to have a few extra children with the expectation that one or two would not live to adulthood.

Likewise, death rates are high for a multitude of reasons. In stage one, the overall population has a very low life expectancy. The lack of modern medicine and health care, limited sanitation, low nutritional standards, and the effects of hazards such as famine and war all contribute to high death rates and low life expectancy. Hard physical labor and long migrations also had the effect of physically wearing down the body and thus decreasing lifespan. This stage of the DTM corresponds to the first stage of the ETM, during which death rates were high due to a combination of diseases, like the plague, and poor medical knowledge.

Stage One Today?

Are there any stage one countries in existence today? Occasionally, yes. Typically we see that Third-World countries engaged in long periods of warfare have late stage one characteristics. When they are peaceful, Third-World agricultural countries generally have stage two birth rates and death rates. The AIDS epidemic in Southern African countries has historically created stage one demographic conditions and likewise harmed the economic development of the region. As of this printing, however, no country is demonstrating a death rate of higher than 20, meaning no countries meet the criteria for stage one based on current demographics.

Overall, though while no countries are officially in stage one, there are some small, isolated communities that do qualify. A few indigenous groups in the Amazon, sub-Saharan Africa, and Southeast Asia certainly meet the criteria. On the whole, however, humanity has advanced to the next stage—a good reason to be optimistic about the future!

Let's Review

	Birth Rates	Death Rates	Life Expectancy	RNI
Stage One	High (25–50)	High (25–40)	Low (33–50)	Low–Moderate (–0.1–1.9%)

Stage Two

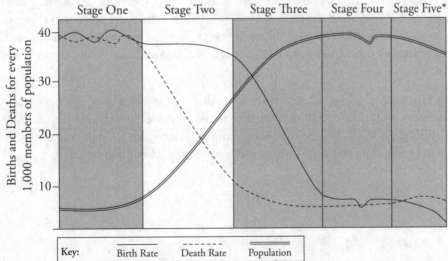

Demographic Transition Model

*Note that Stage Five is theoretical.

Stage two countries are typically agriculturally-based economies. In this economic context, in which agriculture for trade (as opposed to subsistence) is the focus of the economy, birth rates remain high while death rates decline over time. As a result, the rate of natural increase (RNI) goes up significantly as birth rates and death rates diverge. Therefore, as a country advances, population growth explodes. This is why rapid population growth has been a concern when examining the quality of life in Third-World countries. Life expectancy increases as the death rate declines, but it is still low compared to that in the First World.

Babies Are Us

Birth rates remain high as stage two countries develop in a more organized fashion around a formalized agricultural economy. Compared to stage one, children are even more important as a source of labor on farms. Infant and child mortality is still an issue due to a lack of medical care and poor nutrition for expectant mothers and infants. The vast majority of populations in stage two countries live in rural regions as a result of agriculture's economic prominence. Most cities in these countries are far from reaching their population growth potential.

Not Dead Yet!

Death rates decrease due to a number of factors. Populations engaging in the expanded agricultural economy tend to permanently settle in farming areas, and seasonal migrations become far less common. This, along with improved farming methods and the domestication of draft animals, reduces the incidence of death from excessive labor and travel by foot. Likewise, the expanded trade in agricultural goods means there is a larger and more varied food supply available to the general population. This relative increase in food volume, year-round availability, and nutrient quality means that people live longer.

The Stage Twos

Yemen, on the Arabian peninsula, is a good example of a stage two country. It has a high birth rate of 28, but its death rate has plummeted to only 6 over the past 50 years. As a result, the rate of natural increase is very high at 2.8 percent growth per year, and the life expectancy has increased to 66. An example from Asia is Nepal. The birth rate is 20 and the death rate 6, with an RNI of 1.4 percent annual population growth and a life expectancy of 71.

Both of these countries focus on agriculture as their main source of economic productivity. Statistically, this is evident in the rates of urbanization. In Yemen, 64 percent of the population still live in rural areas. Most employed Yemenis work in agriculture. Landlocked Nepal has an even starker lack of urbanization with 81 percent of the population living in rural regions of the country.

These countries are expected to experience a population explosion over the next few decades. Yemen's current population of 30 million is expected to more than double in size to about 60 million by 2050. While Nepal isn't growing quite as quickly due to high emigration, its population should grow from about 29 million today to around 36 million by 2050.

Review and Compare

	Birth Rates	Death Rates	Life Expectancy	RNI
Stage One	High (25–50)	High (25–40)	Low (33–50)	Low–Moderate (–0.1–1.9%)
Stage Two	High (25–50)	Decreasing (8–25)	Increasing (<70)	Highest (1.5–3.5%)

Hey! My Textbook Uses Different Names

Different human geography textbooks use different terms to describe the stages of the model. Some call the stages "phases." Don't be concerned; they're the same thing. Also, some might refer to stage one as pre-agrarian instead of pre-agricultural, or to stages two and three as "transitional." The names we use here relate the model to economic factors far better than general terms like "transitional."

Stage Two and a Half-ish: Newly Industrialized Countries

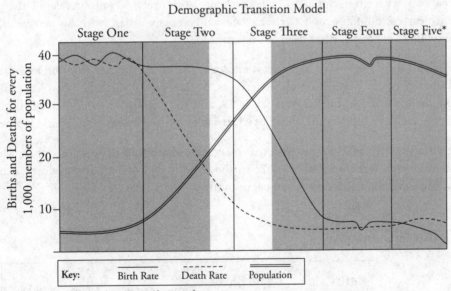

*Note that Stage Five is theoretical.

NICs are characterized by economies that are transitioning their focus away from agriculture to manufacturing as the primary form of economic production and employment. This has two distinct effects on the population. One is that there is rapid population growth in NICs. Looking at the model, you can see that it's in this range between stages two and three where birth and death rates are furthest apart, resulting in high RNIs.

The second effect, which is not shown on the model, is the rapidly increasing rate of urbanization. As these countries shift to manufacturing, more factories are being built in urban areas. Migrants responding to the pull factor of employment opportunity rapidly fill the cities to take new and better-paying jobs than those available in rural regions.

Who Has the Time Anymore?

Birth rates begin to decline with urbanization. As families move to cities, they find (in comparison to the rural agricultural lifestyle) that they have less time, less need, and moreover, less space for children. Most countries forbid child labor (it still happens, even in countries where it's illegal) and thus children in cities are less likely to be seen as a source of labor.

Getting Better All the Time

Death rates continue to decline as more urban societies have greater access to food markets, increased (but limited) access to health care and sanitation, reduced physical labor (factories compared to farming and mining), and increased education.

Around the Planet

Mexico is an NIC example where death rates have plunged in recent decades due to increases in the quality of life and access to services. At present, Mexicans have a birth rate of 18 and a death rate of 5, with a resulting RNI of 1.5 percent. With over 130 million people, the population adds nearly 2 million people per year. Mexico is mostly urban, with 80 percent in cities, and the total life expectancy has risen to 76 years old.

On the other side of the world, Malaysia is another NIC where industrialization and urbanization have changed the population characteristics. Malays have a birth rate of 19, a death rate of 5, and an RNI of 1.2. Life expectancy is 75, and the population is 73 percent urbanized. Mexico appears to be just slightly ahead of Malaysia in terms of demographic development.

In long-term growth, Malaysia is expected to increase sharply in population, while Mexico's population growth will slow and stabilize in the coming decades. By the middle of the 21st century, Mexico's population may even begin to drop.

Here's the NIC Review

	Birth Rates	Death Rates	Life Expectancy	RNI
Stage One	High (25–50)	High (25–40)	Low (33–50)	Low–Moderate (–0.1–1.9%)
Stage Two	High (25–50)	Decreasing (8–25)	Increasing (<70)	Highest (1.5–3.5%)
NICs	Decreasing (12–30)	Lowering (5–18)	Increasing (<75)	Higher (1.1–2.7%)

Stage Three

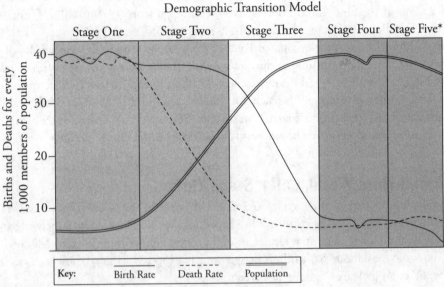

Demographic Transition Model

* Note that Stage Five is theoretical.

Stage three was historically where most "industrialized" or manufacturing-based countries were found in the transition. However, most of these First-World (and many former European Communist Second-World) countries have shifted their economies to a more service-based focus. During this time these same countries have completed the transition—that is, completing the S-curve and moving into stage four. Stage three is what we should expect many NICs to look like as they continue to industrialize.

Baby, Please Don't Go

Birth rates continue to decrease as the effects of urbanization (less space, time, and need factors) along with increases in health care, education, and female employment have negative effects on fertility. Access to health care has an important influence on the **diffusion of fertility control** or the availability of contraceptives in more urbanized and developed economies, as well as reducing the **diffusion of disease** due to medical advances. Women's education and employment also result in fewer children due to the constraints of time and new positions of power gained from their school and job experiences.

Pushing Up the Daisies

In stage three, access to health care, nutrition, sanitation, and education continue to increase life expectancy and decrease death rates. This is a pivotal stage in the ETM, during which both birth and death rates decline due to rapid medical advancements. The advent of antibiotics and vaccines, coupled with the increasing affordability of health care, is a particular hallmark of industrialized countries. However, death rates will never hit zero, for the obvious reason that all humans are worm bait. We all die. The country with the lowest death rate, Qatar, still sees 1.244 deaths per thousand people every year. Life expectancies can extend further in stage four countries, but the death rate stays about the same.

One Child, No Waiting

China, as an NIC, is more advanced demographically than its economic situation would predict. As a result of the One-Child Policy that was enforced from 1979 to 2015, China is more typical of a middle-to-late stage three country, compared to other NICs like Brazil. China's birth rate is 12 and death rate 7, with an RNI of 0.5 percent. The long-term effects of population control in China will continue to slow its growth, despite policies being enforced less often. In fact, China, currently at 1.41 billion people, will likely complete the S-curve in the coming decades. The country is projected to reach 1.45 billion around 2025 and level off, maintaining population levels. Keep in mind that China is only 56 percent urbanized (according to 2015 data, the most recently recorded) because of Mao's "Back to the Land" policy.

Don't Call It Third World, Call It Stage Three

Uruguay also has late stage three characteristics with a birth rate of 13 and a death rate of 9, resulting in an RNI of 0.4. The country's life expectancy is 77, and it is extremely urbanized at 92 percent, as most of the country resides in and around the **primate city** of Montevideo. At present, Uruguay has about 3.5 million people and is expected to grow slowly to 3.7 million people by 2050, an increase of about 11 percent.

Comparisons

	Birth Rates	Death Rates	Life Expectancy	RNI
Stage One	High (25–50)	High (25–40)	Low (33–50)	Low–Moderate (–0.1–1.9%)
Stage Two	High (25–50)	Decreasing (8–25)	Increasing (<70)	Highest (1.5–3.5%)
NICs	Decreasing (12–30)	Lowering (5–18)	Increasing (<75)	Higher (1.1–2.7%)
Stage Three	Lowering (12–20)	Low (5–12)	Higher (<78)	Lowering (0.5–1.2%)

Stage Four and Stage Five

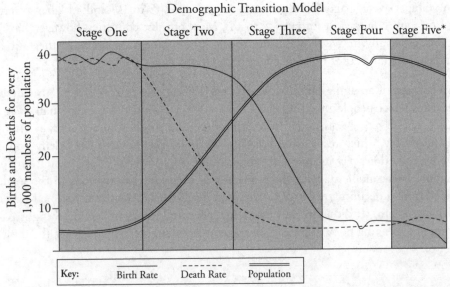

Demographic Transition Model

*Note that Stage Five is theoretical.

In stage four, birth and death rates converge to result in limited population growth and even population decline. Here we expect to find First-World countries with service-based economies. As we discuss elsewhere, it's okay to think of them as "industrialized" countries, but keep in mind that these are service industries like finance, insurance, real estate, health care, and communications that drive the economy. Manufacturing is a dying breed in these countries. For example, in the United States, services are 80 percent of the **gross domestic product (GDP)** and manufacturing is only 20 percent. These are highly urbanized countries (over 70 percent) possessing the longest life expectancies, with some populations averaging over 80 years.

Gone, Baby, Gone

Both the final stages of the DTM and ETM occur when birth rates bottom out into the lower teens. Not only is there a high degree of access to medical care, but the roles of women in society are such that most adult women are engaged in the labor force and are empowered politically and socially within the communities. The result is that fecundity is greatly reduced. When birth rates reach the same level as death rates, this is when you have **zero population growth (ZPG)** and an RNI of 0.0 percent. Birth rates can decline to a point where they're actually lower than death rates. This results in a negative RNI and a shrinking population.

The classical DTM has four stages. However, when this model was created nearly a century ago, scientists didn't anticipate the low death rates and very low birth rates that we now see in some developed countries. Many scholars have proposed adding a fifth stage to the DTM to reflect this potential for a negative RNI and shrinking population. Countries theoretically in or approaching this stage include Japan and Germany. Japan, with an RNI of –0.2 percent, is facing a potential population crisis due to a rapidly aging population and fecundity well below replacement rate.

Don't Fear the Reaper

Death rates remain low and vary slightly depending upon the age structure of the overall population. A younger average age will result in low death rates (5 to 10) and a higher average age will result in slightly higher death rates (7 to 14). Most of these countries, however, have aging populations, especially in Western Europe and in Anglo-North America. In these situations, there tends to be a large, over-65, dependent population.

The consequences of an aging population are vast, particularly in economics. An elderly population means fewer people investing their money—e.g. taking risks, even small ones—and more people conservatively sitting on their cash. This results in less money actually circulating through the society, which results in stagnation. Furthermore, because the elderly population rarely works, they don't pay income tax, which results in a lower tax base to support the rest of the nation. For example, Japan, which has one of the oldest populations in the world and has suffered from a declining tax base for decades, decided to increase the national *sales* tax to address this problem. (It didn't work, because people simply stopped buying things!) Another consequence of an aging population is a shortage of labor supply, which carries the same negative effect on an economy.

Hockey Fans Wanted!

Canada, with a birth rate of 10 and a death rate of 8, grows only around 0.2 percent per year. The population is 38 million, but by 2050 it should be around 42 million. Wait a minute, that doesn't seem quite right. How can a country with such a miniscule RNI be projected to add 7 million people to its population in the next few decades? The answer is this: the rate of natural increase does not include migration into a country. Canada, like the United States and the United Kingdom, has positive net migration, and many international migrants go to Canada, especially those from other British Commonwealth countries. Also keep in mind that migrant populations tend to have much higher fertility rates compared to the general population.

Ciao, Baby? Or Just Ciao!

Italy, like Germany, is another example of a Western European country that has experienced negative population growth in recent years. The birth rate in Italy is 9, its death rate 10, and its RNI is −0.1 percent. Italy, which currently has 59.5 million people, will reach about 63.5 million people by 2050, due to labor immigration. This is where the idea of a DTM stage five gets complicated. In theory, countries with a negative RNI should see shrinking populations. However, many of these countries have positive net migration rates, so their populations remain steady or even continue to grow slowly.

A number of countries that are near or below zero population growth levels offer incentives to citizens to have more children. One of the reasons for this is that with so few children being born, fewer people enter the workforce over time. Many of these countries have become dependent upon foreign **guest workers**, like the *gastarbeiter* in Germany, many of whom have come from Turkey, North Africa, the Middle East, and more recently, the former Soviet Union.

It's also important to recognize that many former Communist countries of Eastern Europe have stage four demographic characteristics. The factors behind this have recently emerged. It appears that many young workers in Eastern Europe and Russia have emigrated for better-paying work opportunities in the West. Despite their recent admission to the European Union, countries like Latvia (RNI –0.4 percent), Lithuania (RNI –0.2 percent), and Hungary (RNI –0.4 percent) have shrinking populations. Some have also pointed to the lingering social effects of Communism on the population in these countries. **Economic restructuring** has brought economic, political, and social hardship to many communities. During the Communist era, people received incentives from the state to have children. With government subsidies gone, many couples don't see any motivation to have a larger family.

Other countries that have enacted **pronatalist** policies include Sweden, Japan, and Germany. These countries have offered such benefits as free childcare, assistance with certain medical expenses, and tax cuts for large families. Some pronatalist policies are put in place because of religious or cultural beliefs that encourage larger families or discourage the use of contraceptives. It may sound funny, but some governments and non-governmental organizations mount advertising campaigns and even propaganda urging people to climb into bed with one another!

On the other side of the coin are **anti-natalist** policies, which are enacted by national governments to restrict the growth of the population. These policies are often found in countries that have concerns about extreme overpopulation, and they range from restrictions on the number of children a family can have to comprehensive family planning education, including contraceptive use. India, Kenya, and China have instituted anti-natalist policies. China in particular has become a popular example of anti-natalism because of its famous One-Child Policy, which began in 1980 and limited families to exactly that: one child. It worked, as China's birth rate did decline. However, due to a cultural preference towards males, many pregnant women chose to abort female fetuses, leading to a lopsided male-to-female ratio that itself carries many unknown consequences yet to come. The One-Child Policy ended in 2015.

Got It? Good!

Well, that was hopefully not too painful. The point here is to understand *why* the model works, as opposed to just memorizing the lines on a graph. Here is a review of the numbers and the complete model one more time, just to give you a last look:

	Birth Rates	Death Rates	Life Expectancy	RNI
Stage One	High (25–50)	High (25–40)	Low (33–50)	Low–Moderate (–0.1–1.9%)
Stage Two	High (25–50)	Decreasing (8–25)	Increasing (<70)	Highest (1.5–3.5%)
NICs	Decreasing (12–30)	Lowering (5–18)	Increasing (<75)	Higher (1.1–2.7%)
Stage Three	Lowering (12–20)	Low (5–12)	Higher (<78)	Lowering (0.5–1.2%)
Stage Four	Low (8–16)	Low (5–12)	Highest (<82)	Low to Negative (0.8 to –0.6%)
Stage Five	Very Low (<12)	Low (5–12)	Highest (<82)	Negative (<0%)

And the Model, One Last Time

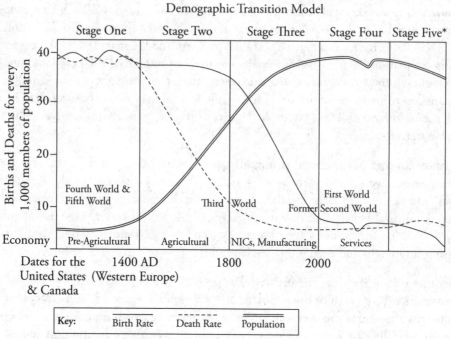

Demographic Transition Model

*Note that Stage Five is theoretical.

MALTHUSIAN THEORY

Englishman Thomas Malthus published *An Essay on the Principle of Population* in 1798. His main idea was that the global population would one day expand to the point where it could not produce enough food to feed everyone. He predicted this would happen before 1900. The Malthusian catastrophe did not happen by 1900 or even by today, but some more recent thinkers (neo-Malthusians) feel it still could in the future.

Why did he have this idea? At the time the math made sense, as the United Kingdom was engaged in the Industrial Revolution and people were being born at a high rate. If we look at the demographic transition model timeline, Britain was moving from stage two to stage three. As we see in NICs of today, Malthus saw rapid migration to the cities and a population explosion.

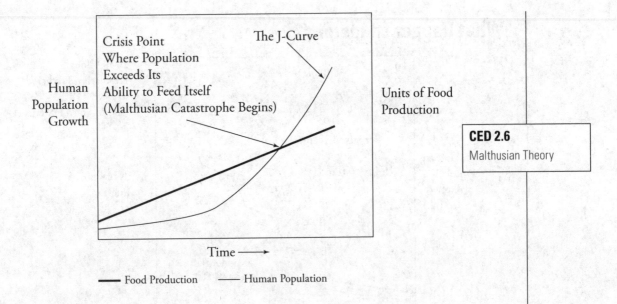

Malthus' Prediction Regarding Population and Food Production

CED 2.6
Malthusian Theory

It Was in the Numbers

Mathematically, what Malthus saw was that food production did grow over time but in a slow arithmetic manner. In this context, arithmetic means that each year another unit of food production was added to the overall volume of agricultural products. Think of it like a "volume + 1" situation or a constant rate of change from algebra class. Meanwhile, human population grows in an exponential manner. Here, exponential means that a couple has a few children and then their children all have a few children, and so on through generations. So rather than undergoing a constant rate of change, the population may, for example, double every few decades, resulting in a logistic curve, or **J-curve,** of exponential population growth on the graph. Looking at the numbers of the time, Malthus figured population was going to catch up fast.

What Happened Instead?

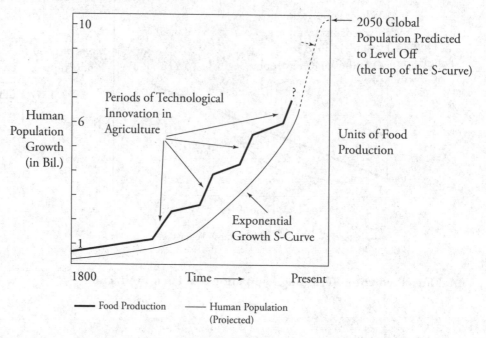

It wasn't that Malthus was wrong, but that he couldn't have predicted that agricultural technology was going to boost food production several times over in the coming century. By 1900, massively important inventions such as the internal combustion engine, artificial fertilizers, pesticides, irrigation pumps, advanced plant and animal hybridization techniques, the tin can, and refrigeration were developed. As each of these new products and methods was adopted, another large volume of food would be added to global production and supply. Mathematically, this meant that food production has continued to stay ahead of population growth. For how long this will occur, we don't know. Let's hope that by 2050 or so, when the global population is predicted to level off at around 10 billion (completing the top of the S-curve), the world has food production in good working order.

What About Genetics? Avoid the Trap!

In the early 1800s, Gregor Mendel was the first to research and write about genes and plant reproduction. However, the science of genetics did not make any impact on global food production until the 1950s and genetically modified foods did not enter markets until the 1980s. If you are asked about why Malthus was wrong, talk about new technologies including plant and animal hybrids, but not genetics, since that has affected agriculture only in much more recent years.

Neo-Malthusians: Be Afraid, Be Very Afraid!

Neo-Malthusians are more recent theorists who warn that a Malthusian catastrophe could still occur. You might think that things don't seem too bad now and that within a generation or two, the global population will level off. Won't we just come up with new technologies to meet future food demands? Three important points are made by the neo-Malthusians:

1. **Sustainability.** When the world does reach 10 billion people, there may be problems keeping up with food demand over the long term. Already, many major agricultural regions have significant ecological problems like soil erosion and soil nutrient loss and, in arid regions, depletion of irrigation sources and soil salinization. If too many of the world's current growing areas are damaged, can food production keep up with the increased demand?

2. **Increasing *Per Capita* Demand.** Globally, the amount of food consumed per person is rising. Why? The average First-World citizen consumes around eight times the amount of food and resources that a person in the Third World does. As the Third World continues to develop economically, consumers there will increase their demand for food and other products several times over. Can the planet provide enough food when all 10 billion of us eat like the First World does today?

3. **Natural Resource Depletion.** Food is not the only concern of neo-Malthusians. Theorists like Paul Ehrlich have also warned about our over-consumption of other resources such as timber, minerals, energy, and other nonrenewables. Can a world with 10 billion people have enough material to house everyone, enough fuel to heat all the houses, and enough food to feed everyone? If not, we need to continue to conserve and look for alternatives so that we can stretch out supplies over time—until we have *Star Trek*-esque replicators to make food for us and fusion reactors to make energy.

THE POPULATION PYRAMID

It sounds like a game show or a seriously geeky board game. Population pyramids are a graphical way to visualize the **population structure** of a country or place. More specifically, population pyramids reveal the **gender** and **age distribution** of the population. Like a country's position on the demographic transition model, the shape of the pyramid can tell you a lot about that country's level of economic development.

> **CED 2.3**
> Population Composition

General Principles

Males are always on the left of the pyramid and females are on the right. Each bar is an **age cohort,** generally made up of five-year sets: 0–4, 5–9, 10–14, and so on. The origin (0-value) of each bar graph is the center and increases in value as you move left or right outward from the center. The single colored bar right or left of the origin is an **age-sex cohort**, with just one gender of that age group. (Note that age-sex cohorts may not always be colored on the exam.) Gaps, where there is an unexpectedly small bar, are important to recognize. A gap in a male cohort but not in females of the same age group is most commonly a sign of a past war that was fought outside the country. A gap in data for both males and females is likely a sign of past war inside that country, epidemic disease, or famine. When comparing the number of males and females in a population of cohort, the **sex ratio** tells you the number of males per 100 females.

One Pyramid to Another

Not all population pyramids look the same. Depending upon who drew them, there may or may not be a column down the middle. Seeing the overall shape of the pyramid is what's important. We'll use both methods here so that you are used to seeing it both ways. You never know what they are going to put on the exam.

Check the Type of Data

Be aware of whether the bars on the graph show the *percent* of the total population or the total *number* of people in the age-sex cohort.

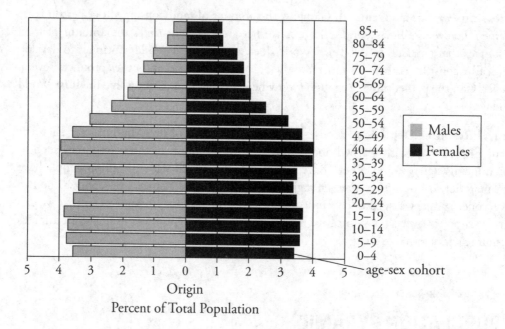

Percent Age-Sex Structure of Indiana, 2000

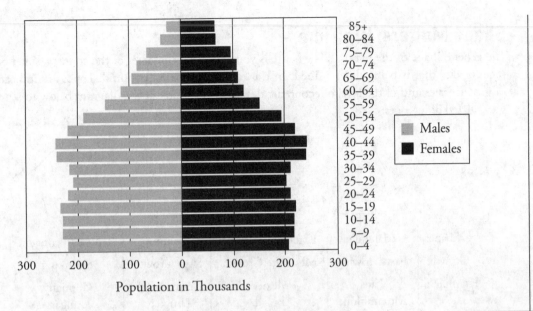

Population in Thousands

Total Population Age-Sex Structure for Indiana, 2000

While the two pyramids look the same, we need to be sure when referring to the data that we recognize what kind of numbers (percent versus total) we are talking about—this is especially important if asked on the free-response section. What about those pyramids with the column down the middle? Here is what the percent data would look like:

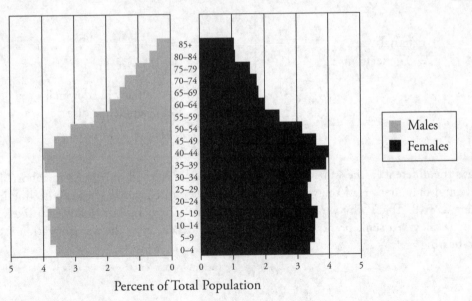

Percent of Total Population

U.S. Census Bureau data

Percent Age-Sex Structure of Indiana in 2000 with Central Column

Shape Matters, Big Time

The general shape of the pyramid is what tells you about the character of the country, state, province, or city that is being diagrammed. In the case of countries, pyramid shapes are indicators of growth rates and of the level of economic development. Look at the diagram below to see the generalized differences:

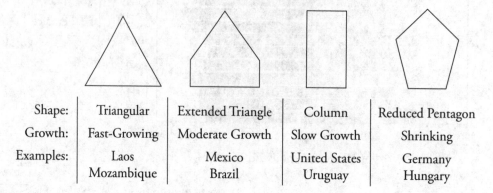

Shape:	Triangular	Extended Triangle	Column	Reduced Pentagon
Growth:	Fast-Growing	Moderate Growth	Slow Growth	Shrinking
Examples:	Laos Mozambique	Mexico Brazil	United States Uruguay	Germany Hungary

The Gaps and the Busts!

What does a gap look like and what does it mean? Take a look at this generalized example. See the possible explanations for these gaps:

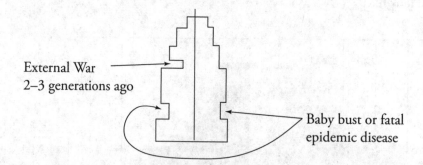

External War
2–3 generations ago

Baby bust or fatal
epidemic disease

What's the difference? The war is a given event in that it affected only one age cohort significantly and only men. Had the war happened in this country, you'd see some decline in the women as well. That's why we refer to it as "external." The baby bust followed a likely postwar baby boom. At some point, booming fertility will recede after the war generation exceeds child-bearing age.

Who's on Top?

Old folks, that's who. Of course, increased mortality from disease and old age causes significant declines in the **elder population**. That's why the top shrinks so quickly. You will notice that the male side of the pyramid declines in number far more quickly than that of the female side. Why? Fair or not, women live 4 to 5 years longer than men on average.

Countries, States, and Cities, Oh My!

You can have population pyramids for many different scales of population. Most commonly countries are shown, but states and cities may also show up on the exam. Let's first look at some country examples:

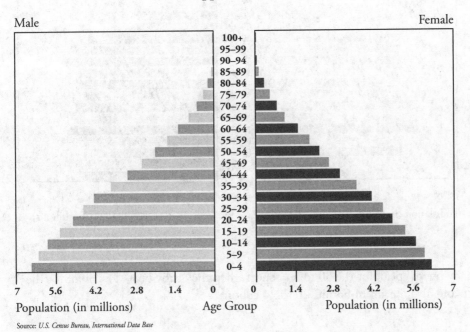

Philippines: 2014

Male / Female

Age groups: 100+, 95–99, 90–94, 85–89, 80–84, 75–79, 70–74, 65–69, 60–64, 55–59, 50–54, 45–49, 40–44, 35–39, 30–34, 25–29, 20–24, 15–19, 10–14, 5–9, 0–4

Population (in millions): 7, 5.6, 4.2, 2.8, 1.4, 0 | Age Group | 0, 1.4, 2.8, 4.2, 5.6, 7

Source: *U.S. Census Bureau, International Data Base*

> The Perfect Pyramid, a Fast-Growing Philippines (RNI = 1.9 percent)

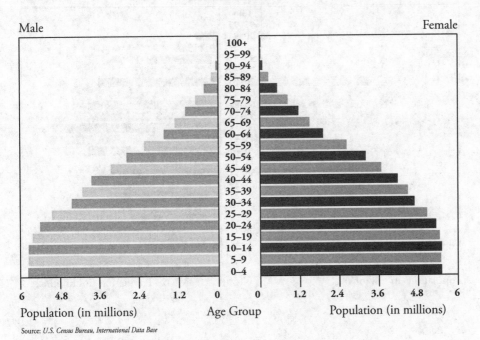

Mexico: 2014

Male / Female

Age groups: 100+, 95–99, 90–94, 85–89, 80–84, 75–79, 70–74, 65–69, 60–64, 55–59, 50–54, 45–49, 40–44, 35–39, 30–34, 25–29, 20–24, 15–19, 10–14, 5–9, 0–4

Population (in millions): 6, 4.8, 3.6, 2.4, 1.2, 0 | Age Group | 0, 1.2, 2.4, 3.6, 4.8, 6

Source: *U.S. Census Bureau, International Data Base*

> Starting to Slow, an NIC Mexico (RNI = 1.4 percent)

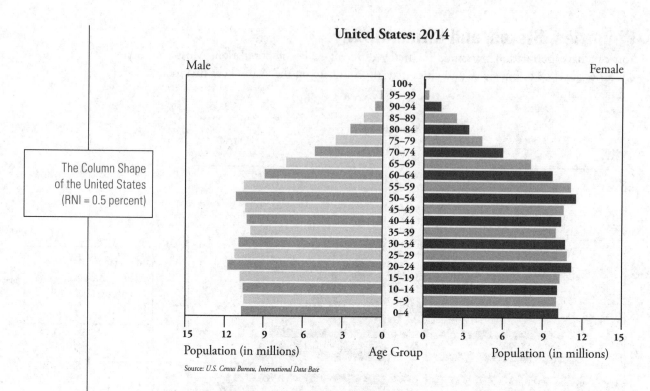

United States: 2014

Male / Female

The Column Shape of the United States (RNI = 0.5 percent)

Population (in millions) — Age Group — Population (in millions)

Source: *U.S. Census Bureau, International Data Base*

Note the "baby boom" peak for the 50 to 54 cohort, then the "baby bust" low point for the 35 to 39 cohort, and also the "mini-boom" 20 to 24 cohort.

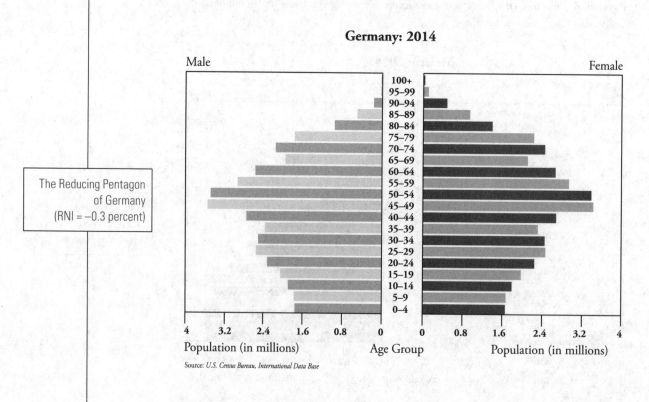

Germany: 2014

Male / Female

The Reducing Pentagon of Germany (RNI = −0.3 percent)

Population (in millions) — Age Group — Population (in millions)

Source: *U.S. Census Bureau, International Data Base*

See those gaps? The 65 to 69 cohorts (both male and female) lived in Germany during World War II. Women suffered mortality in great numbers since many of the war's final years were fought on German soil. The baby boom in Germany lasted much longer than it did in the United States and peaked much later. This late peak is likely due to the food rationing that continued for several years after the war.

The States

Let's look at two U.S. states from 2000 to see each end of the population growth spectrum:

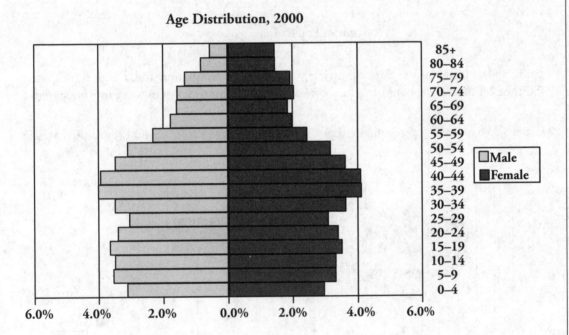

Age Distribution, 2000

Rhode Island, above, is the slowest-growing state in the country. The TFR is 1.6 (0.5 children per female below the replacement rate). Despite a small mini-boom, the child-age population is declining significantly. Within a decade, population structure in Rhode Island could look more like Germany or Italy.

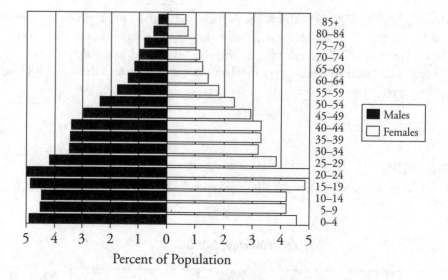

Percent of Population

Utah, above, is one of the fastest-growing states due to immigration and a high fertility rate (TFR of 2.4). Here, the boom and bust cycles are at different times than those in Rhode Island.

Cities also have some interesting patterns. Here are three cities from around the United States:

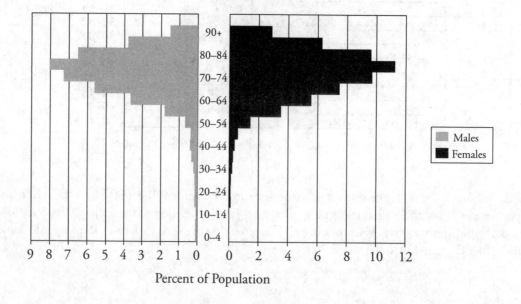

Percent of Population

Sun City, Arizona (shown in the graph above), is a suburb of Phoenix that has long been a retirement destination for older Americans. Notice how there are almost no children.

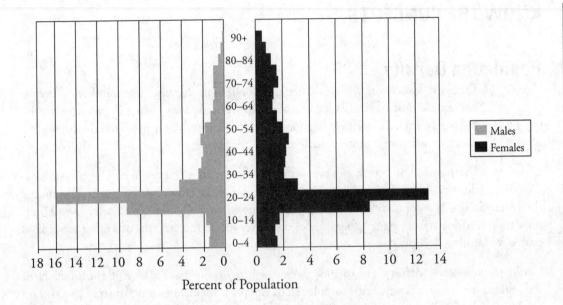

Morgantown, West Virginia (shown in the graph above), is home to West Virginia University. The city's structure is cross-shaped because of the large college-age cohort.

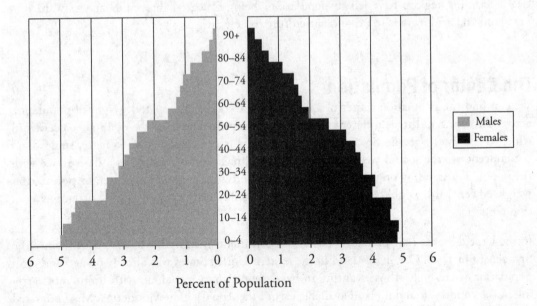

Brownsville, Texas (shown in the graph above), has an age structure more similar to that of Mexico, just across the Rio Grande, than to that of the rest of the United States. Immigrant communities in border towns can have a great effect on population growth.

KNOW THE CONCEPTS

Population Density

CED 2.1
Population Distribution

There are two main ways to calculate population density. The number of people per square unit of land is known as **arithmetic density**. Most island nations and microstates have extremely high arithmetic densities. Consider also the high arithmetic densities of countries such as India, Bangladesh, Japan, and South Korea.

The number of people per square unit of *farm* land is known as the **physiologic density.** Physiologic density can be seen as a more practical tool in understanding the sustainability of a population of a certain region or country. Physiologic density is especially important in understanding the geography of countries where the amount of **arable land**, land usable for farming, is limited.

Limits to physiologic density can include overcrowding on farms or a lack of abundant farming regions due to geography. For example, Iraq, Egypt, Uzbekistan, and Pakistan are all arid countries that have narrow farming regions around river systems and deltas.

In countries like the United States and China, arable land sits in the eastern third of the country and the west is dominated by mountain and desert regions. There, high physiologic densities in farming regions have led to populations being squeezed into cities or westward into grassland and arid regions to expand agriculture to new areas.

The Center of Population

We can find the population center of a country by averaging the spatial weight of population across the country. This is different from the **geographic center** of the country, or **centroid**, which is simply the geometric center of the country's irregular polygon. To better understand the concept of "the spatial weight of population," imagine the country as a flat surface with the population standing on top in their home locations. The population center, or **population-weighted centroid**, would be the point where you could balance that weighted surface without tipping over.

In the United States, the population center has continuously moved west each decade since the first census in 1790. Originally, land in the eastern United States was already owned and farm populations were high. Those wanting to have their own farms, along with immigrants arriving in the country, found no land available east of the Appalachian Mountains. Most migrated westward into the Midwest and Great Plains regions to settle and start their own farms. For this physiologic reason, the arithmetic density and population center moved westward through World War II.

After World War II, the population shifted south and west due to the Sunbelt migration. See more on the Frostbelt to Sunbelt shift starting on page 182.

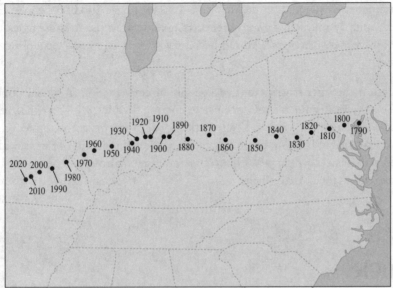

Source: U.S. Census Bureau, International Data Base

Historic Population Centers from Each Decennial Census

Note the southwestern shift from 1950 onward, toward the Sunbelt.

Population and Sustainability

The most important concept to understand about the **sustainability** of the global population is **carrying capacity**. At the global scale, we can ask this question: how many people can the Earth sustain without triggering a **Malthusian catastrophe**? Similarly, at the regional scale we can examine the sustainability of certain **population densities**.

CED 2.2

Consequences of Population Distribution

Across the **ecumene**, the living space of humans on the Earth's surface, there are certain limits to how many people an environment can support in terms of the availability of food, water, and natural resources. Some regions support **human settlement** better than others. For instance, temperate grasslands support far more people than deserts do. That seems obvious, but why then are so many people, in this day and age, moving in greater number into **arid regions**? Secondly, how long before dry regions are pushed to their limits, especially in terms of fresh water?

Overpopulation is a major concern both in resource-poor regions and across the globe. Several neo-Malthusian warnings have been issued regarding the excessive consumption of natural resources worldwide. The message is that certain resources such as clean water, endangered plant and animal habitats, and nonrenewable energy sources like oil will be depleted if **conservation** efforts and **population control** methods are not mandated by governments. Some theorists have expressed a need for the goal of zero population growth worldwide to stem the tide of resource depletion. To do this, some have proposed large-scale family-planning and contraceptive programs. However, many have rejected these ideas based primarily on religious or political beliefs.

Another benefit arising from population control would be alleviating concerns over decreasing amounts of **personal space** as population densities increase. Some worry that too many people crammed into densely packed urban areas will lead to social unrest and, potentially, armed conflicts.

Furthermore, increased population density leads (in cities over 500,000 people) to increased spending per capita by municipal governments, so taxes tend to rise in those cities. And if that population density increases *rapidly*, things become very, very strained—economically, socially, and otherwise.

Other population theorists have examined the role of conservation in global population sustainability. To achieve sustainable resource use in coming decades, with an expected 10-billion-person global population, massive and systematic global programs enforcing recycling, energy conservation, sustainable farming practices, and a wholesale reduction of **personal consumption** are believed to be necessary. Without conservation, many resources could be depleted before we have the chance to save them.

MIGRATION

Migration is common and can take several different forms. **Interregional,** or **internal, migrants** move from one region of the country to another. This is the case with rural-to-urban migrants, who move from farmland to cities within the same country. There are intraregional migrants who move from one area to another within the same region, but they're not very interesting. There are also variations within international migration. **Transnational migration** occurs when migrants move from one country to another.

Migrants can take many forms, from an enslaved person to a job-seeker to a refugee. Humans move for many reasons and there are several theories to explain the practice of migration, both between countries and internally. On the international side, the human capital theory of migration contends that humans take their education, job skills, training, and language skills (*also* called human capital) to a country where they can make more money and reap a higher net return. Higher levels of human capital (education, training, language skills) increase the expected net gain from migration. This flow of human capital from one country to another causes wages to fall in the destination country while pushing wages up in the sending country. Migration between the two countries stops only when the individual expected net earnings and costs of migration are the same.

Who's Who?

CED 2.11
Forced and Voluntary Migration

Migrants are generally those who voluntarily move from location to location. However, there are forms of **forced migration**. Some people may be taken or coerced from their homes for forced labor through human trafficking or enslavement. The largest forced migration in history was the Atlantic slave trade, which displaced millions of Africans between the 15th and 19th centuries. Governments can order their citizens to move to another place. Other people forced to move by war, disasters, or fear of government repression are known as **refugees**. Certain countries have official programs to receive refugees from other countries and grant them **asylum**, either temporarily (until danger at home subsides) or permanently. For example, many countries had asylum programs in the 1990s for people escaping **ethnic cleansing** in the former Yugoslavia, Rwanda, and Burundi. The host country often faces enormous economic burdens in providing a new home for refugees. Basic food, water, sanitation, and safety needs are often barely met in the host country if it is a developing nation already struggling to provide for its own people.

In most countries, people who come seeking refuge or employment opportunities but do not have government authorization (like a work visa or official refugee status) are considered **undocumented immigrants**. Some countries have **amnesty programs** allowing undocumented immigrants the opportunity to apply for official status or citizenship without facing arrest or deportation.

Steps to a Better Life

There are a few particular patterns of migration and specific ways that people migrate. **Step migration** occurs when people move up in a hierarchy of locations, with each move to a more advantageous or economically prosperous place. For example, a family might move from a farm to a neighboring town; then from that town to a regional city; then to the outskirts of a larger metropolitan area; and from there closer to the center of the city, each time to take advantage of better work opportunities. They might then move again closer to the center of the city once they achieve economic stability and want to have full access to the central business district. Along the way, **intervening opportunities** for work and economic improvement will increase the farther migrants travel.

Building the Chain

Chain migration occurs when a pioneering individual or group settles in a new place, establishing a new migrant foothold. These people send information back to friends, family, and business contacts. The pioneer provides information on employment opportunities, furnishes access to markets or social networks, and encourages others to migrate to the location. Over time, more and more people move in and a growing immigrant community is established.

Cyclic Movement and Remittances

Some who migrate purely for employment purposes have a pattern of **cyclic movement**. In the case of transnational labor migrants, foreign employees work for a limited period of time before returning to their home countries. Sometimes this is also called **periodic movement** if it is on an annual or seasonal basis—for instance, agricultural workers coming from Mexico to the United States for different harvest periods and then returning home to help out during harvest on their family farms. Cyclic movement can last several years and even span the career of an individual. In some cases, foreign workers come to a country to find a job that they work through to retirement, and then they return to their home countries when they reach old age.

The receiving countries benefit from the flow of cheap labor into their economies. The socioeconomic cost of receiving this flow of immigrants cannot be ignored: it includes expanding unemployment services, building cultural adaptation and social welfare programs, and even addressing national security concerns. As for the sending countries, the loss of highly skilled workers poses a big challenge to those countries losing the migrants. The largest positive economic effect of migration is the sending of remittances. Remittances are monetary and other cash transfers sent from **transnational migrants** to their families and communities back home. Often, more money flows back home in the form of remittances than the sending country receives in official development assistance. Remittances create a strong positive impact in the migrant's home country. In rural Mexico, hundreds of communities are supported purely by the remittances of transnational labor migrants from their communities working in the United States.

Frostbelt to Sunbelt Shift

Keep in mind that someone does not have to cross international borders to be considered a migrant. Many countries experience internal migrations that significantly change the countries' population distributions. A common example is the Frostbelt to Sunbelt migration in the United States that has taken place over the past few decades. With declines in manufacturing employment, especially in the northeastern United States, many people left the colder, more populated regions of the northeastern upper Midwest for new service employment opportunities and better climates in the South and Southwestern United States.

If you examine the map on page 179 (Historic Population Centers), you'll notice that the average center of U.S. population has moved to the south and the west over the past 50 to 60 years. This is due to the growth of large Sunbelt cities such as Atlanta, Orlando, Dallas, Houston, San Antonio, Albuquerque, Phoenix, San Diego, Los Angeles, and Las Vegas. We can even include places you wouldn't normally consider the Sunbelt, such as Denver, San Francisco, Salt Lake City, Portland, and Seattle.

Life-Course Changes

When people move because of major changes in the course of their lives, these are referred to as **life-course changes**. Internal migration within a country is often explained by looking at life-course changes, such as going to college, moving for a better job, or retiring. Life-course changes can occur in many ways. Older people sometimes move when they retire. Almost 10 percent of Americans aged 60 and older migrated between counties in the five-year period between 1995 and 2000. But don't be misled. Young people are more likely to pick up and move than senior citizens. From the time they leave home for college, young people begin a series of migrations that are based as much on life-course changes as on the amenities of place and quality of life.

The Pros and Cons of Migration		
	Country of Emigration	**Country of Immigration**
Pros	Family members receive remittances from emigrants	Immigrants fill unwanted jobs; the country benefits from both unskilled and educated immigrants
Cons	The country loses intellectual capital (brain drain) and physical capital (labor supply)	Immigrants require housing, schools, language development; some feel threatened by the changing original culture

Push and Pull Factors

Newly industrialized countries (NICs) experience rapid internal rural-to-urban migration. Employment at urban manufacturing locations appears to be the main intervening opportunity for these internal immigrants. However, research has shown that a number of both push and pull factors cause people to leave a rural agricultural lifestyle and move to a city. **Push factors** are specific things about the rural agricultural landscape and livelihood that force people off the farm. **Pull factors** are specific things about cities that draw people to the urban landscape. It is important to remember that the opposite of a pull factor is not a push factor. For example, a pull factor cannot be the lack of employment opportunities in rural regions.

CED 2.10
Causes of Migration

CED 2.12
Effects of Migration

Push Factor: Armed Conflicts

Push factors include a number of issues related to the hardships faced in rural areas. One significant push factor is armed conflict. When rebel movements initiate military campaigns against governments, it is often in rural regions. When conflicts emerge in rural regions, many people flee and become refugees to the safety of cities. Terrorism and drug trafficking activity can have a similar effect and can frighten people off the land.

Push Factor: Environmental Hazards

Environmental pollution is another push factor. Excessive use of agricultural chemicals can poison soils and water supplies. In addition, improper usage of pesticides can lead to birth defects in children, forcing parents to move to cities to seek constant medical care for their children. Natural disasters can also work as push factors. A flood or drought can destroy a whole year's income and cause people to leave farming as their primary source of income.

Push Factor: The High Cost of Land

Increased land costs can also force people off the land. In newly industrialized countries, prices inflate, especially in markets for land. Farmers who own land may suddenly have the opportunity to sell their land and make far more money than they could in several years of farming. This money can then be used for migration to urban areas and pay for new city housing. In the cases in which farmers are renting land, rents can increase significantly. Sometimes the farmers can no longer afford to pay rent or make enough money to support their families. Often these migrants arrive in cities homeless and are forced into squatter settlements (see Chapter 8). Even though land and other commodity prices may increase over time, basic food crop prices tend to change very little over the long term, making farming far less profitable for small family farms.

The Pull Factors

The pull factors that draw people to cities are mainly employment-related. The higher number of job opportunities, higher pay rates, and the regularity of pay can be influential factors that motivate migrants to move to the city. Keep in mind that farmers generally make money only at the end of the growing season, when crops are sold. Having regular paychecks creates better financial security for migrants.

The AP exam loves to ask both multiple-choice and free-response questions about push and pull factors.

Make sure to read where and how people in Latin America live as new urban migrants in Chapter 8.

The Pull of Services

Other factors that pull workers into the city include access to services such as medical care or education, and service access to utilities such as electricity. Entertainment is often cited by migrants as a reason for moving from rural regions. Television, movies, festivals, and sporting events are all attractors to urban areas.

Clean Water: Don't Get Caught in the Trap

The unfortunate reality for many Third-World rural-to-urban migrants is that the water quality in rural regions may actually be better than the water quality in cities. Even when there are municipal water systems in the Third World, water systems are often contaminated. The lesson here is this: if you are asked about access to services in Third-World cities, clean water is not a valid answer, especially when talking about rural-to-urban migration factors.

OTHER RESOURCES

- World Population Data Sheet from the Population Reference Bureau at www.prb.org.
- The U.S. Census Bureau at www.census.gov.

CHAPTER 4 KEY TERMS

rate of natural increase (RNI)

demographic equation

birth rates

death rates

immigration statistics

emigration statistics

population growth

crude birth rate (CBR)/natality

annual statistic

death rate

life expectancy

Green Revolution

natural increase rate (NIR)

fecundity

double-income no-kid (DINK)

net migration rate (NMR)

total fertility rate (TFR)

dependency ratio

demographic transition model (DTM)

population dynamics

economic context

epidemiological transition model (ETM)

predictive capability

population projection

Industrial Revolution

deindustrialization

service-based economies

newly industrialized countries (NICs)

more developed countries (MDCs)

agricultural economy

manufacturing-based economy

S-curve

carrying capacity

equilibrium

subsistence farming

transhumance

feudal political economy

child mortality

infant mortality

diffusion of fertility control

diffusion of disease

primate city

gross domestic product (GDP)

zero population growth (ZPG)

guest workers

gastarbeiter

economic restructuring

J-curve

population structure

gender distribution

age distribution

age cohort

age-sex cohort

sex ratio

elder population

arithmetic density

physiologic density

arable land

geographic center (centroid)

population-weighted centroid

sustainability

carrying capacity

Malthusian catastrophe

population densities

ecumene

human settlement

arid regions

overpopulation

conservation

population control

personal space

personal consumption

interregional (internal) migrants

transnational migration

forced migration

refugees

asylum

ethnic cleansing

undocumented immigrants

amnesty programs

step migration

intervening opportunities

chain migration

cyclic movement

periodic movement

transnational migrants

life-course changes

push factors

pull factors

CHAPTER 4 DRILL
See the end of this chapter for answers and explanations.

1. All of the following may be reasons behind forced migration EXCEPT

    (A) war and terrorism
    (B) natural or environmental disasters
    (C) lack of employment opportunities
    (D) government orders to move
    (E) fear of government persecution

2. Zero population growth occurs when

    (A) the birth rate is greater than the death rate
    (B) a country has a negative rate of natural increase
    (C) the birth rate is equal to the death rate
    (D) a country has a positive rate of natural increase
    (E) the death rate is greater than the birth rate

3. During which stage of the demographic transition model does the diffusion of fertility control begin to play a significant role?

    (A) 1
    (B) 2
    (C) Between stage 2 and stage 3
    (D) 3
    (E) 4

4. All of the following are signs of negative RNI (rate of natural increase) EXCEPT

    (A) a highly urbanized population
    (B) the deterioration in the status of homemaker
    (C) an increased rate of divorce
    (D) an increased rate of immigration
    (E) an increase in DINK households

5. Societies in stage 2 of the demographic transition model are often

    (A) agricultural societies with increasing death rates
    (B) agricultural societies with decreasing death rates
    (C) agricultural societies with increasing birth rates
    (D) industrial societies with increasing birth rates
    (E) industrial societies with decreasing birth rates

6. The main reason that the catastrophe predicted by Thomas Malthus hasn't occurred yet is

    (A) human population grew in an arithmetic manner, not an exponential one
    (B) the J-curve of population always exceeds the J-curve of food production
    (C) soil erosion has limited food production capabilities in many parts of the world
    (D) changes occurred in the quantity and quality of food consumption in First-World countries
    (E) the invention of agricultural technology boosted the value of food production

7. Push factors that result in migration away from rural agriculture include all of the following EXCEPT

    (A) political rebellions in rural areas
    (B) use of agricultural chemicals
    (C) better opportunity for employment in urban areas
    (D) natural disasters such as drought or flooding
    (E) the increasing cost of renting arable land

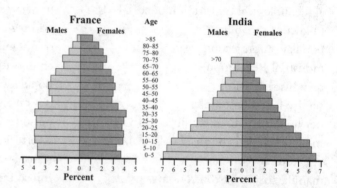

8. According to the pyramid above, the primary difference between France and India is

    (A) their experience with a baby bust
    (B) their history of external war
    (C) their gender imbalance
    (D) their respective rates of growth
    (E) their economic development

9. An optimal TFR for a society is 2.1. The TFR of many Western European countries ranges from 1.4 to 1.8. In those countries, this subreplacement fertility rate has been largely offset by

   (A) longer lifespans
   (B) greater rate of childhood mortality
   (C) lack of antibiotics
   (D) increased immigration
   (E) a higher rate of divorce

10. The Dependency Ratio describes

    (A) the number of people too young or old to work compared to the number of people in the work force
    (B) the population of a country with declining fertility rates compared with the population of a country with rising fertility rates
    (C) the decimal value by which a population with suboptimal fertility rates is beneath 2.1
    (D) the overall balance between imports and exports
    (E) the net emigration from a country versus the net immigration to a country

11. All of the following are true about the geographic center and the population-weighted centroid of a country EXCEPT

    (A) one can change with time, while the other cannot
    (B) one measures a geometric center of a nation, whereas the other averages the spatial weight of the population
    (C) Canada is the only country in which both occupy the same point
    (D) the population-weighted center of the United States has been slowly moving westward
    (E) the mean center and the median center are different

CHAPTER 4 DRILL: ANSWERS AND EXPLANATIONS

1. **C**   While many migrants do leave their homes in search of better job opportunities, such a move is considered voluntary migration. Forced migrants are those who must leave their homes either by government order or because of unsafe conditions.

2. **C**   Zero population growth occurs when a country's birth rate reaches the same level as its death rate. Accordingly, the correct answer is (C).

3. **D**   Contraceptives become available, or the diffusion of fertility control begins, when an economy becomes more urbanized, the economy becomes more developed, and access to health care increases. All of the aforementioned are characteristics of a society in the third stage of the demographic transition model, (D).

4. **D**   A society's RNI refers to how quickly its population is growing. A negative RNI means that the population is shrinking. Signals of a decreasing population include more people living in cities, (A), for the simple reason that urban families tend to be smaller than agricultural families. Other signs that birth rates are shrinking include women turning away from the traditional domestic role of mother, (B), and the traditional role of wife, (C). DINK refers to double-income-no-kids, which clearly isn't contributing to a birth rate. Eliminate (E). Only increased immigration would result in a positive RNI. Choose (D).

5. **B**   According to the demographic transition model, stage one societies are pre-agricultural. The shift to an agricultural society is the hallmark of stage two, so eliminate (D) and (E). Another hallmark of stage two society is the divergence of birth rates and death rates—typically the birth rate remains high while the death rate decreases, owing to better nutrition and health care. Eliminate (A) and (C). Choose (B).

6. **E**   The Malthusian prediction was simple: at some point in the future, the increase in human population would outstrip the increase in food production. This would result in massive hunger and eventual population decline. While his calculations were correct for his era, there was one thing that would arise that he couldn't have foreseen—the growth of revolutionary advances in agriculture. The reaper, thresher, internal combustion engine, pesticides, and other agricultural innovations all made large-scale farming a possibility. Choose (E).

7. **C**   A *push factor* is a specific thing about the rural agricultural landscape and livelihood that forces people off the farm. A *pull factor*, on the other hand, is a specific thing about an urban environment that draws people to it. Of the five answer choices, the only pull factor is the *better opportunity for employment in urban areas*. Choose (C).

8. **D**   A population pyramid reveals the gender and age distribution of the population. Because the genders are roughly equal in each country, eliminate (C). Baby busts and external war cause indentations in at least one cohort. Although it's not apparent from India's pyramid, both countries have a history of external war. Eliminate (B). While there are a couple of small indentations in France's pyramid, we would be hard-pressed to call them baby busts. Eliminate (A). The far more obvious difference between the two pyramids is the overall shape, which indicates growth rates. While economic growth can sometimes be gauged from a population pyramid, the far safer bet is the rate of growth. The population shaped like a triangle is experiencing a much higher rate of growth than the population shaped like a rectangle. Choose (D).

9. **D**   The European countries that have featured the lowest total fertility rate, such as Germany and France, have also been the ones most welcoming to immigrants. This infusion of a foreign population has kept the overall population of those countries high. However, it has also led to a conservative backlash, particularly against Muslim immigrants.

10. **A**   In a population with a low dependency ratio, there is low financial burden placed upon those who work. In a population with a high dependency ratio, there is a heavy financial burden placed upon those who work. In most of the world, including the United States, the dependency ratio has been climbing for many years, largely because the percentage of the population under the age of 30 has increased.

11. **C**   Neither Canada nor any other nation has exactly the same point for both measures. Regarding (E), it is worth mentioning that the mean center is the centroid, whereas the median center is the intersection of the median longitude and median latitude.

Summary

- ○ There are lots of statistics used to analyze population growth; key concepts to know are the rate of natural increase (RNI), doubling time, and the demographic equation:

  - • The RNI compares the birth and death rates of a country:

    $$RNI = \frac{Birth\ Rate - Death\ Rate}{10}\ \%$$

  - • Doubling time measures how long it takes a country to double in size:

    $$Doubling\ Time = \frac{70}{Rate\ of\ Natural\ Increase}$$

  - • The demographic equation is used to calculate a country's population growth rate:

    $$Population\ Growth\ Percentage\ Rate = \frac{(Birth\ Rate - Death\ Rate)\ +\ Net\ Migration\ Rate}{10}\ \%$$

- ○ The demographic transition model defines population changes over time and offers insight into a country's level of economic and social development. The classical model has four stages, but many modern social scientists have proposed adding a fifth stage reflecting the negative RNI of some developed countries.

- ○ Malthusian theory predicted that the global population would expand beyond its capacity to produce a large enough food supply to support itself before 1900. We've avoided this catastrophe so far thanks to technological innovation in agriculture, but neo-Malthusian theorists think it could still happen.

- ○ Population pyramids graphically represent the age and gender distribution of a place's population. The shape of a pyramid, like the DTM, can reveal a lot about growth rates and economic development in the place it represents.

o   Population density can be calculated arithmetically or physiologically.

o   Carrying capacity is the population that an environment, or the whole Earth, can sustain without a Malthusian collapse occurring. In areas with exploding populations or poor natural resources, sustainability and conservation efforts are major concerns.

o   Migration can take place on a variety of scales: interregional, rural-to-urban, or transnational.

o   Most migration is voluntary, for reasons such as education or better economic opportunities.

o   Some migrants are forced to move by government order or by displacement from war, natural disasters, or fear of persecution. Those who are displaced for such reasons are considered refugees. Human trafficking and slave labor are also considered forms of forced migration.

o   Push factors are often negative forces that compel migrants to leave their homes. These can include poor economic conditions, armed conflict, environmental hazards, and increased land costs.

o   Pull factors are traits, generally perceived as positive, that draw migrants to a location. The most significant of these are better employment and economic conditions, although access to services and entertainment can also attract migrants to urban areas.

Chapter 5
Cultural Patterns
and Processes

CHAPTER OVERVIEW

This chapter is intended to help you better understand the diversity of cultures across the globe. First, the chapter presents the various components of culture. Then, each component is described in terms of its relevance to the AP Human Geography Exam. Each component is detailed with examples both domestic and international. This is followed by discussions on the spatial aspects of cultural identity, cultural change, adaptation, globalization, and conflicts based on cultural differences.

WHAT IS CULTURE?

CED 3.1
Introduction to Culture

While there isn't a singular answer to this broad question, human geography textbooks typically give a definition like this:

Culture is the shared experience, traits, and activities of a group of people who have a common heritage.

While a definition of culture technically exists, it's too abstract in nature to be of any use. Therefore, instead of trying to tell you what culture is, we'll give you the many components of the cultural landscape.

To prepare for the AP Human Geography Exam, it is more effective to examine the categories of cultural expression than to try to define culture in a couple of sentences.

THE CULTURAL LANDSCAPE

Almost everything we see and hear in the human landscape expresses some form of culture. Culture is complex, and trying to take it all in and make sense of it can be confusing. To get a better grip on culture, we first have to understand how it is found on the **cultural landscape**. We can see the cultural landscape in the form of **signs** and **symbols** in the world around us—which is a general way of saying that there are different ways customs are imprinted on the several **components of culture**. Here is a list of the components of culture (in the order in which we'll discuss them in this chapter) to give you a simpler way of understanding culture in general and how it is expressed:

Art	Clothing
Architecture	Social Interaction
Language	Religion
Music	Folklore
Film and Television	Land Use
Food	

Each component of culture is expressed in a multitude of ways that signify and symbolize cultural influences. These historical influences can be as simple as the language used on a street sign or as complex as the cooking methods and spice mix in Louisiana Cajun food. To prepare you, this chapter will detail each relevant component of culture and provide examples that will help you answer cultural geography questions on the exam.

Reading the Cultural Landscape

In some ways, we can think about the cultural landscape as a form of text that can be read. We can read the signs and symbols that we see within the different components of culture and understand that place's cultural background and heritage. This takes a keen eye to see, and it helps to know some history of the place to translate what you are seeing.

What we find is that some things are original to a single culture, but most things in the cultural landscape are the product of **cultural synthesis,** or **syncretism**—the blending together of two or more cultural influences.

> **CED 3.2**
> Cultural Landscapes
>
> **CED 3.8**
> Effects of Diffusion

Hey, Y'all

An example of cultural synthesis is country music in the United States and Canada. It is often thought of as a product of American culture and is strongly tied to **folk music** traditions such as bluegrass. However, when we research the origins of country music, we find a culmination of influences from the Scots-Irish, the German, and African immigrants and enslaved people in the American South and Appalachia following the American Revolution. The mixture of musical sounds, vocabulary, rhythms, and instruments from these four culture groups came together to form a new style of music, as well as later developing into other American musical styles like jazz, the blues, and rock and roll.

The Components of Culture Explained

Whether something is original to a single culture or is the product of cultural synthesis, it is important to understand the underpinnings of the things we see in the cultural landscape. Combined, the many components come together to identify and define a single **culture group,** or **nation**.

Not all of these components are going to be questioned on the AP exam. For each relevant component, we will give you detailed geographical examples from **Anglo-America** and international locations to help broaden your perspective on the subject.

Art

Different artistic forms are important signs of a cultural imprint on the landscape. However, art is not a subject that the AP Human Geography Exam tests. Be able to express art's importance as an identifier of groups and a source of local pride if asked a general question on cultural landscape.

Architecture

Unlike art, architecture questions have appeared on the exam, so you need to be aware of a number of architectural styles. Housing types and religious buildings are especially relevant. These questions are most likely going to fall in the multiple-choice section of the exam and will have a picture or diagram to examine or decipher.

Concepts

Within the **built environment** of the human landscape, we find a multitude of **architectural forms** that are the product of cultural influence. When new buildings are constructed, much news is made over innovative designs in **modern** and **contemporary architecture**. This is in contrast to the existing forms of **traditional architecture,** some of which have been used for centuries. Building designers also distinguish between **introvert architecture**, which conceals, and **extrovert architecture**, which reveals.

Modern Versus Contemporary Architecture

As in the art world, architects have a distinct modern period of architecture which differs from new, or shall we say contemporary, forms. Be specific when describing a home or building type. *Modern* means architecture developed during the 20th century that expresses geometric, ordered forms such as the 1950s homes of Frank Lloyd Wright (seen below) or the rectangular steel and glass skyscrapers built in the 1970s and 1980s.

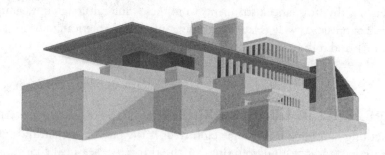

In contrast, the *contemporary* architecture of the present is more organic, with the use of curvature. **Postmodern** is a category within contemporary that means that the design abandons the use of blocky rectilinear shapes in favor of wavy, crystalline, or bending shapes in the form of the home or building. Contemporary architecture can also incorporate **green energy** technologies, **recycled materials**, or nontraditional materials like metal sheeting on the exterior. This is exemplified in the Frank Gehry design of the Guggenheim Museum in Bilbao, Spain, or the Walt Disney Theater in Los Angeles (seen on the next page).

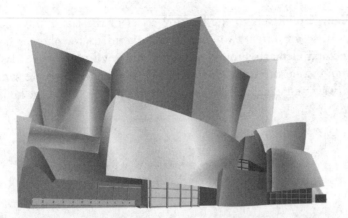

Traditional Architecture

Traditional architecture can express one of two patterns in building type. One form of traditional architecture seen in new **commercial buildings** incorporates the efficiency and simplicity of modern architecture into a standard building design with squared walls and utilizes traditional materials like stone, brick, steel, and glass. The other expression of traditional architecture is seen in **housing** based upon **folk house** designs from different regions of the country. New homes built today often incorporate more than one element of folk house design like a hybrid Swiss chalet–Williamsburg-style home covered in stucco, with a clay tile roof. Let's go over the basic **traditional housing style** forms that could appear on the exam.

Housing Types

New England: Small one-story pitched-roof **Cape Cod** style or the irregular roof **Saltbox** with one long pitched roof in front and a sort of low-angle roof in back (seen below).

Urban Design and Gender

Cultural attitudes towards gender have an impact upon the built environment as well. In other words, the design of cities reflects the power relations between men and women in that culture. In many traditional patriarchal cultures, for example, urban areas are used primarily for males, and the needs of women, children, and others are ignored or minimized. However, in contemporary Western culture, women enjoy mostly equal footing with men. This is evident in the needs that are more specific to women, such as lighted streets for nighttime safety, increased public health, and an emphasis on caregiving (instead of commuting) via workplace-based child care centers.

Federalist or Georgian: Refers to the housing styles of the late 1700s and early 1800s in Anglo-America. These are often two- or three-story urban townhomes connected to one another. Architectural elements around windows and rooflines feature classical Greek and Roman designs and stone carvings. As stand-alone buildings, these are symmetrical homes with central doorways and equal numbers of windows on each side of the house (seen below).

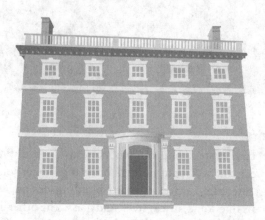

The I-house: A loose form of Federalist and Georgian influence on the average family home in the United States and Canada. Simple rectangular I-houses have a central door with one window on each side of the home's front and three symmetrical windows on the second floor (seen below). However, as the I-house style diffused westward, the rectangle shape and symmetry was lost. Later I-houses have the door moved to the side and have additions onto the back or side of the house. The I-house giveaways are the fireplaces on each end of the house and an even-pitched roof. The loss of form as the I-house moved across the Appalachian Mountains to the Midwest and across the Great Lakes to the Prairie Provinces is an example of relocation diffusion.

Religious Buildings and Places

Another area of architecture the AP Human Geography Exam tests is religious architecture. Here are the major world religious groups and their representative architectural forms for places of worship.

Christian: Traditional houses of worship tend to have a central steeple or two high bell towers in the front of the building. The steeple is typical of smaller churches, and bell towers are found in larger churches and cathedrals. Basilicas, like St. Peter's in the Vatican or St. Paul's Cathedral in London, have central domes similar to the U.S. Capitol building. Symbolically, older churches, cathedrals, and basilicas feature a cross-shaped floor plan.

<table>
<tr><td>Fun Fact
There is a sculpture of Darth Vader on the west tower of the National Cathedral in Washington, D.C.</td></tr>
</table>

Chapel, Cathedral, Eastern Orthodox

National Cathedral, Washington, D.C.

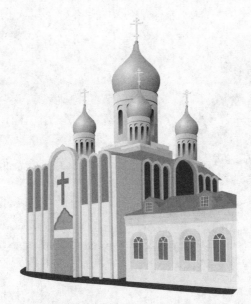

Holy Virgin Orthodox Cathedral, San Francisco, California

Hindu: Temples and shrines tend to have a rectangular-shaped main body and feature one or more short towers of carved stone. The towers often feature stepped sides and display carvings of the heads and faces of deities. The most famous example of this design is the temple complex of Angkor Wat in Cambodia. The Kashi Vishwanath Temple in Varanasi, India, is shown below.

Hindu Temple at Varanasi, India

Buddhist: Temples and shrines vary depending on which Buddhist tradition is followed in the region. In Nepal and Tibet, a temple can be a **stupa**, with a dome or tower featuring a pair of eyes. In East Asia, the tower-style **pagoda** has several levels, each of which features winged roofs extending outward. Temples and shrines in China and Japan feature one- or two-story buildings with large, curved, winged roofs (seen below). Temples are often guarded by large lion statues, such as those at the Temple of the Sun and Moon in the Forbidden City of Beijing. Temples in Southeast Asia tend to have several towers with thin pointed spires that point outward at an angle (seen below).

Stupa, a type of Vajrayana
(Tibet, Nepal, Bhutan)

Mahayana Buddhist Temple (China, Japan)

Theravada Buddhist Temple (Thailand)

Islamic: Mosques can take a variety of forms, though many have central domes. The giveaway feature of a mosque is one or more **minarets**, narrow towers that are pointed on top. Famous mosques include the Al-Kaaba Mosque in Mecca, the most holy place in Islam, an open-air mosque with a large black cube at its center (seen below).

The third most holy place in Islam is the Al-Aqsa mosque in Jerusalem that sits alongside the Dome of the Rock, an eight-sided mosque with a high central dome and thin spire on top featuring a crescent moon. Another large mosque is the Hagia Sofia in Istanbul. A former Eastern Orthodox cathedral, it has a broad central dome and four spires, one in each corner of the square-shaped building. Almost all mosques are built on an angle that places the main prayer area toward Mecca.

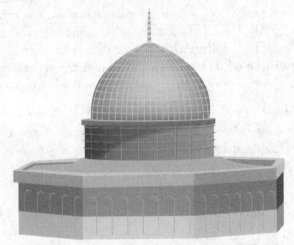

Dome of the Rock (Temple Mount in Jerusalem)

Judaic: There is not a common architectural design style to synagogues. The most holy place in Judaism is the Western Wall of the former Temple of Solomon, next to the Dome of the Rock. Known as the **Wailing Wall**, the old foundation walls feature large rectangular stone blocks where Jews pray and place written prayers in the cracks between the blocks.

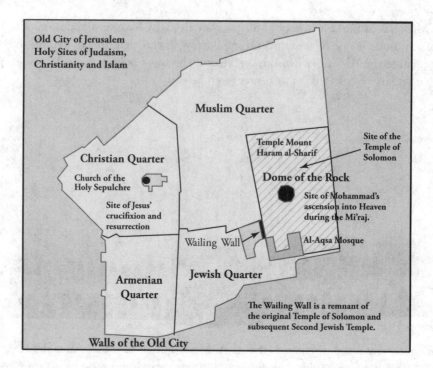

Old City of Jerusalem
Holy Sites of Judaism,
Christianity and Islam

Muslim Quarter

Temple Mount
Haram al-Sharif

Site of the
Temple of
Solomon

Christian Quarter

Dome of the Rock

Church of the
Holy Sepulchre

Site of Mohammad's
ascension into Heaven
during the Mi'raj.

Site of Jesus'
crucifixion and
resurrection

Wailing Wall

Al-Aqsa Mosque

Armenian
Quarter

Jewish Quarter

The Wailing Wall is a remnant of
the original Temple of Solomon and
subsequent Second Jewish Temple.

Walls of the Old City

Language

When we think about language, we most often think about the common tongue of the country that we live in. In terms of **official languages**, the United States federal government has not designated one. Some states have English-only laws and provisions. These affect education standards and state government publications such as driver's licensing exams, since much of the United States tends to be **monolingual** (knowing one language only—in this case, English). Other states, such as California, accept that they have a large **multilingual** immigrant population and have made provisions (especially for public safety) to provide some services in multiple languages including Spanish, Chinese, and Vietnamese.

In Canada, there are two official languages: English and French. Therefore, Canada is **bilingual**. Another example of a multilingual society is the Netherlands. In school, students not only learn their native Dutch, but are also required to learn English, French, and some German. Likewise, it's common in South Africa for citizens to be able to speak varying levels of English, Afrikaans (a Dutch derivative), and one or more African languages such as Xhosa, Sotho, or Zulu.

Aussie, Aussie, Aussie! Oy! Oy! Oy!

Depending upon where you are in a larger **linguistic region**, the way a common language is spoken can sound different depending upon who is speaking it. In the global English linguistic region, **dialect** changes from nation to nation. Although the English spoken by English people and Australian people sounds similar, there is a distinct "strain" of English spoken in Australia with a variety of different **word sounds** and **vocabulary**. Even between the United States and Canada there are subtle differences, such as the strong Canadian "O" in the word *about*, pronounced "a-boat." Within countries, dialect can change from region to region, such as the changes heard when traveling in the United States from New England to the American South.

Cheerio! Or Not!?

Even within Great Britain, varieties of dialect are shaped in part by national heritage. English spoken in England proper is quite different from English in the other nations or culture areas such as Scotland, Wales, Ireland, Cornwall, and the Isle of Man. These variations are due in part to the degree of Celtic influence and the degree to which Anglo-Saxon invaders, who brought their Germanic language with them, settled in the regions during the first millennium C.E. What some refer to as the King's English or "posh" English is linguistically known as **received pronunciation**. Conversely, **Cockney** English is the language of the working-class areas of the East London docklands and surrounding neighborhoods, which sounds distinctly not posh. Cockney is also thought to be very influential in the formation of Australian English.

Baker's Dozen, My Cousin

Cockney rhyming slang is an odd but humorous use of code phrases to describe everyday situations. In slang, "going up the apples" means going up the stairs; stairs rhymes with pears, heard in the fruit markets as "apples and pears," and thus, stairs is replaced with apples. Other examples include "brass tacks" (facts), "chalk farm" (arm), and "round the houses" (trousers).

Pidgin, Creole, and Patois

Slang is similar to other heavily modified dialects of pidgin English. **Pidgin** languages are simplified forms of the language that use key vocabulary words and limited grammar. There are a number of interrelated, English-based pidgin languages spoken in West African countries such as Ghana, Cameroon, and Nigeria. Here, they originated as trade languages between natives and British slave traders and colonists.

> CED 3.5
> Historical Causes of Diffusion

Pidgin language forms can evolve into their own individual language groups over time. In Haiti, **French Creole** is spoken, which incorporates continental French with African dialectal sounds and vocabulary. In fact, many of the French overseas territories (*departments outré mer,* or *DOM)* have their own forms of **patois**, like the ones spoken in the islands of Martinique and Réunion, formed by local or immigrant linguistic syntheses. Pidgin, Creole, and patois can all be thought of as syncretic language forms that integrate both colonial and indigenous language forms.

Eet Iz zee *Lingua Franca,* Monsieur

French itself has long been a language used to bridge the linguistic gap between people of different national heritage. So much so that the term *lingua franca* was coined to describe its utility as a bridge language. Why *franca*? France has long been a center for learning, literature, and diplomacy. There were also a number of French colonies around the world, and Great Britain has long had territorial claims in France, necessitating French literacy among British aristocrats, diplomats, and merchants.

Today, **English** is accepted as the **global *lingua franca*** as different forms of popular culture media, the Internet, and the business world are dominated by the English language. A notable use is that English is the required language of all airline pilots and air traffic controllers around the world. This is done mainly for safety reasons, but is evidence of the United States' and Britain's international business dominance in the post-World War II era.

Major Language Families

Around the world, there are a small number of major **language families** represented by the early or prehistoric language roots. The largest members of these language families are as follows:

- Indo-European (2.9 billion people)
- Sino-Tibetan (1.3 billion people)
- Niger-Congo (435 million people)
- Afro-Asiatic (375 million people)
- Austronesian (346 million people, from Southeastern Asia, Oceania, and Hawaii)
- Dravidian (230 million people, from on and around the Indian subcontinent)
- Altaic (165 million people, from Eastern Europe through Central and Eastern Asia)
- Japanese (123 million people)
- Tai-Kadai (81 million people)

Here is a map of the global distribution of these major language families:

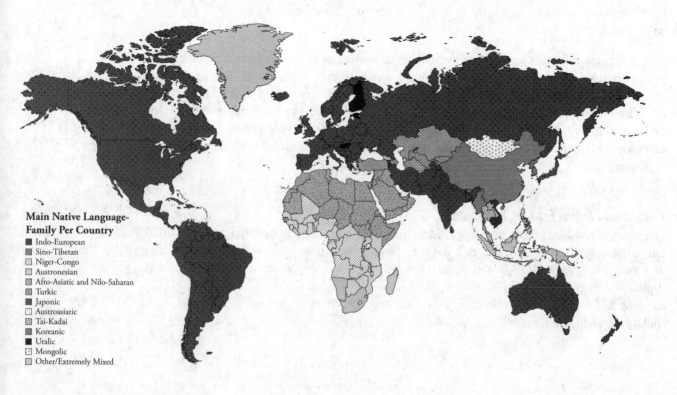

Main Native Language-Family Per Country
- Indo-European
- Sino-Tibetan
- Niger-Congo
- Austronesian
- Afro-Asiatic and Nilo-Saharan
- Turkic
- Japonic
- Austroasiatic
- Tai-Kadai
- Koreanic
- Uralic
- Mongolic
- Other/Extremely Mixed

Each language family can be broken into **language groups**. Some larger language families, such as the Indo-European and Sino-Tibetan, can be broken down into **language subfamilies** and then into smaller language groups. For example, the English language draws from the Indo-European family, Germanic subfamily, and Western Germanic group, along with German, Dutch, and Afrikaans. Hindi is also from the Indo-European family, but from the Indo-Iranian subfamily and Indian group, along with Bengali and Nepali. The Indo-European concept is derived from linguistic analysis and genetic evidence of **prehistoric migrations** from the Indian subcontinent into Europe. These early immigrants brought their Indo-European root language with them, which then divided locally and evolved into the contemporary European languages of today.

Anatolian or Kurgan Theories

There are two competing theories regarding the origins of European language, each with its own **hearth**, or launching point. The **Anatolian theory** holds that this group of migrants from the Indian subcontinent, and their language, were for some time concentrated in the peninsula that makes up most of present-day Turkey, known historically as Asia Minor or Anatolia. From there, a large migration crossed the **Hellespont** into continental Europe and spread outward into what was possibly a relatively unpopulated region.

The **Kurgan theory** holds that the same group of migrants from the Indian subcontinent instead made their way into Central Asia, and then migrated across the **Eurasian steppe** into Central and Western Europe, taking their language with them. Without significant archaeological discovery or possibly extensive genetic research, it will be difficult to prove whether either theory holds true. (See the map below.)

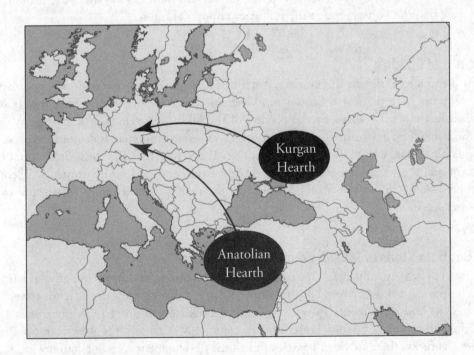

In the twentieth century, the term **Aryan** was adopted, manipulated, and badly abused by Nazi Germany. The original term is thousands of years old, referring to a now-lost group of people on the Iranian-Indian plateau who spoke a now-lost early Indo-European language. The Aryans never actually went anywhere near Europe!

Europeans from India?

Genetic research shows that almost all Europeans are derived genetically from populations that inhabited the Indian subcontinent in prehistoric times. There are a number of hypotheses as to why this light-skinned population, similar to many light-skinned Aryan Indians, pulled up their roots and moved west. But we can tell that they did take their language and genes with them. Unusual genetic markers, such as the Celtic trait for red hair, are drawn from the Himalayan foothills of what is today northern India and Pakistan, where people with red hair can still be found. Genetics can do some fascinating things!

Music

Like language, music is a form of nonmaterial culture that has geographic roots and regional variation. You should know a few things about the geography of musical culture, since it can show up on the AP exam.

Folkies and Pop Stars

Music that is original to a specific culture is categorized as **folk music**. Folk music traditions often incorporate instruments unique to that region or have orchestrations that are specific to that culture. **Folk song** lyrics often incorporate cultural stories and religious tradition, which can be described as **folklore**. It tends to be "unplugged" as well, without electronic instruments.

By contrast, **popular culture** generates a global flow of **pop music** that often has the effect of drowning out local folk music traditions from radio and other media. In the cases where you do hear electronic instrumentation in folk music, this indicates a form of acculturation in which folk traditions are accepting the influence of popular music.

Fiddlin' and Pickin'

As was mentioned earlier in this chapter, American folk music and contemporary popularized country music have origins in Scots-Irish, German, and African culture. Folk traditions in **Appalachia** are often realized by the playing of the fiddle, a variant of the European violin, and the banjo—an instrument of African origin. The most popular folk music type in the region is **bluegrass**, which originated in Kentucky (known as the "Bluegrass State" after both the plant and the music). In bluegrass, fiddle and banjo are the lead instruments. There are a number of other folk styles across Appalachia; the region stretches from Mississippi to the Maritime provinces.

"We Got Both Kinds of Music: Country and Western!"

Bluegrass has heavily influenced contemporary country music, and more recently, so has rock and roll. The difference between bluegrass and country is that country music tends toward the guitar as the lead instrument. The guitar is linked back from country to Western music and, from there, back to the Spanish Americans of colonial Mexico and the American Southwest. Besides Kentucky, there are other hearths, or historic development cores, of country music.

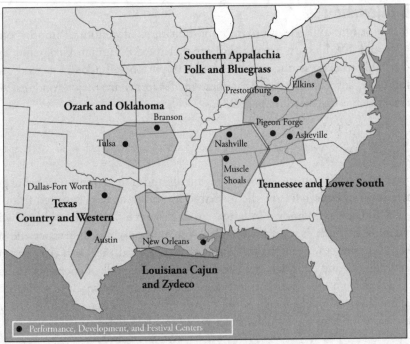

Hearths of American Country Music Styles

Folk Music Forms and World Music

Many of the recordings sold today in the United States and Canada as World Music are actually products of folk musicians from other culture groups. Of these, one of the most popular groups is the top-selling Gypsy Kings. The band is from France, but their families had left Spain decades earlier due to persecution by the Franco-led fascist government of the **Roma** or Romani people (who are more commonly known as "gypsies"). The Gypsy Kings play from a variety of folk traditions and languages, including their native Roma to Spanish flamenco, as well as Basque and Catalan folk songs, which they have popularized.

> The term "gypsy," although still in use, has negative connotations and is considered a slur by the Roma people.

Celtic folk music traditions are played anywhere Celts, Irish, Welsh, Scots, Manx (from the Isle of Man), (Spanish) Galicians, or (French) Bretons or their migrant descendants are found. Irish Celtic music has a particularly large following. The traditional music features a multitude of instruments including the fiddle, flute, tin whistle, harp, concertina accordion, bodhrán drum, and "Uilleann" or Irish pipes—the smaller cousin of the Scottish bagpipes. Today, it is common to hear Pan-Celtic music that draws from more than one Celtic region and utilizes other non-Celtic instruments like guitar, banjo, and bouzouki (a Greek mandolin).

The next time you listen to country or bluegrass music, see if you can pick out the Celtic Scots-Irish folk musical influence.

Film and Television

Different forms of film and television are important signs of a cultural imprint on the land. However, film and TV, like art, are not subjects that the AP Human Geography Exam tests. You should be able to express film and television's importance if asked a general question on cultural landscape. Also, understand that these media forms are major conduits for cultural globalization, which is discussed on page 233.

Food

Food is a material form of culture that varies regionally and is rooted in a number of geographic ways. **Continental cuisine** refers to the formal food traditions that emerged from mainland Europe in the 1800s. It is embodied in **haute cuisine**, French for "high cooking," where traditionally a main meat course is served with a flour-, cream-, or wine-based sauce and side dishes of vegetables and potatoes. Some haute cuisine dishes favored in North America are duck à l'orange, filet mignon, and chocolate mousse as a dessert. This style of cooking can also include regional influences from folk traditions in France such as *escargots* (snails in garlic butter) from Provence in Southern France and *coq au vin* (rooster in red wine sauce) found in a number of regions—these are foods of the French farmer raised to a higher form.

And You Thought Arnold Schwarzenegger Was the Only Austrian in Malibu...

Nouvelle cuisine is the contemporary form of the continental styles mainly from France, Spain, and Italy. Although there is a strong nouvelle style in France, the lighter, fresh fare of California-style cuisine has become very popular worldwide. Gone are the heavy sauces in favor of healthier sauce applications with citrus juices, olive oil, or white wine atop a lighter variety of meats including salmon, chicken breast, or mahi mahi. These have been popularized by celebrity chefs such as the Austrian-born Californian, Wolfgang Puck, who utilizes a number of **Mediterranean** agriculture products such as avocados, artichokes, olives, and citrus fruits in his dishes.

Wolfgang Puck is also seen as a proponent of **fusion cuisine**, in which more than one global tradition is incorporated in dishes. Japanese-American celebrity chef Roy Yamaguchi in Honolulu is one of the leaders of the fusion movement that integrates dishes and flavors from Japan, China, Southeast Asia, Polynesia, and Europe. Hawaii's location makes it a place of heavy immigration from these parts of the world, where cultural synthesis in food and other cultural components, such as music, takes place.

Folk Dishes From Around The World: Japanese Sushi

Of course, all of these forms are based on original forms of **folk food** dishes. Sushi is a simple but artistic form of folk food from Japan. The simplest sushi is *sashimi*, raw fish cut in a special manner to sever potentially harmful parasitic worms—did we just ruin the *maguro* for you? Sashimi on a small pat of rice is another simple folk form called *nigiri*. Sushi has also become stylized in the contemporary form with special rolls, *makizushi* or just *maki*: Inside seaweed wraps (*nori*) are sticky rice and a variety of ingredients like raw, smoked, or fried seafood and fresh vegetables. The condiment *wasabi* is also part of this folk food tradition; it's pickled Japanese horseradish root, and it's spicy!

Moroccan Hummus

The **Moroccan** folk food tradition utilizes a number of regional ingredients from the Mediterranean and North Africa. Main dishes incorporate familiar meats such as chicken and lamb, since cattle are rare in North Africa and pork consumption is *haraam*, or banned by Islam. Permitted meats must be slaughtered under religious rules to be *halal*, or fit for consumption by Muslims. Meat is often served with couscous (a very small-grained pasta), chickpeas (garbanzo beans), and root vegetables grown in the high Atlas Mountains. Food is flavored with a variety of spices including cinnamon, turmeric, and saffron and is often cooked in a traditional clay pot known as a *tajine*. Chickpeas can also be ground and mixed with a sesame seed paste called *tahini,* along with olive oil, salt, and lemon to make *hummus*, which is increasingly popular in Europe and Anglo-America as a dip served traditionally with toasted pita bread. (Don't get it confused with humus, the organic material in soil.)

Clothing

Different clothing styles are other signs of a cultural imprint on the landscape. However, clothing, like art, is not a subject on which the AP Human Geography Exam tests students. You should be able to express clothing's importance, if asked a general question on cultural landscape, since the way people dress is an important sign of their ethnicity. Note also that clothing, like film and TV, is a conduit for cultural globalization, discussed on page 233.

Social Interaction

Different types of **social interaction** are **culturally constructed**, meaning they are traditions devised by a specific culture group. Physical **greetings** are a basic example of culturally different social interaction. In the West, a **handshake** is a common physical greeting, whereas in Japan, the **bow** still holds as the primary formal greeting. The traditional New Zealand Maori physical greeting is the pressing together of the foreheads and noses.

Smoochy, Smoochy!

Formal, non-touching **cheek kissing** is another example. Kiss four times in Paris, France, upon greeting, twice on each side; in Serbia and the Netherlands, three times, right side first; twice in Spain, Austria, and Scandinavia; no kisses in Germany and the United Kingdom; and a variable number of kisses in Italy and Greece, where if you don't know the local rules, it's better to just extend a handshake.

Personal Space Violation?

Personal space also varies from country to country. If you like a large personal space bubble, you'll feel uncomfortable in Peru, where it's considered rude not to sit in an empty seat next to someone, even if they're a stranger. Think about this the next time you select a seat at the movie theater or on a bus.

RELIGION

CED 3.7

Diffusion of Religion and Language

Religions, also referred to as **belief systems** by some social scientists, are as numerous as languages. Like languages, specific religions are drawn from a number of larger global groups. Categorically, religions can be characterized by their expanse. **Universalizing religions** accept followers from all ethnicities worldwide; as opposed to **ethnic religions,** which are confined to members of a specific culture group. All organized religions have one or more books of **scripture**, said to be written of **divine origin**. They also have formal **doctrines** that govern religious practice, worship, and ethical behavior in society.

Religions and their component **denominations** can also be understood by their ability to compromise and change ideologically. **Compromising religions** are often cited for the ability to reform or integrate other beliefs into their doctrinal practices. **Fundamentalists**, on the other hand, are known to have little interest in compromising their beliefs or doctrines and strictly adhere to scriptural dictates.

Before we dive into the specifics of each religion, here is a map of the predominant belief systems around the world:

The Religions of the World

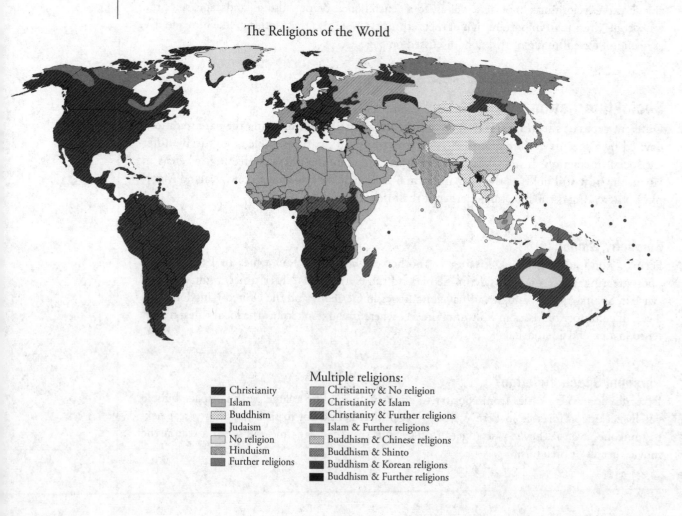

Multiple religions:

- Christianity
- Islam
- Buddhism
- Judaism
- No religion
- Hinduism
- Further religions

- Christianity & No religion
- Christianity & Islam
- Christianity & Further religions
- Islam & Further religions
- Buddhism & Chinese religions
- Buddhism & Shinto
- Buddhism & Korean religions
- Buddhism & Further religions

Know Your World Religions

At the most basic level, there are three major traditions of belief systems, from oldest to most recent:

Animist Tradition: Various ethnic, tribal, and other forms of nature worship
- Though geographically unrelated, these groups have common themes, worship practices, and morality tales, which define a right and ethical way to live.
- *Animus* means spirit in Latin. Animists share the common belief that items in nature can have spiritual being, including landforms, animals, and trees.

Hindu-Buddhist Tradition: Hinduism, Buddhism, Jainism
- The oldest universalizing religions began with Hinduism 5,000 years ago. These **polytheistic** (believing in more than one supreme god) denominations spread throughout Asia by the 1200s C.E.
- The commonalities are that there are many levels of existence, the highest being **nirvana**, where someone achieves total consciousness or enlightenment.
- One's soul is reincarnated over and over into different forms. **Karma**, the balance between good and evil deeds in life, determines the outcome of reincarnation into a lower, similar, or higher form of existence in the next life.

Abrahamic Tradition: Judaism, Christianity, and Islam
- Each of these religions has similar scriptural descriptions of the Earth's genesis and the story of Abraham as a morality tale of respect for the will of God or Allah.
- Each is a **monotheistic** belief system with a singular supreme being. There can also be sub-deities such as saints, angels, and archangels.
- Significance is placed upon prophecy that predicts the coming or return of a messianic figure that defeats the forces of a satanic evil for souls of followers.

These traditions can be further broken down into major religious groups. Here is a quick and basic comparative guide to the world's major religious groups, with diagrams of their diffusion patterns.

Animist Religions

There are hundreds of animist belief systems. Here are two that are commonly described in human geography:

Indigenous American
- *Who?* The pre-Columbian civilizations in the Americas and some descendants
- *When?* From the last period of glaciation (18,000 years before present)
- *Where?* Alaska to the Tierra del Fuego

- *Scripture*: None. System based upon belief in a supreme or Great Spirit that oversees the universe. Instead, spiritual interpretation is provided by **shamans,** sometimes referred to as "medicine men" who are practitioners that lead worship and religious rites.

- *Doctrine:* Depends upon tribal following. Prayers or appeals to sun, moon, animal spirits, and climatic features (wind and rain) are significant in most practices.

- *Denominations:* Hundreds of different tribal interpretations

- *Historical Diffusion:* By **migration diffusion** north to south through the Americas

Voodoun (Voodoo)

- *Who?* West African, Afro-Brazilian, and Afro-Caribbean descendants

- *When?* From prehistory to present

- *Where?* Nigeria, Benin, Ghana, and other states in the region; Haiti, Cuba, Dominican Republic, Brazil, and other small communities in the region

- *Scripture:* None. System based upon multiple deities that control different parts of the inhabited world. Like other animist groups, **shamanism** is part of the system of worship.

- *Doctrine:* Depends upon the community. Common practices often attempt to bring worshippers in contact with deities and family ancestors in the spiritual world through different ceremonies, dance, and sacrificial practices.

- *Denominations:* Different depending upon region and the degree of influence from parallel Christian worship by Voodoun followers.

- *Historical Diffusion:* Relocation diffusion by forced migration under European-directed enslavement from West Africa to the Caribbean and coastal American mainland areas such as northern Brazil, Belize, and Louisiana.

Hindu-Buddhist Religions

Hinduism

- *Who?* South Asians and some Southeast Asians

- *When?* Earliest forms 7,500 years before present

- *Where?* Mainly India; also today in Indonesia, London, Manchester, and other parts of the former British Empire, with significant populations in Guyana, Trinidad, Fiji, Malaysia, and South Africa

- *Scripture:* Vedas, Upanishads, Bhagavad Gita, and other early Sanskrit religious texts

- *Doctrine:* The main personal practice is to work continuously toward multiple reincarnations and eventually nirvana. Practice of temple-based worship and festivals to praise particular supreme gods, including humanistic forms Vishnu, Shiva, Krishna, and animal forms Ganesha (elephant god) and Naga (serpent gods). Several doctrinal writings depict the historical moral traditions and practices.

- *Denominations:* Different denominations are often based on cults to deities as well as on a hierarchical **caste system**. This system is based on the reincarnation principle, in which people are born into a particular social level where they remain for the rest of their lives.

- *Historical Diffusion:* Expansion diffusion from the Hindu hearth in Northern India. Later relocation diffusion across the Bay of Bengal to Southeast Asia (consider the historical Hindu temple complex at Angkor Wat in Cambodia) and to Indonesia, where a remnant population is found today on the island of Bali.

Jainism

- *Who?* A fundamentalist interpretation of Hinduism
- *When?* Around 2,900 years before present
- *Where?* Western India
- *Scripture:* Several texts collectively known as **Agamas**. The most commonly cited is the Tattvartha Sutra.
- *Doctrine:* At the core of religious practice is the complete respect for all other animal life, in that every living soul is potentially a divine god. Followers are strict vegetarians and often wear face masks to prevent the inhalation of insects.
- *Denominations*: Three main groups exist that differ in practice and worship.
- *Historical Diffusion:* Some Jain communities relocated to places such as Great Britain during the colonial period, 1830s to 1940s. Mohandas Gandhi's mother was a devout Jain and her compassion for all life influenced her son's civil rights and peace activism.

Buddhism

- *Who?* An ideological following that rejected the caste system and other Hindu practices
- *When?* About 2,500 years before present
- *Where?* Hearth in the Gangetic Plain (Ganges river basin) of North Central India and spread throughout Asia (see map on the following page)
- *Scripture:* Early Hindu texts combined with the Tipitaka (aka "Pali Canon"), part of which contains the life and teachings of Siddhartha Gautama, the founder of Buddhism.
- *Doctrine:* A main doctrinal difference with Hinduism is the belief that nirvana can be achieved in a single lifetime, via intensive study, meditation, and moral thought. This is through an understanding of the effects of suffering on human life and the following of a "Middle Way" or non-extremist pathway toward enlightenment. Buddhism also rejected the Hindu caste system as oppressive and not in line with Buddhists' view of human suffering.
- *Denominations:* Three distinct traditions: Tibetan (Vajrayana); Southeast Asian (Theravada); and East Asian (Mahayana), each broken into smaller regional and philosophical denominations. Tibetan Buddhists tend to be universalizing, accepting westerners into their community but uncompromising in their beliefs. Theravada tends to be far less universalizing and does not compromise their

traditions; Mahayana Buddhism is both universalizing and compromising. This tradition, which includes Japanese Zen Buddhism, incorporates tenets from a number of other Eastern philosophies such as Confucianism, Shinto, and Taoism.

- *Historical Diffusion:* Several examples of Buddhism **relocating** across physical barriers: Tibetan Buddhism across the Himalayas and Tarim Basin desert to Siberia and Mongolia; Theravada from Sri Lanka across the Bay of Bengal to Southeast Asia; and Mahayana across the Himalayas to Eastern China.

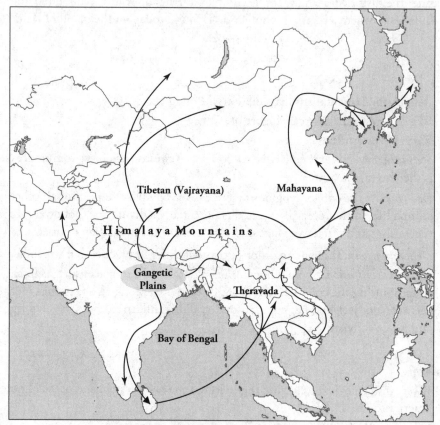

Arrows show the diffusion of Buddhism across the
Himalayas and the Bay of Bengal

Caste System in India

The Hindu scriptures describe a **cosmology** (a belief in the structure of the universe) in which there are several levels of existence, from the lowest animal forms to human forms and then higher animal forms. Such sacred animals include elephants, horses, and—of course—cows, which are seen as aspects of Mother Goddess Earth and symbols of selflessness. According to this cosmic structure, all souls undergo **reincarnation** multiple times, learning new things each time. Whether a person is elevated in each new life depends upon his or her **karma**, which is the balance between the good and bad deeds that he or she has committed in his or her previous life.

Once a person is born into a caste, he or she remains there for the rest of his or her life, no matter the changes to his or her fortune. The lowest human forms, *Dalits* (also known as the *untouchables*), are considered least holy due to their distance from **nirvana**, which is the ultimate state of transcendence and release from the cycle of death and rebirth. At the other end of the scale, the priestly *Brahmans* are considered the highest human form because of their closeness to this elevated state. Above the dalits are four other classes, or varna, of human existence in Hinduism. The varna provide the framework for India's caste system. Here are the five castes (from highest to lowest):

1. Brahmans
   - The priestly caste. Brahmans are responsible for temples and leading religious worship.
   - Some can be selected as high government officials. Others may eschew all material possessions to live as monks or meditating hermits, or as ascetics who sit on sidewalks and perform prayers for those who provide their food donations.
2. Kshatriyas
   - The aristocratic and warrior caste. Despite their political power, hereditary princes and kings still bow to the Brahmans.
   - Many are landowners, government leaders, and wealthy businesspeople.
3. Vaishyas
   - The merchant and professional caste, including doctors, lawyers, accountants, and government bureaucrats.
   - Mahatma Gandhi was born into this caste and trained as a lawyer before becoming a human rights activist.
4. Shudras
   - The caste of farmers, laborers, and artisans, including potters, jewelers, and glassworkers.
   - With no leisure time and near-total illiteracy, this caste was traditionally forbidden from studying the Vedas.
5. Dalits
   - The "untouchables," a name derived from their low position in the system and considered unholy by higher castes. Dalits were often segregated from other Hindu housing areas and social networks.
   - Dalit sub-castes were divided among trades and duties in the community such as leather work (cattle are sacred, and only the lowest-caste humans could handle their flesh) and cleaning of train stations and sewers.
   - Elected in 1997, Indian President K. R. Narayanan was born into the dalit caste, and he has been a symbol of affirmative action for the untouchables.

Caste, varna, social class—these terms are often used interchangeably when describing the traditional Hindu social structure. One other term, *jati,* is sometimes used as well, but this term is more complicated, since it derives from an ancient Sanskrit word that refers to any group of things that have generic characteristics in common. Today, *jati* can also refer to subgroups within the castes, such as leather workers. And some even argue that it is a philosophical term that shouldn't refer to anything in the caste system whatsoever.

Since India gained independence in 1947, its government has initiated a number of efforts to eliminate the caste structure in Indian society. There have been several programs to elevate the social and political standing of the lower castes, including compulsory elementary education, and opening public trade schools, high schools, and universities to large numbers of lower-caste members who had been discriminated against in the past.

Caste difference in Indian cities has become minimal, while it is still recognizable in rural India. Among many Indian families, marriage is still one area in which there is an emphasis on caste, as most traditional parents desire their children to marry within their caste.

Judaism

- *Who?* Larger groups including European Ashkenazi Jews, Sephardic Jews from North Africa and the Middle East, and Native Israelis known as *Sabra*.
- *When?* Over 5,700 years before present. January 1, 2021, was during the year 5782 on the Hebrew calendar.
- *Where?* Hearth in Israel, peripheral communities in Europe, United States, and Canada, particularly the metropolitan area around New York City and other urban areas worldwide, such as London, Antwerp, Paris, Los Angeles, Toronto, and Cleveland
- *Scripture:* Torah (includes several books also used in the Christian Old Testament) and Talmud
- *Doctrine:* Varies between groups. Shared between all is the annual atonement for sins during Yom Kippur.
- *Denominations:* Hassidic, Orthodox, Conservative, Reform, and Reconstructionism
- *Historical Diffusion:* The Jewish Diaspora begins in 70 C.E. with the Roman destruction of the Temple in Jerusalem, where Jews were forced out to other parts of the Empire. The post-WWII era following the Nazi Holocaust marks the beginning of the Jews' movement to Israel from Europe. Conflicts in the 1950s and 1960s caused migrations from North Africa and the Middle East to Israel.

Christianity

- *Who?* Originates in the Roman Empire but not recognized officially until the 4th century C.E.
- *When?* Following begins around 30 C.E.; begins expansion outside the Mediterranean in the 6th century.
- *Where?* Europe, the Americas, sub-Saharan Africa, Philippines, Austronesia
- *Scripture:* Bible, divided into an Old Testament, a modification of the Torah and sharing major dictates such as the Ten Commandments; and a New Testament, which depicts the messianic life of Jesus of Nazareth and includes the writings of his disciples and early followers
- *Doctrine:* Varies depending on the denomination. Typically involves communion practices and baptisms.
- *Denominations:* Eastern Orthodox, Armenian, Antiochian, Greek Orthodox, Coptic, Roman Catholic, Protestant; each can be subdivided into further denominations.

- *Historical Diffusion:* From the Mediterranean hearth, Christianity diffused hierarchically to large cities such as Rome, Constantinople, Alexandria, and Marseilles. From there, missionaries spread the religion to other towns and cities where it diffused to smaller communities. These patterns of diffusion become recognizable through the hierarchy of the Holy See, archbishoprics, bishoprics, and local parishes.

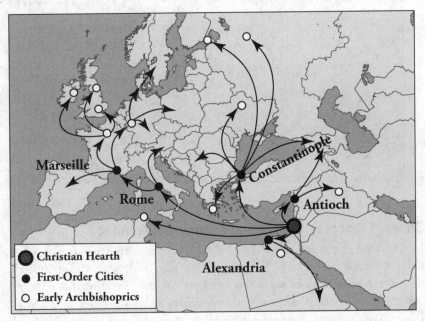

Islam

- *Who?* Originates with the peoples of the Arabian Peninsula along the Red Sea, particularly Mecca, Medina, and Jeddah

- *When?* Early 600s C.E.

- *Where?* Today the Islamic realm spans from Mauritania in West Africa; east to Indonesia and the Philippine Island of Mindanao; north to Chechnya, Kazakhstan, and Xinjiang in Western China; and south to Tanzania

- *Scripture:* Koran (Quran), the scriptures received by Muhammad

- *Doctrine:* Haddith, the recorded sayings of Muhammad. All sects emphasize at least five pillars of Islam, if not more.

- *Denominations:* Sunni (85 percent) and Shia (15 percent) sects with a number of denominations within, such as the Ismaili Shiite and Wahabi Sunni. Differences between the two major sects are based upon the emphasis by Shiites on the necessity for **Imams** (religious leaders) to have a direct blood line back to Muhammad.

- *Historical Diffusion:* From Mecca, Islam diffused in an expansion pattern in all directions very quickly. By 700 C.E., all of the Middle East and much of North Africa was adherent to Islam. Further expansion into Europe and Asia occurred through the 1600s. Some relocation diffusion was seen, such as that to Indonesia in the 1200s (seen on the following page).

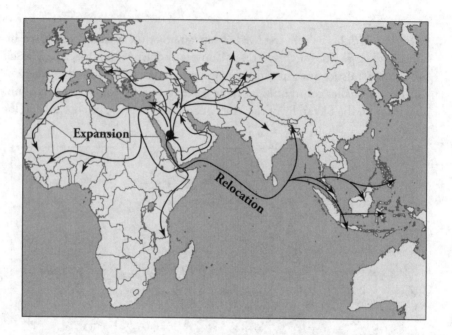

Islamic States: Theocracy, *Sharia,* and Secular Governance

You may have learned that a few countries in the Middle East are **theocracies**, where religious leaders hold the senior positions of governance. In fact, only Iran has a supreme religious council that serves as the **head of state** and can overrule the elected parliament and president. Some, but not all, Middle-Eastern states are **republics** or **monarchies** that abide by *Sharia,* or Islamic law, based on the Koran and Haddith. A few absolute monarchies (that, unlike constitutional monarchies, have no elected parliament) have all-powerful kings and large aristocracies, who in turn enforce religious standards on the populace.

Other states in the region are more **secular**, meaning they are not directly governed in a religious manner and, instead, often utilize French or British legal tradition and government structure. Even in these states, the influence of religion on government policy remains, and tension between the secular government and religious activists can cause difficulty or violent conflict.

Here are a few Middle-Eastern examples of each case:

Theocracy:	Iran, formerly Afghanistan under the Taliban
Sharia States:	Saudi Arabia, Kuwait, Yemen
Secular States:	Jordan, Turkey

Moral Principles in the Abrahamic Traditions: The Five Pillars of Islam

The Judeo-Christian system has its Ten Commandments from the Book of Exodus, which serves as a basic moral code for all followers. Likewise, the Koran emphasizes five pillars that guide followers with a moral system. The **Five Pillars of Islam** are as follows:

1. Five Daily Prayers
   - The call to prayer is heard on loudspeakers in cities throughout the Muslim world at designated hours.
   - For the devout, all work stops and prayer mats are unrolled.
   - Prayer is done facing Mecca. Islamic astronomers and geographers have worked for centuries to determine the azimuth, the angle of direction, from Mecca to other parts of the Earth.

2. Islamic Creed
   - "There is only one god, Allah, and Muhammad is his prophet."
   - The creed is a statement of monotheism. Prior to Muhammad's religious conversion of the Arabian peninsula, many of the peoples in the region believed in polytheistic Animist or tribal religions.
   - Muslims believe in a number of prophets shared with the Judeo-Christian traditions, such as Moses, Isaac, Ishmael, and Jesus, but Muhammad is the supreme prophet, as he is the author who received the Koran from Allah.

3. Alms to the Poor
   - It is the duty of all Muslims to care for and donate to the poor and sick within their communities.
   - Large charitable foundations in the Islamic world help alleviate poverty, extend health care, and educate children.
   - Many of these international charities have come under increased scrutiny by the U.S. government following September 11, 2001, due to accusations that charities were being used to funnel money to terrorist groups.

4. Observance of Ramadan
   - Ramadan is a period of spiritual cleansing and repentance for past sins.
   - During Ramadan, there is fasting during daylight hours, with plain evening meals of sparing quantity.
   - Ramadan, like the Christian Easter and Lenten period, the Jewish holidays, and Buddhist New Years, is set on a lunar calendar. The lunar month of Ramadan can fall during a wide range of months in our Gregorian calendar.

5. The Hajj
   - Each Muslim who is able must make at least one pilgrimage to Mecca during his lifetime. "Haji" is an honorific name for those who make the journey.
   - The Hajj pilgrimage takes place during the Islamic month of Dhu Al-Hijjah (or Dhul Hijjah), which is typically in June or July.
   - Even prior to the 20th century, Hajis made multi-month-long voyages across deserts and oceans to complete the pilgrimage.

> The geography of religion can be further broken down by denomination and region. There are important sections later in this chapter and in Chapter 6 regarding religious-based conflict. There is also some discussion on religion and ethnicity in urban American neighborhoods in the Know the Models discussion of the sector model in Chapter 8.

Syncretic Religions

There are some religions, known as syncretic religions, that synthesize the core beliefs from two or more other religions. Examples of these include the **Druze,** who incorporate both Christian and Islamic principles, and the **Sikhs,** who incorporate principles from both Islam and Hinduism. Like Buddhists, Sikhs reject the concept of a caste-based social hierarchy.

Folklore

Folklore is the collected stories, spoken-word histories (such as Norse sagas), and writings that are specific to a culture and tell the societal histories and morality tales that define a culture's ethical foundations. The morality tales serve a purpose similar to religious scriptures, dictating culturally constructed rules of behavior. **Aesop's fables** are an example of folklore from the classical Greeks. Each fable had a moral to the story, a lesson to be learned regarding proper behavior. A fundamental element of American folklore, tall tales such as Paul Bunyan, John Henry, and Mike Fink incorporate unbelievable elements or exaggerated versions of actual events to relate stories of a strong work ethic, a product of Puritan Protestantism.

When a culture's history and its folklore intersect, it can often lead to distortions of reality in the lives of historical figures, like the myth of George Washington chopping down his father's cherry tree. Also see the stylized tales of American frontiersmen like Daniel Boone or Davy Crockett, whose Hollywood movie depictions have furthered fictions and half-truths about the long-dead historical persons.

Cristóbal Colón, American Hero? The Historical Geography of Folklore

In many parts of the Americas, a folklore has been built around the life and travels of Christopher Columbus. The myths and facts are intertwined and the folklore varies from country to country. Here's a comparison of the folklore and truths regarding Columbus from the United States' point of view:

"Columbus Discovered America."

- Archaeological evidence shows that Norsemen (Scandinavian Vikings) established settlements on the northeastern tip of Newfoundland at L'Anse aux Meadows around 1000 C.E. These were likely abandoned 100 years later when a significant global climate cooling event resulted in crop failures. Settlers likely evacuated to other settlements in Greenland or Iceland.

- Columbus never saw or set foot on the mainland United States. He did explore the Bahamas, Cuba, and Hispañola, and also landed on the mainland of South America.

"Columbus sailed the ocean blue with his ships the *Nina, Pinta,* and *Santa Maria.*"

- Well, sort of. These are the ships he departed with in 1492 from Seville in Spain on his first voyage. What you might not know is that the *Santa Maria* struck a reef off the northern coast of what is today Haiti, the island Columbus named *Hispañola*.

- The shipwreck forced Columbus to leave behind 40 men at a colony named for the Spanish Queen, Isabella. This was in part to establish trade with the indigenous people who lived there. Upon Columbus' return 366 days later on his second voyage, not a single sign of the 40 men was found at the village. This caused severe grief for Columbus and the other crew who had returned to rescue their comrades.

"Columbus was a famous Spaniard who gained the title 'Admiral of the Seas.'"

- First, Columbus was Genoese (from Genoa—a coastal city in what is today northern Italy).

- Columbus sought funding for his expedition to the Indies (today's India, Indonesia, and China), but was turned down by a number of potential donors when he proposed sailing westward across the Atlantic instead of around Africa, as was already done by the Portuguese.

- The Spanish Royal Court of Ferdinand and Isabella was receptive to Columbus' plan for two reasons:

  ○ Spain was nearly bankrupt from years of war trying to remove the Muslim Moors from the southern Iberian Peninsula and needed the new trade route to raise money for their treasury. The western sailing route to land had been long rumored. Basque fisherman had likely sailed off the coast of Brazil and Canada following cod fish and Columbus was aware of their land sightings—and assumed they were India.

  ○ The Portuguese were keen on protecting their African trade route and would likely fight to protect it. They also possessed sailing charts of the route, maps to which the Spanish did not have access.

- Columbus did receive the title of "Admiral of the Seas" but did not receive the promised 10 percent of treasure from the New World that the position was entitled to. Only after his death were his sons able to extract money from the Spanish government. Columbus was not a folk hero in Spain; he died blind in Spain in 1506 at the age of 54.

> In recent years, increased attention has been given to Columbus's legacy of brutality in the Caribbean, challenging the enduring perception of him as a national hero. He enslaved the indigenous Taino people, forcing them to mine gold and punishing them with mutilation or even death if they did not collect enough. Of the Taino, Columbus wrote, "They do not carry arms or know them...they should be good servants."
>
> Furthermore, the Spanish forced the encomienda system upon the Taino and others, separating families, destroying communities, and ending cultures.

This may seem like a "historical" example. However, the Columbus myth and the settlement of Latin America is an area of extensive research in cultural geography. This kind of thing is fair game on the exam, and you need to be prepared for it. Read Carl Sauer's *Northern Mists* about the Nordic voyagers and *The Early Spanish Main* for an accurate description of the Columbus voyages and the first Spanish settlement in the New World.

Land Use

Land survey techniques can also reveal something about the cultural landscape. How property is utilized, shared, or divided can say something about culture through its imprint on the landscape.

Farming Practices

Cultural differences in agriculture are not limited to the types of food produced. How farming is done can also be culturally specific and is heavily influenced by technology. It is, after all, agri-*culture*. Cultural farming practices range from **swidden**, or a "slash and burn" style of agriculture seen in forest regions, to the highly technological large-scale farming seen in the First World. Keep in mind, traditional farming practices seen in the Third World are quickly disappearing in favor of modern, mechanized farming.

Blue Sheep's Milk?

Also, don't forget that in the First World there are still some significant culturally specific and low-tech farming practices. Examples of this can be found in Vermont with the production of maple syrup from trees. Or look to Europe for the production of regionally specific cheeses, such as Roquefort (a blue sheep's milk cheese) in France, or Parmagiano Reggiano (a hard cow's milk cheese) in Italy. These are high-value **appellations** that designate a culturally specific farm product that brings high value. These appellations, including Champagne and Vermont Maple Syrup, have their name usage protected by international trade laws. Find out more about appellations and specialized agriculture in Chapter 7.

Residential Patterns

How living space is distributed is also an important indicator of culture, especially in rural and tribal areas. Often, cultural traditions impose rules on living space that depend on singular clan relations, extended family units with more than one clan, or whole tribal communities with multiple clans living in one shared residential area. For the distribution of urban land use, see Chapter 8.

Land Ownership

As was mentioned in Chapter 3, in Europe, much of Latin America, and Anglo-America east of Central Ohio and Ontario, land surveys used natural landscape features to divide up land on a system of metes and bounds that had been developed in Europe centuries earlier. Metes and bounds are also evidence of the European feudalist political economy (see Chapter 6 for more details). In its early form, the irregular property boundaries were the territorial claims of large aristocratic landholdings.

Over time, these landholdings became subdivided via partial land sales or by nationwide land reform efforts. Land reform often divided properties into smaller polygons. France and French colonial areas such as Québec and Louisiana have **long-lot patterns.** These have a narrow frontage along a road or waterway with a very long lot shape behind.

As mentioned in Chapter 3, new techniques in the 1830s were transferred from sea navigation to land survey; land survey in the United States and Canada used a rectilinear township and range survey system based on lines of latitude and longitude. This produced the block-shaped property lines and the geometric shape of many western U.S. states and Canadian provinces. It is also evidence of the impact of technology on the cultural landscape.

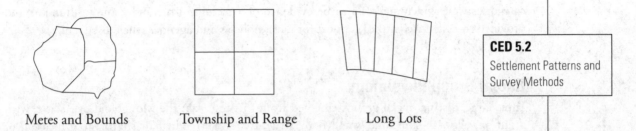

Metes and Bounds   Township and Range   Long Lots

CED 5.2
Settlement Patterns and Survey Methods

CULTURAL IDENTITY

How people are identified and how they identify themselves is another important aspect of cultural geography. This section examines the several dimensions of identity that may appear on the exam.

Nation and Ethnicity

The term *nation* is used loosely in normal conversation. However, cultural geographers and political geographers have a specific definition for the term. A nation, in its most basic definition, is a population represented by a singular culture. Another term for nation would be a culture group. What defines a nation is a common identity, which is a complex mix of genetic heritage and political allegiance embodied in the term **ethnicity.** Ethnic groups often claim a single identifiable lineage or heritage, which all members tend to identify with as a common social bond. Keep in mind, as with our prior example of the English language, several ethnicities can exist within the same linguistic region. Likewise, within a single ethnicity more than one language can be used, such as among the French Canadians, South Asian Indians, or Belgians.

Not all nations have a representative state, as a state in its most simple form is a population represented by a single government. This is the case with our previous music example of the Roma, or Romani, peoples of Europe. Likewise, the Kurds of northern Iraq, southeastern Turkey, northeastern Syria, and western Iran are similar in that they are defined groups with no official government. The Kurds are attempting to establish a Kurdistan in what is today northern Iraq and northeastern Syria. However, the geopolitical relationship between the United States and Turkey prevents the Kurds from being recognized as a sovereign independent state.

Ethnicity can be modified in the process of migration. In the United States and Canada, there are many migrant groups, including Italian-Americans and Irish-Canadians. This modified ethnicity is more than symbolic, and can be evidence of acculturation by immigrants to their new home country. See the section on acculturation later in this chapter.

Race

Ethnicity and race are two commonly confused cultural identifiers. Whereas ethnicity represents the national or cultural heritage of an individual, **race** refers to the physical characteristics of a common genetic heritage. The concept of race was developed by physical anthropologists in the 1800s. Researchers categorized racial groups based on a number of variables including skin color, bone structure, and the shape of the hair shafts (straight, wavy, or curly). These categories were widely believed to be evidence of a biological hierarchy among humans and provided so-called "scientific" support for racist policies and agendas (such as eugenics).

Racial Group Physiology

Three large, distinct racial groups emerged from this research: the Mongoloid or Asiatic, with a tan or yellowish skin tone, small body structure, and straight hair shaft; the Caucasoid or Indo-European, with a light to dark skin tone, medium body type, and wavy hair shaft; and the Negroid or African, with a dark skin tone, medium body shape, and a curly hair shaft.

The Names Explained

Mongolians appeared to have physical features common to all Asians. Native Americans, who were at the time hypothesized to be from Asia, shared many Asiatic features with Mongolians. Archeological and genetic research has since added to a body of theory connecting Native Americans to origins in Asia. The Caucasus Mountains region, which separates Europe from Asia, is believed to have been a major migration route from the Indian subcontinent to Europe during the prehistoric era. The term *negro* is derived from the Latin word for "black."

The Pacific Islands

In addition, four small populations of physical anthropological groups were identified within the Pacific Islands. **Melanesians**, found in New Guinea, New Caledonia, and Fiji, so named because of their dark skin coloration, have comparatively thin bodies and angular facial features, with a curly hair shaft. **Polynesians**, living in Tonga, Samoa, New Zealand, Tahiti, and Hawaii, have a lighter brown skin color, heavyset body shape, and curly hair shafts. **Micronesians**—the name coming from the small island atolls of the Marshalls and Caroline Islands—have a light brown skin color, medium body shape, and curly hair shafts. And **Aboriginals** in Australia have light brown skin, a medium body type, and wavy hair shafts.

Race and Identity

Oppression and discrimination based on race was popularly opposed and legally deregulated in many countries during the latter part of the 20th century. In the contemporary era, it would seem that racism is less of a barrier to success. The 2008 and 2012 elections of Barack Obama to the presidency of the United States was a visible sign of progress. Still, disparities in treatment and outcomes in the U.S. court and medical systems (to name just a few examples), provide evidence that structural racism persists into the 21st century.

Mixed-Race Cultures

In many parts of the world, identity is based on a single race being the **indigenous population** —the people who originally settled an area. In other parts of the world, identities are defined by multiple mixed races. In Latin America and the Caribbean, for example, identity based on mixed races is the norm. Across the region, several thousand terms are used to describe varying degrees of mixed heritage.

For the purposes of the exam, we focus on the larger representative groups. **Mestizos** are people who have cultural and genetic heritage from European and indigenous backgrounds. **Mulattos** are people who have mixed African and European heritage. (This term has fallen out of favor and use because of its history as a derogatory term.) There is one significant group of mixed indigenous and African peoples, known as the **Garifuna**. The Garifuna live on the Caribbean islands of St. Vincent, Dominica, and Trinidad, as well as the coast of Honduras, including Roatan Island.

Creole is a term used to describe people or culture that is derived from all three racial groups— European, Native American, and African. Originally, the term in Spanish meant someone who was born in the New World, regardless of heritage, and could refer to colonists with two European parents. Creole heritage and culture is mainly found in the Greater Antilles (Cuba, Haiti, the Dominican Republic, Puerto Rico, and Jamaica), as well as coastal Louisiana, Texas, Mississippi, Belize, Colombia, and Brazil. An example of the Creole food culture would be gumbo. It's a French Mediterranean soup similar to bouillabaisse, with *file*, a spice used in Native American cooking made of sassafras. The rice first used in American cooking of gumbo in the 1600s was West African red rice.

Environmental Determinism and Racism

In the 1800s, at the same time anthropologists were establishing the physical characteristic of race, human geographers developed the concept of environmental determinism to explain cultural differences around the world. **Environmental determinism** is the former scientific ideology that states that a culture's traits are defined by the physical geography of its native hearth or culture region. Contemporary human geography as a science was originally based on deterministic philosophies. The *Anthropogeographie* of the German geographer **Friedrich Ratzel**, considered the father of modern human geography, and his students, such as American Ellen Churchill Semple, built a large body of research claiming that all aspects of culture were defined by physical geographic factors such as climate, landforms, mineral resources, timber, food, and water supplies.

The problem with environmental determinism was that science was being used to reinforce the racist ideologies of the 1800s and early 1900s. An example of this racist logic would be that people from extremely hot tropical regions are considered lazy, as they would not want to work during the midday heat. Conversely, people from colder regions had to be physically and mentally hardier to survive the cold winters. Although these ideas may seem plausible, they are scientifically incorrect and based on flimsy evidence. In truth, different races and culture groups are essentially the same physiologically, and each can survive in a multitude of climates and environments.

The Determinism Debate and Possibilism

Despite the global elimination of enslavement by the late 1800s, racism and environmental determinism were widely accepted both socially and scientifically. To change the scientific perspective, human geographers including **Carl Sauer** debated and opposed the environmental determinists. **Possibilism** was the revised concept proposed by Sauer and other like-minded geographers. This ideology stated that cultures were to a *partial* degree shaped by their environment and the material resources available to them. However, culture groups have the ability to adjust and modify the environment. The research of Sauer and others from the 1920s onward showed that in many cases, cultures made massive modifications to the landscape to meet their food and resource needs, often destroying the natural environment in the process.

Nazism and Determinism: Be Careful What Science Creates!

Despite Sauer's contribution of possibilism to the science of human geography in the 1920s, the deterministic ideas first proposed by Ratzel had become ingrained in the European society and psychology. The concepts of Nazism proposed by Hitler in the 1920s and put into practice in the 1930s were in part based on Ratzel's concept of *lebensraum*, in which the living space for each distinct nation was based upon the optimal physical geography of the culture group. Hitler's idea was to expand the living space of the Germanic or Aryan race across the European landscape. Of course, this was at the expense of other European ethnic groups, who, by the way, were also Caucasians.

Despite Germany's defeat during World War II, Nazi ideologies still persist among some extremist groups in the United States and Europe. This neo-Nazism is not based on *lebensraum* or ethnicity, but is instead violent racism against non-whites and immigrants. This is also a violent expression of **xenophobia,** the fear of outsiders.

Ethnocentrism: A Feature, Not a Bug

Ethnocentrism is defined as the belief in the superiority of one's nation or ethnic group, and in the inferiority of other nations or ethnic groups. It typically grows fiercest in the earliest and most dominant settlement group, whose characteristics strongly influence the initial social and cultural geography of an area. Often demonized—and rightfully so—this belief is nonetheless a permanent characteristic of a portion of any given population.

The resurgence of white nationalism in both the United States and Europe is the latest, most regrettable example of Western ethnocentrism. It exists elsewhere too, however. In Asia, the former leader of Myanmar, Aung San Suu Kyi, was stripped of her Nobel Peace Prize—which she'd received while spending a decade as a political prisoner—after she supported a campaign of ethnic cleansing against the Rohingya, an ethnic minority, in her own country.

On the other hand, cultural relativism is the idea that an individual's beliefs and activities can only be understood in the context of that person's culture. It is the polar opposite of ethnocentrism.

Internal Versus External Identity

How people express their identity is dependent on the audience with which they are communicating. **Internal identity** is used by individuals to express their cultural heritage, ethnicity, or place of origin to people who share their heritage or place of origin. **External identity** is used by individuals to express their cultural heritage, ethnicity, or place of origin to people who do not share a common cultural or geographic background.

Egyptian or Arab?

For example, imagine an Egyptian in London being introduced to another person of Egyptian descent. Immediately the conversation includes geographic specifics such as local place-names, family names, and culturally specific language. Compare this to that same Egyptian an hour later, meeting someone from Canada. In this conversation, there is little geographic specificity; just basic identifiers such as Egypt or terms like "near Cairo."

On the other side of the conversation, the Canadian may have her own misconceptions, which can further distance the cultural goals between the two people. For instance, by referring to Egyptians as Arabs, the Canadian may lose face, as many Egyptians consider themselves a single culture group as opposed to those who live in the Arabian Peninsula, a few hundred miles away, despite their common language. From the Egyptian's point of view, she might as well refer to the Canadian as an American. It is quite possible that we use external identity to compensate for the lack of cultural knowledge from one group to another.

SPATIAL CONCEPTS IN CULTURAL GEOGRAPHY

Cultural Region

The world is covered with several overlapping culture regions that create multiple layers on the local to global scale. As stated in Chapter 3, a region is an area of bounded space with a homogeneous characteristic. In the case of **culture regions**, the homogeneous characteristic can be one or more components of culture, such as language. Likewise, the cultural concept of a nation or ethnicity can also represent the culture region. In these cases where ethnicity defines the culture region, look for a multitude of cultural components with which to define a number of homogeneous characteristics as a complex of factors.

The Fuzzy Borders of Cultural Regions

One of the things that sets apart cultural regions from other types of regions is their border characteristics. Cultural regions tend to have what are called **fuzzy borders.** They are referred to as fuzzy because it's hard to tell where one cultural region ends and another begins. In addition, the transition from one cultural region to another is not easily measured, as compared to the way you can measure the transition between one bioregion to another. The fact is that cultural regions overlap in an irregular manner.

An example of a fuzzy border would be where **Dixie** ends and the American Northeast or Midwest begins. Some try to apply a political boundary to it, like the Mason-Dixon Line, but this is a very poor definition. The Mason-Dixon Line actually runs south and west of Delaware and north of Maryland. These are **border states** where one part of the state is decidedly Southern and another part seems more Northeastern. There's no one place where you could put a road sign saying, "Welcome to Dixie!"

Others have attempted to quantify certain cultural symbols in the hope of determining Dixie's regional boundary. If you were to estimate the concentration of NASCAR fans or the market areas of country music listeners, you might be able to see the extent of the Dixie culture region. However, you would find much inconsistency along its edges, and you would find that the phenomena of NASCAR and country music extended far beyond the South proper.

Culture Hearths

Our Ties to Ancient Culture Hearths

The **culture hearth** is based on the idea that every culture has a localized area where it originated or has its main population center. **Contemporary culture hearths** exist in today's world. Human geographers also discuss the concept of **ancient culture hearths**, which developed ideas and technologies that still exist today. The most common of these technologies is the domestication of **staple food crops**.

In the ancient world, staple food crops were very important, as they fed the conquering armies of empires, provided sustenance for the labor force, and were the primary commodity for commercial trade networks. Most large ancient civilizations had a single staple food, which they either domesticated or utilized heavily. The following table provides some examples of ancient culture hearths and their staple food crops:

Culture Hearth	Staple Food	Civilizations
Nile River	Wheat	Ancient Egyptian
Mesopotamia	Wheat*	Sumerian, Assyria, Babylon
The Indus Valley	Wheat	Harappan
Mesoamerica	Corn	Olmec, Maya, Aztec
The Andean Highlands	Potato*	Inca
Northeast China	Rice	Ancient Chinese
West Africa	Yams*	Malian, Songhai

*Indicates place of original domestication.

The classical civilizations of Rome and Greece were also major consumers of wheat. However, wheat had been domesticated long before, in Mesopotamia. Archaeologists believed this occurred in what is present-day northern Iraq and southeastern Turkey. The culture hearth of ancient Greece and Rome drew much of its cultural traditions, such as Greek and Roman shared mythology, from the earlier Minoan culture of Crete. Likewise, Western societies today draw upon much from Greek and Roman politics, such as the concepts of democracy and the republic.

Culture Hearths of Today: Core and Periphery of Mormonism

Hearths can represent the core of a **contemporary culture region**. An example of a region with a distinct core and a wider periphery is the Mormon culture region of the American West. The **Latter-Day Saints (LDS)** religion, of course, is the homogeneous characteristic shared by the region.

The population and cultural core of the region is the Salt Lake City-Ogden-Provo metropolitan area, a long, continuous north-south urban corridor also known as the Wasatch Front. The area has around 1.5 million people, the majority of whom are practicing church members. At its cultural heart is Temple Square in downtown Salt Lake City, where the church has its main offices, a large convention center, and a historic temple and tabernacle.

Outside of the Wasatch Front, the region is predominantly rural and agricultural. The peripheral Mormon culture region spreads across the irrigated farms and dry ranchlands of Utah and the border regions of the surrounding states of Idaho, Wyoming, Colorado, Arizona, and Nevada, and extends with significant populations in rural eastern Oregon and suburban Southern California. As you head farther away from the Wasatch Front, the cultural signs (the ward church house) and symbols (the beehive of industry) become fewer, especially when you leave Utah's borders. But even in this peripheral region, Mormonism is still detectable and existent in the population. Las Vegas, Idaho Falls, Boise, Denver, Phoenix, and Los Angeles all have large active Mormon communities.

Formal or Functional Culture Region?

As we discussed in Chapter 3, there are both formal regions, with homogeneity across the region, and functional or nodal regions, with a distinct central place. Functional regions can be defined as organized networks with a distinct node at the center and connections radiating throughout the region.

In the previous example, we could argue the Mormon culture region as both functional and formal to some degree. As a formal region, Mormon culture is evident through the population of followers who are concentrated in the Intermountain West. Even though not everyone who lives there is LDS, Mormons in the region are a large and distinguishable populace. Conversely, the Salt Lake City-based Church of Jesus Christ of Latter-Day Saints, the largest denomination in the LDS faith (there are a few much smaller LDS faiths), is a very well-organized and hierarchical network of neighborhood ward, local, state, and regional church administration that is coordinated from the Salt Lake City headquarters. As such, the Mormon culture region is also a functional or nodal region.

The Global Islamic Culture Region: Culture Hearth Versus Population Center

The culture hearth of Islam is the region along the Red Sea coast of Saudi Arabia. Inland from the sea, at its heart, is the most holy city of Islam, Mecca, where Muhammad was born. But don't forget Islam's second-most holy city of Medina, where Muhammad received a portion of the Koran. As centers of Islamic learning and traditional philosophy, these are the spiritual centers of the faith.

However, the Middle East is not a very well-populated area compared to other parts of the Islamic world. Combine the Islamic populations of Pakistan (184 million), India (195 million), Bangladesh (144 million), Malaysia (20 million), Nigeria (90 million), and the world's largest Muslim state, Indonesia (220 million). Add to that number the Muslim populations of several smaller countries, as well as Muslims living in non-Muslim countries. The result: out of nearly 2 billion Muslims in the world, more than two-thirds do not live in the Middle East!

CULTURAL CHANGE

Sequent Occupance

Long-term cultural changes can be seen in all of the world's populated regions. One way this is observed is through the concept of **sequent occupance**. That is, for a single place or region, different dominant cultures replace each other over time. To visualize this, think of layers of culture building up on top of each other, much like layers of sediment building up a geologic stratigraphy. When we examine the cultural landscape of a place, we often see remnants of previous cultural influences.

An example would be European architecture found in former colonial cities of Africa like Lagos, Nigeria. Deposited upon this is a postcolonial Nigerian landscape with modern buildings, a product of globalized architecture, and place-names and street names with Nigerian references that replaced the British colonial names after independence in 1960.

New York City was at one point under British colonial rule (think of neighborhood place-names such as Greenwich Village, Williamsburg, and the borough of Queens). But prior to this, the city was controlled by the Dutch (with place-names like Harlem, Van Cortlandt, and Stuyvesant). And before that, several indigenous groups populated the shores of New York Harbor, which were rich in oysters and other seafood. Strata can be seen in construction site excavations along the waterfront where shell middens, large garbage dumps of mainly oyster shells and other artifacts of indigenous life, are uncovered. Atop all these layers are signs and symbols of the postcolonial and modern American cultural occupants.

Cultural Adaptation

The cultural landscape also retains the imprint of minority and immigrant groups. The ethnic neighborhood is the best example of how these groups make their way into the layers of sequent occupance at a much smaller scale. In the case of New York, Little Italy or Chinatown immediately come to mind. You can also cite the example of Spanish Harlem, where Puerto Rican and Dominican immigrants settled from the 1950s onward.

Acculturate or Assimilate—Which Is It?

When European immigrants came to America in the early part of the 20th century, they adopted many new beliefs and behaviors in their new home. They still kept much of their original culture, but they learned American norms as they adjusted to life in America. This is an example of **acculturation**—the process of adapting to a new culture while still keeping some of one's original culture. Usually acculturation is a two-way street, with both the original and the incoming culture group swapping cultural traits.

Assimilation is more of an "all-or-nothing" process. Assimilation is a complete change in the identity of a minority culture group as it becomes part of the majority culture group. A clear example of assimilation occurred when the U.S. government adopted a policy of "forced assimilation" of the indigenous population. The government forced the indigenous people to move to reservations where they were taught in government-run schools. The people were made to learn English and give up their native tongue. The government insisted they adopt the dress, manners, language, and ways of the dominant American culture. The "old ways" were forbidden. This total absorption into the dominant culture is one-way and usually "encouraged" by government policy when the new residents (or original inhabitants, in the case of the Native Americans) are forced to learn the new languages and embrace the new ways.

Cultural Survival

In other parts of the world, national cultures have historically been threatened by outside influences, such as military invasions, mass migrations, or the decline of indigenous cultures. The term **indigenous** means the people who were the original occupants of a place or region. The **indigenous culture** is, therefore, the original culture of that same region. The loss of indigenous culture has become a significant concern among citizens and a major policy issue among governments. In some cases, the indigenous culture is merely threatened by external cultural influences. Yet in many other cases around the world, cultures are in danger of extinction if something is not done to help protect and promote the **preservation of cultural heritage**.

William Denevan and the Depopulation of Native Americans

One of the most important bodies of research on the destruction of indigenous culture groups is the work of geographer **William Denevan** on the depopulation of Native Americans in the early colonial era after 1492. By collecting years of archaeological research on the extent and productivity of agriculture by indigenous people, Denevan and allied researchers have established that the **pre-Columbian** population of North and South America combined was approximately 54 million people. By comparison, their research into colonial census data, collected journals, and colonial government reports revealed that the total native population had declined to around 5 million people by 1635.

Understanding what caused the massive indigenous population decline was the next part of Denevan's research. By examining Spanish colonial-era documents, such as the journals of Jesuit priests, the logs of ship captains, and the personal diaries of other individuals, Denevan found that diseases of European origin were the main culprit behind the decline, which in some cases wiped out whole native culture groups. Diseases such as influenza, measles, and cholera were unknown to the Americas prior to the arrival of European colonists. Native Americans had no immune system defense against these pathogens to which they had not been previously exposed. As a result, diseases like the flu, which normally has very low mortality rates, resulted in deadly **epidemics** with very high mortality rates among indigenous groups. Research has shown that deaths from European diseases vastly outnumbered all other causes of death including warfare, forced labor, and relocation combined.

From a cultural perspective, disease epidemics had a devastating effect on the survival of many unique and advanced civilizations in the Americas. In addition to the large Aztec and Inca empires that the Spanish systematically eliminated through military conquest, there is a growing body of theory that a large agrarian civilization existed in the Amazon basin that may have been completely wiped out by European disease. The difference here is that Amazonian peoples did not utilize stonework construction. Over time, the rapid physical deterioration of wooden houses and buildings in the tropical environment left little evidence of what is believed to have been a large and extensive agricultural society.

To learn more about ancient Amazonian civilization, look for research into *terra preta* soil formations, which are the focus of archaeological and geographic research. In short, *terra preta* means black earth, which was formed by combining charcoal, bone, and manure to increase the soil fertility.

CONTEMPORARY CULTURAL CONFLICTS

Today, a number of indigenous cultures around the world are under threat from a variety of forces that have the potential to eventually wipe them out. The concept of **cultural survival** is used to describe the efforts to research, understand, and promote the protection of indigenous cultures. In addition to protecting the identity and promoting the livelihood of indigenous peoples, indigenous cultures are seen as invaluable to the social, anthropological, and geographical composition and diversity of humankind. Thus, indigenous cultures are important to their people and representative governments, as well as to researchers.

An example would be the current research of geographer Kendra McSweeney. She investigates the cultural and economic livelihood of the Miskito indigenous people along the Caribbean coastal region of Honduras. The Miskito live in an environmentally sensitive tropical forest region that is under threat from a number of development interests, including plantation agriculture for crops such as bananas and sugar, and land development for new towns, mining, and ranching. McSweeney's research from both environmental data and field interviews shows that there is continuous encroachment, both physically and economically, on the traditional territory of these indigenous people. Without official protections instituted by the Honduran government, the Miskito will continue to suffer from the shrinkage of their indigenous territory and their culture and way of life will be threatened.

Cultural Globalization

Another set of factors that can harm indigenous cultures and threaten the constitution of national cultures is **cultural globalization**. A number of influences such as literature, music, motion pictures, the Internet, and satellite and cable television, mainly from English-language sources, combine to diminish and potentially eliminate the media and culture of other linguistic groups. Other globalizing factors such as architecture, transportation infrastructure, food retailing, clothing styles, and the missionary efforts of **proselytic religions** (those that actively seek converts) also threaten many unique cultures around the world.

The problem with cultural globalization is that when people are fully immersed in globalized popular culture, they are denying the importance of their own ethnic cultures. Over time, unique and socially important traditions can be forgotten and lost. People who lose their connection to their heritage are also losing part of their personal **connection to nature**. This can leave people feeling disconnected from the natural world and humanity, causing social and psychological problems— things that we geographers will leave to psychologists to better understand and explain.

Economically, culture has value. By protecting national cultures from the negative effects of globalization, a nation can promote its own cultural economy and products from creative arts and media. At a basic level, these artistic products can be a significant draw for cultural tourism. At its most valuable level, whole media industries can generate large amounts of employment and value. An example would be the Bollywood movie industry based in Mumbai, India (formerly Bombay, hence the name *Bollywood*).

National Regulations and Laws

To combat the negative effects of cultural globalization, a number of national governments around the world have instituted laws and regulations that lessen the impact of foreign influence on their home cultures. These laws and regulations in many cases restrict certain types or limit the volume of foreign media and other external cultural influences. In some cases, there are attempts to completely ban external cultural influence.

As a First-World example, the French government has taken a number of steps to significantly limit the volume of English-language films and television programs released or broadcast within France. Furthermore, the French government, through its Culture Ministry, provides funding to develop and promote French-language media for internal release and export. These media exports are intended for both Francophone countries and non-French-speaking countries, in an effort to push back against the English-dominated global media. Similar programs exist in Québec, where the Canadian and Québécois governments provide special funding for French-Canadian media.

Perhaps the most extreme case is the country of Bhutan, which places a number of limits on the importation of foreign media. Set in the Himalayan foothills and surrounded by northeastern India with China to its north, Bhutan severely limits the number of entrance visas for foreigners. This is an effort by the royal government to preserve the ancient Buddhist culture and protect its people from the undue influence of popularized global media brought in and demanded by foreign visitors.

Causes of Cultural Diffusion

CED 3.6
Contemporary Causes of Diffusion

Despite these regulations, culture behaves much like water, in the sense that it seeps across borders despite the best attempts of authorities to limit it. This is **cultural diffusion**. Today, as in the past, culture is transmitted through a number of different methods:

- **Trade**. Interconnectedness increases along popular trade routes. Renaissance Italy, for example, rediscovered many of its own great ancient works by trading with the Arabic world.

- **Colonialism**. Though the Mormon church began in Utah, it spread itself around the world via mandatory missions conducted by its young members. It's become one of the world's universalizing religions.

- **Conflict**. Better known by its other name—war—conflict often sees soldiers and armies invading or even occupying foreign cultures. For example, during World War II, American GIs returned from the South Pacific with a newfound taste for Polynesian culture. As a result, many opened tiki bars and popularized floral-patterned shirts, bringing a wave of South Pacific culture into the U.S. for the first time.

- **Migration**. Immigrants carry their own culture to their new country and blend them with preexisting bits of culture. This explains many aspects of American life, but most especially things like Korean tacos.

Ethnic and Religious Conflicts

Cultural conflicts have existed throughout human history and unfortunately are still with us today. Some cultural conflicts are continuously negotiated between groups and do not result in violence or armed conflict. However, in a number of cases, bloodshed has resulted merely from the cultural differences of people occupying the same region.

Places such as the former Yugoslavia, the Caucasus Mountains, East Timor, Rwanda, Burundi, the Darfur region of Sudan, and Syria have been in the international eye for the bloody armed conflicts between their inhabitants. Yet, what can lead to war is something as simple as differences in language or as complex as differences in religion.

Yugoslavia

The former Yugoslavia was created as a state during the post-World War I **Treaty of Versailles** in 1919. Prior to that time, there was no such thing as a Yugoslav either politically or culturally. This part of the Balkan Peninsula contained a multitude of different overlapping ethnic regions, including groups such as Serbs, Croats, Bosnian Muslims, Slovenians, Montenegrins, Kosovars, and Macedonians. The victors in World War I (Britain, France, and the United States) thought the best plan of action was to put them all together as one state. In historical terms, the idea was short-lived.

Following the 1980 death of the country's longtime Communist leader, Josip Tito, there was a power vacuum that left no particular individual or group in control. Tito was born a Croat, but fought alongside Serbians against the Germans during World War II. In this way, he was a representative of an artificial Yugoslav identity, which did not exist before the 20th century.

After his death, with no Yugoslav heir apparent, people and politicians began to revitalize their centuries-long ethnic and religious arguments.

Croats, as an ethnic group, are predominantly Roman Catholic. Serbians are Eastern Orthodox Christians. Despite their shared Christianity and Serbo-Croatian language, these are two separate ethnic groups from two very different religious traditions. In 1989, localized fighting broke out in northern Yugoslavia between these groups. Croats forced Serbs out of Serbian enclaves in Croatia and Serbs did the same, forcing Croats to leave northern Serbia. Here we see the first mention of the term **ethnic cleansing,** where people of one ethnic group are eliminated by another, often under threat of violence or death.

Despite this conflict being quickly resolved by international diplomacy, by 1990, fighting and ethnic cleansing had flared up in Bosnia between ethnic Croats, Serbs, and Bosnian Muslims who fought to control various parts of the mountainous country. Several thousand men and older boys were executed in Bosnia just for being potential combatants in war. The war was curtailed in 1994 by the **Dayton Peace Accords**. Today, roughly 20,000 foreign peacekeeping troops are on duty in Bosnia and neighboring Kosovo (southern Serbia).

Since then, several political and military leaders have been charged with **crimes against humanity** for their war crimes in Bosnia. In late 2008, Radovan Karadžić, a Bosnian Serb leader, was arrested after living several years in bearded disguise as an herbal medicine practitioner in Belgrade. He has been charged with ordering the genocide of Bosnian Muslim males in Srebrenica, where several mass graves have since been uncovered.

Never Again?

Genocide, a large-scale systematic killing of people of one ethnic group, has been seen in a number of ethnic conflicts. Most famous is the **Holocaust** of Jews at the hands of the Nazis in World War II when six million were killed. More recent cases involve the deaths of several hundred thousand Tutsis by Hutu Extremists in Rwanda during 1994. And today the genocide label has been applied to the situation in the west Sudanese province of Darfur, where Christians and Animist people have been killed by Muslim militia groups known as *Janjaweed*. See more on culture as a source of conflict in Chapter 6.

Taking an AP history exam? Check out our books, *AP World History Prep, 2023, AP European History Prep, 2023,* and *AP U.S. History Prep, 2023,* on sale now!

OTHER RESOURCES

- For more cultural geography material, see *The Human Mosaic* by Terry G. Jordan-Bychkov, Mona Domosh, Roderick P. Neumann, and Patricia L. Price.

- Also see *Cultural Geography in Practice* by Alison Blunt, Pyrs Gruffudd, Jon May, and Miles Ogborn.

CHAPTER 5 KEY TERMS

culture
cultural landscape
signs
symbols
components of culture
cultural synthesis (syncretism)
folk music
culture group (nation)
Anglo-America
built environment
architectural forms
modern architecture
contemporary architecture
traditional architecture
postmodern
green energy
recycled materials
commercial buildings
housing
folk house
traditional housing style
New England style
Cape Cod
Saltbox
Federalist (Georgian) style
I-house
stupa
pagoda
minarets
Wailing Wall
official languages
monolingual
multilingual
bilingual
linguistic region
dialect
word sounds
vocabulary
received pronunciation
Cockney
Cockney rhyming slang
pidgin
French Creole
patois

lingua franca
English
global *lingua franca*
language families
language groups
language subfamilies
prehistoric migrations
hearth
Anatolian theory
Hellespont
Kurgan theory
Eurasian steppe
folk music
folk song
folklore
popular culture
pop music
Appalachia
bluegrass
Roma or Romani
continental cuisine
haute cuisine
nouvelle cuisine
Mediterranean
fusion cuisine
folk food
Moroccan
social interaction
culturally constructed
greetings
handshake
bow
cheek kissing
personal space
religions (belief systems)
universalizing religions
ethnic religions
scripture
divine origin
doctrine
denominations
compromising religions
fundamentalists
animist tradition

Hindu-Buddhist tradition
polytheistic
nirvana
karma
Abrahamic tradition
monotheistic
shamans
migration diffusion
shamanism
caste system
Agamas
relocating
cosmology
dalits
varna
Imams
theocracies
head of state
republics
monarchies
Sharia
secular
Druze
Sikhs
Five Pillars of Islam
Aesop's fables
swidden
appellations
metes and bounds
long-lot patterns
township and range
ethnicity
race
racism
Melanesians
Polynesians
Micronesians
Aboriginals
indigenous population
mestizos
mulattos
Garifuna
Creole
environmental determinism
Friedrich Ratzel
Carl Sauer

possibilism
lebensraum
xenophobia
internal identity
external identity
culture regions
fuzzy borders
Dixie
border states
culture hearth
contemporary culture hearths
ancient culture hearths
staple food crops
contemporary culture region
Latter-Day Saints (LDS)
sequent occupance
acculturation
assimilation
indigenous
indigenous culture
preservation of cultural heritage
William Denevan
pre-Columbian
epidemics
terra preta
cultural survival
cultural globalization
proselytic religions
connection to nature
Treaty of Versailles
ethnic cleansing
Dayton Peace Accords
crimes against humanity
genocide
Holocaust

CHAPTER 5 DRILL
See the end of this chapter for answers and explanations.

1. Which of the following styles is associated with houses having one long pitched roof in front and a low-angle roof in back?

   (A) Cape Cod
   (B) Federalist
   (C) I-house
   (D) Georgian
   (E) Saltbox

2. Minarets are prominent in the architecture associated with which of the following religions?

   (A) Judaism
   (B) Buddhism
   (C) Islam
   (D) Christianity
   (E) Hinduism

3. Which system of land division relies on the use of natural landscape features?

   (A) Long lot
   (B) Caste
   (C) Township and range
   (D) Belief
   (E) Metes and bounds

4. An example of cultural synthesis would be

   (A) the practice of building a church upon the location of a mosque
   (B) the creation of a new style of music from the traditions of two separate groups of immigrant colonizers
   (C) a pidgin language that uses simplified vocabulary and verb conjugations
   (D) a village that has refined a single recipe for many generations
   (E) a system of rigid social classes inherited from colonial occupiers

5. The type of religious architecture that does NOT have a common design style is

   (A) Islamic mosques
   (B) Hindu shrines
   (C) Jewish synagogues
   (D) Christian cathedrals
   (E) Buddhist pagodas

6. The Altaic language family encompasses both

   (A) Turkish and Mongolian
   (B) Korean and Japanese
   (C) Yoruba and Zulu
   (D) Farsi and Urdu
   (E) Tibetan and Burmese

7. The Abrahamic tradition is most distinct from the Hindu-Buddhist tradition in

   (A) the willingness of Abrahamic devotees to slaughter members of other religions
   (B) the belief in a higher plane of existence
   (C) the belief in continued existence after death
   (D) the absence of the Abrahamic tradition from Southeast Asia and the Oceanic regions
   (E) the difference between monotheism and polytheism

8. All of the following are examples of Creole societies EXCEPT

   (A) Cape Verde
   (B) Seychelles
   (C) Louisiana
   (D) Brazil
   (E) Argentina

9. Contemporary architecture typically features all of the following EXCEPT

   (A) recycled materials
   (B) green energy technologies
   (C) nontraditional materials
   (D) symmetrical design
   (E) use of curvature

10. A *lingua franca* refers to

    (A) the use of French in the field of diplomacy
    (B) an archaic expression for French kissing
    (C) any language that is used as a bridge between speakers whose native languages are different
    (D) the difficulty of pronouncing French vowel sounds, particularly at the ends of words
    (E) the practice of acquiring a second language

11. All of the following are examples of products from appellations of origins EXCEPT

    (A) Champagne from France
    (B) maple syrup from Vermont
    (C) prosciutto di Parma ham from the Emilia-Romagna region of Italy
    (D) pizza from Naples
    (E) tequila from Mexico

CHAPTER 5 DRILL: ANSWERS AND EXPLANATIONS

1. **E**   A Saltbox home, (E), has one long pitched roof in front and a low-angle roof in the back. Make sure you qualify all of the clues in the question stem, as a Cape Cod house, (A), has a pitched roof, but not the other identifying features. Both Federalist, (B), and Georgian homes, (D), have rooflines that feature classical Greek and Roman designs, and an I-house, (C), has chimneys on opposite ends of an evenly pitched roof.

2. **C**   Mosques, places of worship associated with Islam, have one or more minarets, which are narrow towers that are pointed on top. Minarets are not a prominent feature in the architecture of the other religions, so (C) is therefore the only valid answer.

3. **E**   Land surveys that use natural landscape features to divide up land are a system of metes and bounds, (E). The long-lot system, (A), splits land into very long lots with narrow frontage along a road or waterway. The caste system, (B), is a social hierarchy system present in India. Township and range surveys, (C), split land into block shapes. Belief systems, (D), have to do with religions, which should pretty obviously be irrelevant to a land division question.

4. **B**   Cultural synthesis is the practice of blending together two or more cultural influences. Clearly bringing two styles of music together to form a new style of music falls under this definition—for example, the African rhythms and Scots-Irish song structures that blended to form American blues. Choose (B).

5. **C**   Mosques famously have minarets, while Hindu shrines have rectangular-shaped main bodies and short towers of carved stone. All cathedrals feature a steeple, bell tower, or a cross-shaped floor plan. Buddhist pagodas feature several levels with winged roofs. Jewish synagogues, however, follow no single design, perhaps because of the constraints of anti-Semitism throughout history. The correct answer is (C).

6. **A**   The Altaic language family, named after the Altaic Mountains, spans the entire Asiatic continent, including Turkey and Mongolia. Experts believe that both languages descended from a common proto-Altaic language that existed thousands of years ago. Korean was originally a spoken language, a linguistic isolate with a supposed background in Manchuria (northeast China), and Japanese is unrelated to both Korean and Altaic. Yoruba and Zulu are members of the Niger-Congo family, while Urdu is a descendant of Farsi, the Iranian language. Tibetan and Burmese are members of the Sino-Tibetan family. Choose (A).

7. **E**   While Buddhism is the religion most associated with non-violence, Buddhist monks have conducted several campaigns of slaughter, particularly in Myanmar. Both traditions believe in either heaven/hell or reincarnation, which can be defined as higher planes of existence and continued life after death. Lastly, the largest Islamic (meaning Abrahamic) country in the world is in Southeast Asia: Indonesia. Abrahamic religions are monotheistic (one god), while Hindu-Buddhist traditions are polytheistic (many gods). Choose (E).

8. **E** Defined as a people or culture that is derived from European, African, and local indigenous groups, Creole is found primarily in regions that were colonized by European powers using enslaved African workers. While Argentina was certainly colonized and populated by Spanish and Italians, its African slaves were either shipped to other countries or eventually died off. Likewise, the European colonists eradicated virtually all the native population. Today, the country claims 97% European descent. The correct answer is (E).

9. **D** Symmetrical design was typical of traditional architecture, going all the way back to the Greeks, the Romans, and up through more recent folk styles such as Cape Cod, Federalist, and I-house design. Contemporary designers such as Zaha Hadid and Frank Gehry reject it outright.

10. **C** The term *lingua franca* derives from the time when France was considered to be the most powerful cultural hub of the world. Civilizations around the world imitated its design, its food, its literature, its diplomacy—and so they used French as a language to communicate with speakers of other foreign languages because of its perceived high value. Today, it has been usurped by English as the global *lingua franca*.

11. **D** An appellation of origin is designated primarily to places that can boast a single product that is farmed or grown there, such as wine or tequila or ham. A pizza, because it's assembled out of many different ingredients in a kitchen and then baked, wouldn't qualify.

Summary

- Culture is made up of the shared experiences, behaviors, and practices of a group of people with a common heritage. The cultural landscape includes a wide range of traits and activities such as language, religion, folklore, and various forms of the arts.

- Languages can be organized into several major families—and from there, into groups—based on their prehistoric roots. Even within a single linguistic region, various dialects can carry drastically different accents and vocabularies. On the AP exam, these distributions and patterns may be depicted on maps, charts, or language trees.

- Religions may be characterized as ethnic or universalizing, depending on their expanse and openness:
  - Ethnic religions are limited to members of a particular culture group and are generally found near their hearths or spread by relocation diffusion.
  - Universalizing religions accept followers from all ethnicities and cultures, and so may spread by either expansion or relocation diffusion.

- There are three major world religious traditions which can be broken down further into major religious groups:
  - Animist religions are ethnic or tribal. They share common themes and practices, and engage in varying degrees of nature worship.
  - Hindu-Buddhist religions are polytheistic and believe that one's soul is reincarnated into different levels of existence.
  - Abrahamic religions are monotheistic, with emphasis on the prophesied coming or return of a messianic figure to save followers' souls from the forces of evil.

- Be sure you understand the difference between ethnicity—a blend of common genetic heritage and cultural identity—and race, which is the physical manifestation of a shared genetic lineage. The categorization of racial groups in the 1800s has been used to justify racist forms of oppression and suffering throughout the world.

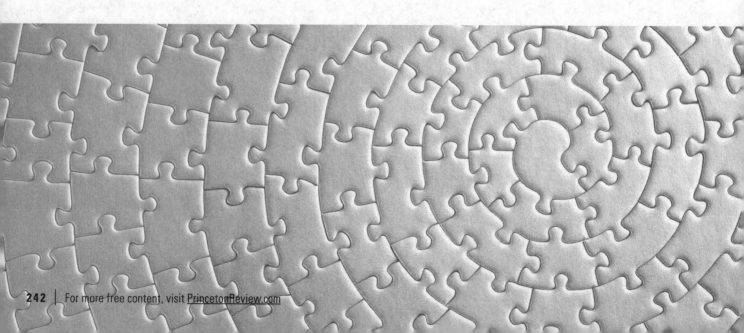

o   Cultural regions, unlike other types of regions, typically have fuzzy borders and may overlap. However, the shared cultural characteristics of a region contribute to a strong sense of place.

o   Language, religion, ethnicity, and many other aspects of society diffuse from cultural hearths. While we often think of the ancient culture hearths such as Mesopotamia, contemporary cultural hearths exist as well.

o   Cultural globalization has contributed to the tension between folk and popular cultures. Folk culture is based in the traditions of a specific region; popular culture is changeable and contemporary, and may diffuse globally. When this happens, the local folk culture can be threatened.

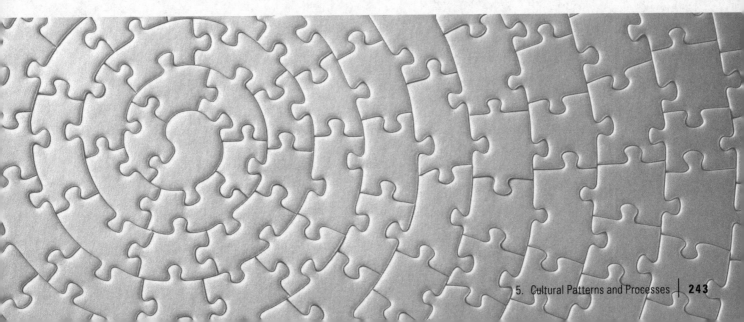

Chapter 6
Political Patterns and Processes

CHAPTER OVERVIEW

CED 4.1
Introduction to Political
Geography

This chapter is divided into two major parts: Know the Concepts and Know the Models. The concepts section contains examples of political state units and nationalism, the organization of states, spatial concepts and borders, electoral representation, political-economic systems, and finally, geopolitics. The models section details Mackinder's Heartland-Rimland model, Cohen's Shatterbelts, and Cold War containment theory.

KNOW THE CONCEPTS

UNITS OF POLITICAL ORGANIZATION

There are a number of political geography terms such as *nation* and *state* that we use in everyday speech as synonyms. However, the technical definitions of these terms have specific and important meaning in the geography of politics. Here's how to keep them straight:

Country: an identifiable land area
Nation: a population with a single culture
State: a population under a single government
Nation-state: a single culture under a single government

A nation is the same as a **culture group**. "State" implies that there is a **sovereign territory**. Sovereignty generally means that a state is fully independent from outside control, holds territory, and that it has **international recognition** from other states or the United Nations. Use these examples to keep the differences in your mind:

Nations	State Name	Country
England, Scotland, Wales, Northern Ireland, Isle of Man, and the Channel Islands	United Kingdom of Great Britain and Northern Ireland	Great Britain or the British Isles
Han, Manchu, Zhuang, Miao, Uygur, Tibetan, and others	People's Republic of China	China
Anglo-Canadian, Québécois, and First Nations	Canada (former name Dominion of Canada)	Canada
French, German, Italian, and Romansch	*Confoederatio Helvetica* (in Latin)	Switzerland (French: *Suisse*) (German: *Schweiz*)

These examples, the United States, and most other sovereign states are **multi-national states** made up of a number of different nations represented by the multitude of culture groups who have migrated and intermixed around the world. Multinational states, sometimes called **multiethnic states,** are most common in the Americas, where there are no nation-states.

CED 4.2
Political Processes

Nation-States

There are a number of nation-states in which one culture group is represented by a singular government. Many are smaller states or island countries. Although no nation-state is truly made up of only one cultural group, places such as Japan, Iceland, Tonga, Ireland, Portugal, and Lesotho (pronounced Lesu-too) are places that have not seen permanent invasion or mass immigration from other culture groups in their histories.

The term nation-state is also applied, theoretically, to multinational states where the state has come to represent a singular and contemporary culture, as opposed to the ancient cultures from which the population originates. One could argue that there is an identifiable American culture in the United States, or a unique Brazilian culture in Brazil. In both of these cases, the new political nation is the result of the blending of several culture groups together along with the idea of political nationalism.

Nationalism

Nationalism can derive from an existing culture group that desires political representation or independence, or from a political state that bonds and unifies culture groups. Politicians use nationalism as motivation to support the state and oppose foreign or other political influences. Individuals tend to take pride in their nationalist identities, even though they or their neighbors may be from a mix of different ethnic backgrounds.

Stateless Nations

Although many culture groups are politically represented or are part of larger political entities, there are some **stateless nations,** where a culture group is not included or allowed a share in the state political process. Here are a few examples.

Kurds are an ethnic group spread across northern Iraq, western Iran, eastern Syria, and southeastern Turkey. A semi-autonomous Kurdistan has existed in Iraq since the U.S.-led invasion in 2003. However, full independence is limited geopolitically due to Turkish government resistance to their sovereignty, based upon Kurdish Marxist rebels, the PKK, who have been fighting in Turkey for several decades. Since the start of the Syrian Civil War, Kurds have taken territory and started a semi-autonomous government.

Basques are an ethnic group in northern Spain and southwestern France who do not have Celtic or Latin cultural or language roots. In fact, their people's origin is poorly understood by historians. Spain has granted limited autonomy to the Basque region around the city of Bilbao, but many Basque nationalists seek full independence and statehood. A militant group, ETA, has used terror tactics to fight against Spanish rule.

Hmong are mountain peoples who have existed in rural highlands isolated from others in Laos, Vietnam, Thailand, and southern China. However, their alliance with the United States against the Communists during the Vietnam War caused many families to leave their traditional homeland. Today many Hmong (pronounced "mung") have resettled in the upper Midwestern states of Wisconsin and Minnesota. Hmong immigrants are featured in the 2008 film *Gran Torino*.

Other stateless nations include the Karen (primarily of Myanmar), Roma (or Romani), Karelians, Tartars, Tuvans, Chechens, Sami, Uygurs, Tibetans, and Tamils. Some groups have been granted limited autonomy, while others have active nationalist and independence movements. See the section on irredentism in this chapter for more on independence and sovereignty in the post-Soviet era.

| CED 4.7 |
| Forms of Governance |

ORGANIZATIONS OF STATES

The Big Fellas

Federal states and **confederations** are a common approach to government. The United States, Australia, Canada, Germany, Brazil, Russia, and Mexico are all confederations of several smaller states or provinces under a federal government. Like an umbrella, the federal state provides military protection, administers foreign diplomacy, and regulates trade as well as a number of internal administrative (executive branch), legislative, and judicial services across the country. The states each have their own governments, legislatures, regulations, and services. The overlapping roles in the administration may seem redundant, but each has its own division of responsibilities. For instance, the federal government regulates interstate trade, whereas states can make rules about the sale of goods within each state.

Many other states adhere to a **unitary** system with a single centralized government. While some power may be delegated to regional or local governments, the ultimate authority lies with the central government. The United Kingdom is one example: although Scotland, Wales, and Northern Ireland all have some degree of autonomy, that power is granted—and may be altered or overturned—by the British Parliament. Other states, such as Ireland, grant no subnational power at all. Many smaller states are able to adhere to the unitary system due to their size, but the largest unitary state by far is the vast People's Republic of China.

The Wee Fellas

At the other end of the international scale, **microstates** are sovereign states that despite their very small size still hold the same position as much larger states like the United States or Canada. Many are island states, ports, or city-states, or they sit landlocked with no access to the sea. The following table provides a list of microstates that are full members of the United Nations (UN):

State	Geography
Andorra	Landlocked
Antigua and Barbuda	Islands
Bahrain	Islands
Barbados	Island
Comoros	Islands
Djibouti	Port
Dominica	Island
Grenada	Islands
Liechtenstein	Landlocked
Luxembourg	Landlocked
Malta	Islands
Monaco	Port and City-state
Nauru	Island
Palau	Islands
St. Kitts and Nevis	Islands
St. Lucia	Island
Samoa (Western Samoa)	Islands
San Marino	Landlocked
Singapore	Port, Islands, and City-state

The Vatican City is also a sovereign microstate but is not a member of the UN. It is not a nation-state despite the common religion of its residents, who are mostly clergy drawn from around the world.

Autonomous Regions

Certain parts of certain nations have been granted freedom from central authority, usually for historical, geographical, religious, or linguistic reasons. These are known as **autonomous regions**, and they occupy a special place in human geography. For example, the Basque region of northeastern Spain boasts its own language, Euskara, which is thousands of years old and is unrelated to any of the Romance languages that surround it. The Basques are technically part of Spain but govern themselves, with little obligation to Madrid. **Semi-autonomous regions** have the same freedom as autonomous regions, but to a lesser degree.

Multi-State Organizations

Supranationalism is the concept of two or more sovereign states aligned together for a common purpose. A number of **supranational organizations** have been formed for the purposes of trade alliances, military cooperation, and diplomacy. The largest of these is the **United Nations** (193 member states) whose purpose is primarily diplomatic. The UN also provides a number of services internationally through its World Health Organization (WHO), Food and Agriculture Organization (FAO), Development Program (UNDP), International Children's Education Fund (UNICEF), peacekeeping forces, and other smaller directorates such as the UN High Commissariat for Refugees (UNHCR). Each of these units is an important supranational organization in its own right.

Detailed Example: The EU

Another important supranational organization with several purposes is the **European Union** (EU). In 2013, the EU grew to 28 member states with a small number of applicant states awaiting membership. The EU was named in 1991 under the Treaty of Maastricht, which expanded the organization's role beyond trade relations. Prior to that, the European Coal and Steel Community (created in 1957) helped strengthen steel production between Italy, France, Luxembourg, Belgium, and the Netherlands. The success of this limited free-trade network encouraged the development of the European Economic Community, "the Common Market" or EEC. By 1973, the EEC eliminated all tariffs on trade goods between its 12 Western European member states.

Today, the EU acts like a federal government for Europe but lacks some of the administrative aspects of other confederations like the United States. The modern EU serves five main purposes:

- **Free-trade union:** No taxes or tariffs are charged on goods and services that cross the internal borders of the EU. By eliminating these fees, European businesses can save money and be more economically competitive with the United States and Japan.

- **Open-border policy:** Between EU member states, there are no longer any border-control stations for immigration or customs inspections. People and commercial vehicles cross internal EU borders without stopping. This began with the **Schengen plan** in 1985 when West Germany, France, Belgium, Luxembourg, and the Netherlands opened their borders to one another. Workers can now take jobs in other EU states without applying for work permits (some professions may be protected from this).

- **Monetary union:** In 2000, the first EU members began converting to the Euro and phasing out their old forms of money. This eliminated the costs of currency exchange fees. Only 12 members retained their own currencies. The United Kingdom kept the British pound due to its high value—converting to the less-valuable Euro would have caused significant financial problems in the United Kingdom. New member states have to meet strict EU economic regulations before they can join the monetary union. However, the world financial crisis of 2008 revealed some weaknesses of the Euro as indebted countries were unable to devalue the Euro as they had been able to with national currencies. Countries like Greece, Ireland, and Portugal received bailouts as part of the Eurozone crisis. These events have forced countries to question the desirability of using the Euro currency.

- **Judicial union:** The European Court of Justice in Luxembourg provides a legal venue for cases between litigants in separate EU member states. With the increase in cross-border trade and labor, there were bound to be lawsuits and contract issues that would require the EU's decisions. In addition, a European Court of Human Rights has been established to preserve civil rights regardless of their member states' local laws.

- **Legislative and regulatory bodies:** The 751-seat EU Parliament was established to propose and approve laws within the union. The European Commission is a separate council with one seat for each member state. Each year the presidency shifts to one member state, allowing it to set the year's policy agenda. The European Commission also acts as the executive branch of the union to enact programs and enforce regulations set by the EU Parliament and Council. The EU Commission president is appointed by the European Council.

In sum, EU governance has been successful in creating a singular economy through free trade, open borders, free movement of labor, free exchange of currency, and a level playing field for business and labor in terms of laws and regulations. Instead of many small economies, the EU acts as one state economy that is highly competitive with China, the United States, India, the Association of Southeast Asian Nations, and Japan. In terms of gross domestic product (GDP), the EU had an economy of $17.1 trillion and China had an economy of $17.7 trillion as of 2021.

Something Rotten in Denmark?

Despite the economic success of the EU, a number of problems have emerged from the perspective of its citizens and member states. Even though free trade, open borders, and the Euro reduced the cost of doing business and reduced the cost of goods and services, the EU government's main source of revenue is a standard 20 percent sales tax, known as the **value-added tax (VAT)**. Many complain that the cost of EU governance has significantly increased the cost of many items in Europe. Member-state governments have also complained that the European courts have threatened the sovereignty of national and local courts and laws.

Likewise, open borders have made it difficult to control crime and terrorism. Once someone gets inside the EU's borders, he or she can move around freely regardless of citizenship, making it difficult to stop and apprehend criminals. Externally, the EU has had to strengthen its borders against undocumented immigration and the flow of contraband. The term **Fortress Europe** has been used to describe the concept of sealing EU borders. This is a rather difficult problem, since many of the eastern borders of the EU are undefended and only road and rail border crossings are inspected by immigration or customs officers.

In June 2016, the UK voted to leave the EU in a referendum commonly called "Brexit." Despite the EU's economic success, the issues of immigration, open borders, and British sovereignty in the face of an increasingly centralized European government led many voters to favor a split with the EU.

No Constitution for You! Yet...

In terms of further expansion of the EU system of governance, a **European Union Constitution** was proposed for ratification in 2004. The complex 65,000 word document was

You Need to Know the EU

The EU is a common topic in both the multiple-choice and free-response question sections. Make sure you are familiar with all things EU.

poorly understood by the citizens and members of parliament who had to vote on the constitution. Concepts like a common EU foreign policy among all states were unclear. Many voters and politicians were concerned about the continued loss of sovereignty for member-state governments. Political leftists saw the constitution as being too pro-business. And right-wing sentiment against Turkey in the EU also resulted in "No" votes against ratification. The constitution was voted down in the Netherlands and France in 2005, thus forcing the European Commission to go back to the drawing board.

Other Examples of Supranational Organizations	Purpose
North Atlantic Treaty Organization (NATO)	Military
Organization of Petroleum Exporting Countries (OPEC)	Oil Pricing Cartel
Organization of African Union (OAU)	Regional Diplomacy
World Bank and International Monetary Fund (IMF)	Government Loans

SPATIAL CONCEPTS OF POLITICAL GEOGRAPHY

Territoriality is the expression of political control over space. The concept of the state implies that the government controls land and the people who live there. **Citizenship** is the legal identity of a person based on the state where he or she was born or where he or she was naturalized as an immigrant. Keep in mind that when citizens go outside their state's political borders, they retain their citizen status and thus become an extension of their state (unless they apply for new citizenship as immigrants). This is why we strictly define the state as a population represented by a single government, without mentioning territory. However, don't forget that space matters; it's not much of a state if it has no land, which can happen in the case of a government in exile, such as the Dutch or Polish governments during World War II.

CED 4.3
Political Power and Territoriality

Political Borders

The borders between political states and political sub-unit areas (counties, parishes, parliamentary districts, and city limits) are strictly **finite lines**. Political boundaries, as expressions of political control, must be definable and clear. Sometimes the **physical geography**, such as rivers or other water bodies, defines boundaries, and sometimes borderlines are measured surveys based on treaties or other agreements between states. Non-physical boundaries often reflect **cultural divisions,** but these are not always accurate. Such borders can be the result of aristocratic land holdings from Feudalistic eras, or they can be the front lines at the cessation of armed conflict between states—however, treaties can change these lines.

Outside the Lines

Countries with large **expatriate** populations (citizens living outside of their borders) have to provide consular services in large foreign cities. Citizens living in foreign countries often have to visit their country's embassies or consulates to process legal documents, passports, and visa applications. When citizens get trapped in war zones or disasters in foreign countries, it's up to their government's diplomats and military to get them out.

Enclave and Exclave

Borderlines may be finite, but they can become quite irregular in pattern especially where the cultural borderlines become fuzzy. An **enclave** is a minority culture group concentrated inside a country that is dominated by a different, larger culture group. This could be as simple as an ethnic neighborhood or a large area such as Québec. As part of the 1994 Dayton Peace Accords, several enclaves were formally established within Bosnia to separate warring Serb, Croat, and Muslim communities.

An **exclave** is a fragmented piece of sovereign territory separated by land from the main part of the state's territory. Occasionally, neighboring states attempt to claim exclaves in the name of cultural nationalism. Often, armed conflicts result, but sometimes diplomatic negotiations result in official permanent exclaves. Other times, states purchase territory or receive fragments of territory under peace treaties. Islands are not considered exclaves. Examples of exclaves follow.

Exclave	Controlling State	Separated by
Alaska	United States	Canada
Point Roberts	United States	Canada
Kaliningrad (Koenigsberg)	Russia	Lithuania, Belarus
Nagorno-Karabakh	Armenia	Azerbaijan
Nakhchivan	Azerbaijan	Armenia
Cabinda	Angola	Dem. Rep. of Congo
Musandam	Oman	United Arab Emirates
Llívia	Spain	France
Ceuta and Melilla	Spain	Morocco

Water Borders at Sea

Historically, borders at sea were poorly defined, and each country had its own laws regarding where territorial claims began and ended. Often, more than one sovereign state claimed the same piece of water. This all changed in 1982 with the **United Nations Conference on the Law of the Seas** (UNCLOS), which proposed standard oceanic boundaries for all UN member states, and was fully ratified in 1994. The border system under UNCLOS is in the following two parts:

Territorial sea: Sovereign territory includes the area of sea from shore out to the 12-nautical-mile limit. Within 12 nautical miles, all the laws of a country apply.

Exclusive Economic Zone (EEZ): Exclusive economic rights from shore out to the 200-nautical-mile limit. Within 200 nautical miles of its shores, a state controls all aspects of natural resource exploration and extraction. This includes fisheries, oil and gas production, salvage operations, and permits for such activity. Two hundred nautical miles is beyond the shallow water **continental shelf** in almost all cases.

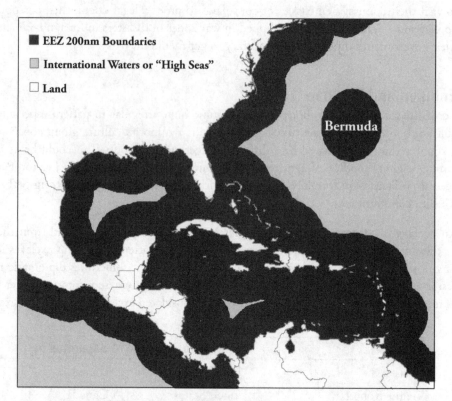

EEZ Boundaries and High Seas off the Eastern United States

The **high seas** are technically outside of the 12-mile limit. Past that line, cruise ships can open their casinos and ship captains gain the authority to marry couples or arrest thieves onboard their ships. These are provisions made under **admiralty law**, a part of international law that dictates legal procedures on the high seas. Beyond the 200-mile limit, international fishing fleets can hook or net whatever ocean life they choose and in unregulated amounts.

The only exceptions are when international treaties limit the capture of certain species. The 1986 **International Whaling Commission** moratorium on commercial whale hunts banned whaling after centuries of hunting dangerously depleted populations. Norway and Japan still hunt whales, claiming their hunts are for scientific research. This claim is heavily criticized by environmental organizations who state that whale meat still makes its way to market in these countries.

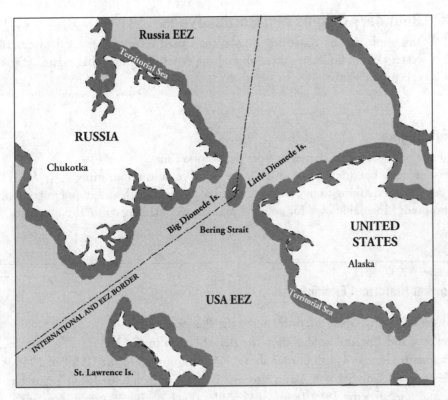

International Political Borders Compared to EEZs and Territorial Seas

Political Borders on the Map, Not EEZs

When you look at the map above, you can see that normal political boundaries and the real EEZ boundaries are very different. The cartographic borders are often rectangular around islands. In reality, territorial seas and EEZs create circular boundaries, especially around islands —each of which extends a country's EEZ out another 200 nautical miles.

Overlapping Borders at Sea and Disputes

The UNCLOS makes provisions for a UN **arbitration board** to settle disputes regarding boundaries at sea. Often, countries with overlapping sea claims generally agree to split the lines halfway. Where it becomes difficult is when uninhabited small islets, exposed reefs, and sandbars above water are claimed by more than one country. It can take years of negotiation to settle such disputes, and occasionally troops are deployed to precariously small pieces of land, just to claim rights to the surrounding EEZ. For example, two areas of the South China Sea, the **Spratly Islands** and the **Paracel Islands,** are claimed concurrently by China, Vietnam, Indonesia, the Philippines, Malaysia, and Brunei. Oil is believed to be under both island groups, and these are areas of potential future armed conflict if arbitration fails.

CED 4.4

Defining Political
Boundaries

Boundary Origins and Border Types

This topic can be confusing due to the varied terminology used to describe processes behind boundary creation and the types of borders that exist. Let's see if we can simplify this:

Boundary Origins

Antecedent: Boundary lines that exist from prehistoric times
Relic: Former state boundaries that still have political or cultural meaning
Subsequent: Lines resulting from conflict or cultural changes, such as war and migration
Superimposed: Lines laid down for political reasons over existing cultural boundaries

Important Historical Examples

Antecedent: French-Spanish border along the Pyrenees
Relic: Scotland-England border after The Act of Union in 1652
Subsequent: German-Polish border after 1945; Kaliningrad to the USSR in 1946
Superimposed: Sub-Saharan Africa after the Berlin Conference of 1884; Yugoslavia and Iraq after the 1919 Treaty of Versailles (Each of these resulted in recent conflicts.)

Boundary Process

Definition: When borders are claimed, negotiated, or captured
Delimitation: When borders are put on the map
Demarcation: When markers are placed on the ground to show where borders lie

It's Not (Just) What You Know...

Remember, it's not enough to simply memorize definitions. You must be able to relate concepts to historical and current events on the AP Human Geography Exam.

Border Type

Physical: Natural boundaries—rivers, lakes, oceans, mountains, or deserts
Cultural: Estimated boundaries between nations, ethnic groups, or tribes
Geometric: Boundaries surveyed mostly along lines of latitude and longitude

Border Disputes

Definitional: When border treaties are interpreted two different ways by states
Locational: When the border moves, like a river changing course or a lake drying up
Operational: When borders are agreed on, but passage across the border is a problem
Allocational: When a resource lies on two sides of a border. Who gets what?

Important Historical Examples:

Definitional: Russian-Japanese Kuril Islands under Soviet control in 1945
Locational: India-Bangladesh territory along the Ganges-Brahmaputra River Delta
Operational: New passport requirements for entry into the United States after
September 11, 2001
Allocational: Mexico-United States river allocations for irrigation and drinking water
on the Colorado River and Rio Grande (Rio Bravo)

Border Conflicts: Frontier War or Peace?

Historically, when land was either unexplored or unsurveyed, the term **frontier** was used to describe the open and undefined territory. There are a few disputed small frontier regions in the world today. The only remaining large land frontier is Antarctica, where the Antarctic Treaty (1959) has set aside the continent (actually several large islands covered by an ice cap) for scientific research and prohibits any military action and commercial mineral or energy extraction.

CED 4.8
Defining Devolutionary Factors

Peaceful Resolution to Border Conflicts

Prior to the 1846 Oregon Treaty that set the border at 49° North latitude, the western border between Canada and the United States was undefined. Much of the frontier region of what is today Montana, Idaho, Oregon, Washington, Alberta, and British Columbia was claimed concurrently by Great Britain and the United States. Diplomacy was the key to a peaceful settlement of the border dispute, but it nearly led to war as many in the United States were heard to say, "Fifty-Four Forty or Fight!"—the claim that the U.S. border should be 54°40' North. Not all parts of the world have been so lucky to resolve their frontier claims peacefully. In fact, many border treaties have led to violence later on.

Postcolonial Boundary Conflicts

An international example of a former frontier dispute that has led to conflict today is in Central Africa. The **Conference of Berlin** (1884) was a diplomatic meeting between the European colonial powers to set the internal political boundaries in Africa, which was one of the last areas of European colonial expansion. Most colonies were in coastal areas, but the interior of the continent had only recently been explored by Europeans. Diplomats at the conference went about carving up the continent's interior and settling disputed claims. The final agreed-upon map is very similar to the political boundaries in Africa today. However, there are many problems with the 1884 border design that did not emerge until after **decolonization** in the late 20th century. Most African colonial states achieved **self-determination** as fully independent sovereign states between 1960 and the early 1990s.

The main problem with the European-set boundaries in Africa is that they do not match the cultural boundaries. This **superimposed boundary** situation is what Africans refer to as the **Tyranny of the Map.** Instead of the large artificial nation-states that the Europeans envisioned, the reality is that political allegiance in sub-Saharan Africa is based upon tribal identity, and at a much smaller relative scale. The result within postcolonial African states has been that a number of tribes—some with long precolonial histories of conflict—have been grouped together into confined areas.

Tyranny of the Map Example: Rwanda

An example of one such postcolonial conflict zone is Rwanda, where in 1994 ethnic Hutus and Tutsis fought to control the small landlocked and mountainous country. Tutsis had migrated to the region some 400 years earlier, but upon independence from Belgium in 1962, Hutus went about **ethnic cleansing,** forcing many Tutsi refugees into the former Zaire and to Uganda. In 1994, after a plane carrying the presidents of Rwanda and neighboring Burundi was shot down, large-scale reactionary violence erupted by Hutus against local Tutsis, who were blamed for the crash. In response, Tutsi refugees flooded back into the country to fight back. In the end, each ethnic group lost around 500,000 people to the violent **genocide**.

CED 4.9

Challenges to Sovereignty

In the years following, Hutu versus Tutsi violence has spilled over to Burundi and eastern parts of the Democratic Republic of the Congo, where ethnic-based violence and fighting continue today. The Eastern Congo is seen by many researchers to be the next area of widespread **armed conflict in Africa**. Due to ethnic fighting in and along the Democratic Republic of the Congo and invasion by the armies of Uganda and Zambia, the region's 1884 borders are all but meaningless lines on the map. Other postcolonial frontier border disputes are highlighted in the following table.

Frontier	States in Dispute	Cause or Reason
Kashmir	India, Pakistan, China	Mountainous region and British Partition in 1948 (Remains in conflict)
Empty Quarter	Saudi Arabia, United Arab Emirates, Oman	Open sand dune desert (Rub al-Khali) (Saudis and Yemen settled in 2000)
Neutral Zones	Saudi Arabia, Iraq, Kuwait	Uqair Protocol of 1922 and open desert (Saudis and Kuwait settled in 1970) (Saudis and Iraq settled in 1991)

Territorial Morphology

The shape of a country is often what helps you identify it on a map. To some degree, the shape of a country also impacts its society and external relations with other countries. Here is a list of the major types of state **morphology** (shape):

Type	Description	Examples
Compact	Shape without irregularity	Nigeria, Colorado
Fragmented	Broken into pieces; archipelagos	Philippines, Newfoundland
Elongated	Appears stretched-out, long	Chile, Tennessee
Prorupt	Has a panhandle or peninsula	Italy, Michigan
Perforated	Has a hole(s) (country, large lake)	South Africa, Utah
Landlocked	Has no sea or ocean borders	Switzerland, Wyoming

The Swiss Navy?

Although Switzerland can register and flag **merchant ships**, due to its landlocked morphology, it has never had a navy. Humorously, the term "Swiss Navy" is either an oxymoron or pure absurdity. The latter appears to be the historical case. In the early 1990s, pilots from the Swiss Air Force were the first outside of the U.S. Navy and Marines to fly the F-18 Hornet aircraft. The United States gave permission for the Swiss Air Force to use all existing American F-18 training programs and facilities. For some this went as far as the ultimate in military flight training, carrier landing school. Upon completion of carrier training, some pilots were awarded certificates that had "Swiss Navy" printed on them.

Territorial Change

In addition to wars and other subsequent border changes, there are a few other ways in which state territory can change shape. Decolonization after World War II significantly reduced the area and number of territorial and colonial holdings of the European powers and the United States. Although most areas were granted independence, some colonial holdings were incorporated and residents integrated with full citizen status. Examples include Hawaii, Alaska, and the French *departments* of Guadeloupe, Martinique, Réunion, and French Guyana. Residents of these places have full voting rights, pay taxes, and receive benefits just like the other citizens of the United States and France.

Annexation is another term used to describe the addition of territory as a result of a land **purchase** or when a territorial claim is extended through **incorporation**. The United States originally purchased Alaska from the Russian Empire in 1867 for $7,000,000 in gold—a bargain of Manhattan-esque proportion—and it became a full state in 1948. The U.S. Virgin Islands resulted from a cash sale of St. Thomas, St. John, and St. Croix by a financially strapped Danish government in 1917 (during World War I).

Capitals

We can't forget that each state has to have a capital city. Why? There will always need to be a **seat of government** where political power is centered. In a way, political power is a form of currency just like money. And just as market areas need financial centers of exchange, politicians need a place to have organized exchanges of power. Occasionally they make laws and have elections, as well. Federal states can have several scales of capitals, just as they have several scales of sub-state units.

Federal State Example	
Place, Description	**Relative Scale**
Akron, county seat of Summit County, Ohio	Local, County, or Parish
Columbus, state capital of Ohio	State, Provincial, or Regional Scale
Washington, D.C., capital of the United States	National (nation-state), Federal

Most countries have one national capital, but some have more than one. Often this is done to share power across different regions of the country. Here are a few examples of countries with more than one capital:

State	Capitals
South Africa	Pretoria, Bloemfontein, Cape Town
Bolivia	La Paz, Sucre
Netherlands	Amsterdam, The Hague
Ivory Coast	Abidjan, Yamoussoukro

Occasionally countries change the location of their capital. Sometimes this is due to a shift in political power, or it can be due to congestion in the old capital. Some new capitals are often **planned capital cities,** which are located in places where cities did not previously exist:

Planned Capital City Examples		
New Capital	**Old Capital**	**State**
Washington, D.C.	New York City	United States
Brasilia	Rio de Janeiro	Brazil
Canberra	Sydney	Australia
Abuja	Lagos	Nigeria

Other capitals were moved to existing cities for political reasons.

Other Historical Capital Changes			
New Capital	**Old Capital**	**State**	**Reason**
Berlin	Bonn, East Berlin	Germany	Reunification
New Delhi	Kolkata (Calcutta)	India	Center of colony
Ankara	Istanbul	Turkey	Congestion, centrality
Moscow	St. Petersburg	Russia	Russian Revolution
Jerusalem*	Tel Aviv	Israel	Israeli annexation of West Bank

*Many countries do not officially recognize this and locate their embassies in Tel Aviv instead.

Electoral Politics and Internal Boundaries

CED 4.6
Internal Boundaries

Who Can Vote?

Suffrage in terms of age, race, and gender has varied historically from state to state. The Nineteenth Amendment to the U.S. Constitution granted American women the right to vote in 1920. Women in other parts of the world gained the right to vote in these selected examples:

Fun Fact
Did you know that the Twenty-Sixth Amendment lowered the voting age in the United States from 21 to 18 in 1971?

State	Year Women's Suffrage Granted
New Zealand	1893
Canada	1917
United Kingdom	1918 (but only after age 30 until 1928)
United States	1920
Mexico	1947
Honduras	1955
Paraguay	1961

In addition to gender, race has historically been a barrier to voting rights. Apartheid in white, minority-ruled South Africa, which racially segregated almost all aspects of life and residential geography, also denied the voting rights of non-white citizens. In 1994, the first full and free elections in South Africa resulted in the presidency of former political prisoner and civil rights activist Nelson Mandela, who was from the African Xhosa tribe (pronounced Ho-sah). This was the world's last case of official government restriction, or *de jure* (by law) restriction on voting due to race. However, in many countries there is still *de facto* (a matter of fact) racial and ethnic discrimination that restricts voting by minority citizens, via fear and intimidation tactics.

Voting for Local and Regional Representation

All democracies have some form of parliamentary system in which at least one lawmaking body or house has **popular representation.** Each country has its own system regarding the number of seats and the size of **voting districts.** In the United States, division of the 435 seats of the House of Representatives is apportioned relative to each state's population. Every state is divided into a number of congressional districts, each district having one seat in the Congress; California has the most, at 53, and the least-populated state, Wyoming, has 1. In the United Kingdom and Canada, members of parliament (MPs) are selected from local constituencies based upon population, but unlike in the United States, these are averaged from across the country. Due to its relatively dense population, Ontario holds 106 of the House of Commons' 308 MPs. Senators in Canada are appointed.

The Electoral College

In the United States, presidential elections are decided through voting by the **Electoral College.** After the November presidential election, electoral votes are assigned state by state in December, based on the popular vote in each state. Most states are "winner takes all," but a few, like Maine and Nebraska, split electoral votes in proportion to the popular vote. The number of electoral votes is based on the total number of representative seats, plus the two senators' seats from each state—the District of Columbia also has 3 electoral votes. It follows that California has the most electoral votes, with 55, and Wyoming the least, at 3. It takes at least 270 (> 50 percent) electoral votes to win the presidential election. If the candidates tie or have fewer than 270 due to a third party, then Congress chooses the new president.

Every ten years following the census, the United States **reapportions** the 435 seats of the House of Representatives. In many states, this generally causes some changes to the number of congressional seats and, as a result, the number of electoral votes a state has. If the number goes up or down (and sometimes even when the number doesn't change), state governments draw new congressional district borderlines to reapportion districts into equal-sized populations.

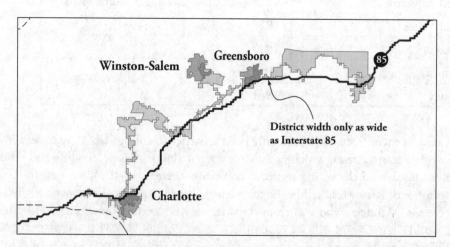

Map of the North Carolina 12th Congressional District

Gerrymandering

Sometimes reapportionment mapping is done in a straightforward manner with regional or compact districts. Other times the shapes of new or redrawn districts are very irregular. The irregularly shaped districts that are highly elongated and prorupt are often referred to as **gerrymandering**, named for Massachusetts Governor Elbridge Gerry who first attempted irregularly shaped districts in 1812.

In 1990 and 2000, a number of gerrymanders were attempted that tried to stack votes guaranteeing congressional support for one particular party within each district, making the outcomes of elections predictable and in the favor of the political majority in state government. Others were attempted that created "minority-majority districts," where lines were drawn to encompass only minority population centers.

In the 1992 case of North Carolina, Republican state leaders drew the new 12th district along Interstate Highway 85, connecting a number of African American communities along a narrow corridor over 200 miles long. The reapportionment was challenged in court and, in 1993, the U.S. Supreme Court found the redistricting unconstitutional, resulting in a redrawn district for the 1998 election cycle.

> ### Did You Know?
> A prorupted state is a compacted state with a large projecting extension, like Florida.

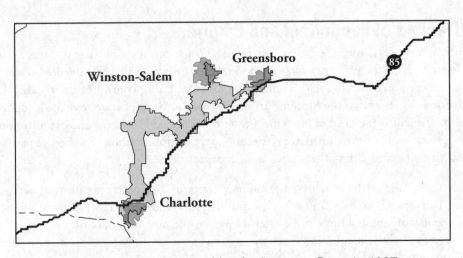

Redrawn Map Approved by the Supreme Court in 1997

POLITICAL ECONOMY

In terms of current and historical context, it is important to keep in mind the concept of political economy when you are discussing a country (especially on the FRQs). Why political economy? For one, it's often difficult to discuss the political situation in a state without explaining the economic aspects. In addition, these political-economic systems have important links to other parts of the AP Human Geography material. Here are the major categories to consider, with examples:

Feudalism and Its Decline

Feudal political economies operated with the vast majority of land and wealth being controlled by an **aristocracy**—a **peerage** of lords, earls, marquis, barons, dukes, princes, kings, and queens. Conversely, the vast majority of the population, as peasants, commoners, serfs, or slaves, were poor farmers and laborers who worked the land controlled by aristocrats. Peasants paid rent and had their harvests taxed for the right to live on and work the land. This system kept peasants in a cycle of debt, known as **debt peonage,** as they were never able to fully pay off rents and taxes.

Feudal states tended to have **absolute monarchy,** in which the supreme aristocrat, a king, prince, or duke, was both **head of state** and **head of government,** and therefore did not share power with anyone. Like medieval-style feudalism, the concept of absolute monarchy has diminished over time and mostly exists in the Islamic world. Only a few absolute monarchies exist today: Saudi Arabia, Brunei, Morocco (limited power-sharing), and emirates within the United Arab Emirates.

The Decline of Feudalism and Empires

Revolutions and wars from the late 1700s to the 1900s forced many feudal states to accept some form of democracy. Events such as the French Revolution of 1789 inspired many monarchs to accept power-sharing with commoners to avoid losing control of their states. Under **constitutional monarchy,** the supreme aristocrat remains head of state, but the leader of the elected parliament is the head of government, with integrated legislative and executive powers. In most cases, this is a **prime minister** or **premier,** who appoints senior members of parliament to be ministers or secretaries of executive-branch departments.

In most constitutional monarchies, the monarch retains the power to dismiss parliament; appoints judges, ambassadors, and other officials; is commander and chief of the military; and retains significant land holdings and estates. However, the monarch's political power is mostly diminished to a symbolic role, and he or she holds a small but important position in dictating policy and proposing laws.

Here are some examples of constitutional monarchies:

- Great Britain
- Belgium
- The Netherlands
- Japan
- Norway
- Denmark
- Sweden
- Spain
- Thailand
- Luxembourg
- Kuwait
- Jordan
- Bahrain
- Monaco
- Cambodia

Example: The British Aristocracy and Government

The current form of constitutional monarchy in Great Britain has been in place since the Magna Carta was signed in 1215. Feudalism has reigned throughout but, in the Magna Carta, there was some degree of power-sharing with the aristocracy and later with commoners voting in elections (1689).

Today, feudal rents to local aristocrats are still technically paid in a number of rural areas of the United Kingdom, although many are symbolic and small fees. A majority of Britons live in urban areas and are not subject to these fees. Many rural farms are now owned privately, though some may still be required to pay feudal rents.

The British aristocracy's structure and role has also been modified in recent years. Traditionally, aristocratic peers sat in the **House of Lords,** the upper house of parliament, which also serves as the supreme court. The House of Lords numbers more than 760 members. When the king or queen elevated someone to the peerage, a new seat was added. Eventually, they had too many members. Beginning in 1999, Queen Elizabeth II reformed the house with two types of members. Hereditary peers, who at death pass their title and seat to their firstborn son, were reduced in number and life peers, mainly senior public servants who were rewarded with a title, kept their title and seat for their lifetime only.

Since the late 1600s, the power of the **House of Commons**, the lower house of parliament, has steadily increased. The Commons has 650 seats apportioned to local districts across the United Kingdom; Scotland, Wales, and Northern Ireland also have regional parliaments of their own. The Prime Minister (PM) is head of government, but is also a member of parliament (MP). Generally the PM is the political leader of the party with the most MPs. Other senior MPs from this **ruling party** serve as ministers of the executive branch of government. This is another example of how parliamentary democracy integrates the three branches of government.

Commonwealth Countries

Most, but not all, member states of the **Commonwealth of Nations** (independent former parts of the British Empire) retain the British monarch as their head of state. These commonwealth countries have their own parliaments and prime ministers as head of government. Each also has a royally appointed governor-general as the crown representative in the country. The governor-general's role, like the monarch's, is mostly a symbolic and ceremonial position. These countries are nonetheless considered independent sovereign states. Yet they do retain some minor political link to the United Kingdom—most provide military support to the United Kingdom in times of war. The following countries claim the British monarch as head of state:

- Canada
- Jamaica
- Dominica
- St. Vincent and the Grenadines
- New Zealand
- Australia
- Fiji
- Papua New Guinea
- Belize
- Guyana
- Bahamas
- Antigua and Barbuda
- Grenada

India, Pakistan, Sri Lanka, Nigeria, and Kenya are a few of the commonwealth members that do *not* claim the British monarch as head of state. However, all commonwealth nations have parliamentary governments, which integrate executive, legislative, and judicial powers, like that of Great Britain. In addition, the Commonwealth of Nations is an important supranational organization that provides special trade, education services, government funding, and preferred immigration status between member governments and citizens.

Some former colonies are now dependent territories (not sovereign states) of the United Kingdom. They are not Commonwealth members but are still controlled from London with limited local governance. These colonies include Anguilla, Cayman Islands, Turks and Caicos, British Virgin Islands, Bermuda, Montserrat, the Falkland Islands, St. Helena, and Ascension Island.

Political Economy: Free-Market Democracy

Generally, countries with elected-representative parliamentary systems such as the United States, the United Kingdom, commonwealth countries, and other constitutional monarchies or republics are classified as **free-market democracies**. Internal to a state, this system generally relies upon balancing the relationship between the elected-representative government, its citizens, and business interests. In most cases, there is a variable system of regulation and taxation by the state. As a result, the marketplace is not totally free, as it would be in a completely unregulated *laissez-faire* economic system, but it's close enough.

Government regulatory influence of the private lives of its citizens and practices of businesses is usually limited to areas concerning public safety and economic protections. The point of democracy is that people have a say in who makes the rules and thus have some influence over the rule-making process.

What's a Republic?

Without going too deeply into your AP Government material, keep in mind that France, Germany, Italy, and many former colonial states are technically republics, under the broader category of free-market democracy. Some republics, like France, are centrally governed from a single capital. Others, like Germany or the United States, are confederations that apportion some government power of legislation and administration to their component states or provinces (*Lander* in Germany). The main thing to keep in mind is that **republics** are free of aristocracy or monarchal control. The governments are fully under the control of the "common" people, as opposed to hereditary monarchy. By this definition, neither Canada nor Australia are republics, since both still recognize the Queen of England as the unelected, hereditary head of their states. On the other hand, another former British colony, Barbados, became the world's newest republic in November 2021 when it officially removed Queen Elizabeth as its official head of state and elected its first president, despite having been independent since 1966.

Unlike parliamentary systems that assign legislative, executive, and judicial power to the same people, republics generally have a **separation of powers.** Here, the executive, legislative, and judicial branches of government are held by separate groups of people that keep each other in check. This may seem less efficient, but it reduces the potential for corruption of the whole government. If one branch's leadership fails or its practices are called into question, the other branches can act to correct problems or replace leadership if necessary.

Problems Within Republics

This is not to say that republics are perfect systems, as you might feel if you read too much Plato. The written **constitutions** of these governments need to be flexible enough to allow governments to deal with political and other crises when they occur. The United States has had two constitutions, the former being the Articles of Confederation, which did not work out. The French have had five different types of government since the revolution, and the current government system in France is known as the "Fifth Republic." There is no perfect constitution, but a constitution can be refined over time by the addition of amendments. Another problem is that wealthy businesspeople and corporations have replaced the aristocracy in terms of the control of money, land, and resources. Their personal and corporate **political influence** overshadows that of many thousands of private citizens. The purchase of political favoritism to influence the setting of regulations is a constant problem in republics, as it is in other democracies, especially within the legislative branch. This has created uneven power relations in free-market democracies.

Another type of separation that is sometimes employed to blunt the **power of the executive branch** is to have separate presidents and prime ministers (or chancellors in Germany). In the United States, Mexico, and Argentina, the president is both head of state and head of government. In most other republics, there is executive separation. Depending on the country, this can be done in a couple of ways. In France, the president is head of government and the prime minister is head of state, but it's the opposite in Italy. Ay! There are too many variables to keep straight, but make sure to know a couple of examples.

Political Economy: Marxist-Socialism

Under **Communism**, Karl Marx's political-economic theories attempted to right the wrongs of feudalism and inequalities of capitalism in free-market democracies. One of the main goals of **Marxism** was to create a class-free society where there were no inequalities in terms of wealth or power. To do this, the state would own all land and industry, the government would direct economic productivity, and everyone would earn the same amount of money regardless of labor position.

The key to this working was the **planned economy**, which did not rely on supply and demand like capitalism. The central government would calculate the economic needs of the state, its industries, and people. Then the government would set **quotas** for each individual operational unit of agricultural or manufacturing production to meet these needs. Theoretically, the productivity of the economy would result in a collective wealth that would be shared equally across the population. It's a utopian ideal that the system should create a harmonious peaceful social existence, but Communism in practice failed to reproduce Marx's utopia.

What Happened with Communism?

You may have heard the statement, "A good idea in theory but not in practice." This is true for Communism. Marx died in 1883 and the first Communist country, the Union of Soviet Socialist Republics (USSR or Soviet Union), was established in 1917 with the fall of the czar's absolute monarchy in Russia. This time gap is significant. Had Marx seen how his ideas were put into practice, he'd have "blown a fuse," "had a cow," "had kittens"—pick your own analogy. On a free-response question, you could describe him as upset or disapproving.

There were a number of unintended consequences to the Russian revolution, including a protracted and bloody civil war, human rights violations, murders on the part of the Communist government, and forced resettlement of over a million citizens. Despite all this, Soviet Communism emerged functioning under Marx's basic principles. Under Stalin, the USSR developed **Five-Year Plans,** which were comprehensive long-term economic plans that dictated all production in minute detail. In the 1930s, when the rest of the world was suffering through the poverty of the Great Depression, the Soviets were doing comparatively well.

However, 50 years later the USSR was falling apart. The **devolution** of the Soviet system was due in part to several political-economic problems in the USSR. One thing that would have caught Marx's eye was that, in reality, **three classes of Soviet citizens** emerged early in the Soviet Union. Most were workers, as Marx had envisioned his **proletariat.** However, to achieve an important position in Soviet society, such as that of a government official, professor, or factory manager, you had to join the **Communist Party**. Party members made up about 6 percent of the USSR population and enjoyed many perks such as special stores, nicer homes, and personal cars. Likewise, a **military officer class** emerged that had a similarly high quality of life in comparison to the regular working class.

Working-class people were resentful. But what could they do? Heavy-handed secret police and laws that made public protest punishable by hard labor in prison camps (known as *gulags*) kept open criticism to a minimum. Creative, inventive, and industrious people stagnated. Another reason for this was that there was a **lack of incentive** in the system that would motivate people to have better lives. It didn't matter if you were a brain surgeon or a garbage man; you got the same monthly pay. Sure, there are some perks to being a doctor, but were these enough to struggle through examinations and years of training with no financial reward? This was a problem.

The lack of incentive also affected economic productivity. Neither farms nor factories had any reason to produce more food or products than what was stipulated in government quotas. This resulted in a **lack of surplus**, leaving many stores with few items on the shelves and lines of people waiting to receive rations for food and clothing. More details about the effects of the Cold War on the devolution of the USSR are ahead in this chapter.

These problems have also plagued other communist countries, and now only two cases of Soviet-style Communism remain: Cuba and North Korea. Despite the historic restoration of diplomatic relations between Cuba and the United States in 2014, Cuban president Raul Castro continues to declare Cuba a communist state. To see what has happened with economic reforms in Communist China and Vietnam, see Chapter 9.

What About the Socialism Part?

The positive things that came out of Communism were mainly in the realm of infrastructure and social welfare. Health care is a good example. Prior to Communism in the Soviet Union, China, and Cuba, there had been almost no health care available to the common people. Socialism meant that everyone had a right to health care, and hospitals, clinics, and rural traveling doctor programs were established early on. Similarly, infrastructure programs for public schools, free universities, drinking water, care for the elderly, and public transit were established to improve the efficiency and quality of life in communist society. It may not look glamorous today, but it successfully replaced the utter poverty that existed under the former feudal and corrupt capitalist societies in these countries.

These socialist successes impacted the non-communist world as well during the latter 20th century. Government leadership and control of health care, education, and pensions are Marxist-socialist ideals which have since been incorporated in Western free-market democracies like Canada and Great Britain.

GEOPOLITICS

The term **geopolitics** refers to the global-scale relationships between sovereign states. Here are a number of other important geopolitical issues that you need to be prepared for on the exam.

Centrifugal and Centripetal Forces

These are two terms that students mix up all the time. Here are the definitions and a way to remember which one is which:

CED 4.10
Consequences of Centrifugal and Centripetal Forces

- **Centripetal forces** are factors that hold together the social and political fabric of the state. Think *pedals make a bike go.*
- **Centrifugal forces** are factors that tear apart the social and political fabric of the state. Think *a centrifuge separates blood into its different parts.*

Centripetal and centrifugal forces are a favorite topic for both multiple-choice and free-response questions. Make sure you know the difference!

In every country, there are a number of forces at work that both reinforce and destabilize the state. When the balance shifts too far in the category of centrifugal forces, the survival of the state is at risk and indicates the likelihood of **armed conflict**—in the form of an **internal civil war**, or the possibility of conflict spilling over into **external cross-border war**. Centripetal forces come with their own set of consequences—while we're quick to think of the positive outcomes such as a sense of unity and a well-run economy, an overabundance of centripetal force may lead to nationalistic movements and xenophobia.

Examples of Centripetal Forces:	Examples of Centrifugal Forces:
• Political beliefs of nationalism • A strong and well-liked national leader • An effective and productive economy • Effective government social welfare programs	• Ethnic, racial, or religious differences or conflicts • Political corruption • Failing economic conditions • Natural disasters or a wartime defeat

Example: Yugoslavia

As we mentioned in the Cultural Conflicts section of Chapter 5, Yugoslavia was an artificial state created after World War I that had several different ethnic and religious groups living within its borders. The post–World War II communist leader of the country was the Croatian Josip Tito. As a Croat who fought alongside Serbians against the Nazis, Tito was a good choice as president. He became a centripetal force representing the two largest ethnic groups in the country. A strong nationalist belief in Communism among Yugoslavians helped Tito build an economically strong and socially harmonious multiethnic society. These were additional centripetal forces that held the state together.

When Tito died in 1980, the lack of an effective multiethnic leader to replace him created a political **power vacuum** that opened the way for different nationalist leaders representing different ethnicities to attempt to seize power for themselves and their constituents. These disparate groups not only differed in ethnicity and religion, but also shared a history of conflicts and warfare.

These differences became powerful centrifugal forces that ripped apart the Yugoslav social and political fabric and, in combination with the fall of Communism in Europe, doomed the country to ethnic violence and dissolution. In a way, you can think of Tito's death as a centrifugal force in itself.

The Cold War's a Hot Exam Topic

The theme of political-economic conflict between democracies and communist countries during the Cold War (1945–1991) is a common topic of geopolitical questions on the AP Human Geography Exam. This will be covered in more detail in the Know the Models section at the end of this chapter.

Balkanization and Irredentism

The case of the former Yugoslavia is also an important example of **balkanization**. This is due to the fact that Yugoslavia sits in the Balkan Peninsula, which has historically been divided among a large number of ethnic and religious groups. The term *balkanization* refers to a situation in which the political landscape goes from a larger state to several smaller states. In the last 100 years of European history, the continent has geopolitically gone from being dominated by large **empire states** to being dominated by several small **nation-states**. In 1909, there were 27 sovereign states in Europe; today, there are 50.

After World War I, many of the early cases of balkanization were due to a realignment of German borders and the dissolution of the Austro-Hungarian Empire into six sovereign states. After World War II, some borders changed but the number of states changed only slightly. It was after the fall of Communism in Eastern Europe and in the Soviet Union in 1991 that the political landscape began to break apart.

Examples of Balkanization		
Old State (end date)	**New States**	
Yugoslavia (1991–2008)	Slovenia Croatia Serbia Bosnia-Herzegovina	Montenegro Macedonia Kosovo (disputed)
Czechoslovakia (1993)	Czech Republic	Slovakia
Austro-Hungarian Empire (1918)	Poland (part) Czechoslovakia Hungary	Austria Yugoslavia (part) Liechtenstein
USSR (1991)	Russia Belarus Ukraine Estonia Latvia Lithuania Moldova Georgia	Armenia Azerbaijan Kazakhstan Uzbekistan Tajikistan Kyrgyzstan Turkmenistan

Irredentism as the Cause of Balkanization

Irredentism tends to follow one of two definitions: when a minority ethnic group desires to break away from a multiethnic state and form its own nation-state, or break away and align itself with a culturally similar state. Almost all of the cases of balkanization discussed in the previous section fall into these two categories. Cases of irredentism continue, and Russia is one of the most significant situations where a number of groups are seeking independence or annexation by a neighboring sovereign state that is culturally similar.

Chechnya is one such place. Chechens, like more than 25 other **autonomous republics** in Russia, were granted limited local self-governance by the Russian Federation. However, Chechens are ethnically Turkic peoples who are predominantly Muslim—very different from Slavic, Eastern Orthodox Christian Russians. It stands to reason that both religion and ethnicity are the centrifugal forces in this case.

Soon after the fall of Communism, Chechens began to declare independence from Russia. As a result, the Russian government moved in troops and a regional armed conflict has ensued. Russia fears the loss of oil resources and pipelines in the region, but a larger geopolitical issue looms. If Russia were to allow Chechnya to become independent or be annexed by Azerbaijan, then many of the other autonomous republics would push for secession, leaving the Russian Federation without much of its current land and resources.

Recent Irredentist Conflicts		
Location	Island of Timor	Ossetia
Irredentists	East Timorese (Catholic)	South Ossetia (Muslims)
Resistant State	Indonesian (Muslim)	Rep. of Georgia (Christian)
Status	Independence in 2002 after UN intervention with Australian peace-keeping troops	Russian military as of 2008 protects the Ossetian autonomous region in Georgia

Reunification

In a few irredentism cases, nations or culture groups were torn apart into separate states as a result of war or other historical events. In the post-Cold War era, there have been a few cases of **reunification** of note: (East and West) Germany, Yemen (North Yemen and Yemen Democratic Republic), and the return of the Canal Zone to Panama. Some places, such as China/Taiwan and North/South Korea, occasionally talk of reunification, despite the potential for armed conflict.

Speak Softly and Carry a Big Stick

Neocolonialism, meanwhile, describes a contemporary form of colonialism—one based not on political control, but on *economic pressure*. Exhibit A: The United States of America. While it possesses very few political territories, it has long waged economic control over nearly every nation in the Western Hemisphere, often by granting favored-nation trade status to those neighbors who play by its rules. This type of power is often used by developed countries to control developing countries and their precious resources.

The best current example is China. That rising superpower has been busy building neocolonial control over many African nations. It does so via Chinese state-controlled corporations that dole out valuable construction contracts—new ports, new roads, etc.—to those African leaders willing enough (or desperate enough) to do China's bidding.

KNOW THE MODELS

HEARTLAND-RIMLAND MODEL

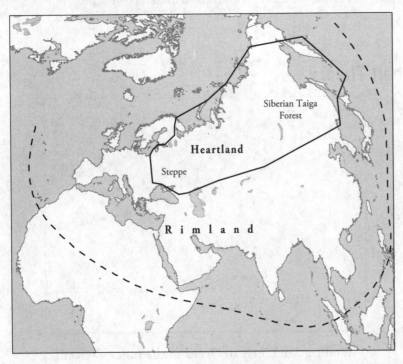

The Agricultural and Resource Heartland Is Surrounded by Rimland

The main geopolitical model in the AP Human Geography course encompasses both world wars and the Cold War. In 1904, British geographer Halford Mackinder proposed what would become known as the **Heartland-Rimland model**. Mackinder's model was an effort to define the global geopolitical landscape and determine areas of potential future conflict. He identified agricultural land as the primary commodity that states were interested in. Several states with limited land area wanted to expand their territory—as they had done by expanding their colonial empires. However, they also eyed one another's European farming areas.

The largest of these was the **Eastern European steppe**, a very productive area of grain cultivation mostly controlled by the Russian Empire at the time. This, combined with the mineral and timber-rich region across the Urals into Siberia, was identified by Mackinder as the **Heartland.** It was this portion of the Earth's surface that states bordering **Rimland,** such as the German Empire, the Austro-Hungarian Empire, and Romania, might potentially invade. The Rimland also contained other **landwolves** eager to grab at neighboring territory, such as France and Italy. Likewise, there were **seawolves,** such as Great Britain and Japan, who would use their navies to leverage geopolitical power.

Predictive Power of the Model

In effect, Mackinder accurately predicted the battle lines of the Eastern Front during World War I. In 1921, he revised the model, expanding the Heartland further into Central Europe. In essence, Mackinder stated that the same geopolitical situation remained, with land still being the primary **commodity of conflict**: the thing that countries were willing to fight over.

From 1904 onward, Mackinder points out that the areas of future conflict are the borderlines between the Heartland and Rimland. This prediction comes true again with the 1931 invasion of Manchuria by the Japanese, which some Asian scholars identify as the actual start of World War II. The European border conflict areas in the model are also realized with the 1939 German invasion of Poland, a country within the redrawn Heartland.

Shatterbelt Theory

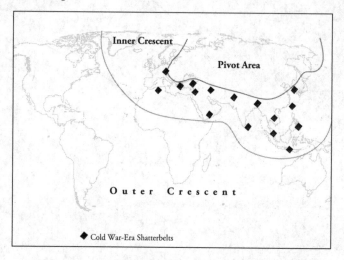

Conflicts Are Likely to Occur in the Inner Crescent

The Cold War: Shatterbelts and Containment Theory

Mackinder died in 1947, but his legacy lived on in Cold War-era geopolitical models and theory. In 1950, American geographer Saul Cohen proposed the **Shatterbelt theory**. He modified Mackinder's Heartland into the **Pivot Area** and Rimland into the **Inner Crescent.** The rest of the world became the **Outer Crescent,** including the United States. His land-based concept was that Cold War conflicts would likely occur within the Inner Crescent. He pointed out several Inner Crescent areas of geopolitical weakness that he called Shatterbelts. Like Mackinder's earlier predictions, Cohen's Shatterbelts accurately identified numerous areas where wars emerged between 1950 and the end of the Cold War in 1991.

Containment Theory

Some of these conflict areas were ones that the Soviet Union and the People's Republic of China would attempt to capture to create **buffer states,** lands that would protect them by creating a surrounding buffer of sympathetic countries. Influenced by Mackinder and Nicholas Spykman's theoretical work, U.S. diplomat George Kennan first proposed the strategic policy of **containment** to the American government in 1947. In this proposal, the United States and its allies would attempt to build a containment wall around the core communist states. Anytime the USSR or China attempted to expand the realm of influence politically or militarily, the forces of NATO and other democratic state allies should be deployed to stop them.

This was a successful strategy at first, and communist movements were thwarted in Greece, Iran, and Malaysia. At the same time, West Germany, Italy, and Japan were rebuilt as industrialized free-market democracies as part of the containment wall, under the Marshall and MacArthur Plans. However, communists reached a military stalemate in Korea in 1953, and won military victories against the French (1958) and Americans (1975) in Vietnam. These combined with quick communist takeovers of Hungary (1956), Czechoslovakia (1969), as well as Angola (1975), Cuba (1959), and Nicaragua (1979) were evidence of containment theory's limitations put into practice, as communism spread even to parts of the Outer Crescent.

The United States and allied states had to contain these Soviet-supported **satellite states** to prevent Communism from spreading further. They feared a **domino effect,** where one state would fall to Communism and then inspire and support communist uprisings in neighboring states.

Containment's Long-Term Success

Despite the failings of the containment approach, Communism was limited to a large degree to the Pivot Area and a number of buffer states. The containment effort had a devastating effect on the economy of the Soviet Union and its allies. At certain points during the Cold War, it is estimated that upwards of 50 percent of the USSR's gross national product was focused on military production and other activities to support the expansion of Communism. This stressed the Soviet economy to the breaking point and created further shortages of food and consumer goods for its citizens, which in turn created further problems within Soviet society and the communist government.

For more political geography material, see *Key Concepts in Political Geography* by Carolyn Gallaher, Carl T. Dahlman, Mary Gilmartin, Alison Mountz, and Peter Shirlow.

By the 1980s cracks began to appear in the social fabric of the USSR. Numerous dissidents publicly criticized the government's expansion efforts and costly nuclear arms arsenal. Similarly, the mothers of the Red Army soldiers killed in the **War in Afghanistan** (1979–1989) publicly protested in the streets of Moscow, despite the potential of arrest and deportation to Siberia. They learned that not even the most coldhearted communist leaders could jail the mother of a soldier killed in action. Continuing the containment tradition, monies spent by the United States in the 1980s to arm Afghan Mujahideen rebels with arms, including Stinger shoulder-launched anti-aircraft missiles, paid off in the end with Soviet troops returning in defeat. This was a centrifugal force that reverberated throughout the USSR, and its government fell two years later in 1991.

Terrorism

Which is harder to do, define "terrorism" or prevent it? Both are proving to be very challenging. The use of terrorism—planned violent attacks on people and places to provoke fear and cause a change in government policy—is as old as time. **State terrorism** occurs when governments use violence and intimidation to control their own people. Roman armies attacked Carthage in 146 B.C.E. and totally destroyed the city and its inhabitants. They even threw salt on the fields so no food could be grown. Nazi Germany, the Stalinist Soviet Union, and Pol Pot's regime in Cambodia are all sad examples of state terrorism during the 20th century.

CHAPTER 6 KEY TERMS

country
nation
state
nation-state
culture group
sovereign territory
international recognition
multinational states
multiethnic states
nationalism
stateless nations
Kurds
Basques
Hmong
federal states
confederations
microstates
supranationalism
supranational organizations
United Nations
European Union
free-trade union
open-border policy
Schengen plan
monetary union
judicial union
legislative and regulatory bodies
value-added tax (VAT)
Fortress Europe
European Union Constitution
territoriality
citizenship
finite lines
physical geography
cultural divisions
expatriate
enclave
exclave
United Nations Conference on the
  Law of the Seas
territorial sea
Exclusive Economic Zone (EEZ)

continental shelf
high seas
admiralty law
International Whaling Commission
arbitration board
Spratly Island
Paracel Islands
antecedent boundaries
relic boundaries
subsequent boundaries
superimposed boundaries
definition
delimitation
demarcation
physical border
cultural border
geometric border
definitional border disputes
locational border disputes
operational border disputes
allocational border disputes
frontier
Conference of Berlin
decolonizaton
self-determination
superimposed boundary
Tyranny of the Map
ethnic cleansing
genocide
armed conflict in Africa
morphology
merchant ships
annexation
purchase
incorporation
seat of government
planned capital cities
suffrage
popular representation
voting districts
electoral college
reapportions
gerrymandering

aristocracy
peerage
debt peonage
absolute monarchy
head of state
head of government
constitutional monarchy
prime minister (premier)
House of Lords
House of Commons
ruling party
Commonwealth of Nations
free-market democracies
republics
separation of powers
constitutions
political influence
power of the executive branch
Communism
Marxism
planned economy
quotas
Five-Year Plans
devolution
three classes of Soviet citizens
proletariat
Communist Party
military officer class
lack of incentive
lack of surplus
geopolitics

centripetal forces
centrifugal forces
armed conflict
internal civil war
external cross-border war
power vacuum
balkanization
empire states
irredentism
Chechnya
autonomous republics
reunification
Heartland-Rimland model
Eastern European steppe
Heartland
Rimland
landwolves
seawolves
commodity of conflict
Shatterbelt theory
Pivot Area
Inner Crescent
Outer Crescent
buffer states
containment
satellite states
domino effect
War in Afghanistan
state terrorism

CHAPTER 6 DRILL
See the end of this chapter for answers and explanations.

1. An identifiable land area is known as a

   (A) country
   (B) nation
   (C) state
   (D) nation-state
   (E) culture group

2. Which of the following is NOT a primary purpose of the European Union?

   (A) Allow free trade amongst member countries
   (B) Institute open-border policies within the union
   (C) Establish a monetary union amongst member countries
   (D) Reduce the threats of terror cells in member countries
   (E) Propose and approve laws within the union

3. Allocational border disputes occur when

   (A) border treaties are interpreted two different ways by states
   (B) a border moves due to geographical changes
   (C) cultures argue over different religious locations
   (D) borders are agreed upon, but physically crossing the border is troublesome
   (E) a resource lies on two sides of a border

4. The Basque people, who live in both Spain and France and who speak their own ancient language called Euskadi, would be described as an example of

   (A) a confederation
   (B) a stateless nation
   (C) a supranational organization
   (D) a nation-state
   (E) a sovereign territory

5. The border system for oceanic boundaries is divided into

   (A) high seas and low seas
   (B) national waters and international waters
   (C) physical borders and geometric borders
   (D) territorial seas and the Exclusive Economic Zone
   (E) antecedent boundaries and superimposed boundaries

6. The Kashmir region of India is primarily known for

   (A) its allocational border dispute
   (B) its postcolonial frontier border dispute
   (C) its unusual territorial morphology
   (D) its annexation of Pakistan
   (E) its planned capital city

7. North Korea is one of the few remaining examples of a

   (A) feudal economy
   (B) free-market economy
   (C) Marxist-socialist planned economy
   (D) balkanized political system
   (E) reunified society

8. According to the Heartland-Rimland model, a region with a strong agricultural belt would also have

   (A) a region with an equally strong manufacturing sector
   (B) a political movement demanding annexation of surrounding states
   (C) an Inner Crescent and an Outer Crescent
   (D) a predatory neighboring state eager to grab the fertile territory
   (E) a policy of containment of one's geographic enemies

9. The border between India and Pakistan, a country that was formed during the Partition of 1947, would be an example of a type of boundary that is

   (A) antecedent
   (B) relic
   (C) subsequent
   (D) superimposed
   (E) temporary

10. An example of annexation is

   (A) Hitler's invasion of Poland
   (B) Thomas Jefferson's Louisiana Purchase
   (C) King Leopold II of Belgium's arrival in the Congo
   (D) the monastery at Angkor Wat
   (E) the construction of the Great Wall of China

11. All of the following are examples of a centrifugal force EXCEPT

   (A) the success of the U.S. Federal Emergency Management Agency under President Clinton
   (B) the Japanese defeat in World War II
   (C) the falling value of Argentina's currency
   (D) Venezuela's Hugo Chavez firing ten thousand civil servants who opposed him
   (E) the vandalization of Jewish cemeteries

CHAPTER 6 DRILL: ANSWERS AND EXPLANATIONS

1. **A** An identifiable land area is known as a country, (A). Eliminate both (B) and (E) because they refer to populations with a single culture, not location. A state, (C), sounds good, but the term is primarily used to represent a population under a single government, which makes it a weaker answer that can be eliminated; the same goes for a nation-state, (D), which is a single culture under a single government.

2. **D** The European Union serves five main purposes: to establish a free-trade union, allow open-border policies, create a monetary union, establish a judicial union, and establish regulatory bodies to propose and approve laws within the union. Accordingly, (A), (B), (C), and (E)—which are correct—can be eliminated. Reducing the threats of terror cells in member countries, (D), is not a primary purpose of the EU.

3. **E** Allocational border disputes occur when a resource lies on two sides of a border, (E). Choice (A) refers to a definitional border dispute, (B) refers to a locational border dispute, and (D) refers to an operational border dispute. As for (C), it refers to religious conflict and can also be eliminated.

4. **B** A stateless nation exists wherever a cultural group is prohibited (or prohibits itself) from joining in the state political process. The Basque region of Spain has very limited sovereignty but is seeking full independence. Choose (B).

5. **D** The territorial sea is defined as all water 12 miles out from land. It belongs to that country, and the country's laws apply. From shore to 200 miles out is the EEZ, in which the country owns the exclusive rights to natural resource exploration and extraction—fish, oil, etc. The correct answer is (D).

6. **B** The mountainous region of Kashmir, in the north of India, has been hotly contested by India and Pakistan ever since the famous British Partition of 1948, which resulted in the largest mass migration in human history. Both countries consider it an integral part of their societies, and for years Kashmiri insurgents have risen up against the Indian government over the question of autonomy. Choice (B) is the correct answer.

7. **C** North Korea is one of only two centrally planned Soviet-style Marxist economies remaining. North Korea was originally founded shortly after World War II with support from newly Communist China. Today, the central state, controlled by the Kim regime, still controls all food production and distribution—which means, lately, people are getting only two meals a day. There are signs that this is beginning to change, particularly with the arrival of private markets. Cuba is the other such economy. Choose (C).

8. **D** According to the model, the Heartland (agriculture) would always be surrounded by other states that sought to annex it. McKinder called these states the Rimland. A good example would include the Ukraine, long known as the breadbasket of Europe, and controller of the port of Crimea. Russia unilaterally annexed the Crimean peninsula in 2014, and then invaded Ukraine outright in February 2022, alienating itself overnight from almost every nation in the world. The correct answer is (D).

9. **D** A superimposed boundary is a line that has been laid down for political reasons on top of cultural boundaries. The Partition was famous for being the largest forced migration in human history—nearly 15 million people, mostly Muslims living in India, were forced to move across an imaginary border.

10. **B** Annexation is a term used to describe the addition of territory as the result of a land purchase or when a territorial claim is extended through incorporation. Clearly, Jefferson's purchase, which doubled the size of the United States, qualifies. Illegal invasions and edifices themselves do not qualify as annexations.

11. **A** A centrifugal force is any factor that tears apart the social and political fabric of a society. Those forces can result from racial or religious differences, political corruption, poor economic conditions, or wartime defeats. The only answer that indicates a factor holding together the fabric of society is a strong governmental reaction to a natural disaster.

Summary

- A nation-state is one identifiable cultural group represented by a single government.

- Some culture groups are identified as stateless nations because they are denied a share in the state political process due to ideological or ethnic conflicts.

- Supranationalism is the alliance of two or more states for a common purpose, such as trade agreements, military cooperation, diplomacy, and other factors. The largest supranational organization is the United Nations; others include the European Union and NATO.

- Political boundaries are clear and definable. They often—but not always—coincide with cultural boundaries. When they don't, conflicts can erupt.

- Internal boundaries, such as voting districts, influence elections at various scales. Gerrymandering is the creation of irregularly shaped voting districts in an attempt to stack votes to favor one political party.

- Major forms of political economies include feudalism, free-market democracies, and Marxist-socialist systems such as Communism.

- Centripetal forces are generally positive factors that hold together a state's social and political fabric. They may be uniting forces in the economic, political, or cultural dimension.

- Centrifugal forces are mostly negative factors that tear at the state's social and political fabric. They may originate from economic, political, or cultural conflicts. When they become too strong, the likelihood of armed conflict and devolution increases.

- The Heartland-Rimland model and Shatterbelt theory defined the geopolitical landscape and accurately predicted areas in which conflict was likely to break out.

Chapter 7
Agriculture and Rural Land-Use Patterns and Processes

CHAPTER OVERVIEW

First we will go through the general concepts of the geography of agriculture. Then we'll discuss several revolutions in global agriculture to give the necessary historical perspective on innovations in farming. This is followed by a section on contemporary issues within specialized agriculture. At the end of the chapter is a detailed presentation on the sole model in agricultural geography, von Thünen's Model.

KNOW THE CONCEPTS

The Links Across Human Geography

Agriculture is one of the activities that makes up the **primary economy**, which also includes timber, fisheries, and mineral and energy resources. These other areas are discussed in Chapter 9, "Industrial and Economic Development Patterns and Processes." Agriculture is connected to the **demographic transition model** and **Third-World countries**. In stage two of the model and in the Third World, agriculture is the primary mode of economic productivity. That means that in stage two and in the Third World, the majority of the population is engaged in agriculture for **employment** and the majority of the countries' **gross domestic product (GDP)** comes from the sale of agricultural products.

Concepts: Intensive Versus Extensive

Agricultural activity can be classified by how concentrated the labor and area of activity is for a particular type of farming. There are two main classifications:

- **Intensive agriculture:** Requires lots of labor input, or is focused on a small plot of land, or both

- **Extensive agriculture:** Requires limited labor input, or is spread across large areas of land, or both

Pre-agricultural Society

CED 5.3
Agricultural Origins and Diffusions

The earliest forms of agriculture emerged from **hunting and gathering societies** in prehistoric times. These peoples traveled the land, making seasonal migrations to areas where food and water were periodically abundant. This is the concept of **transhumance,** where groups moved seasonally not only to avoid harsh climates, but also to follow animal herds and walk to areas where native plants were in fruit. This activity is associated with stage one of the demographic transition model.

Animal Domestication

Hunting of animals eventually led to the live capture and eventual domestication of cattle, horses, pigs, donkeys, sheep, goats, reindeer, llamas, alpacas, and water buffaloes. These herd animals could be raised for meat or milk, or used as draft animals to carry or pull loads and plow fields. Birds that were captured, domesticated, and kept for meat and eggs included chicken, turkey, guinea hen, duck, goose, and pigeon.

The domestication of herd animals led to **pastoralism**, or agriculture based on the seasonal movement of animals from winter to summer pastures and back again. Also known as **nomadic herding**, in this practice, whole communities would drive their herds from one seasonal grazing area to another following an annual cycle that was repeated over centuries. Over time, a tradition of **ranching**, or grazing livestock in a single large area, has evolved in some places such as the American West. Don't forget the domestication of dogs to help in driving and protecting livestock. Just a few border collies can replace the work of several human shepherds.

Plant Domestication

Seasonal migrations to different plant habitats revealed fruits and grains that could be harvested from wild plants and trees. The seeds of these plants could be replanted along seasonal migration routes to provide food during transit. Eventually, people learned to domesticate and grow more abundant plants, which led to more permanent and organized farm settlements. Over time, other plant **cultivars** were added to these early farms so that there were a variety of crops. People used the plants for food, and used plant fibers to make clothing out of flax and cotton. Plant and animal domestication is discussed further in the section First Agricultural Revolution later in this chapter.

Subsistence Farming

The **multi-cropping** approach was more secure than single-crop **monoculture**. If one crop failed or was damaged by pests, another crop would provide a backup food supply. However, monoculture became common in the era of early political civilization and empires, when farms produced a **staple crop** in large order to feed whole societies and armies with a basic carbohydrate. Grain staple crops, like wheat, also dried on the stalk and could be preserved. These, along with tubers and root vegetables such as rice, potatoes, and yams, could be kept in dry storage for many months before being cooked or ground into flour to make bread.

Early crop farmers added domesticated animals to their holdings, resulting in **mixed farming**. This is also referred to as **general farming**, where multiple crops and animals exist on a single farm to provide diverse nutritional intake and non-food items, such as bone for tools and leather for different materials such as saddles, rope, and coats.

Intensive mixed farming that provides for all of the food and material needs of a household is commonly called **subsistence agriculture**. A single farm can produce staple grain crops, fruits, and vegetables along with meat, eggs, milk, wool, and leather, having animals pull plows during planting and loads during harvest. Essentially all the daily needs of the household could be provided for on the farm. This allows people to settle permanently and subsist without having to migrate seasonally. Even when most of the farm's production is focused on staple crops to pay taxes or fulfill government quotas, other plants and animals are grown to fulfill the subsistence needs of the farming family.

Extensive subsistence agriculture occurs when there are low amounts of labor inputs per unit of land. This is more likely to occur in less-populated regions such as South America or in less-habitable areas where pastoralism is common, such as Siberia or Sahelian Africa (the dry grassland areas just south of the Sahara Desert).

Today, most subsistence agriculture is usually very intensive and done on small plots of land. In much of the Third World, the **physiologic density**, or number of people per unit of **arable land** (farmable land), is very high compared to the First World. This means that more people have to be fed off of much less land in the Third World. This makes many rural communities much more susceptible to famine from drought or armed conflicts.

Food Preservation

Subsistence practices require farmers to have knowledge of plants, animals, soils, and climate and the ability to preserve foods for long-term consumption and for times of need. **Food preservation** via drying, pickling, cooking, and storage jars has been a necessity for survival for thousands of years. It has also led to many cultural variations in food consumption.

As a result, many **specialized crops** were grown for both immediate consumption and preservation. For example, cabbages soaked in saltwater were buried in clay storage jars to make *kimchi* in Korea starting eight thousand years ago. Likewise, cucumbers were grown in Eastern Europe and preserved in either lime or salt water to make pickles. Meats are preserved by drying, smoking, sugar-curing, or salting for long-term preservation. These storage and preservation techniques did not require refrigeration—don't forget that we have had refrigerators only for the last one hundred years.

Specialized and Nutritious (for Long Life)

Over time, people learned that certain foods lead to improved health. What they didn't know was the science of nutrition. For example, pickled cabbages such as sauerkraut and *kimchi* are an important source of vitamin C. People didn't know this, but they did know they didn't get scurvy when they ate them. Today we are dependent on citrus, such as orange juice, to provide vitamin C. Imagine what it was like in earlier times when nutrients were harder to come by. Link this to what you know from the demographic transition model in stages one and two, where people have poor nutrition and, as a result, much lower life expectancies.

Non-Subsistence Agriculture

The opposite of intensive subsistence farming is **cash-cropping** to sell farm goods at market. This is a form of extensive agriculture in which harvested crops are exchanged for currency, goods, or credit. The credit is then used to buy equipment or seed for the next planting season and in part to buy food, clothing, and other necessities for the farm family. The **commercial crops** are transported, sold at other markets, and finally preserved or processed into other goods for sale. That describes small-scale cash-cropping, but large-scale corporate operations also engage in non-subsistence farming. In addition, farming under communism was also done on a non-subsistence basis, with much of the food grown being produced collectively in farm communities and distributed across the country.

Communism and Agriculture

Throughout much of human history, wealthy landholders and aristocrats (in **feudal** political economies) owned most of the arable land. Yet, these people made up only a small part of the population, around 5 percent. This meant that upwards of 90 percent of the population were peasants, serfs, and sometimes enslaved people who farmed land that they never owned. Peasants were forced to pay rent to farm land that sustained their families and produced goods for the landowners. In the late 1700s, both the American and French revolutions rejected this system that had created a large **income disparity** between rich and poor.

In the late 1800s, armed with knowledge from Karl Marx and Friedrich Engels's *The Communist Manifesto* (1848), peasants staged uprisings in Eastern Europe that called for a rejection of not only aristocracy and landlords, but also the whole capitalist system. The Russian Revolution in 1917 had a number of political and military causes combined with a crisis of poverty in many rural Russian farming communities. The prescribed solution under the Marxist-socialist political economy was the collectivization of farms and elimination of privately owned land. The **communes** that resulted were large farms where several families were organized as labor units. The land was owned collectively by the whole state. Similar collectives and communes were established in Eastern Europe, China, and other Soviet satellites after World War II.

How the Communist System Worked

The collectivization of agricultural production often had the initial effect of leading to food shortages due to disorganized production networks. However, over time, farming communes began to produce crop yields similar to those in capitalist economies. Communes were assigned **quotas** by the government that detailed exactly how much each farm should produce each year. Falling short of the quota meant government reprisals and penalties, but making the quota was met with celebrations and awards.

The main problem with this system, compared to the capitalist system, was that there were no **incentives** to produce over the quota or produce other crops or products outside the mandated crop, which usually encouraged monoculture. The result was a system that had no surplus food and not much variety available to consumers. Stores and food shops tended to have very limited supplies of basic food products, and lines often formed in front of stores for items like bread and toilet paper. Fruits and summer vegetables were a rarity. The lack of surplus was exacerbated by the heavy food demands of the Soviet military. In times of regional drought, food had to be transferred from other areas, causing nationwide shortages.

These and other problems combined to cause the downfall of Soviet Communism in 1991. See Chapter 6 for more on this subject.

Human Ecology: Farming Techniques

CED 5.1
Introduction to
Agriculture

The term **human ecology** is used to describe human interactions with nature. Earlier geographic research in the 1940s and 1950s focused primarily on the "man to land relationship" specific to farming. *Human ecology* as a term has since fallen out of favor, and now the broader term *human-environment interactions* is more commonly used to describe forestry techniques, fisheries, and environmental regulation in addition to farming practices.

Our ecological relationship to the land can be conceived of as a **food web** in which each type of crop and animal is dependent on a number of human inputs, soil and climate conditions, and other crops. The term **food chain** describes the order of predators in the animal world and is also used to describe several integrated human and mechanical inputs, from developing seeds to planting, fertilizing, harvesting, processing, packaging, and transporting food to market and finally to your dinner plate.

Much of what you need to know for the exam has to do with specific farming practices. The following section provides a number of key words in relation to farming practices.

Types of Cropping

Crop rotation occurs when one crop is planted on a plot of land and then switched to another plot in subsequent years. The rotation cycle will vary back and forth due to one or more factors. Soil nitrogen quality is a common factor in North American farming. Corn is a heavily nitrogen-dependent plant and often requires artificial fertilizers to maintain soil quality. However, soybeans "fix" nitrogen in the soil, meaning the roots of soy plants emit nitrogen back into the soil. Farmers can rotate between corn and soybeans, thus saving money since they won't have to buy as much fertilizer.

Multi-cropping involves the planting of more than one crop on the same plot of land. In contrast to monoculture, this is an intensive strategy in which either crops are planted together simultaneously or one crop is planted right after another in the same row. For instance, after summer vegetables are harvested, winter vegetables and cold-tolerant plants like kale and spinach can be planted and harvested before the freeze. **Double cropping** implies planting two crops one after another on a single plot in a year, and **triple cropping** means three crops in the same year. These practices often rely on fertilizers and irrigation, especially in dry-land growing areas such as Southern California's Imperial Valley.

Growing Seasons

Each crop has its own specific **growing season**, but the general rule is to plant in spring, grow in summer, and harvest in fall. However, some crops have variations, such as spring wheat and winter wheat. **Spring wheat** follows the normal growing season. It is planted in the spring and harvested in late summer. Spring wheat is grown in northern areas such as Minnesota, the Dakotas, Alberta, and Saskatchewan. By comparison, **winter wheat** is grown in more southern areas of the Great Plains, where ground freezing is less likely. Winter wheat is planted in the fall, lies dormant in the winter, and then grows in the spring to be harvested by the start of summer. Kansas, Oklahoma, and Colorado make up most of the winter wheat production in the United States.

Irrigation Agriculture

The practice of **irrigation** opens up more land to cultivation than would normally be possible in arid climates. Irrigation agriculture is responsible for close to three-quarters of world freshwater use and up to 90 percent of freshwater use in the most poverty-stricken countries of the world. Governments often heavily subsidize irrigation agriculture with the result that the crops produced are often worth less than the water. The Nile Valley in Egypt is an example of heavily subsidized irrigation agriculture. Unfortunately, the water for these irrigation farms comes from underground water tables called aquifers. These **aquifers** are being depleted at a rapid rate and large-scale grain-producing countries such as India, China, and the United States are examples of those caught in this predicament.

Sustainable Farming

Farming practices can be criticized for their dependence on external inputs such as fuel and agricultural chemicals like pesticides and fertilizers, and the effects of farming on soil erosion and local water usage. As soils become depleted and water becomes the Earth's most precious commodity, a new movement has grown and spread to conserve and protect these resources. **Conservation** is the practice of preserving and carefully managing the environment and its natural resources. A new method of farming, **conservation agriculture**, has become increasingly important as a way of providing a sustainable farming system without sacrificing crop production. One of the methods used involves not plowing the soil (called "no-tillage") so that soil erosion is greatly reduced and soil fertility is increased by retaining natural vegetation. Crop rotation and inter-planting are two other methods used to increase soil fertility and discourage pests. **Inter-planting** means planting fast-growing crops alongside slow-growing crops. Inter-planting allows a farmer to harvest the fast-growing crop before the slow-growing crop shades it out. **Sustainable yield** describes the amount of crops or animals that can be raised without endangering local resources such as soil, irrigation, or groundwater, or it describes what can be raised without too many expensive inputs that would make farming unprofitable. Thus, **sustainability** can be viewed in both environmental and economic terms. Either way, by reducing inputs and using ecologically sound methods, farmers can reduce the risk that their farming practices may lead to long-term environmental or economic problems.

Non-Food Crops

Not all agriculture is done to create human food; a number of crops are raised for industrial use, **textiles** (clothing), or **animal feed**. Cotton and flax have long been used to make cloth and linens. Soybeans have been used since the 1950s to make paints, ink, and synthetic polymers like nylon. Even the parts of animals that are not eaten are utilized to make products like leather (animal skins), soaps (from fats and bone meal), and organic fertilizers (fish parts).

Alternative energy crops have become important as oil prices have increased over time. Since the 1970s, corn has been used to make **ethanol**, an alcohol that can supplement gasoline and make it burn cleaner. In the last few years, demands for wholly alternative vehicle fuels have opened markets for corn-based E85 ethanol fuel to replace gasoline and be used in "flex-fuel" vehicles. In Brazil, a large percentage of cars run on sugar cane-derived alcohol fuels that have reduced the country's dependence on oil imports. Likewise, **biodiesel** from soybeans and vegetable oils (even waste oil from fryers) has become an alternative to petroleum-based diesel fuel for trucking in the United States, Canada, and Europe.

Shifting Cultivation

In many parts of the agricultural Third World, farming occurs in environmentally sensitive areas such as tropical rainforest or dry grasslands. Traditionally, **slash and burn agriculture** (also known as **swidden**) has occurred in tropical rainforest regions with farmers shifting from one plot of land to another every few years as soil nutrients become depleted. Land abandoned by farmers was allowed to **fallow**, and natural vegetation would return and increase the nutrient biomass of the area. This cycle of cutting and fallowing has occurred throughout human history and, until the population explosion of the 20th century, was ecologically sustainable because of the small number of active areas. Today, slash and burn is considered unsustainable due to the large amount of forest land burned.

The Problem of Tropical Deforestation

CED 5.10

Consequences of Agricultural Practices

Contrary to popular belief, rainforest soils are very poor due to the water and nutrients in the environment being sapped up by the natural vegetation. When rainforest is cut today, large trees are sold to logging companies and the remaining vegetation is burned to create a nutrient layer of ash atop the soil. People who have moved to the forest to claim their own land and escape overcrowded cities in countries like Brazil or Indonesia often discover that they can farm for only a few seasons before soil nutrients are sapped or eroded by heavy tropical rains. The forest settlers often have to sell their farms to cattle ranchers and move to another plot of land to continue the cycle. The problem is that tens of thousands of farm families are now doing this, which puts dangerous pressure on a very sensitive and valuable natural resource. Rainforests are often considered the lungs of the Earth because of the large amounts of oxygen produced and CO_2 consumed by trees.

Desertification

Extensive pastoralism, the shifting of animal herds between grazing pastures, has remained popular in several arid parts of the world, especially Africa, the Middle East, and Central Asia, where dry grassland is the common landcover. The contemporary problem is similar to that of rainforest destruction, since too many people and too many animals are placing **population pressure** on too little land. **Overgrazing** has led to significant amounts of dry grassland being denuded, eroded, and as a result, desertified. **Desertification** is any human process that turns a vegetated environment into a desert-like landscape. In addition to overgrazing, deforestation and **soil salinization** can also lead to desertification.

Soil Salinization

One of the risks of farming in dryland and desert regions is that the evaporation of water can trap **mineral salts** on the surface soil layer. High daytime temperatures cause water vapor to be drawn out of irrigated farmland. As evaporation continues over several growing seasons, the amount of mineral salt can build to toxic levels and poison crops. The land has to be either abandoned or flooded by about 18 inches of fresh water over a couple of months to draw out the salts. Fresh water, though, tends to be expensive and in short supply in these dry areas.

Agricultural Practices: Cultural Views and Available Resources

Agriculture is not divorced from culture, since cultural practices affect how food is grown. For example, religion plays a role in determining agricultural practices, given pray-for-rain scenarios that Western farmers are familiar with. Religion can affect agricultural trade as well. Dietary restrictions can limit the trade of beef (to India, for example) or pork (to Islamic societies).

Family history plays other types of roles in agriculture. For instance, first-generation farmers may view planting differently than second- or third-generation farmers, since they have less received wisdom to depend on. The first-generation farmers are therefore more likely to be open to innovative ideas—as are societies in which technological progress is seen as a virtue.

Furthermore, culture determines different levels of societal support for farmers, many of whose fortunes often rise and fall based on the weather. Countries with larger governmental safety nets tend to support farmers in a more socialistic manner, while countries with smaller safety nets don't.

Agricultural practices, too, change based on available resources. In water-scarce regions, irrigation becomes necessary. In water-abundant regions, flooding is a concern.

KNOW YOUR AGRICULTURAL HISTORY

The Agricultural Revolutions

Think of these revolutions as significant innovations in farming. These new farming methods are important since they often reduced the amount of labor needed to produce goods and increased the amount of goods harvested per unit of land. Relate these practices and technological innovations to the Know the Models section on criticism of Malthusian theory in Chapter 4.

Note that these revolutions did not occur all at once. Instead, these changes occurred in different places at different times. The general historical pattern is that revolutions began in one place and diffused around the world over time—sometimes an innovation could take many decades before being adopted elsewhere. In fact, there are still a few hunting and gathering societies found today, such as the Bushmen of the Kalahari in Southern Africa and the highland tribes of Papua New Guinea, who are untouched by these changes.

First Agricultural Revolution

After thousands of years of humans hunting, gathering, or fishing for food, people transitioned to an organized form of farming. The prevailing theory of early farming is **vegetative planting,** where the shoots, stems, and roots of existing wild plants were collected and grown together. Later on, this became **seed agriculture**, where the fertilized seed grains and fruits of plants were collected and replanted together.

Over time, early farmers rejected the poorly growing crops, and took cuttings or seeds from the more productive, better-tasting plants to grow future generations. The **domestication of plants** took place in this way. Domestication led to early forms of **horticulture**, where plant varieties that thrived in different soil or climate conditions were cultivated. Specific varietals were selected for different sizes, colors, flavors, foliage, and fruit. As a result, regions of agriculture emerged where certain crops were grown under optimal conditions for the specific cultural tastes of the area's inhabitants.

The areas where most of this early agricultural activity originated are called **hearths of domestication,** which just so happen to have been located in or around the ancient culture hearths we discussed in Chapter 5. (Remember those?)

An Ideal Husband

Animal domestication also took place in different areas at different times in history. Just as with plants, wild breeds were first taken captive. The most productive of these were purposely interbred or hybridized to be reproduced through **animal husbandry.** The diffusion of animal hybrids was also specific to certain regions—those with specific climatic and natural vegetative conditions that allowed them to thrive.

Geographic Considerations

The **growing areas** of crops and livestock expanded as domesticated varieties were traded and diffused across the landscape. However, there were geographic limits to this diffusion. Keep in mind that most plants grow in particular habitats. These growing areas are usually defined by the amount of rainfall and temperature range. In temperate climates, the growing season of many vegetables and fruits is also limited by periods of freezing. And there were cultural limits to crops and animals that did not meet the tastes of certain societies.

Early farms produced at a very small scale and were mainly for the subsistence of the family or local community. Until the 1900s, the vast majority of the world's population lived in rural farming areas and was dependent upon local crop production to survive. This type of farming was a labor-intensive form of farming, especially compared to the commercial mechanized farming of today. Relate this to what you learned from the demographic transition model in Chapter 4. In stages one and two, birth rates are very high because children are seen as additional farm labor. The more children you had, the more labor that could be done, and the larger the herd or area of land that could be farmed.

The Columbian Exchange

There's another important historical event in the history of agriculture that you need to know for the AP Human Geography Exam. With the conquest of mainland Central and South America in the early 1500s, a number of domesticated New World crops made their way to the rest of the world through **relocation diffusion.** We call this the **Columbian exchange**, as it is historically symbolized by diffusion that occurred after the voyages of Christopher Columbus. Animals also diffused during this time, but mostly in the opposite direction from plants. Many Old World animals made their way to the New World. Explorers took animals to the New World and brought plants back with them. Here are a few agricultural examples of the Columbian exchange:

New World to the Old World	Old World to the New World
Maize (corn)	Wheat
Cayenne pepper	Rice (initially red rice from Africa; later Asian white rice)
Bell peppers	Coffee
Potato	Apples
Tomato	Citrus
Manioc (tuber also known as yuca or cassava)	Horses
Tobacco	Cattle
Rubber	Hogs
Peanuts	Chickens
Cacao (chocolate)	Sheep
Turkeys	Goats

The Second Agricultural Revolution

From the beginning of the Industrial Revolution in the late 1700s, technological changes in agriculture were enabled by parallel innovations in manufacturing. Devices such as Whitney's cotton gin in 1793 or the McCormick reaper in the 1830s drastically reduced labor requirements and increased the scale of farm production.

> **CED 5.4**
> The Second Agricultural Revolution

However, bigger changes came in the mid-1800s to early 1900s with the development of specialized **hybrids**, artificial **chemical fertilizers**, early **chemical pesticides,** and **mechanization** in the form of trucks, tractors, and pumps. **Tractors** were originally driven by steam and then in the early 1900s by the internal combustion engine. They were used to plow, plant, fertilize, and harvest crops, and they radically eliminated the need for large numbers of farm laborers. Combine harvesters that remove cobs or grains from plant stalks, mechanical hay balers, and a number of mechanized food-processing devices made vast improvements in crop yields for farmers through labor reduction.

As the technological innovations of the Second Agricultural Revolution has increased food production, it has allowed for better diets and therefore longer life expectancy. From the early 1900s to today, agricultural chemicals, hybridization, and large-scale highly mechanized farms around the world have enabled the global population to expand from two billion to more than six billion in just over one hundred years.

The Smaller They Are, The Harder They Rise

In addition to the development of mechanical devices, modern science has had a critical role to play in horticulture and chemistry. Scientific horticulture uses laboratory techniques to develop plant and animal hybrids that grow larger or under certain climatic conditions to meet the needs of farmers in different regions. **Dwarf varieties** were an important plant hybrid innovation. Shorter breeds of both wheat and rice were found to be hardier and more productive because the plant spent less time and energy growing a stalk, resulting in more and larger grains on each head.

Dead Bugs

Chemists in Germany were the first to synthesize both artificial fertilizers and chemical insecticides. Ammonium nitrate was first mass-produced as a fertilizer in 1909 to replace lost nitrogen in soils, mainly for corn and wheat farming. Pesticides were developed during the 1840s from natural sources and from synthetic chemicals in the early 1900s. They include insecticides, fungicides, herbicides, rodenticides (rat and mouse poisons; rodents cause huge amounts of crop damage, both in fields and in crop storage), and nematocides, which kill harmful worms either in soils or within foods.

Geographic and Historical Considerations

These technical innovations led to larger farms and fewer farmers. Link this to early stage three in the demographic transition model in Europe and North America. During industrialization in the 1800s and early 1900s, there was rapid rural-to-urban migration. As work opportunities were eliminated in agriculture, manufacturing job opportunities increased. However, these innovations took decades to reach the Third World.

Green Revolution in the Third World

The technical innovations in farming that took place in Europe and North America in the 1800s and early 1900s did not diffuse to most of the Third World until after World War II. The **Green Revolution** occurred in the 1950s and 1960s when tropical plant and animal hybrids and chemical fertilizers and pesticides began to be used in Third-World agriculture.

CED 5.5
The Green Revolution

Mechanization has, by comparison, been much slower to diffuse, mainly due to the high cost of large-scale farm equipment as well as tractors or combines and the small-scale farm plots that are still maintained by hand labor. An exception to this would be **irrigation pumps** that can be purchased at low cost to move water to dryland farming regions.

The other thing to remember about the Green Revolution is that its impact on the Third World has made for far greater amounts of crop production on small plots of land. The technology transfer from First to Third World has also enabled the expansion of populations in Third-World countries. Without **expanded food production**, the rapidly growing populations in the post-World War II developing world would have led to disastrous global food shortages, as opposed to the periodic regional famines that occur within some countries, often initiated by drought or civil war.

While the Green Revolution has been invaluable to the growth and development of the Third World, there have been drawbacks as well. Some modernized practices have done significant environmental damage. Water supplies have been depleted from irrigation and contaminated by chemical pesticides, herbicides, and fertilizers. Much of the expanded agriculture in Third World countries heavily focuses on exportable cash crops, which results in a loss of biodiversity as well as soil degradation if plots of land are not carefully managed. Finally, the rising cost of seeds, equipment, and chemicals forces many small farmers into debt.

That's Some Bull

An example of a Third-World innovation is the **Brahman cattle** (or Brahmas), which is a hybrid of European cattle and the Zebu cattle of India. This beef cow produces far more meat than other tropical cows. And the Zebu's heritage allows it to thrive in higher temperatures and humidity, conditions which lead to illness in European cattle breeds. As a result, Brahmans have diffused to many warmer regions of the world including Africa, South Asia, and even south Texas, where they compete economically with the prized Texas longhorns.

Modern Commercial Agriculture

The Third Agricultural Revolution marked the start of a more inclusive way of farming as well as the internationalization of industrialized farming. Modern commercial agriculture is now more than just growing one or more crops. Farmers now produce one or more crops (primary economic activity), process the crop (secondary economic activity), and advertise and market it through a farmer's co-op or other market as well (tertiary economic activity). This broader economic activity is the first important fact you should remember about the Third Agricultural Revolution.

The use of larger, more powerful agricultural machinery is the second hallmark of modern commercial agriculture. Use of more powerful equipment started to replace both human and beast in the early 20th century in the United States and then spread to Europe after World War II. The third and last important fact you need to know about the Third Agricultural Revolution is that research in biotechnology and food processing has made agribusiness a truly "big business." As technological innovations have made large-scale farming feasible, it has increased **economies of scale,** meaning that these large-scale producers are able to achieve lower per-unit costs. Therefore, large industrial farms are typically far more profitable than small family-run operations. (You'll read more about economies of scale in Chapter 9.)

The Green Revolution, starting in the 1940s with the arrival of agricultural scientists in Mexico to export wheat-growing technology, was only one part of the Third Agricultural Revolution—the widespread globalization of industrialized agriculture. Higher-yield hybrid seeds, used in conjunction with new, improved chemical pesticides, fertilizers, and herbicides, gave farmers in other regions of the world the ability to greatly increase crop yields. Regions depending on the staple grains of wheat and rice benefited the most from the Green Revolution technologies.

> **CED 5.6**
> Agricultural Production Regions

On the following page is a map of the general global distribution of farming types. While boundaries between farming types are fuzzy and somewhat arbitrary on maps, there are a couple of important patterns that emerge. Note that widespread commercialized farming occurs primarily in First-World countries, while much of the Third World still relies on pastoralism and intensive subsistence agriculture.

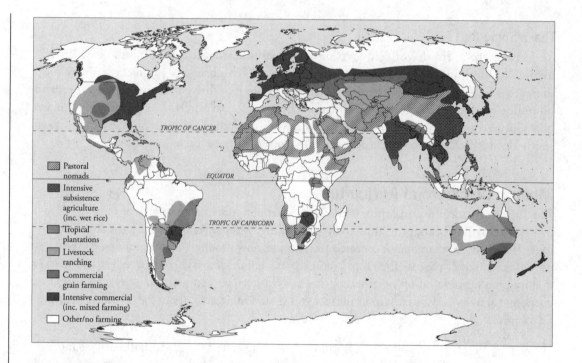

Pastoral nomads

Intensive subsistence agriculture (inc. wet rice)

Tropical plantations

Livestock ranching

Commercial grain farming

Intensive commercial (inc. mixed farming)

Other/no farming

What Do You Get When You Cross a Bacterium with a Corn Plant?

In addition to the previously mentioned Green Revolution technologies, **genetic engineering** has further increased the possibilities and productivity of global agriculture. Veterinary science and **biotechnology** research have developed vaccines, antibiotics, and growth hormones that have reduced farm animal mortality and increased the yields of meat, eggs, and other materials. These factors have all combined to enable industrial agriculture, also known as **factory farming.**

A significant example of genetic engineering is **BT corn**. Genes from *Bacillus thuringiensis,* or BT, a bacterium that produces toxins deadly to certain insects and fungi, have been spliced into the genes of different varieties of corn to make them pest-resistant. This creates significant cost savings for farmers and has environmental benefits due to the reduced need for spraying chemical pesticides. The seeds to grow the corn do cost more than regular seeds, but the fact that farmers don't have to pay for pesticide spraying means there are potentially higher profits.

Franken-cattle?

CED 5.7
Spatial Organization of Agriculture

Biotechnology has had a major impact on the productivity of meat and milk. **Recombinant Bovine Growth Hormone,** or **rBGH,** is used widely in both the production of beef and milk in the United States and some other countries. These are synthetic hormones that mimic the real growth-stimulating hormones produced by a cow's pituitary glands. The result is that cattle grow bigger and cows produce more milk. From the farmer's perspective, an investment in these drugs can significantly increase meat and milk yields, and thus increase farm profitability.

The Egg Factory

The combination of genetically modified chicken breeds, avian (bird) growth hormones, and **antibiotics** to prevent bacterial diseases from spreading in large flocks has made large, indoor egg-farming operations possible. Some egg-production facilities have several hundred thousand hens. Egg producers claim that this is a safe and economical way to produce eggs at very low cost. Keep in mind eggs are not just for scrambling in the morning. Egg powders and proteins are found in everything from cake mix to baby formula to cosmetics. These large-scale farms are necessary to meet the globally increasing demand for egg products.

Recent Turning Points for Farming in the United States and Canada

In Anglo-America today, agriculture is moving toward **extensive monoculture of staple crops**, namely corn, soybeans, and wheat. Corporate ownership of farms is the norm, whereas the family-owned farm is becoming a thing of the past. The high-cost technical developments of the Third Agricultural Revolution have combined with low **commodity prices** of crops and animals to push small-scale farms out of business. However, there has been significant consumer resistance to genetic engineering and biotechnology. This has opened the door for some highly specialized or organic small farms to survive the rise of agribusiness.

Agribusiness

Modern commercial agriculture has radically changed the organization of farming. The dominant form today is **corporate agriculture,** or **agribusiness,** in which large-scale extensive farms of several thousand acres or several thousand animals are controlled by a single regional business.

Large multinational corporations, including seed and agricultural chemical companies, purchase hundreds of thousands of acres that are then leased to local contractors who use the company's seed or chemicals to produce crops. With crop prices at historic lows, one of the few ways to continue farming low-price staple crops like corn, soybeans, and wheat is to consolidate smaller farms under one company to spread costs and create profitability through volume.

The Politics of Agroindustry

Though agriculture, food, and related industries produce only about 5 percent of the United States GDP, corporate agribusiness has significant political power, especially in Midwestern states and prairie provinces. Many of these companies receive the same tax breaks, low-cost loans, and direct government subsidies that family farmers are given to help keep them in business. Cargill, the largest privately owned company in the United States; the Archer Daniels Midland Corporation (ADM); Monsanto; and other firms lobby the government to keep programs running that subsidize their business.

Where the Factory Meets the Farm

To keep costs down, agribusinesses have become increasingly dependent on factory farms. Like the earlier egg farm example, beef cattle, pigs, and poultry are increasingly farmed in large, densely packed facilities where thousands of food animals are bred, grown, and (sometimes in the same location) slaughtered. Poultry are raised indoors in large houses with automated feeding and building-cleaning systems. Dairy cattle are kept outside but are milked two to three times daily in large, increasingly automated indoor facilities where cow health is monitored to prevent potential milk-supply contamination. Hogs are also raised increasingly in indoor facilities but can wind up in large feedlots.

By contrast, most beef cattle are kept for all or part of their lives in large outdoor feedlots which, due to the density of cows, have no natural vegetation. Feed is either dumped from trucks or sent through pipes to feed troughs in a wet slurry. Once the cattle are fattened, they are shipped at night to slaughterhouses that process all their parts. To keep animals healthy enough for animal inspectors, feedlot operations are heavily dependent on antibiotics. **Downer cattle** are beef cows that appear ill or are lame and cannot be used for human consumption, but can wind up in pet food or animal feed instead.

Farm Crisis

Low crop prices and low profitability, increasing fuel costs, and competition from big agribusiness firms have made farming very difficult for the traditional small-scale family farm. Beginning in the 1970s, the United States and Canadian governments extended vast amounts of low-interest loans, price supports, and other subsidy programs to aid farmers who, at the time, had significant political influence in agricultural states and provinces. This was a necessary bailout of farms, which would have shut down without the public supply of credit to buy seed, chemicals, and equipment at the start of planting seasons. Most banks saw farms as risky creditors, and the government had to step in as a lender of last resort.

Death of the Family Farm in America

If the government hadn't bailed out farmers, a mass closure of farms would have led to wild price swings in food, and things were bad enough with fuel prices in the 1970s at then all-time highs. Many farms' mortgages were foreclosed due to the farmers' inability to make money as a result of low commodity prices for crops (the prices set by market traders at mercantile exchanges for volumes of crops like bushels of corn or pork bellies). Eventually, agribusiness stepped in during the 1980s and 1990s, buying up and consolidating many farms into larger holdings. As a result, some farm communities nearly disappeared as people left to find a new life in other parts of the country.

SPECIALIZED AGRICULTURE

Family Farm Survival and the Rise of Specialized Agriculture

For those who wanted to survive the farm crisis in rural areas, there were a few options: start farming as a contractor for agribusiness, buy out other farmers and go into agribusiness for yourself, or stick with your current farm and get into **specialized farm products**.

The increased industrialization of farming by agribusiness has created an important opportunity for farmers who are willing to give up the technological advancements of the Second and Third Agricultural Revolutions, or willing to switch to alternative and nontraditional crops. The public and consumers resistant to **genetically modified organisms (GMOs)**, skeptics of artificial hormones, and those concerned about **animal welfare** have rejected many of the farming practices used by agribusiness and other farmers. As a result, a large market for so-called **natural food products** has emerged, and many small family farms have restructured their operations to meet the rapidly increasing demand for such products. Small farms have also benefited from **"eat local"** movements that encourage consumers to purchase food products from nearby farmers.

> **CED 5.11**
> Challenges of Contemporary Agriculture

Non-GMO Foods

By raising crops or animals that are not themselves GMO or the offspring of genetically engineered organisms, farmers can certify their products as non-GMO. In the United States and Canada, this can bring a premium price from natural foods processors and consumers looking for the non-GMO label. By contrast, in the European Union, food from GMOs must carry a label warning consumers of the product's contents. All other products are assumed to be non-GMO and do not carry special labels. Many small American family farms market their non-GMO crops and meats to EU markets and food processors.

> **Did You Know?**
> The Non-GMO Project is a nonprofit organization that offers North America's only third-party verification and labeling for non-GMO food and products.

Note that there is no evidence that GMOs cause harm to humans, but many consumers have health concerns regarding GMOs. Many also worry that genetically modified plants and animals could interbreed and contaminate natural food supplies or the environment, thus doing potential long-term harm.

Organics

In most places, including the United States and Canada, to be labeled **organic,** crops and animals must not be grown using genetic engineering, must be free of pesticides, antibiotics, and synthetic hormones, must not use artificial fertilizers, and must feed on completely organic crops. The organic label brings even higher prices than the non-GMO label, since it is far more costly to grow crops and animals without artificial inputs. For instance, a gallon of regular milk costs roughly $2.75 to $3.40 in a grocery store, whereas a gallon of organic milk in the same store can cost anywhere from $5.80 to $7.50. Small family dairy farms can make far more money per cow compared to traditional dairies, thus increasing their profitability and making farming economically possible. Organics are also seen as a much more **sustainable** form of farming due to the lack of artificial chemicals, which have lingering downstream effects on natural ecology.

Antibiotic- and Hormone-Free

When farmers cannot guarantee that milk or animals are not genetically modified or that fertilizers or feed are not organic-quality, they can still market their products as "antibiotic- and hormone-free." Poultry, meat, and cheeses designated as such are now widely demanded by U.S. consumers and often cost less than organics.

Heirloom Varieties

Many crops have been so highly modified by hybridization that only a few commercial varieties are available to consumers, despite the fact that many older and less commercially known varieties exist. Russet apples, black Russian tomatoes, blue corn, and fingerling potatoes are often found for sale in farmers' markets and at specialty food stores where consumers are often willing to pay four to five times more for heirlooms than the going price for standard commercial varieties. One former heirloom varietal, Silver Queen corn, has become so popular that it is widely sold in regular grocery stores during the summer months.

Free Range

Concerns over animal welfare and loss of flavor in agribusiness-produced meats and eggs have led to increased consumer demand for free-range poultry, eggs, and beef. To attain this designation, farmers must have open pastures or large outdoor poultry pens where natural vegetation grows. Free-range labels attract consumers who have ethical positions against factory farming and inhumane treatment of animals. Free-range animals can still eat feeds from non-organic and genetically modified sources.

Grass-Fed Beef

Grass-fed cattle have also brought significantly higher prices to gourmet consumers who seek the more natural-tasting beef, as corn- and soy-based cattle feed has been blamed for less flavorful beef. There are also concerns that even cattle feeds labeled as organic can have protein supplements made from other animals. Nerve and brain tissue from other animals has been blamed for outbreaks of Bovine Spongiform Encephalopathy (BSE), otherwise known as Mad Cow Disease. Grass-fed animals would not be at risk for BSE.

Alternative Livestock

Although lamb, goose, and duck are consumed widely and aren't that "alternative," many small farms have expanded or switched to these meats since they also produce wool and feather down for clothing and housewares for added farm earnings. However, other "exotic" animal products and clothing fibers have emerged as economic options for small-scale specialty farmers. Examples include ostrich for meat and feathers; bison for low-fat meat and skins; llamas and alpaca as draft animals and for specialty wools; goats for meat, milk, and cheeses; and kangaroo for meat and leather to make athletic cleats.

Value-Added Agriculture

Likewise, there is increased consumer demand for value-added agricultural products, where food is processed on the farm and significantly increases in value, and more money goes to the farmer. Examples of value-added products are wine, specialty cheeses, olive oil and nut oils, fruit and tree syrups, and smoked and dried meats. Chocolate has also become a **cottage industry** in dairy farming areas. The quality of chocolate is highly dependent on the quality of the milk used. Chocolates using non-GMO or organic whole milk are of very high quality and can fetch high prices.

Many value-added products are advertised by their **appellation**, the local or regional geographic name for the product. Napa or Sonoma wines from California are associated with a particular high quality that consumers are willing to pay for. These names are protected so that only products produced in the local area or region can have the appellation on the label.

Wine and Cheese Parties: Big Money for European Farmers

Champagne can be labeled as such only if the grapes are grown and bottled in the Champagne region of France. Imitators must bear the label "sparkling wine" or "*methode champagnoise,*" but not "Champagne"; otherwise, they'll find themselves in court being sued by the French government for violating international trade agreements. Likewise, you can sell Parmesan cheese made in Wisconsin, but don't dare label it **Parmigiano-Reggiano** or you'll face similar litigation. This type of cheese can carry the specific appellation only if it is made in the area surrounding the city of Parma in Italy.

The key with appellations is the higher price these place-names bring at market. A basic sparkling wine from Spain or California will cost $10 per bottle, while an actual French Champagne will fetch anywhere from $35 to $180 in stores, and only the true wine afficionados can tell the difference. Similarly, domestic Parmesan costs about $8 per pound, whereas the Italian appellation will cost $18 per pound. These high prices keep French and Italian grape and dairy farmers in business and help them maintain competition with big agribusiness.

Fair Trade

Concerns over the human impact of major agribusiness extend beyond supporting small, local family farms on a domestic scale. In an effort to maximize profits, some corporations pay producers at the base of the supply chain extremely low wages, forcing them to work long hours in often difficult and potentially unsafe working conditions to make a living. This is especially true for crops grown in developing countries, such as chocolate, bananas, and coffee. The **fair trade** movement focuses on ensuring that small farmers and artisans are paid a fair price for their products. Businesses that want to source fair trade products typically undergo a certification process with one of several international fair trade federations and work with cooperatives of small farmers to ensure fair prices, living wages for workers, and safe and environmentally sustainable working conditions. Some companies and cooperatives also establish funds for the education and health care of workers and their families. The fair trade certification may also apply to craft goods, such as clothing and textiles.

Aquaculture

Fish farming may not seem like traditional agriculture, but it is a rapidly growing industry that small farmers can engage in and be profitable. Large catfish farms have been developed in Arkansas, and tilapia, a South American fish, is being farmed in California and Texas. These fish are popular because they don't cost much to raise but fetch a high price at the market. In the Pacific Northwest, New England, and the Maritime Provinces, aquaculture in bays and estuaries has resulted in very profitable small-scale oyster and salmon farms. Even geoducks (pronounced gooey-ducks), a large species of clam, are now farmed in the tidal mudflats of Washington state and British Columbia. Why? The Japanese will pay $25 per pound to get geoducks for their sushi restaurants.

Specialized Agriculture in General

In contrast to staple grain farming of corn, rice, soybeans, and wheat, specialized crops play an important role in the diversity of foods in terms of both farm economy and the cultural specificity of consumers. Both small family farms and commercial farms grow specialized crops that bring much higher amounts of money per acre than basic grain staples. These farms tend to be smaller than grain farms, but specialized crops can still be produced in large-scale operations.

Truck farms in the eastern United States and Canada grow specialty crops during the summer growing season and are important sources of earnings, since much industrial dairy production has moved to the upper Midwest (Wisconsin). "Truck" comes from the old term for agricultural exchange of goods. Examples of these highly profitable crops are tomatoes, lettuce, strawberries, and tree crops like apples and peaches. These can be sold fresh in stores, canned, or frozen for later use. **Suitcase farmers** are those farm owners who have city jobs but still own land in rural areas. They also tend to engage in specialty crop farming for added personal earnings and to keep old family traditions and farms alive. Small farms can also distribute produce through **community-supported agriculture (CSA)** programs. In CSAs, produce and other farm products are delivered directly to individual consumers, often on a weekly or monthly basis. You might think of it as a food subscription service.

Meeting Demand Throughout the Year

In Florida, South Texas, and Southern California, specialty crops can be grown year-round with two and sometimes three growing seasons depending on the crop. These, along with crops grown in areas of northern Mexico (lettuce, tomatoes, broccoli, green beans) and imports from Chile (grapes, berries) and even as far as New Zealand or Australia (lamb, apples, kiwifruit), keep American and Canadian stores stocked with fruits and vegetables. Even in the winter, salad bars have fresh produce and, if you so choose, you can pay $4.00 for a half pint of fresh Chilean raspberries.

Specialized Crops: Mediterranean Agriculture

The areas of Africa, Asia, and Europe that surround the Mediterranean Sea have a warm, dry climate with short periods of rain in winter and spring. In this region, the domestication of plants has specialized certain varieties of crops that today bring significant value to farmers. Here is a short list of **Mediterranean agriculture** crops that have been domesticated and continuously grown in the region:

Crops	Details
Citrus	Oranges, lemons, limes, grapefruit, blood oranges
Nut trees	Pistachios, almonds
Palms	Different varieties produce dates, palm oil, hearts of palm
Olives	Many varieties for both eating and pressing for oil
Artichokes	Flowers sold fresh for cooking or hearts preserved in oil
Avocados	Dark-skinned Hass variety and larger green Florida type
Grapes*	Raisins and fresh fruit pressed for wine production

*Wine is often identified with the Mediterranean, but wine grapes also grow in cooler temperate regions such as northern France and Germany. Thus, grapes are not exclusively grown in Mediterranean climates.

Other parts of the world with climates similar to the Mediterranean have also adopted these specialized crops. Some growing regions are small but produce these valuable crops in large order for domestic cash crops and export. Here is a list of areas outside of the Mediterranean that have a similar climate and produce Mediterranean crops:

Southern and Central California
Central Florida
South Texas
Southern and Central Brazil
Southern China and Southeast Asia
Hawaii

Northern Argentina
Uruguay
Central Chile
Black Sea Coastal Areas
South Africa
Southern Australia

Plantation Agriculture

In the tropical and sub-tropical climates of the world, it is common to find extensive **plantation agriculture**, specialized crops intended for both **domestic consumption** and for **export** to other parts of the world. These plantations tend to be large, extensive monoculture farms that are reliant upon low-wage labor and, historically in the United States until 1865, slave labor.

Today, tropical plantation export crops are still found the world over, mainly in Third-World locations. They still serve much the same purpose they have historically: to export value from large-scale monoculture.

Here are some examples and locations:

Plantation Crop	Countries
Banana	Brazil, Dominica, Costa Rica, Honduras
Cane Sugar	United States (Florida), Brazil, Cuba, China
Coffee	Ethiopia, Kenya, Colombia, Brazil, United States (Hawaii)
Tea	Sri Lanka, India, China, Thailand
Rubber	Brazil, Malaysia, Indonesia, Mexico
Cacao (chocolate)	Ghana, Brazil, Mexico, Indonesia
Palm Oil	Indonesia, Malaysia, Nigeria, Thailand

As exports, these crops can produce a significant amount of economic value for their countries. However, frequent fluctuations in the commodity prices for these goods can make them highly profitable one year and then unprofitable the next. As a form of monoculture, plantation production can prove to be a risky financial investment for many countries. This has led to attempts to diversify the types of crops grown for export and thus reduce the potential for national economic downturns due to losses from a single crop.

Plantation-Style Agriculture Declines in the United States

In the United States, cotton and tobacco were Southern plantation crops that sold domestically and for export. In the 20th century, these were replaced by other crops such as soybeans, peanuts, and yellow pine trees for timber. Cotton production in the South was severely damaged by boll weevil infestations in the 1890s through the 1920s. Today, most of the cotton in the United States is grown in California. Tobacco production was cut back in the 1990s after tobacco industry litigation in which state attorneys general pointed out the costly health dangers of smoking. Like other family-owned farms in the United States, old plantations are a dying breed in the face of large corporate farms.

Specialized Crops: Dairy

Dairying is done mainly with cows but can also be a specialized agricultural activity using goats and buffalo for cheese production. Dairying cow's milk is today a massive global operation that yields milk for drinking, cheeses, yogurt, butter, and cream. A major concern with milk is spoilage, hence the long history of producing cheeses and yogurt to preserve excess milk for long-term usage.

With the development of pasteurization in the 1860s by French scientist Louis Pasteur, milk that was briefly heated to kill potentially harmful bacteria had an increased shelf life from a couple of days to up to two weeks. This development expanded the amount of area that could be served by dairies. In terms of travel time and distance, the region around a city to which **fresh milk** is delivered without spoiling is known as the **milkshed**. Multiple large dairies are necessary to supply large cities.

Processed dairy like cheese and yogurt production in the United States has continually moved westward over the last 150 years. Formerly, New England dominated cheese production in the late 1800s and early 1900s. But the wider availability of cheap land and the need for larger dairy farms has driven large-scale cheese production westward over time to "America's Dairyland," Wisconsin, and other parts of the upper Midwest. Most of the milk produced in Wisconsin is processed, whereas most of the milk produced in New England today ends up in jugs and cartons to be sold at stores in nearby urban areas.

I'll Have a Skinny Latte, No Foam

Milk is sold in a number of grades based on the amount of fat content. Whole milk has had the cream removed from the raw milk. This cream is sold separately. Reduced fat milk is healthier, since it reduces the potential for heart disease from excess saturated fat and cholesterol consumption. Skim milk has all of the milk fat removed and is considered the most healthful for humans age four and older. Parts removed from the raw milk are highly valuable; milk fat is used to produce butter, and milk solids are used in making glue, cosmetics, and moisturizers. Milk is often enriched to increase the nutritional complement of the fat-soluble vitamins A and D to people's daily consumption. Milk is often homogenized—mixed in large batches—to create a consistent flavor.

In the 1980s a new milk preservation method called **ultra-high temperature (UHT) pasteurization** was devised. Here milk is flash-pasteurized at very high temperatures and under pressure to keep the water in it from turning to steam. This is then stored in a sterile box container that is sealed in plastic to prevent contamination. These UHT packages can keep milk fresh for up to a year. As a result, UHT milk has a global milkshed.

> **CED 5.12**
> Women in Agriculture

Women in Agriculture

Women play an essential role in global agricultural production, yet almost everywhere they face a gender gap in pay equity and access to resources. They may be unpaid workers on family farms or paid (or sometimes unpaid) labor on other farms. On average, women make up 43% of the agricultural labor force, a figure that rises to over 50% in parts of East Asia and sub-Saharan Africa and even 80% in some developing countries where small farming and subsistence agriculture are still a common way of life. However, women own just 2% of land worldwide—the number of female landowners is dwarfed by that of male landowners, and the land that women do own is frequently in smaller plots and of lower quality. In some areas, women are barred from inheriting family land. Those who purchase land may be required to have a male relative give consent or co-sign on the purchase.

This same inequality presents challenges when it comes to production for women farmers. Agricultural extension services and training exclude women in many developing countries. Female-headed farms are also less likely to be extended credit than male-owned farms. Without this credit, they have less access to essential inputs like tools, machinery, fertilizers and pesticides, and improved seeds. With fewer and lower-quality inputs, their agricultural yields may be 20-30% lower than those of male farmers—not because they're less skilled at farming, but because they have poorer access to the resources required to run successful farming operations. This gap has a significant impact on the total agricultural output and food security in developing countries. Another obstacle that female farmers may face is access to markets: rural women, especially in developing countries, may lack convenient transportation or decent infrastructure to reach market centers in more populated areas.

Additionally, there's a clear correlation between gender inequality and world hunger. Areas in which women face greater barriers in farming also tend to have higher rates of undernourishment. It's estimated that the increased output from allowing women farmers in the developing world equal access to resources could reduce the number of undernourished people by anywhere between 100 million and 150 million. As such, many organizations, like the Food and Agricultural Organization of the United Nations (FAO) and non-governmental groups, have begun to focus on increasing training and resources for women in agriculture. Such initiatives include education in farming and management practices, encouraging participation in niche and value-added agriculture, funding through microloans, and increased access to tools and other inputs.

Global Systems of Agriculture

CED 5.9

The Global System of Agriculture

While importing and exporting agricultural goods is a practice that dates back centuries, the technological advances of the Agricultural Revolutions combined with increasing globalization have made the global agricultural economy more vast and complex than ever. Much of that economic activity occurs in poor and developing countries, so the ability to grow and export crops can have an enormous impact on economic growth in those areas.

Commodity Chains

Virtually every agricultural product (or any good, for that matter) follows a multi-step path from farm to consumer. These links between producers and consumers in the journey from raw material to delivery of a finished product are called **commodity chains**. On a local level, an agricultural commodity chain may be as simple as a farmer growing a crop and selling it directly to the consumer at a farmers' market. However, in the age of globalization and multinational agribusiness firms, many commodities follow a **global supply chain**. Consider what it takes to get your favorite chocolate bar into your hands. Odds are, the raw cacao your candy bar is made of was produced not in your backyard, but on another continent. The process required to not only transform this raw material into a finished good, but also deliver it to consumers like you, is complex and involves numerous parties.

While the commodity chain can involve many players at various points, it can be broken down into five general stages:

1. **Inputs:** Aside from seeds, farming requires a number of elements to maximize both the size and quality of crop yield. Many are consumable, such as fertilizers, pesticides and insecticides, and water. Inputs can also be tools and mechanical equipment such as tractors and plows. Since knowledge is essential to increasing agricultural productivity, even activities such as training, certifications, and research & development can fall into the input category.

2. **Production:** When you think of agriculture and farming, this is the stage that probably comes to mind—growing and harvesting crops. In the age of agribusiness, producers may be independent farmers, small farmers who often contract with corporations, or large commercial operations with their own harvesting and processing facilities. In many cases, the farmers and laborers who work to raise crops receive only a tiny share of the selling price of the end product. For example,

cocoa farmers receive an estimated 7 percent of the value added to each ton of cocoa beans they produce. In top cocoa-producing countries like Ghana, that amounts to roughly 2 dollars per day. By and large, production workers are the lowest-paid actors in the commodity chain.

3. **Processing:** Raw agricultural goods are turned into consumer products. At this stage, agribusinesses may contract with outside industries for services such as marketing, packaging, and transport. The processing stage can be cost-intensive and complex. It may involve numerous players, although the amount of processing depends on what the final product is. Fresh produce may only need to be packaged and labeled, while other crops require additional steps to turn them into an edible product. Consider your chocolate bar again: after cocoa beans are harvested, dried, and fermented by farmers, they are sent to processing plants to be roasted and ground. They are then transformed into semi-finished cocoa products (powder, butter, and liquor). Finally, these key ingredients are either sold to outside chocolate manufacturers or, increasingly more often, sent to another plant owned by the same corporation, where they are combined with other components like milk and sugar to produce the finished product.

4. **Distribution:** Agricultural products are sent to market. Again, this step frequently involves contracting with outside transport providers. There are a variety of distribution markets for agricultural commodities. On the smallest scale, this may mean an independent farmer loading a van full of produce or meat and driving it to a farmers' market. In many other cases, products are sold to a wholesaler for distribution to retailers and restaurants. On a global scale, exporters and importers distribute goods internationally. Returning to the example of chocolate (are you hungry yet?), the multinational corporations that control most chocolate production have multiple distribution channels. They may sell the semi-finished products to other companies for further processing, transport their finished chocolate to their own factories to make and package various types of chocolate products, or sell that finished "industrial" chocolate to exporters and wholesalers. In turn, those middlemen distribute it to retailers, bakers, or confectioners who use the chocolate in their own products.

5. **Consumption:** Retailers and restaurants sell the final product to you, the consumer. Let's eat!

Outside Influences on the Global Supply Chain

With so much of food distribution and consumption occurring on a global scale, the supply chain can be deeply affected by other factors such as infrastructure, political relationships, and economic and trade developments.

Infrastructure is an essential piece of being able to move goods around a country. This can especially impact less developed countries, where roads may be in poor condition and technology is often lacking. Without functional infrastructure, it becomes difficult to get needed inputs to farmers in inaccessible locations and for those farmers to get their products to market. It's often even more difficult to get goods to a point from which they can be distributed globally to profitable export markets.

Both internal and external political developments may impact the functionality of a supply chain. Some popular agricultural commodities such as coffee and cocoa are grown in countries with volatile political situations. For example, Côte d'Ivoire is the world's largest cocoa producer, accounting for 30% of the world's supply. However, since the outbreak of a five-year civil war in 2002, its political landscape has remained unstable. The periodic outbursts of political strife can create obstacles for the production and sourcing of cocoa, thus cutting into revenues for both chocolate companies and local farmers.

Global political and economic relationships can also put a strain on the supply chain. Free trade agreements can stimulate the economies and agricultural production of trade partners. On the other hand, shifting policies and political tensions often lead to reduced trade activity and, in extreme cases, **embargoes** that completely ban trade or commercial interaction with a particular country. This makes it more difficult for producers in the embargoed country to distribute their goods, as well as more difficult for consumers on the other end to get the goods they want.

Supply chains can be vulnerable to numerous challenges, whether political, economic, or environmental. The more diversified an economy is, the more stable it will be. A country is considered **commodity-dependent** when a single product or type of good accounts for more than 60% of its exports. Commodity dependence is not uncommon; about 54% of the world's nations are heavily reliant on a single export. However, the share of commodity-dependent countries sharply increases as the level of development decreases. Only about 13% of more developed countries (including Australia, New Zealand, and Norway) are commodity-dependent, while that share skyrockets to 85% of the world's least developed countries. Reliance on a single good leaves an economy vulnerable to financial crisis. For example, when commodity prices dipped between 2013 and 2017, it created an economic slowdown in 64 countries, throwing several of those into a recession. Without the financial resources needed to diversify its economy, a country remains trapped in a vicious cycle of commodity-dependence.

Here is a map of commodity-dependent countries. Note the proportion of them that are in the developing world:

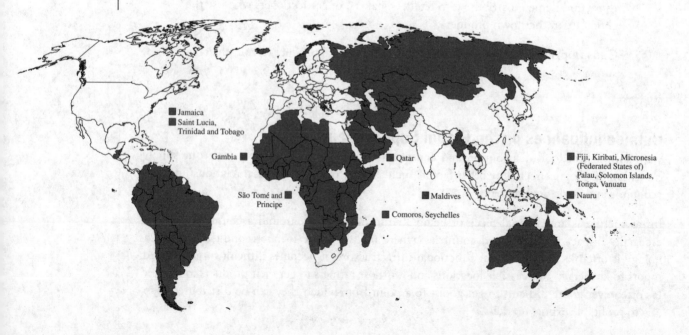

KNOW THE MODEL

Von Thünen's Model

Johann Heinrich von Thünen wrote his book *The Isolated State* in 1826. In it, he described the pattern of agricultural land use surrounding a theoretical European town, village, or city. In terms of context, von Thünen was writing about the agrarian geography of Europe, despite publishing his work in the early industrial period.

The key to understanding von Thünen's model is that land use (the type of farming) is determined by how **labor intensive** the type of farming is. Crops or animals that require lots of attention are going to be closest to the town, and the ones that require the least attention will be farthest.

Von Thünen's Model

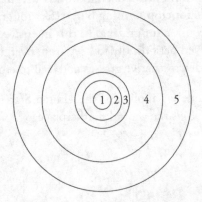

> **CED 5.8**
> Von Thünen Model

1: Town, village, or city as the central place
2: Intensive farming: Vegetables, dairying, market gardens
3: Village forest or "wood"
4: Extensive farming: Grain crops, hay fields
5: Grazing lands, meadows

Each Ring Explained

1. **Village.** Even though this model predates Walter Christaller by a hundred years, today von Thünen's model is considered a type of **central place model** due to the organization of a central marketplace and place of consumption for the agricultural goods produced in the surrounding area.

2. **Labor-intensive crops** include fruits, garden vegetables, herbs, and anything that required constant tending or weeding or that needed to be picked for market at a particular time to ensure ripeness. **Labor-intensive animals** include dairy cows and egg-producing poultry. Dairy cows require twice-daily milking and, being perishable, milk needed to be near markets to prevent spoilage. **Medicinal crops,** such as herbs, were grown along with vegetables in town **market gardens** for local sale.

3. A **managed forest** was needed to meet the energy and lumber needs of the community. Due to wood's weight and bulk, these trees were located close to town to minimize transportation costs. Managed cutting and replanting of trees was often done in a highly sustainable manner, allowing these town woods to be used continuously as a local **renewable resource**.

4. **Labor-extensive crops** require far less tending. Crops like wheat, barley, and rye (the grain crops commonly grown in von Thünen's Germany) require little tending other than planting and harvest. Why? These species, like corn, are members of the grass family (*Poaceae*), and grasses tend to dominate their growing environment, choking out most potential weed invaders. Large plots of land are required to grow these staple food crops that are needed in much larger volumes than vegetables. Thus, this ring covers a very wide area.

5. **Grazing** land is the least labor-intensive. A single shepherd could tend to well over 100 head of beef cattle (as opposed to dairy cows) or sheep. Of course he was not alone, since domesticated herding dogs were used to drive herds from pasture to pasture and provide security from predators like wolves. **Highlands** in peripheral areas were often not suitable for crop farming but perfect for grazing. Like grain farming, lots of land was required for grazing. In this intensive form of pastoralism, animals have to be moved periodically to keep from overgrazing meadows and pastures, which could destroy native grasses and lead to erosion.

Below is a map of von Thünen's model as applied to the United States. It assumes that New York City, as the largest city in the US, is the central marketplace.

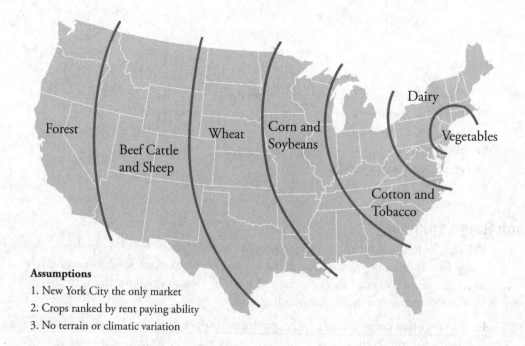

Forest

Beef Cattle
and Sheep

Wheat

Corn and
Soybeans

Dairy

Vegetables

Cotton and
Tobacco

Assumptions
1. New York City the only market
2. Crops ranked by rent paying ability
3. No terrain or climatic variation

Now here is the same map adjusted for climatic variation. This version recognizes that the American South has a warmer climate than the North, making it better suited for certain intensive farming crops such as cotton, tobacco, and tropical specialty crops (like citrus) that can be grown in the warmest areas of Florida and southern California.

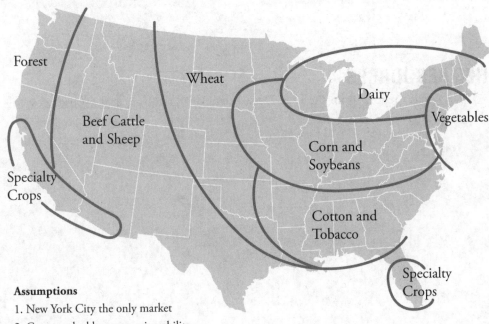

Assumptions

1. New York City the only market
2. Crops ranked by rent paying ability
3. No terrain variation
4. Climatic variation considered

Land Economics of von Thünen's Model

From an economic perspective, you can say that von Thünen's model explains the **cost-to-distance relationship** in agricultural land use. It can be described as an inverse relationship between the value of labor and the distance from the center of the model; the higher the total labor costs, the closer it is to the center, and the lower the labor costs, the farther it is from the center.

Labor costs can be equated to the price of rent paid by peasants to farm a piece of land generally owned by aristocrats under the political economy of feudalism. The more labor input required, the higher the rent paid on land to produce a specific good. As a result, prices for goods in markets are a product of rent and labor inputs. Thus, fruits and vegetables are much more expensive by volume than wheat.

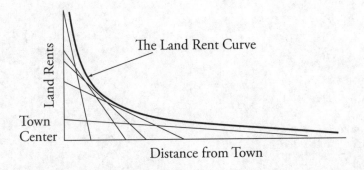

If you chart the price of rent for different locations on the model, you can draw a line to represent the cost-to-distance relationship for each of the rings. The combined lines create a cost surface upon which you can draw the **land-rent curve,** a mathematical function that shows the changes in rent prices across the model. Notice how rents for grazing and grain farming are relatively low, and that rent prices jump exponentially as you move toward the town's center.

OTHER RESOURCES

- Agency reports from the U.S. Department of Agriculture at www.usda.gov

CHAPTER 7 KEY TERMS

primary economy

demographic transition model

Third-World countries

employment

gross domestic product (GDP)

intensive agriculture

extensive agriculture

hunting and gathering societies

transhumance

pastoralism

nomadic herding

cultivars

multi-cropping

monoculture

staple crop

mixed farming

general farming

subsistence agriculture

extensive subsistence agriculture

physiologic density

arable land

food preservation

specialized crops

cash cropping

commercial crops

plantation agriculture

domestic consumption

export

feudal

income disparity

The Communist Manifesto

communes

quotas

incentives

human ecology

food web

food chain

crop rotation

double cropping

triple cropping

growing season

spring wheat

winter wheat

aquifers

irrigation

conservation

conservation agriculture

inter-planting

sustainable yield

sustainability

textiles

animal feed

alternative energy crops

ethanol

biodiesel

slash and burn agriculture (swidden)

fallow

extensive pastoralism

population pressure

overgrazing

desertification

soil salinization

mineral salts

vegetative planting

seed agriculture

domestication of plants

horticulture

hearths of domestication

animal domestication

animal husbandry

growing areas

relocation diffusion

Columbian exchange

hybrids

chemical fertilizers

chemical pesticides

mechanization
tractors
dwarf varieties
Green Revolution
irrigation pumps
expanded food production
economies of scale
Brahman cattle
genetic engineering
biotechnology
factory farming
BT corn
Recombinant Bovine Growth Hormone (rBGH)
antibiotics
extensive monoculture of staple crops
commodity prices
corporate agriculture (agribusiness)
downer cattle
specialized farm products
genetically modified organisms (GMOs)
animal welfare
natural food products
sustainable
organic
cottage industry
appellation
Champagne

Parmigiano-Reggiano
fair trade
truck farms
suitcase farmers
Mediterranean agriculture
fresh milk
milkshed
processed dairy
ultra-high temperature (UHT) pasteurization
embargoes
commodity-dependent
gross domestic product (GDP)
commodity chains
global supply chain
Johann Heinrich von Thünen
labor intensive
central place model
labor-intensive crops
labor-intensive animals
medicinal crops
market gardens
managed forest
renewable resource
labor-extensive crops
grazing
highlands
cost-to-distance relationship
land-rent curve

CHAPTER 7 DRILL

See the end of this chapter for answers and explanations.

1. Which of the following requires a lot of labor, focuses on a small plot of land, or both?

   (A) Extensive agriculture
   (B) Pastoralism
   (C) Hunting and gathering
   (D) Nomadic herding
   (E) Intensive agriculture

2. All of the following can contribute to desertification EXCEPT

   (A) overgrazing
   (B) slash and burn agriculture
   (C) deforestation
   (D) soil salinization
   (E) extensive pastoralism

3. Which of the following was introduced to the Old World as part of the Columbian exchange?

   (A) Wheat
   (B) Apples
   (C) Horses
   (D) Peanuts
   (E) Goats

4. The concept of transhumance is associated with

   (A) stage 2 of the demographic transition model
   (B) Buddhist spiritual practices
   (C) pastoralism
   (D) subsistence farming
   (E) hunting and gathering societies

5. What effect did the publication of *The Communist Manifesto* have upon Russian agriculture?

   (A) An improvement in the standard of living for all farmers everywhere
   (B) The eventual collectivization of farms by the Soviet system
   (C) An immediate decline in the level of agricultural efficiency
   (D) A return to a feudal arrangement wherein wealthy aristocrats owned most of the land
   (E) The selection of wheat over corn because of its perception as the grain of the common man

6. The most important reason for the rising use of alternative energy crops such as ethanol and biodiesel has been

   (A) the rapid increase in the price of oil
   (B) the public relations efforts of alternative energy advocates
   (C) the large amount of waste oil from deep fryers
   (D) the slash and burn agriculture occurring in Brazil that has seen the growth of millions of acres of new sugar cane
   (E) the improvement in irrigation techniques

7. All of the following characteristics mark the Third Agricultural Revolution EXCEPT

   (A) the internationalization of industrialized farming
   (B) the use of larger, more powerful agricultural equipment
   (C) research in biotechnology and food processing
   (D) the invention of artificial chemical fertilizers and pesticides
   (E) the growth of the Green Revolution

8. A small-scale farmer who successfully survived the farm crisis in rural areas would NOT have

   (A) initiated a marketing campaign demonstrating his commitment to animal welfare
   (B) begun to sell non-GMO certified products
   (C) switched from a diverse range of crops to corn-and-soybean monoculture
   (D) invested in heirloom varieties of produce
   (E) purchased open pastures or large outdoor pens for free-range poultry

9. Subsistence agriculture is LEAST likely to be

   (A) very intensive
   (B) marked by high amounts of labor inputs
   (C) performed on small plots of land
   (D) conducted in areas with high physiologic density
   (E) susceptible to famine caused by drought or armed conflict

10. During the Columbian exchange, which one of the following products found its way from the Old World to the New World?

   (A) Tobacco
   (B) Potatoes
   (C) Citrus
   (D) Cacao
   (E) Turkey

11. According to von Thünen's model, land use is defined primarily by

   (A) walkable communities that do not rely upon motorized transportation for daily life
   (B) the commodification of highlands and other peripheral areas for grazing
   (C) a greater density of medicinal crops than edible crops
   (D) the replanting of forests at greater distance from town than tradition dictates
   (E) an inverse relationship between the value of the labor and the distance from the center of town

CHAPTER 7 DRILL: ANSWERS AND EXPLANATIONS

1. **E** Intensive agriculture, (E), both requires a lot of labor input and is focused on a small plot of land. Extensive agriculture, (A), requires limited labor input, is spread across large areas of land, or both. Pastoralism, (B), and nomadic herding, (D), are types of agriculture based on the seasonal movement of animals. Finally, hunting and gathering, (C), is a nomadic form of subsistence, in which individuals move to areas where food and water are abundant.

2. **B** Overgrazing, deforestation, soil salinization, and extensive pastoralism can lead to desertification, so they can all be eliminated. Slash and burn agriculture, (B), is generally related to rainforests and involves the cutting and burning of forest plants to create fields. While bad in its own right, slash and burn agriculture does not lead to desertification.

3. **D** When Central and South America were conquered in the early 1500s, a number of crops and livestock were transferred to the New World from the Old World and vice-versa. Choices (A), (B), (C), and (E) are all examples of things that came to the New World from the Old World. The only item that was introduced to the Old World as part of the Columbian exchange was peanuts, (D).

4. **E** During stage one of the demographic transition model, groups of hunters and gatherers moved seasonally to avoid cold, escape flooding, follow animal herds, and find native plants in season. This is the idea behind transhumance. Stage two of the DTM, pastoralism, and subsistence farming are all signs of more advanced civilizations. Buddhist spiritual practices are irrelevant. The correct answer is (E).

5. **B** Published in the middle of the 19th century, *The Communist Manifesto* fueled the Communist Revolution. A major part of that was the collectivization of farms, one of the first Five-Year Plans to be introduced in the Soviet Union by General Secretary Joseph Stalin in the late 1920s. It was a way, according to the policies of socialist leaders, to boost agricultural production through the organization of land and labor into large-scale collective farms (known as *kolkhozy*). At the same time, Stalin argued that collectivization would free poor peasants from economic servitude under the *kulaks* (wealthy, prosperous farmland owners). However, Stalin resorted to mass murder and wholesale deportation of farmers to Siberia in order to implement the plan. Millions who remained did not die of starvation, but the centuries-old system of farming has destroyed one of the most fertile regions of the world. Choose (B).

6. **A** From 1998 to 2013, the price of oil nearly quadrupled. This put intense pressure upon communities to discover alternate forms of energy that weren't as expensive. Brazil struck upon ethanol, a sugar-cane derivative that powers its vehicles. Biodiesel is made from vegetable oil. Driving behind a biodiesel vehicle smells like driving behind a fast-food restaurant. Select (A).

7. **D** While fertilizers and pesticides may seem to be modern inventions, they've actually been around for many decades. The first pesticide, DDT, was invented in 1939, while Justus von Liebig promoted the use of ammonia in agriculture as far back as the 1850s. Both dates fall within the Second Agricultural Revolution, which also included drastically reduced labor requirements thanks to the invention of trucks, tractors, and pumps. Choice (D) is the correct answer.

8. **C** You can't beat the giants of agribusiness at what they do best—and what they do best is corn-and-soybean monoculture. They've got efficiencies of scale that small-scale farmers can only dream of. Instead, small-scale farmers tend to succeed based on specialty niches either based on nontraditional products or nontraditional, ancient techniques. Choose (C).

9. **B** Extensive subsistence agriculture occurs in places where there is not much labor put into the land. This is owed to lack of modern technology, lack of population, or lack of arable land. Therefore, there are low amounts of labor input in these regions, not high.

10. **C** While we often associate the Spanish discovery of the Americas with the looting of mines and plundering of agricultural products, the Americas also benefited from the arrival of many European products. Citrus is one of them, which had been grown in the Mediterranean for thousands of years. Also arriving for the first time to the New World were most modern varieties of livestock, including horses, cattle, sheep, goats, and even chickens—as well as all the diseases that are associated with those animals.

11. **E** If you think about it, von Thünen's model measures land using common sense—the land closest to the town would require the most work. This assumes that humans don't want to walk any more than necessary. The proximity to human settlements is also a factor in the cost of that product when it arrives to market.

Summary

o Agriculture is one part of the primary economy and the predominant means of economic productivity in stage two and Third-World countries. It can be classified as either intensive or extensive.

o While the natural environment can influence agricultural regions, farming practices can also dramatically affect the landscape for better or worse. Sustainable farming aims to conserve natural resources and maintain economic stability, while poor farming practices can do irreparable environmental damage.

o There have been several agricultural revolutions throughout history:
   • First Agricultural Revolution: Humans transitioned from hunting and gathering to organized planting, which led to the domestication of plants and the development of horticulture.
   • Second Agricultural Revolution: Technological advancements in agriculture during and after the Industrial Revolution drastically increased food production while reducing labor requirements.
   • Green Revolution: The innovations of the Second Agricultural Revolution reached Third-World countries in the 1950s and 1960s. The expanded agricultural output supported a population boom that would have otherwise been unsustainable.
   • Third Agricultural Revolution: The dawn of industrialized agribusiness, the use of larger and more powerful machinery, and expanded economic activity around farms.

o Agribusiness, or corporate agriculture, is the predominant form of agriculture today; large-scale farms run by multinational corporations are replacing small family farms.

o Specialty farming products such as non-GMO, organics, heirloom varieties, and free-range and pasture-fed livestock offer small, independent farms a means of staying in business.

o Von Thünen's Model describes a pattern of land use in which the most labor-intensive crops and animals are located closest to the central village.

Chapter 8
Cities and Urban Land-Use Patterns and Processes

CHAPTER OVERVIEW

This chapter is organized into the following three parts: Know the Theory, Know the Models, and Know the Concepts. The section on theory contains an explanation of central place theory and related concepts. The models section details the concentric zone model, the sector model, the multiple-nuclei model, the galactic city or peripheral model, and the Latin American city model. The concepts section includes parts on suburbanization, gentrification, city types, urban change, economies, and sustainability issues.

KNOW THE THEORY

CED 6.4

The Size and Distribution of Cities

Central Place Theory

Central to spatial analysis and at the heart of all urban models is the basic concept of **central place theory**. Explained simply, central place theory holds that all market areas are focused on a central settlement that is a place of exchange and service provision.

The **market areas** of settlements, also known as **hinterlands,** overlap one another at different scales. Large settlements have larger market areas, but they are few in number, whereas small settlements have smaller, more numerous market areas. In terms of the size of market areas, large settlements have a larger number of services, which consumers are willing to travel large distances to access. Small settlements have a smaller number of services, which are closer to consumers.

Research in the 1920s by German theorist **Walter Christaller** showed that there is a hierarchy of places (seven levels, from a small hamlet to the large regional service-center city) across the landscape that follow a regular pattern. Christaller used hexagons to represent individual market areas. Then, he overlapped smaller-scale patterns with larger-scale layers of hexagonal market areas. The diagram below is a cutaway of three layers of this **urban hierarchy** as a basic example of Christaller's theoretical principles. In this example, the city's market area (or hinterland) contains three towns and five villages. One village and one town lie outside the city's market area.

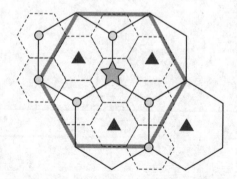

○	Village	---	Village Market Area
▲	Town	—	Town Market Area
★	City	▬	City Market Area

Use the market areas of food stores as an example to understand the principle. Describe the village with a convenience shop (such as a 7-11, Circle K, Wawa); then represent the town with a grocery store (Safeway, Kroger, Albertsons); and finally, define the city with a big-box warehouse store (Sam's Club, BJ's, Costco). People are willing to travel different distances for the service of food retailing. These market areas are based on the number of goods available in the store and the volume discount received when purchasing in bulk.

Need a bottle of soda? Just go to the local convenience store for a 20-ounce bottle for $1.29. Head further to a grocery store if you desire a 2-liter bottle for $1.09. And go all the way to the big-box warehouse store if you want a case of twenty-four 20-ounce bottles for $17.00.

Threshold and Range

The **threshold** of a service is the minimum number of people required to support a business. The **range** is the maximum distance that people are willing to travel to gain access to a service. Keep in mind that these concepts are modified by income and travel time, respectively. Threshold is partly calculated based on the earnings of the local population. For example, a luxury car dealership will have somewhat larger population requirements than a regular car dealer, but will exist in an area only if the population's income will support the business.

Range is calculated not in terms of distance but in **travel time** that a consumer needs to get to a service location. People are poor judges of actual distance, but they can tell you how long it takes to get somewhere. Sometimes traffic patterns become more important than distance in terms of how long it takes to reach a destination. Like the soda bottle example, decisions regarding access to a service are dependent on the amount of travel time and the necessity of the service. The convenience store is mainly for immediate consumption, the grocery store for the week's consumptive needs, and the warehouse store for the month's consumptive needs.

Agglomeration

Why then do we often find the same types of businesses in the same locations? **Agglomeration** exists when similar business activities are found in a local cluster. In heavily populated areas, competition within markets is common. Also, planning and zoning rules often push some types of businesses with similar building space requirements into the same local areas. In the case of manufacturers and corporate services, firms will often locate near one another in search of technical knowledge and labor-sharing. Likewise, there may be some local advantage for certain types of companies to all locate in one place.

The following are some examples of agglomeration:

- Computer hardware and software firms in the **Silicon Valley** area south of San Francisco: this is due to close proximity to the high-tech **growth poles** of Stanford University and the NASA Ames Research Center.

- Automobile companies in **Detroit**: this was originally due to manufacturing **cost advantages** of location on the Great Lakes for iron-ore delivery by water, and proximity to coal in the Midwest and Appalachia.

- Banks in **South Dakota**: the state of South Dakota has **limited banking regulations** and no corporate taxes. Some national banks have facilities where large corporate and institutional accounts are held to avoid the high auditing costs and banking profit taxes of other states.

Urban Origins

Why do settlements form where they do? For this section, think back to when the cities we know today were just settlements. This section will review the spatial concepts related to central place theory that historically discuss why cities are located in a particular place and how they became prominent places among the mass of other similar settlements.

The origins of an urban place often have to do with one of two categorical factors: access to resources and access to transportation. Towns and cities that were founded due to access to natural resources are known as **resource nodes**. Similarly, places that were founded as settlements due to their location as intersections of two or more lines of transportation are known as **transport nodes**. Lines of transportation can include oceans, rivers, bays, trails, roads, and rail lines. Airports are also transportation nodes. Below is a basic diagram to help you better visualize this concept:

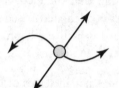

Resource Node   Transport Node

The Gold Rush Example: California

Resource node: **Transport node:**

Sacramento, California (gold)   San Francisco, California (port)

In 1839, Sutter's Fort was established as a trading post in what is today downtown Sacramento. The site of the fort was right at the base of the Sierra Nevada Mountain foothills, where gold was discovered at Sutter's Mill in 1849. San Francisco, despite its historical association with the gold rush, had been founded in 1776 at the tip of the peninsula that separates San Francisco Bay from the Pacific Ocean. The literal transport node is the narrow natural canal between the bay and the ocean called the Golden Gate, hence the name of the bridge that spans it. From San Francisco Bay, riverboats moved people and goods inland to Sacramento and brought gold back, forming the resource node that later became the state capital.

Settlement Patterns

Patterns of rural settlements are generally described as being clustered or dispersed. **Clustered rural settlements** are communities in which all of the residential and farm structures of multiple households are arranged closely together. **Dispersed rural settlements** are where households are separated from one another by significant distances. Clustered communities are commonly seen in Europe and New England, where peoples of the same culture group or clan settled nearby one another for social interaction, use of common land holdings, and security. In contrast, the farm regions of the American South, Midwest, and Great Plains generally have dispersed patterns of settlement, where large land holdings spread homes far apart. Here, many settlers had no cultural or family relations on the agricultural frontier. Thus, they were less likely to settle near one another.

In addition, clustered patterns can have circular or linear settlements. **Circular settlements** are generally a circle of homes surrounding a central open space. Examples of these can be found in medieval-era German and English towns as well as the enclosed villages of tribal herding communities in sub-Saharan Africa. **Linear settlements** tend to follow along a road or a stream front, such as the French long lots (see Chapters 3 and 5 for more on land survey patterns).

Site and Situation

The concept of **site,** in terms of urban origins, has to do with the physical characteristics of a place or its absolute location. In the same terms, **situation** has to do with a place's relationship with other locations, or its relative location.

> **CED 6.1**
> The Origin and Influences of Urbanization

Example: New York City

New York City's site characteristic is that it lies on a large, deep, enclosed water harbor at the end of the navigable Hudson River. Other colonial ports had large harbors but lay far inland (Baltimore or Philadelphia), or were not connected to inland waterways (Charleston, South Carolina or Boston). This site characteristic gave New York an economic advantage during the colonial and postcolonial era.

The city's access to Albany gave traders in New York City a link to large volumes of natural resources and the early manufacturing centers of inland New England. Likewise, New York Harbor lies right on the open Atlantic Ocean with access to the wind-driven sailing trade routes coming from Africa, Latin America, and the Caribbean, and those ships heading back to northern Europe. Together, site and situation help explain why New York City's optimal port location became the trade and financial capital of the United States by the early 1800s.

Economic Site Factors Today

Site and situation can still be used today to compare the economic prominence of cities. Economic site factors such as land, labor, and capital can be used to estimate the capacity of industry and services to develop in a particular place. Competition between cities for new business locations and new jobs are intense. How much land is developed, how educated the workforce is, and how much investment capital is available in a city are all important indicators of the potential for urban economic development.

Housing and the Built Environment

Over half of the people in the world live in urban settlements of some type now. Very few North Americans spend more than 10 percent of their time outdoors. This fact means that the built environment (not the natural environment) has become the most important spatial environment for the majority of us. Structures such as houses, schools, stores, workshops, businesses, and recreational facilities make up the built environment. The cities, towns, villages, and suburbs are also our built environment on a larger scale. Most importantly, these places are not just our physical environment, they are our social environment, also called social space, where people meet and interact and carry on their daily activities.

Housing is shelter from the elements and wild animals but it also has another important function. The World Health Organization (WHO) has determined that housing is an important factor in human health. How safe and clean one's housing is directly impacts one's health. Housing needs to keep its residents dry, safe, and warm. Building codes and inspections ensure that safe buildings are built and maintained for home, school, and work use. They also protect us from building near floodplains or dirty, polluted rivers and industries. Housing must be clean and provide safe drinking water and adequate sewage and garbage-removal systems. Housing must finally be attractive and well maintained. It should provide us with a feeling of well-being and have safe places for our children to play and have fun. Other parts of the built environment—schools, stores, workplaces—must contain these necessary elements, too.

KNOW THE MODELS

> **CED 6.5**
> The Internal Structure of Cities

For the AP Human Geography Exam, you will need to know a number of urban models. As with the other models in the course, knowing the structure of the model is only part of the process—that allows you to answer the "where" questions. You also need to be able to explain the "who, why, and how" behind the different parts of the model. And you'll need to give real-world examples of what these theoretical models represent.

> It's not enough just to be able to describe the urban models! You'll need to be able to use them on the AP exam to explain the development, distribution, and size of cities.

If you can explain the different parts of the model and how they are related, then you will easily remember the shape. That is to say, spend more prep time understanding how the models work and what their parts represent, as opposed to trying to memorize the shapes of the models, which will probably be included on the exam.

Another thing that will help you remember and better understand the models is knowing how the models have changed over time, both in terms of how cities have changed historically, and in the different ways geographers have looked at the city. As you go from the concentric zone model to the galactic city model, think of each as an evolutionary step along the way to better understanding the changing urban landscape.

Concentric Zone Model

The **concentric zone model** was first published in 1923 by theorist Ernest Burgess. The model represents the Anglo-American city of the United States and Canada during the height of industrialization. Representations of the model vary but follow this general pattern:

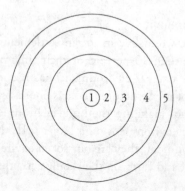

Practical Classifications	Alternate Terms
1. Central Business District	1. CBD, Downtown
2. Manufacturing and Wholesaling	2. Industrial Zone, Factory Zone
3. Lower-Class Housing	3. Working-Class, Blue Collar, Inner City
4. Middle-Class Housing	4. Professional-Class, White Collar, Suburbs
5. Upper-Class Housing	5. Country Estates, Exurbs

Theoretical Classifications	Density Classes
1. Central Business District	1. High-Density Commercial
2. Zone of Transition	2. Low-Density Commercial
3. Zone of Independent Workers Homes	3. High-Density Residential
4. Zone of Better Residences	4. Low-Density Residential
5. Commuter Zone	5. Very Low-Density Residential

The Model Explained

A number of different terms are used to describe the five concentric rings in the model, depending on the textbook or perspective of the researcher. Be familiar with the variations, since you never know how questions or potential answers could be worded. Also, keep in mind that it's a theoretical model and no city is perfectly laid out in nice, even rings. Let's go over some historical and current interpretations of each zone.

> **CED 6.6**
> Density and Land Use

The CBD

All cities possess a **central business district,** or **CBD**. In all models, the CBD contains the highest density of commercial land use. This is characterized by **verticality** of buildings such as the tendency to build skyscrapers that maximize the use of one parcel of urban land. The CBD also contains the **peak land value intersection,** or **PLVI**, the downtown intersection surrounded by the most expensive pieces of real estate.

Industrial Zone

In the concentric zone model, the CBD is surrounded by an area of low-density commercial land that contains space-dependent activities such as factories, warehouses, rail yards, and port facilities. More recently in the era of **deindustrialization**, many American and Canadian cities have rebuilt former industrial areas into **festival landscapes**, converting the spaces and buildings into parks, museums, sports stadiums, arenas, convention centers, and outdoor concert venues. Examples include the Inner Harbor of Baltimore, Skydome in Toronto, and Centennial Olympic Park in Atlanta.

Inner City Housing

When the city model was first developed back in the early 1900s, the average worker did not have a car and some did not have access to public transportation. Since walking and streetcars were the main modes of transport, most people tended to live as close to work as possible. This is why high-density housing surrounds both the CBD and industrial zones.

The types of housing structures ranged from poor tenements and small apartments to row houses and townhouses for better-paid workers. Today, some of these areas have been replaced or renovated through a process of **gentrification,** the economic reinvestment into existing buildings (discussed later in this chapter). However, most of these inner city neighborhoods retain their underdeveloped industrial-era housing or public housing projects and remain low-income areas.

The Suburbs

In the 1870s, the first planned developments with detached single-family homes began to appear on the periphery of American cities. One such place was Riverside, Illinois. Riverside was the design of Frederick Law Olmstead (the designer of Central Park in New York City), and is an example of the Victorian-era **garden city movement**. Homes were designed to look like European farmhouses with front lawns, and were built for the growing urban middle class of Chicago.

Although suburbs also contain garden apartments and townhouses, the detached single-family home has become the most common housing structure. Lots vary in size from a quarter acre to over an acre. We require a comparatively large amount of land for suburban housing. Suburbs continued to grow through the 1920s, but expansion ceased during the Great Depression and World War II.

It was following the war that American suburban growth really took off. The suburbs are home to a mostly middle-class to upper-class population. Today, about 52 percent of the American population lives in suburban areas, compared to 26 percent in inner cities and 21 percent in rural areas. Redrawing the model for today's day and age, we would vastly expand the "zone of better residences" as the suburbs have pushed outward and become the largest of the concentric zones. See the section on **suburbanization** later in this chapter.

The Exurbs

The **commuter zone** represents a wealthy area of people who own large tracts of land outside the city. Some of these could be described as country estates, while the owners of other exurban homes might be better described as **suitcase farmers,** who worked in the city but kept farms outside of town. Not only could these people afford large homes in the early 1900s, but they could also afford a personal vehicle or daily train ticket into town.

Today, many exurbs still retain the feel of the large country estate homes on multi-acre lots. However, many suburban and exurban areas in large cities have pushed well into traditional agricultural areas. This expansion has prompted the development of a number of regulations, including farmland protection laws, minimum-acreage zoning, and development boundary zones.

Related Topic: The Bid-Rent Curve

In addition to being a spatial model of the city, the concentric zone model has particular use as an economic model. The **bid-rent curve** represents the cost-to-distance relationship of real estate prices in the urban landscape. This is very similar to the land-rent curve related to von Thünen's model described in Chapter 7. The bid-rent curve is a cost function that shows the exponential increase in land prices as one moves closer toward the peak land value intersection (PLVI).

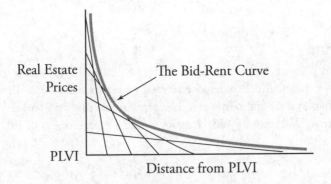

One way to help remember the principle of exponential cost increase is that space for downtown commercial real estate is sold or leased by the square foot. By comparison, land in the suburbs is sold by the acre. Along the curve, you could plot different land uses. Land for a suburban home or space for a suburban apartment building are not much different in price. However, land for that apartment building and land for building downtown are vastly different in price.

Sector Model

The **sector model** of urban structure was first proposed in 1939 by theorist Homer Hoyt. This model also applies to cities in the United States and Canada. In the model, the concepts of the industrial corridor and neighborhood are combined for practical purposes. These result in a much more realistic urban representation compared to the concentric zone model. The model is also used to depict ethnic variations in the city.

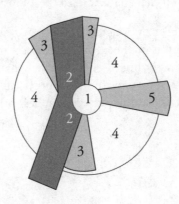

Theoretical Categories	Practical Descriptions
1. Central Business District	1. Central Business District, Downtown
2. Industrial Corridor	2. Rail Yards, Riverfronts, or Harbors
3. Lower-Class Housing	3. Ethnic Neighborhoods
4. Middle-Class Housing	4. Suburbs, WASPs
5. Upper-Class Housing	5. Elite Corridor or "The Boulevard"

The Model Explained

This is a standard central place model with the CBD at the center. Hoyt recognized that outside of the core business district, industrial space tended to be organized as a linear corridor surrounding a main transportation line. This could be a main rail line and parallel rail yard, a riverfront, or a harbor area. Warehouses and factories would be on either side of the corridor with equal access to transport.

In terms of residential space, Hoyt saw that a corridor of upper-class housing extended outward from the CBD of several cities. Examples of this include the Upper East Side in Manhattan, the Chicago North Shore, and Grosse Pointe in Detroit. Working-class neighborhoods also radiate out from the CBD along the industrial corridor. Other theorists recognized these lower-class housing areas as being generally **ethnic neighborhoods**, the result of immigration to industrial cities over previous decades.

By comparison, the middle-class areas of the city are broken into wide, separate areas radiating outward from downtown (remember that suburbs didn't boom until after World War II). At the time, the socio-cultural makeup of these areas tended to be dominated by **WASPs**, white Anglo-Saxon Protestants. WASPs would continue to be the majority in suburban middle-class neighborhoods until the late 1960s, when middle-class inner-city residents, including many white Catholics, began to move out in large numbers.

Related Topic: White Flight: Myth or Misnomer?

Many people, including social scientists, have described the phenomenon of people leaving inner-city areas of the United States as **white flight**. In truth, not everyone that left the city was white, and not all whites left the inner city. Regardless of race, many inner-city residents with middle-class incomes moved out to suburban districts to escape the social unrest and economic blight of deindustrialization that characterized the 1960s and 1970s in the United States.

Although most non-white suburban migrants integrated into mostly white suburban neighborhoods in small numbers, this was not always the case. Some areas, such as Prince George's County, Maryland, feature distinctly mixed suburban neighborhoods with large numbers of African Americans, many of whom are government workers in Washington, D.C. Conversely, inner-city areas in the United States still have large numbers of whites within a diverse mix of ethnicities.

Multiple-Nuclei Model

In 1945, geographers Chauncey Harris and Edward Ullman proposed the **multiple-nuclei model** of urban structure. This represents another evolutionary step in the conceptualization of the Anglo-American city. In the model, we see the first recognition of **suburban business districts** forming on the urban periphery. Below is a simplified graphic to explain the basic principles.

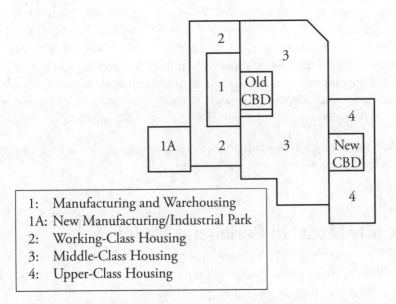

1:    Manufacturing and Warehousing
1A: New Manufacturing/Industrial Park
2:    Working-Class Housing
3:    Middle-Class Housing
4:    Upper-Class Housing

The Model Explained

Like the sector model, the multiple-nuclei model attempts to practically represent the urban landscape with neighborhoods and commercial corridors. However, the main difference is that instead of all commerce being focused on the center of the city as in the sector model, the term "multiple-nuclei" (the plural of nucleus or center) implies that there is more than one commercial center within the city landscape.

New **suburban CBDs** were emerging in post–World War II cities, and as suburbs spread outward, service industries followed. As will be discussed in the section on suburbanization later in this chapter, service providers came to the suburbs to be closer to their consumers and stay near members of the service workforce.

New areas of industrial development were also located on the urban periphery. The area labeled 1A represents the new manufacturing locations that were added for war production and after the war. Expansion to the suburbs was necessary since many downtown factory districts had no room for expansion. The urban periphery offered large tracts of land for heavy industry such as aircraft production and new automobile plants.

Related Topic: The "Death of the American Downtown" in the 1970s

The Old CBD, as it is labeled on the diagram above, was an area at risk in the last quarter of the 20th century. "Deindustrialization" meant old factories and related industry and services in downtown areas closed down. As a result, the labor force moved away and capital investment into downtown real estate dwindled. Having lost many consumers (sources of income and investment), the CBD was no longer the most prominent place in the urban economy.

The country was moving away from a manufacturing-based economy to a service-based economy. As services migrated to the suburbs, so did the money to invest in commercial real estate. Soon the old CBD began to look run-down and dated. Prominent retailers that were once located on Main Street were replaced by discount stores or, in many cases, sat empty. City government efforts at downtown "urban renewal" projects had little impact. City downtowns had additional problems with crime and homelessness that cost money and diverted attention.

On the urban periphery, new malls and shopping centers flourished in suburban areas. Developers continued their focus on suburban expansion and suburban CBD development until the mid-1990s when a renewed focus on downtowns received business and government attention. Downtown property prices had dropped significantly through the 1980s and early 1990s, and cost-effective opportunities to reinvest in downtown real estate began to emerge. We still see many of these "urban redevelopment" projects in cities today and many have become successful as downtowns have become more appealing and, in some cases, trendy.

See more later in this chapter on gentrification. Also see the section on the attempts to create "cool" cities (page 349) in the section on urban geography.

Galactic City Model or Peripheral Model

In the last half of the 20th century, urban geographers noticed that many of the new suburban CBDs in the United States and Canada had become specialized toward a particular industrial or service sector. In many ways, the following model, regardless of what name is used, represents the **post-industrial city** with its several, dispersed business districts. Here is a simplified version:

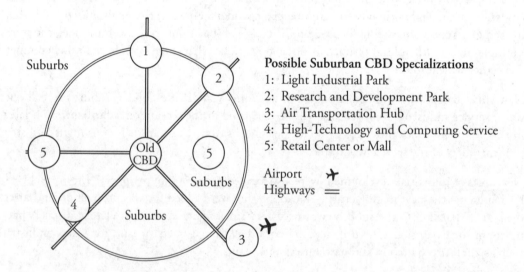

Possible Suburban CBD Specializations
1: Light Industrial Park
2: Research and Development Park
3: Air Transportation Hub
4: High-Technology and Computing Service
5: Retail Center or Mall

Airport ✈
Highways ═

The Model Explained

The model represents a distinct decentralization of the commercial urban landscape as the economy has transitioned to services as the leading form of production. It's not that manufacturing has disappeared; it has just declined significantly and become specialized. This specialization has meant that new manufacturing facilities tend to be much smaller and require low-cost land to afford to operate. Therefore, these new facilities tend to be in specially designated industrial parks on the urban periphery. They are often subsidized by local governments to reduce costs and increase employment opportunities.

Suburban retailing often occurs in multiple locations around the city. The retail center closer to the old CBD is likely an older center from the 1950s or 1960s among older neighborhoods. The retail center located at the intersection of the belt highway and the artery leading out from the old CBD is likely a newer center built late in the completion of the interstate highway in the 1970s or 1980s. The point to take away from this is that **transportation nodes** are common locations for suburban CBDs due to their high level of access. Other types of service specializations are found in suburban CBDs.

Here are a few examples, including those shown on the diagram on the previous page:

High-technology and computing
Research and development
Transportation services
Bio-technology
Hospital centers
Telecommunications and call centers
Banking and finance
Suburban government centers
Universities or branch campuses

Related Topic: The Rise of Dulles

Commercial development around airports is as common as airports themselves. Hub airports, from which airlines service a large number of regional destinations, are especially important for local service and commercial land development.

For example, in the late 1990s, AOL and MCI Worldcom located large corporate headquarter facilities just north of Dulles International Airport in the northern Virginia suburbs of the Washington metropolitan area. These companies chose the D.C. area so they could be close to federal communication regulators and Internet service providers. However, their management workforce needed to travel the country and world on a frequent basis. The Dulles location proved very efficient for business travel.

The only problem was that these immense facilities were built on old farmland where no municipality or mailing address had previously existed. When AOL representatives went to the airport post office to figure out the company's new mailing address, they found out that no postal town or city was listed. The post office's suggestion was to just call it "Dulles." The name stuck and a new place was created.

Latin American City Model

Whereas the previous models depicted the Anglo-American cities of the United States and Canada, there are also models that depict the common urban landscapes of international locations. Only one of these appears commonly on the AP exam. The **Latin American city model** was first presented by Larry Ford and Ernst Griffin in 1980. The model was updated in 1996, but not all introductory textbooks show the changes.

Here is the model as it appeared in its original form:

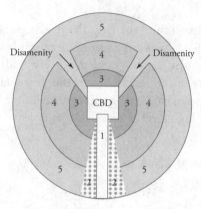

1: The Spine (or Commercial Spine)
2: Zone of Elite Residences
3: Zone of Maturity
4: Zone of *In Situ* Accretion
5: Zone of Peripheral Squatter Settlements

The Model Explained

This model is important as an example of the colonial city. The effects of European colonial rule on many cities in Latin America, Africa, and Asia are significant. Often, colonial powers demolished old precolonial cities and rebuilt them in the European style. In other cases, new cities were built according to specific plans. The Latin American model tends to represent the latter. During the 1500s, the Spanish government in the New World enacted a number of colonial legal codes collectively known as the **Laws of the Indies**. One of these laws dealt specifically with the planning and the layout of colonial cities.

The CBD

Just as it is in Anglo-America, the CBD in Latin American cities is also at the center of the model. Historically, the Laws of the Indies stipulated that each settlement have a central square known as a **plaza**. This was to reproduce the style of European cities such as Madrid, which has at its center the *Plaza Mayor*. Surrounding the plaza, the centers of government, religion, and commerce are located. Today, the CBD remains the primary location for businesses. This is unlike the United States and Canada, where numerous suburban CBDs dominate the economy. CBDs in Latin America are also vertically oriented and most large cities have a cluster of skyscrapers at their core.

The Commercial Spine

The Laws of the Indies also required that a main boulevard be constructed leading from the plaza to the outskirts of the city. In some large cities today, several boulevards radiate outward from the central square. For example, in Buenos Aires, three main boulevards stretch outward from the central *Plaza de Mayo*. In the colonial era, the spine was often the location for the homes of the wealthiest merchants and landowners. Today, many of these old homes have been replaced by office towers and high-rise condominiums. As such, the spine is still an area of wealth and prestige.

The Zone of Elite Housing

Similar to the Sector model, an area of upper-class housing straddles the spine leading outward from the city center. In the colonial era, social status was gained by having your home along these main avenue districts. This remains true today. One of the primary differences between the urban models of Anglo-America and the Latin American model is that in Latin America, the wealthiest people tend to live close to the CBD, whereas in the United States and Canada, the wealthiest people tend to live on the urban periphery.

The Zone of Maturity

This area of middle- to upper-class housing surrounds much of the CBD. The Laws of the Indies segregated housing in Spanish colonial settlements. Only those of European descent were allowed to own homes and live within the city limits or walls. The name "maturity" comes from the type of European architecture and building materials used in homes of this zone. Today, many of the colonial-era homes are being torn down and lost to commercial redevelopment as the CBD expands, or to the proliferation of high-rise apartment buildings surrounding the city centers.

The Zone of *In Situ* Accretion

In the colonial era, this was the area outside of the city limits or walls where people of indigenous or mixed descent made their homes. The name "*in situ* accretion" means growth over time (accretion) in the ground (the Latin, *in situ*). This is meant to describe the building materials and architecture of housing, which relied primarily on local timber and mud brick, known in some areas as *adobe*. Today, these are areas of middle-class and working-class housing. Many are single-family homes surrounded by walls or iron gates. The interiors of these homes may still contain parts of old colonial-era homes that they were built on top of or next to.

The Zone of Peripheral Squatter Settlements

Squatter settlements on the urban periphery are home to most of the urban poor in Latin America. By comparison, in the United States, the peripheral suburbs are dominated by middle-class housing and the poor are generally in the inner city areas. These communities are known by several names such as *colonias* in Mexico, *barriadas* in Peru, or *invasiones* in Colombia and Ecuador.

Squatter settlements did not become a common feature of the Latin American urban landscape until the years following World War II. The rise of industrialization and the numerous civil wars fought in rural regions, among other **push and pull factors**, led to an increase in rural-to-urban migration in the region (see Chapter 4 for more on rural-to-urban migration). For most migrants new to cities, there was little to no available housing. Part of the reason for this is a lack of real estate investment for low-income housing in Latin American cities. This is different from the United States and Canada, where during the 1800s and early 1900s, numerous inner-city dwellings were built to house European immigrant workers.

Squatting and Land Tenure

In Latin America, rural-to-urban migrants have been forced to build their own squatter settlements on the urban periphery. **Squatters** are people who settle on land that they don't own. Often, the land available on the urban periphery is owned by either governments or agricultural landowners. Land that is sitting idle and unoccupied is most commonly targeted by communities of squatters. This is because in many countries, idle land, regardless of who owns it, can be legally squatted upon if the new residents make good use of it. This is the opposite of real estate laws in the United States that favor landowners, but is a common legal standard in many social democracies.

To avoid retributions from landowners and local police, squatters generally settle a new area overnight with a large number of families. This is known as a **land invasion**. A squatter camp can be quickly erected with makeshift homes using available building materials, such as scrap wood, plastic, and blue plastic tarps. These rudimentary homes may give squatters some legal protections, since in some places it is illegal for the government to tear down housing of any type without court authority to do so.

Over time, the squatter homes are improved upon and utilize sturdier materials. A 30-year-old squatter settlement may look like formal housing with brick walls and metal roofs, along with electric power or other utilities. However, as you move through to new squatter settlements farther out of the city, the quality of housing declines, as does the availability of utilities and other services such as bus lines.

Through these tactics, squatters attempt to achieve **land tenure**—that is, legal right or title to the land upon which they build their homes. It can take years if not decades to formalize property ownership. Until then, there is always the risk that squatters could be run off the land. To minimize this risk, squatter communities often pool their resources to pay off landowners, bribe local officials, or if money is short, promise local elected leaders the guarantee of votes in exchange for their protection. These political relationships are also important for later gaining government funding for schools, transit, clean water, and other public services.

Zones of Disamenity

These are squatter communities closer to the center of the city. They are built on land that is deemed unsuitable for standard homes and businesses, including steep hillsides, flood plains, old industrial sites, refuse dumps, and land near airports. They are settled because of their availability and due to their close proximity to work opportunities in the city center. For example, *favelas* in Rio de Janeiro rise up the steep hillsides of the city, some built partially on top of one another. The mountainous coastline leaves land available for low-income homes, as most of the flat land is taken for formal housing and commercial development. One problem with settling these areas is that they are often unstable, and a mudslide, flood, or fire can devastate the whole community.

Related Topic: The Updated Model

The updated model of the Latin American city contains a few additional parts that reflect the growth of the region's economy. In the Zone of Maturity, CBD expansion and the growth of high-rise apartments has caused city residents to be concerned that much of the old city character is being lost. In response, a number of cities have promoted the gentrification of colonial-era homes and remaining neighborhoods. Like historical preservation efforts elsewhere, these neighborhoods have value in their tourist appeal and the protection of local cultural heritage. The updated model adds a slice of the Zone of Maturity, which is labeled "gentrification."

The Zone of Peripheral Squatter Settlements is expanded in the updated model to reflect the influx of rural-to-urban migration. Within this zone, three features have been added to the model. At the outer end of the commercial spine, shopping malls are common in Latin America; thus, a mall is placed here on the updated model. Belt highways have been constructed around a number of major Latin American cities. Therefore, a circular *periférico*, or beltway, is added running through the middle of the zone. Lastly, opposite the mall on the other side of the model is the industrial park zone. These zones are common and prolific on the outskirts of many Latin American cities, including the *maquiladoras* of northern Mexico, where manufacturing boomed following the passage of the North American Free Trade Agreement (NAFTA).

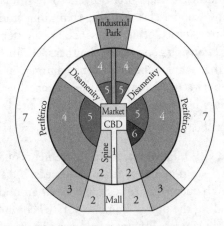

1. Commercial
2. Elite Residential Sector
3. Middle-Class Residential
4. Zone of *In Situ* Accretion
5. Zone of Maturity
6. Gentrification
7. Zone of Peripheral Squatter Settlements

Southeast Asian City Model

Other parts of the world also have characteristic urban landscapes. The **Southeast Asian city model** predates the Latin American city model; it was developed in 1967 by geographer Terrence Garry McGee, who noticed similarities in land use among several Asian cities.

A Generalized Model of Land Use Areas
in the Large Southeast Asian City

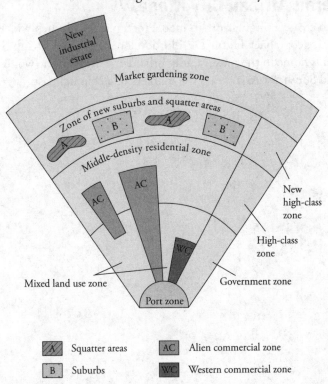

A Squatter areas	AC Alien commercial zone
B Suburbs	WC Western commercial zone

The Model Explained

Southeast Asia contains some of the fastest growing and most densely populated cities in the world. Many are marked by high-rise developments, and some of the tallest buildings on Earth are located in this part of the world. The Southeast Asian model bears some similarities to the Latin American model. Both feature a strip of upper-class housing stemming from the center, middle class residential areas close to the inner city, and the presence of squatter settlements on the periphery. Adjacent to the high-class housing zone in the Southeast Asian model is the zone of government offices, an elite sector that may be likened to the commercial spine in the Latin American model. A major difference between the models is the existence of new suburbs on the periphery, which include middle class housing. This is reflective of the larger middle class, compared to a small middle class in Latin America.

You may also notice the lack of a designated CBD. However, there are elements of a traditional CBD scattered throughout the model. McGee noted that many Southeast Asian cities are focused around the old colonial port zone, characteristic of a city centered around the export business. The mixed land use zone surrounding the port is home to various commercial activities, including light industry and unofficial businesses. There are also two immigrant commercial sectors unique to the Southeast Asian model. The Western commercial zone is functionally a CBD, but is populated primarily by Western rather than local businesses. The alien commercial zone is dominated by Chinese merchants who have migrated to these cities and typically reside in the same buildings as their businesses. Because of the immigrant commercial zones, these cities tend to have blended cultures but also strong ethnic bonds among migrant communities. At the outskirts of the city, beyond the inner city and peripheral residential zones, lie the market gardening zone and a recently built industrial zone, or "estate."

The Sub-Saharan African City Model

While it is difficult to create a singular urban model for a place with such widely varied history and culture as Africa, geographer Harm De Blij developed a model of sub-Saharan African cities in 1968. Africa is home to the most rapidly urbanizing areas in the world and, like much of Latin America and Southeast Asia, bears the markers of a colonial past.

A Model Sub-Saharan African City

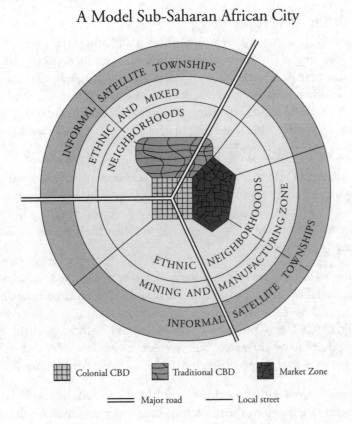

INFORMAL SATELLITE TOWNSHIPS

ETHNIC AND MIXED NEIGHBORHOODS

ETHNIC NEIGHBORHOOODS

MINING AND MANUFACTURING ZONE

INFORMAL SATELLITE TOWNSHIPS

⊞ Colonial CBD   ▨ Traditional CBD   ▦ Market Zone

══ Major road   ── Local street

The Model Explained

The center of the sub-Saharan African city model features three distinct CBDs that reflect the history of African urban development. The former colonial CBD is laid out on a grid pattern like that of many European cities, contains the most vertical development, and is connected to other parts of the city by major, planned roads. The traditional CBD is the center of most commercial activity and is characterized by traditional, mostly single-story architecture. Finally, the market zone is an open-air area in which informal business is periodically conducted curbside or at stalls. The mining and manufacturing zone at the outskirts of the city is indicative of the major industries found in sub-Saharan Africa.

As in Latin American and Southeast Asia, the quality of residences tends to get poorer closer to the periphery; the informal satellite townships surrounding the mining and manufacturing areas are largely composed of squatter settlements, or "**shantytowns**," many of whose residents work in the mines. The prevalence of ethnic neighborhoods reflects the strong sense of tribalism present throughout Africa. Note the lack of apparent upper and middle-class areas, which is indicative of widespread poverty and overall lack of development. However, African cities are rapidly growing and changing, so for this reason the African city model is sometimes criticized as being outdated.

International Urban Diversity

Cities around the world have very different urban forms and structure. Even within a specific region or country, you find many interesting variations. Cities in Western Europe are much more compact in size than U.S. cities. They were developed for pedestrians and are smaller in area to permit residents to easily walk everywhere they need to go. Urban skylines don't generally contain the skyscrapers seen in other parts of the world. Public transportation is well-developed and most people live within walking distance of their schools, work, and shopping.

In Eastern Europe and countries of the former Soviet Union, the flavor of central planning reminds us of the Soviet era. There is a strict division between urban and rural zones and the overwhelming majority of residents live in apartments. The central part of the city (Central Cultural District, or CCD) was not used for retail or commercial purposes but rather for government activities and recreational parks. Zones of uniform housing, called **microdistricts,** provided worker housing near job sites.

Cities in the developing world have widely divergent forms determined in large part by their religious makeup, colonial history, socialist influences, and many other cultural and urban land-use influences. Some of these cities were established as colonial administrative centers: Mumbai (Bombay) and Kolkata (Calcutta), products of the British raj in India, and the French city of Dakar in Senegal. Other capital cities were built to serve as growth poles and were planned to attract people and industry to that specific region of the country (Brasilia, Brazil).

Urban forms vary greatly even within a cultural realm. For example, in South Asia we find several different city types ranging from the traditional bazaar city and military installation to the colonial city and the resort city. There are some important characteristics that ALL developing-world cities possess: a large modern center of commerce, a massive immigrant population from rural regions, rapidly growing rates of natural increase, and huge outer rings of squatter settlements that lack even the most basic amenities.

| CED 6.9 |
| Urban Data |

URBAN DATA

No matter where in the world they are located, cities have one thing in common: they need to monitor themselves. Billions of lives and careers depends upon the quality of their schools and hospitals, the functioning of their roads, their air and water quality, even the happiness of the population. To track their own doings, cities gather two types of data about themselves: **qualitative** and **quantitative data**. Qualitative data is collected through surveys, polls, interviews, and other "soft" forms of questioning. This type of data can be debated because it is so subjective. Quantitative data, on the other hand, is numerical and cannot be argued with. It includes such data as traffic statistics, graduation rates, and incidence of illnesses. Collecting and analyzing both types of data help cities understand how to improve the standard of living for their inhabitants.

KNOW THE CONCEPTS

A large number of urban geography concepts may be tested on the AP Human Geography Exam. Here are a few categories with examples included.

Suburbanization

We'll begin with suburbanization due to its many links to the material in the Know the Models section. As a quick review of what was covered in the models, keep these suburban concepts in mind:

- Though many people live in suburban apartments and townhouses, the detached single-family home is the dominant feature on the American suburban landscape.

- The suburbs are predominantly middle-class, economically. However, many upper-class suburbs exist, as do some lower-class suburban neighborhoods.

- The first suburban single-family homes appeared in the 1890s. One early example is Riverside, Illinois, outside Chicago, which was designed by Frederick Law Olmstead.

- The original American suburbs were culturally populated by WASPs. This changed between the late 1960s and the 1980s when suburbs become more integrated with Catholic and non-white middle-class populations, who formerly lived in inner-city areas.

- According to the American Housing Survey in 2017, just over half of people in the United States describe their neighborhood as suburban.

- Suburbs continue to expand outward and are the largest zones within urban models.

Combine these facts and historical perspectives with the material in the following subsections.

Home Mortgage Finance and Suburban Growth

In post–World War II United States, homeownership increased significantly as a result of **federal home loan programs** such as the G.I. Bill. Several million war veterans and members of the Armed Forces were eligible for guaranteed federal home loans. Other federal programs, such as the Federal Housing Administration and the public finance mortgage corporations Freddie Mac and Fannie Mae, radically increased the number of mortgages available to the American public with regulated interest rates and limited processing fees.

The result was a massive influx in new home construction during the 1950s and 1960s. Prior to World War II, rates of homeownership were limited. After the war, new large-scale housing developments were constructed. Demand was so high that factory-style housing construction methods—using prefabricated parts and specialized construction teams—became common. **Levittowns** were an example of this. In places such as Long Island; suburban Philadelphia; San Juan, Puerto Rico; and other cities, the Levitt Company built large communities of single-family homes in a short amount of time. New Levitt homes could be constructed start to finish in less than 18 days. Many companies copied the Levitt model, and similar communities were constructed around the country during the 1950s and 1960s.

Service Relocation in the Suburbs

The boom in suburban home construction prompted a number of small service providers to locate in suburban areas. As shown in the multiple-nuclei model, limited suburban business districts began to emerge from 1945 onward. These featured **basic services** like food, the family doctor, fuel, and auto repair, as well as **non-basic services** such as dry-cleaning and gift shops. Later, in the 1970s, the combination of **middle-class flight** from the inner city and the deindustrialization of urban manufacturing economies prompted even more and larger service providers to **relocate** to suburban areas.

Two factors causing people to leave cities were at work. First, service providers realized much of their consumer base moved away from the old CBDs that had been the traditional service centers. Simply put, *companies brought the services to where the suburban consumers lived.* Large suburban retail centers and shopping malls became the places of service provision as the same services in the old CBD closed down.

Second, many service firms such as banks, insurance companies, and other white-collar businesses realized their labor force was moving farther and farther out from the old CBD. This influenced many corporate-service offices to relocate to suburban CBDs. *Companies brought the service industry jobs to where the white-collar workers lived.* These two factors worked in concert to establish suburban central business districts as the central places of the post-industrial service economy by the 1980s. As such, the suburban office park replaced downtown office buildings as the contemporary place of business and commerce.

Suburban Sprawl

Suburban **sprawl** is defined as the expansion of housing, transportation, and commercial development to undeveloped land on the urban periphery. In and of itself, suburban expansion is not necessarily a bad thing. The basic question is whether the expansion of suburbs is sustainable. Sustainability within the suburban context can be measured in both economic and environmental terms. Suburban sprawl has been cited as the cause behind a number of problems such as traffic congestion, shortfalls in public school funding, environmental degradation, and economic decline in farming.

CED 6.2
Cities Across the World

A number of suburban political **anti-growth movements** have emerged in the United States and Canada. These groups push for new laws and regulations that slow suburban development and limit approval of new suburban roads and highways. Anti-growth sentiment is especially strong in places where the surrounding rural areas are environmentally sensitive or have historical significance.

An example is Loudoun County, Virginia, where in the 1990s, the county board of supervisors enacted a series of **growth boundaries** that set minimums for the lot sizes of new homes. Supporters were known to exclaim, "Don't Fairfax Loudoun!" in reference to neighboring Fairfax County, which has over a million people in roughly the same-sized area just to the east. On the other side of the argument were real estate agents, developers, and new residents who cited the rapidly increasing home prices in the Washington, D.C., metropolitan area as a reason to increase the local housing supply and loosen the development boundary regulations. Although there have been some changes to the original growth boundaries, much of central and western Loudoun County remains sparsely developed and retains its rural character.

Increased congestion in suburbs from suburban commercial development and sprawl has compelled some suburban residents to move even farther away from the city. **Counterurbanization** is the movement of inner-city or suburban residents to rural areas to escape the congestion, crime, pollution, and other negative aspects of the urban landscape. To maintain their jobs, these people either endure long commutes or participate in the workplace by **telecommuting** and working from home. See more related to sprawl in the section on urban sustainability later in this chapter.

Edge Cities

The concept of the **edge city** was first put forward by journalist (and honorary geographer) Joel Garreau in 1991. Garreau recognized the importance of suburban central business districts to the new service-based economy in the United States and Canada. He also noticed that some suburban CBDs had grown to immense size and economic prominence. Many were built on former agricultural areas and lacked a municipal government, though some were built on towns that expanded into edge cities.

To be considered an edge city, a suburban CBD would have the following characteristics:

- Minimum of 5 million square feet of office space
- Minimum 600,000 square feet of retail space
- No city government, except where built atop an existing town
- High daytime population, low nighttime population
- Located at transportation nodes or along commuter corridors

One effect that edge city growth has had in many large metropolitan areas is the large increase in **lateral commuting** between suburbs and edge cities. In some cases, significant amounts of **counter-commuting** have been detected from downtown residences to edge city locations. Traditionally, transportation planners have worked from a hub-and-spoke model of commuting in and out of the old CBD. Large amounts of lateral commuting and counter-commuting have made it necessary to construct transportation plans that have multiple hub-and-spoke traffic-flow patterns centered on edge-city locations in addition to the old CBD.

The Tyson's Corner Edge City

The quintessential edge city is Tyson's Corner, Virginia. Tyson's is located eight miles west of Washington, D.C., at the intersection of the Capital Beltway and Virginia Routes 7 and 123. The edge-city complex of nearly 18,000,000 square feet of office space contains a number of government contracting and telecommunications firms, as well as the headquarters of the National Automobile Dealers Association, *USA Today,* and Freddie Mac.

At its core are not one but two large regional shopping malls, Tyson's Corner Center, and the up-market Tyson's Galleria. In addition, a long string of big-box retail stores can be found along Route 7. Tyson's Corner has more office and retail space than downtown Miami, Florida (not to be confused with the Miami–Ft. Lauderdale metropolitan area).

This table provides examples of other edge cities in the United States and Canada:

Boston Area	Toronto	Washington (Maryland)
The Route 128 Corridor	Scarborough	Bethesda
Framingham	Markham	Rockville
Quincy-Braintree	Mississauga	Silver Spring
Waltham	Yorkville	New Carrollton

Chicago Area	Houston Area	Washington (Virginia)
O'Hare Airport	Clear Lake	Rosslyn
Northbrook	Greenspoint	Courthouse-Clarendon
Lombard	Greenway Plaza	Ballston
Naperville	Katy Freeway	Reston-Herndon
Oak Brook	Post Oak	Crystal City-National Airport
Schaumburg	Westchase	Dulles Airport

Numerous edge cities can be found in the areas surrounding New York, Los Angeles, and San Francisco. Other metropolitan areas with multiple edge cities include Detroit, Philadelphia, Baltimore, Montreal, Vancouver, Minneapolis, Seattle, San Diego, Dallas-Fort Worth, Phoenix, Atlanta, Orlando, and Miami.

In 2001, urban studies professor Robert E. Lang coined the term "**boomburbs**" to describe incorporated suburbs that have exploded in size to populations of 100,000 or greater. These "accidental cities" are not the major metropolitan centers in their areas and retain their suburban characters, even as their populations outpace those of some established major cities. For example, the largest boomburb, Mesa, Arizona, a population of around half a million more than Minneapolis, St. Louis, or Miami. While boomburbs are similar to edge cities in the sense that both signify rapid development on the fringe of a primary city, they differ in that boomburbs were already established communities that have simply rapidly expanded. As such, they also retain a much higher proportion of residential space compared to largely commercial edge cities.

City Types

In addition to edge cities, described in the previous section on suburbanization, there are a number of city types tested on the AP Human Geography Exam.

Colonial City

Cities with origins as centers of colonial trade or administration are classified together as **colonial cities**. In the postcolonial era of independence, many of these cities retained their European-style buildings and street networks.

However, newly independent governments have often changed street names and place-names to reflect local culture and social history. For instance, India has renamed the major cities of Mumbai, Chennai, and Kolkata from their respective British colonial names of Bombay, Madras, and Calcutta. Other countries such as Brazil have moved their national capitals away from former colonial capitals. In 1960, the Brazilian government moved from Rio de Janeiro to Brasilia, escaping the congestion of the old colonial capital and building a new modern city planned just for the country's government.

Fall-Line Cities

Larger colonial-era cities in the United States and Canada were most often port locations. The term **fall-line cities** is used to describe the ports that lay upstream on coastal rivers at the point where navigation was no longer possible by ocean-going ships. The fall-line is where a river's tidal estuary transitions to an upland stream at the first set of river falls.

As such, these were economic **break-in-bulk points** (or break-of-bulk) where ships were offloaded and then packed with outgoing trade. In the early part of the Industrial Revolution, the waterfalls on these rivers could be harnessed for hydropower. Waterwheels turned to drive industrial production of furniture, textiles, and food processing in these early American cities. Thus, many fall-line cities became both centers of trade and manufacturing in the 1800s.

Industrial Fall-Line Cities in the United States:
- Boston, Massachusetts
- Providence, Rhode Island
- Albany, New York
- Philadelphia, Pennsylvania
- Baltimore, Maryland
- Washington (Georgetown), D.C.
- Fredericksburg, Virginia
- Richmond, Virginia

In Canada:
Montreal, Québec, also lies on the fall-line of the St. Lawrence River. However, it is rarely listed with the other fall-line cities.

Medieval Cities

Medieval cities are urban centers that predate the European Renaissance, roughly 1400 C.E. In addition to Paris, Rome, and London, medieval cities in Europe include Cologne in Germany, Marseille in France, and York in England, all of which were originally settled during the Roman era and developed into significant centers of trade and population during the medieval period.

Outside of Europe, medieval cities include Istanbul, Turkey; Samarkand, Uzbekistan; Kyoto, Japan; and Beijing, China. These all became important centers of trade and governance during the medieval period.

Gateway Cities

Gateway cities are places where immigrants make their way into a country. As a result, gateway cities tend to have significant immigrant populations. Examples of gateway cities include New York City and Miami in the United States; Toronto and Vancouver in Canada; and ports in Europe such as Rotterdam and Hamburg.

Entrepôt

Entrepôt describes a port city in which goods are shipped in at one price and shipped out to other port locations at a higher price, resulting in profitable trade. This type of trade is made possible by the lack of customs duties (import and export taxes) that are common in most other port cities. Entrepôts tend to become large centers of finance, warehousing, and the global shipping trade. Examples include Singapore, Hong Kong, and Dubai.

Megacities

The definition of the **megacity** is a metropolitan area with more than 10 million people. About 28 cities qualify as megacities. You can probably think of the big world centers like New York and Tokyo. However, you should keep in mind places like Mexico City in Mexico (21.6 million), Dhaka in Bangladesh (19.6 million), Cairo in Egypt (20.0 million), and Mumbai in India (20.0 million). Don't try to memorize it, but get to know examples:

Rank	City	Population (in Millions)
1	Tokyo	37.3
2	Delhi	32.1
3	Shanghai	28.5
4	Dhaka	22.5
5	Sao Paolo	22.4
6	Mexico City	22.1
7	Cairo	21.8
8	Beijing	21.3
9	Mumbai	20.9
10	Osaka	19.1
11	Chongqing	16.9
12	Karachi	16.8
13	Istanbul	15.6
14	Kinshasa	15.6
15	Lagos	15.4
16	Buenos Aires	15.4
17	Kolkata	15.1
18	Manila	14.4
19	Tianjin	14.0
20	Guangzhou	13.9

World City Populations 2022

Megalopolis

A **megalopolis** is the merging of the urbanized areas of two or more cities, generally through suburban growth and expansion. The name was given by French geographer Jean Gottmann following his travels through the Northeastern United States during the 1950s. Other megalopolises may form in coming decades, which may challenge Tokyo for the world's largest **conurbation**, or combined city.

Examples of Megalopolises:
- **Northeastern United States**: Boston, Providence, New York City, Philadelphia, Baltimore, Washington (also referred to as BosWash). Can also include Arlington, Richmond, and Norfolk, which are all cities in Virginia.
- **Ruhr Valley**: Essen, Dortmund, Duisburg, Bochum
- **Tokaido**: Tokyo, Yokohama
- **Randstad**: Amsterdam, The Hague, Rotterdam
- **Keihanshin**: Kobe, Osaka, Kyoto

Possible Future Megalopolises:
- **Pearl River Delta**: Guangdong, Shenzhen, Hong Kong, Macau
- **Southeastern Brazil**: São Paulo, Rio de Janeiro, Santos, Belo Horizonte

World City

The **world city** designation signifies a metropolitan area as a global center for finance, trade, and commerce. As such, world cities are ranked in levels of importance, and provide an example of **urban hierarchy** at a global scale. The **first-order world cities** include New York City, London, and Tokyo. The **second-order world cities** include Los Angeles, Washington, D.C., Chicago, Frankfurt, Paris, Brussels, Zürich, Hong Kong, São Paulo, and Singapore. A long list of the **third-order world cities** includes places such as Miami, Toronto, Seoul, Mumbai, Amsterdam, Buenos Aires, and Sydney.

> **CED 6.3**
> Cities and Globalization

Primate Cities

When the largest city in a country has at least twice the population of the country's next largest city, it can be designated as a **primate city**. In some cases, primate cities are several times larger than the next largest city. The situation of **urban primacy** is sometimes blamed when there is uneven economic development within a country. Due to its high population, the primate city can receive a large majority of a country's economic development and investment.

For example, Bangkok, Thailand, is a rapidly developing industrial and service center with an improving quality of life for its residents. By comparison, much of the rest of Thailand remains a chronically underdeveloped rural region without access to many services. Here's another example. To counter the effects of urban primacy, the French government has regulated industrial investment for many years, directing portions of public industrial investment to locations away from metropolitan Paris. Regional manufacturing centers such as Marseille, Lyon, Lille, Clermont, and Bordeaux have benefited significantly from this purposeful **decentralization** of industrial development funding.

Examples of Primate Cities:

Asia/Oceania	North Africa/ Middle East	Latin America	Europe	Sub-Saharan Africa
Seoul, South Korea	Cairo, Egypt	Mexico City, Mexico	Paris, France	Dakar, Senegal
Bangkok, Thailand	Algiers, Algeria	Buenos Aires, Argentina	Lisbon, Portugal	Kinshasa, Dem. Rep. of Congo
Manila, Philippines	Amman, Jordan	Lima, Peru	Vienna, Austria	Nairobi, Kenya
Sydney, Australia	Beirut, Lebanon	Santiago, Chile	Warsaw, Poland	Luanda, Angola

The Rank-Size Rule

Related to the primate city concept is the theoretical notion of the **rank-size rule**. Population geographers have recognized an urban hierarchy of city populations, especially in countries with long social histories. Under the rank-size rule, a country's second largest city is half the size of its largest city; the third-largest city is one-third the size of the largest city; and so on, such that the eighth largest city is one-eighth the size of the largest city.

Be able to recognize the formulaic definition for the rank-size rule:

> The nth largest city is $1/n$ the size of the country's largest city.

However, few countries have city populations that precisely follow the rule. The hierarchy of cities in the United States or in Russia is a close approximation of the rule.

Urban Society

In addition to the ethnic and class-based comparisons within the urban models, a few other urban social concepts are important to know. Two significant areas of study are segregation and urban social change.

Segregation

Ethnic neighborhoods are, in some cases, areas of *de facto* **segregation** where no law requiring ethnic or racial segregation exists, yet they nonetheless remain zones of separation. Historically, legal or "*de jure*" segregation existed in the United States in a number of ethnic and racial situations. The segregation laws against African Americans in the "Jim Crow" American South are an example of *de jure* segregation. Asian immigrants in the 1800s were also segregated by law in cities across the country. Today, **Chinatowns** are often seen as cultural districts, but many have their origins as zones where Chinese, Filipino, and Japanese migrants were forced to live.

African Americans have faced discriminatory real estate practices even in northern and western states. Although illegal today, banks and insurers historically engaged in **redlining,** designating neighborhoods on company maps where home mortgage and insurance applications would be automatically denied. The Federal Housing Administration now enforces rules against redlining and cases continue to be prosecuted.

Restrictive covenants were another means of racial discrimination through the real estate system. At the behest of neighbors and local politicians, homeowners added special covenants to their home real estate titles, restricting future sale of a home to white-only buyers. Some covenants also attempted to restrict Jews from buying homes. Such covenants are illegal today under federal fair-housing laws. However, title research often uncovers covenants in old titles during home sales—by law these must be ignored.

Even following the Civil Rights Act of 1964, some white urban communities openly engaged in **racial steering,** mainly through the use of real estate agents. When non-whites attempted to buy homes, real estate companies or their agents purposefully drove them to racially specific neighborhoods, regardless of their income or ability to pay for a house. At the same time, many real estate agents and developers also profited from racial prejudice in a common practice called **blockbusting**. Agents would convince white homeowners to sell their homes quickly and cheaply by leading them to believe that minorities were moving into their neighborhoods and that property values would consequently decline. They would then sell those homes at a considerable profit to prosperous non-whites looking to escape the inner city. These practices were banned by the Fair Housing Act in 1968, but cases have continued, including three lawsuits in 2006 by state attorneys general against realtors in Illinois, Michigan, and New York.

Urban Social Change

In many cities, a distinct social pattern of **invasion** and **succession** typifies the long-term turnover of neighborhood social and ethnic composition. Over time, one ethnic group or economic class leaves a neighborhood and is replaced by another.

Women and the City

Despite the job losses and outmigration caused by deindustrialization, remaining inner-city populations have changed and adapted to the new urban economic landscape. Gender is an important factor in these changes. The percentage of **female-headed households** in urban areas has increased significantly in recent decades. Working mothers are an important demographic group and are currently the subject of geographic research.

Geographer **Susan Hansen**, in particular, has focused on the urban transportation patterns of working mothers. Her work shows that the commuting patterns of female heads of household are different from male commuters. Specifically, female heads of household are likely to depend on public transportation and thus must live near bus and subway lines. Their patterns of commuting are not just from home into work. Women heads of household also must access food shopping, health care, and other services and plan their home location accordingly.

Overall, it's important to keep in mind that the **roles of women** in American and Canadian society have changed significantly in recent decades. Women make up half of the urban labor force. Women are increasingly equal (but not yet equal) to men in terms of pay, access to management positions, and political power. Today, educational statistics show that women are outperforming men as university students, both in terms of numbers and overall grade performance.

As a result, two sectors of the service economy, health care and education, have seen women surpass men in terms of the number of positions and average pay. Many women hold senior management positions in these sectors, such as those of hospital administrators and university presidents. Furthermore, medical schools in the United States reported in 2008 that entering classes were 50 percent female for the first time.

> **CED 6.10**
> Challenges of Urban Changes

Urban Economies

Beyond those mentioned in the chapter on economic geography, there are some additional urban geography patterns directly related to economic development.

> You may have noticed lots of talk about sustainability in this book, whether in agriculture or in urban living. This has become an important topic of discussion, not just on the AP exam but in everyday life.

Gentrification

Gentrification is defined as the economic reinvestment in existing real estate. In recent history, deindustrialization left many older areas of cities neglected and economically depressed. Real estate prices in these neighborhoods devalued and many residents and businesses left. However, by the 1980s, prices had fallen to such a point that reinvestment in certain neighborhoods became profitable. Initially, many gentrifiers, or "flippers," saw the opportunity to take old homes and storefronts and convert them into attractive modern accommodations.

This pattern began in many historic areas in the 1970s, when people in the **historical preservation** movement began renovating homes in places such as Greenwich Village in New York City and Georgetown in D.C. Many of the renovations were attempts to recreate homes and buildings near to their original form. But consumer demand for gentrified homes with modern amenities increased. By the 1990s, a whole **cottage industry** in gentrification had emerged in which flippers bought old homes at low prices, renovated the homes to contemporary standards, and resold them at handsome profits. Preservation, in these cases, took a back seat to demand for hot tubs, granite countertops, and stainless steel appliances.

In addition to gentrified homes, **commercial gentrification** has occurred in many of the same areas. Formerly shuttered business places were rebuilt as coffee shops, art houses, bars, and restaurants. Mixed-use development is also common. Some old warehouses are converted into stores, office space, and loft apartments in the same building. The phenomenon of gentrification is so widespread that whole newly renovated districts have emerged in many cities.
This table shows a few examples of gentrified areas:

City	Gentrified Areas
New York City	Greenwich Village, SoHo, Williamsburg
Washington, D.C.	Georgetown, Adams-Morgan
Chicago	Wrigleyville, Hyde Park
Los Angeles	West Hollywood, Silver Lake
New Orleans	French Quarter, Garden District
Columbus, Ohio	Short North-Victorian Village, German Village
Salt Lake City	Sugarhouse, the Avenues-Federal Hill

In terms of urban social change, it is important to know that neighborhood-scale gentrification has a negative effect of driving out **low-income residents** from the community. As the number of gentrified homes increases, so does the price of even non-gentrified real estate in the area. For many urban poor people, rents increase to unsustainable levels. This is especially hard on elderly residents who have lived in these neighborhoods all of their lives. Finding new homes often becomes difficult, and **displaced elderly persons** can become a costly social welfare program issue for city governments.

Urban Economic Growth

In general, urban governments and investors are concerned with the **infrastructure requirements** of cities. Economic growth tends to occur only in urban areas where utilities, transportation, safety, health, and education needs are met in terms of access and capacity. City leaders desire to create downtown areas with services such as specialty retailing, art, music, culture, nightlife, and other **cool city** amenities. All of this is done to attract investment to the city in the form of new businesses.

> **CED 6.7**
> Infrastructure

Much of this development is focused on revitalizing old central business districts that have suffered from deindustrialization. Attracting high-paying service industry jobs to old downtowns has become the focus of many city governments. By making the city attractive to young, educated businesspeople, the hope is that major service industry firms in high-paying fields such as technology, computing, research and development, and other **creative industries** such as media and advertising will relocate downtown.

Silicon Valley: Too Much Economic Growth?

Attracting new service firms is not easy, but some places have it easier than others. Companies tend to locate their offices near significant **growth poles** for their industry. Mentioned earlier in this chapter were the high-tech growth poles of Stanford University and the NASA Ames Research Center in the suburbs south of San Francisco. Economic **multiplier effects** around these centers have resulted in a multitude of companies and investment in computer hardware and software development.

The multitude of high-paying technology jobs in recent decades has driven local real estate prices to astronomical levels. Housing there is priced much the same as **rare commodities**. As of 2022, the average price of a home in Palo Alto is nearly $3.7 million. Meanwhile, the average price nationally is only a little over $400,000.

Affordable housing for Silicon Valley residents who are not engaged in the technology economy has become a major urban social issue. This is true for a number of other cities in the United States where high pay and limited housing have created **inflated real estate prices**. Cities such as San Diego; Washington, D.C.; Seattle; Boston; New York; and Portland, saw significant real estate price increases from the late 1990s until 2008. And while prices declined after the 2008 mortgage crash, they have bounced back, so affordable homes still remain out of reach for many urban residents, especially as unemployment has increased.

Urban Sustainability

The sustainability of urban growth and development is measured in economic and environmental terms. Questions of sustainability rarely have simple answers. Political attitudes and practical considerations often create a multitude of problems for urban government leaders and policymakers. Likewise, there tend to be several possible solutions to every sustainability problem. The trick for urban governments is to find solutions that are specific to local needs and that are affordable within the funding capabilities of the city.

> **CED 6.8**
> Urban Sustainability

Economic Sustainability

In addition to the problem of inflated real estate prices, city governments must address economic sustainability in terms of public services like transportation, utilities, health care access, public housing, and the most expensive: education.

Since deindustrialization, large city governments have had the difficult job of balancing depressed commercial tax revenues with the high cost of maintaining municipal services. One area of criticism lodged at city governments is the large size of municipal payrolls. Eighty to ninety percent of municipal budgets go to pay the local public workforce. However, laying off city workers would reduce public services and increase costs of social welfare programs for the unemployed and homeless. New sources of tax revenue are hard to come by, which is why there is a focus on development projects like hotel and convention centers (hotel room taxes), as well as attracting new high-paying service jobs to the old CBD (local payroll taxes).

One approach to combat the high costs of running urban governments is to combine the municipal governments of the core city with the multiple town governments of the surrounding suburbs. The resulting regional municipality would have reduced administrative costs and increased cost efficiency for service delivery. The trick is to come up with a system of shared governance between the involved communities. Regional municipalities have been successful in Canada, where they are common around large cities. In the United States, examples of large regional municipalities include Lexington-Fayette County, Kentucky; Miami-Dade County, Florida; and Denver-Arapahoe County, Colorado.

The Expense of Schools

Suburban governments have similar financial problems. In several areas of the country, the property taxes collected on homes often do not meet the cost and demand for high-quality schools. Think about it: if the typical suburban home produces two children who go into the public education system, and if schools spend upwards of $8,000 per student annually to educate them, then property taxes must raise $16,000 per home each year or be provided by state income taxes. This doesn't include the additional costs of police and fire protection or other local government service programs.

Resistance by homeowners to increased taxes is often expressed by voting down school bond levies, which raise money by increasing property taxes. School systems are caught between a public that does not want to pay higher taxes and parents who demand higher-quality schools. As a result, local school districts are increasingly dependent on state governments to help meet funding needs or are forced to cut extracurricular programs and increase class sizes.

Environmental Sustainability

A number of environmental sustainability issues concern urban governments such as local air pollution, wetlands loss, watershed management, parkland creation, and solid waste management, as well as international issues such as global warming. The problems often center on the question of how urban development will impact the environment.

CED 6.11

Challenges of Urban Sustainability

Urban Transportation

Urban transportation is a frequent topic of environmental sustainability discussion. **Traffic congestion** plagues many cities in the United States and Canada, and there is public pressure on local politicians to come up with solutions. Local leaders are often restricted in what they can do in terms of building highways because of the high cost of road construction and federal clean air regulations that limit emissions. Air pollution from cars has two scales of environmental impact. Locally, **smog** from vehicle emissions is harmful to public health and can create an unsightly haze. Globally, carbon dioxide emissions from cars are a significant source of **greenhouse gases** that contribute to the problem of global warming.

The benefits of **mass transit,** such as having fewer cars on the highway, reduced emissions, and increased accessibility for low-income citizens, have become important for almost all cities. There are many public and political supporters of subways, dedicated busways, and street-level light rail networks. Although these systems use up less land than new highways, some property owners whose land is used for these projects complain about their losses. The cost of construction and vehicles is often more than what can be raised from rail and bus fees alone. Who should pay to subsidize mass transit is a contentious issue. It often falls to local governments to find other sources of tax revenue to pay for it.

New Downtown Housing

In addition to gentrified neighborhoods that add to the "cool" value of cities, many cities desire additional downtown housing. This is environmentally beneficial because it stops suburban housing sprawl from encroaching on farmland or sensitive environments such as wetlands, coastal zones, forests, or habitats of endangered species. By having workers live downtown, close to their jobs, new downtown housing can also have the added environmental benefit of reducing transportation impacts, fossil fuel use, and air pollution.

City governments work with building developers to target idle downtown land like parking lots and former industrial sites for new construction. Many cities are able to simultaneously solve pollution issues and create new space for residential and commercial developments through **brownfield remediation,** a process in which hazardous contaminants are removed or sealed off from former industrial sites. These newly safe properties can then be redeveloped into housing or business complexes. Other types of spaces can be converted as well. Occasionally, even old schools and library buildings are turned into loft apartment complexes. However, the most popular new approach is **mixed-use buildings** that contain both housing and commercial space. Several large mixed-use developments have been constructed in recent years. These types of developments have been referred to as the **New Urbanism**.

Over the last several decades, many cities have enacted zoning laws, which separate commercial and residential space. One of the significant effects of New Urbanism is that it has forced cities to re-examine the sustainability of their zoning codes. Many cities have added new zoning categories that allow for mixed-use development and special planning districts where housing, public transit, and office space is more spatially integrated.

The criticism of mixed-use downtown housing developments is similar to that of gentrification. The purchase and rental prices of many new downtown housing units are so high that only the upper-middle-class income-earners can afford to live there. To combat this issue, some cities require that a certain percentage of new construction be priced specifically for lower- to middle-income buyers and renters.

OTHER RESOURCES

- For more urban geography material, see *Urbanization: An Introduction to Urban Geography, 3rd Edition* by Paul L. Knox and Linda M. McCarthy.

CHAPTER 8 KEY TERMS

central place theory

market areas (hinterlands)

Walter Christaller

urban hierarchy

threshold

range

travel time

agglomeration

Silicon Valley

growth poles

Detroit

cost advantages

South Dakota

limited banking regulations

resource nodes

transport nodes

clustered rural settlements

dispersed rural settlements

circular settlements

linear settlements

site

situation

concentric zone model

central business district (CBD)

verticality

peak land value intersection (PLVI)

deindustrialization

festival landscapes

gentrification

garden city movement

suburbanization

commuter zone

suitcase farmers

bid-rent curve

sector model

ethnic neighborhood

WASPs

white flight

multiple-nuclei model

suburban business districts

suburban CBDs

post-industrial city

transportation nodes

Latin American city model

Laws of the Indies

plaza

push and pull factors

squatters

land invasion

shantytowns

land tenure

microdistricts

federal home loan programs

Levittowns

basic services

non-basic services

middle-class flight

relocate

sprawl

anti-growth movements

growth boundaries

counterurbanization

telecommuting

edge city

lateral commuting

boomburbs

counter-commuting

colonial cities

fall-line cities

break-in-bulk points

medieval cities

gateway cities

entrepôt

megacity

megalopolis

conurbation

world city

urban hierarchy

first-order world cities

second-order world cities

third-order world cities

primate city

urban primacy

decentralization

rank-size rule

segregation

Chinatowns

redlining

restrictive covenants

racial steering

invasion

succession

female-headed households

Susan Hansen

roles of women

historical preservation

cottage industry

commercial gentrification

low-income residents

displaced elderly persons

infrastructure requirements

cool city

creative industries

growth poles

multiplier effects

rare commodities

inflated real estate prices

traffic congestion

smog

greenhouse gases

mass transit

mixed-use buildings

New Urbanism

CHAPTER 8 DRILL

See the end of this chapter for answers and explanations.

1. Which of the following refers to the minimum number of people required to support a business?

    (A) Range
    (B) Threshold
    (C) Travel time
    (D) Hearth
    (E) Spatial perspective

2. A megacity is defined as a metropolitan area with a population greater than

    (A) 1 million
    (B) 5 million
    (C) 10 million
    (D) 25 million
    (E) 50 million

3. All of the following are consequences of urban transportation EXCEPT

    (A) environmental damage due to the release of greenhouse gases
    (B) increased access to mass transit
    (C) increased controversy regarding construction subsidization
    (D) a decline in public health because of vehicle emissions
    (E) traffic congestion due to increased personal vehicle use

4. In the bid-rent curve, it is expected that as the distance from the PLVI decreases

    (A) the crime rate increases
    (B) the crime rate decreases
    (C) the cost of transportation increases
    (D) the price of land increases
    (E) the price of land decreases

5. One advantage of the sector model over other models of urban structure is that

    (A) it portrays a decentralized vision of urban life
    (B) it incorporates both industrial corridors and ethnic neighborhoods
    (C) it implies that there are multiple nodes of business
    (D) it explores the concept of public religiosity
    (E) it relies upon the certainties of mathematical modeling

6. A major difference between an Anglo-American city and a Latin American city is

    (A) the central business district is significantly larger in Anglo-American cities than in Latin American cities
    (B) major boulevards lead out of the central business district in Anglo-American cities, while a patchwork of streets serves the same function in Latin American cities
    (C) the poor are located in the inner city in Anglo-American cities, while in Latin American cities, they're located at the outer periphery
    (D) the wealthy in Anglo-American cities stayed within the city center, while the wealthy in Latin American cities fled to the exurbs
    (E) it takes longer for squatters in Latin America to achieve land tenure than it does for squatters in the United States

7. An edge city contains which of the following?

    (A) Transportation nodes, telecommuting, retail space
    (B) Little office space, much retail space, telecommuting
    (C) Much office space, little retail space, transportation nodes
    (D) Much retail space, weak city government, high daytime population
    (E) Much office space, strong city government, low daytime population

City	Population
Santiago	4,837,295
Puente Alto	510,417
Antofagasta	309,832
Viña del Mar	294,551
Valparaíso	282,448
Talcahuano	252,968
San Bernardo	249,858
Temuco	238,129
Iquique	227,499
Concepción	215,413

8. According to the chart above, Santiago contains nearly ten times as many people as the next biggest city. It can be concluded from this that Santiago must be

(A) an entrepôt
(B) a gateway city
(C) a megacity
(D) a primate city
(E) a world city

9. The garden city movement, which pioneered planned developments with detached single-family homes, was the beginning of the growth of

(A) deindustrialization
(B) central business districts
(C) high-density zoning
(D) gentrification
(E) suburbia

10. Since the 1950s, suburbia has been the predominant model of American life. Its growth can be LEAST attributed to

(A) federal home loan programs
(B) the migration of business districts to the suburbs
(C) the existence of growth boundaries
(D) increasing crime rates in the inner city
(E) the arrival of freeways

11. Which of the following was NOT a method by which segregation was enacted in neighborhoods?

(A) Jim Crow laws
(B) Federal fair-housing laws
(C) Redlining
(D) Restrictive covenants
(E) Racial steering

CHAPTER 8 DRILL: ANSWERS AND EXPLANATIONS

1. **B** The threshold, (B), of a service is the minimum number of people required to support a business. Range, (A), refers to the maximum distance people are willing to travel for a service. Travel time, (C), refers to the amount of time an individual will travel for a service. A hearth, (D), is a region from which innovative ideas originate. And spatial perspective, (E), is concerned with observing variations in geographic phenomena across space.

2. **C** A megacity is a metropolitan area with a population of more than 10 million people. If you don't know the answer to a strict definition question like this, at least try to narrow down choices like (A) and (E) that seem too extreme.

3. **B** Increased access to mass transit, (B), is a potential solution to some of the problems caused by a high volume of vehicles on the road in urban areas. Such problems include environmental damage due to greenhouse gases, (A); controversy regarding construction subsidization, (C); a decline in public health, (D); and traffic congestion, (E).

4. **D** The PLVI, or peak land value intersection, is the point in a city that has the highest value. Therefore, the closer another parcel of land sits relative to the PLVI (meaning decreased distance), the higher the land value rises. For example, as you drive into the center of the city of Chicago, the cost of housing climbs higher. Choose (D).

5. **B** Unlike the multiple-nuclei model or the peripheral model, the sector model actually accounts for variations in the ethnic makeup of neighborhoods. Often, immigrants move into low-income housing, which is often situated alongside the manufacturing and shipping corridors. Choice (B) is correct.

6. **C** The urban poor in Latin America are almost always located at the outer edges of the city. The reasons for this are many, but one significant one is the fact that many of those poor people have resettled in the cities after being forced off their land because of rural political unrest and uprisings. In American cities, the urban poor are usually situated in the center of the city. Select (C) as the correct answer.

7. **D** An edge city is any part of a suburb that is conceived of as a business district. It has grown directly out of the new emphasis on the service sector. Retailers tended to follow the jobs, resulting in the growth of large suburban shopping malls. Many of these suburban business districts have become quite large and are poorly planned, due to the weak or nonexistent city government in these regions. Choose (D).

8. **D** A primate city occurs when the largest city in a country has at least twice the population of the country's next largest city. This can result in uneven national economic development, resentment, and a sense of there being two different classes of people: those who live in the primate city, and those who live everywhere else. This phenomenon has also occurred in Argentina, Egypt, South Korea, and France. The correct answer is (D).

9. **E** The garden city movement began in the 1870s, largely as a reaction to the messiness and chaos of the rapidly growing inner cities. Their innovation was to imitate small European estates on the outskirts of the city, served by streetcar lines into the center—the beginning of modern suburbia. Choices (A), (B), (C), and (D) are hallmarks of urban zones.

10. **C** Growth boundaries are laws enacted by county boards to limit the rapid growth of real estate development in a particular area. These rules often insist that developers maintain a minimum lot size, so that fewer homes may be built in the area. Communities without such rules often result in smaller lots, more housing, and higher population density—precisely the same as the cities they're leaving.

11. **B** While some federal policies certainly encouraged segregated communities, the fair-housing laws are part of a newer generation of federal laws. These are meant to counteract the redlining, restrictive covenants, and racial steering that served as de facto methods of segregation in places where it wasn't explicitly allowed, which the Jim Crow laws symbolized.

Summary

o Central place theory, the basis of all urban models, holds that all market areas are focused on one central settlement. Market areas can come in different sizes, and small markets like towns may also be contained within larger market areas like one centered in a major city.

o Be comfortable with the following urban models:
  • Concentric zone model
  • Sector model
  • Multiple-nuclei model
  • Galactic city (peripheral) model
  • Latin American city model

o Suburbanization has had a tremendous impact on the American urban landscape since the mid-20th century. As new residents flocked to the suburbs, services and major employers followed. Some suburban CBDs have grown into edge cities primarily composed of office and retail space but few residential areas.

o *De facto* ethnic and racial segregation is common in urban areas, although discriminatory practice in real estate and urban planning is illegal in the U.S.

o Gentrification occurs when existing urban areas receive economic reinvestment. While it can help revitalize many neighborhoods that suffered after deindustrialization, many low-income and elderly residents are driven out of those areas when housing becomes unaffordable.

o Economic and environmental sustainability has become a major area of concern amid population booms in both cities and suburbs. The development of mass transit and new downtown housing has helped to some extent by cutting down on suburban sprawl and auto traffic.

Chapter 9
Industrial and Economic Development Patterns and Processes

CHAPTER OVERVIEW

This chapter is broken into four parts: Know the Concepts, Know the Math, Know the Theories, and Know the Maps. In the section on concepts, we discuss sectors of the economy and country-scale levels of development. The math section discusses the development indicators used to measure economic volume and level of development for states. Next, the theory section discusses development theory and location theories along with related theoretical concepts. Finally, the maps section will show the locations and structures of some major industrial regions around the world.

KNOW THE CONCEPTS

Sectors of Production

CED 7.2
Economic Sectors and Patterns

The economy can be divided into different categories known as **sectors**. What composes a sector of the economy can vary depending upon what is being categorized. One common way to group economic activity and employment is by its stage in the production process, from primary production onward. This results in three to five categories. Another way is to categorize sectors by the types of products or services they create, such as mining or communications. This results in a much larger number of categories.

Sector Categories by Stage of Production

Primary production includes agriculture, mining, energy, forestry, and fisheries. These activities and jobs deal with the extraction of natural resources from the Earth.

Secondary production includes the processing of the raw materials drawn from the primary sector. These activities and jobs also include the fabrication of components and the assembly of finished goods. In sum, secondary production reflects all forms of **manufacturing**. Keep in mind, manufacturing is a type of industry, but not all industries are manufacturing. Other industries can include fisheries or service industries.

Tertiary production includes the transportation, wholesaling, and retailing of finished goods to consumers. Commonly, tertiary production can include other types of services that could be categorized as quaternary, such as finance, or quinary, such as government. They are detailed here separately but are collectively categorized as **services** in the tertiary sector:

Although the quaternary and quinary sectors are subsets of tertiary production, the AP exam regularly treats them as distinct categories.

- **Quaternary production** includes wholesaling, finance, banking, insurance, real estate, advertising, and marketing. These are collectively called **business services.**

- **Quinary production** includes retailing, tourism, entertainment, and communications, government, or semi-public services such as health, education, and utilities. These are known as **consumer services.**

All the world's countries include each of these stages. Depending on a country's level of development, one sector will be more prevalent than the others.

Sector Categories by Product or Service Type

Dividing economic sectors by product or service type creates a detailed system and a large number of categories. It is important to consider the cash value of what is produced in one sector compared to other sectors. This helps explain why certain products and services are emphasized in an economy and why others might decline or be abandoned.

Agriculture

Whether it's done by hand in the Third World or mechanized in the First World, it's still agriculture. Economically, what is measured is the combined cash value of what is produced, not the volume in bushels or weight in tons. Of the major product type categories, agriculture is the least valuable, despite the fact that a majority of the world's population still lives in rural agricultural regions.

People obviously need food, but how they get it differs geographically. In less-developed parts of the world, subsistence farming is very common, with agriculture supporting the farm family and local people. Farmers in the Third World who farm plantations or work in cash-cropping generally send crops around in search of buyers. In the more-developed countries, farming is most commonly done on a commercial basis, with processed products sold and distributed globally. Here, company-owned farms have overtaken the family farm as the most common type of agricultural unit.

Commodity Chain

Ever wonder who grew the tiny little tea leaf that contributed itself to your tall, frosted glass of iced tea? Commodity chain analysis explains the links between producers and consumers in the production and distribution of a commodity. **Commodity chains** exist from the small-scale, family-based producers selling directly from the farm or through local farmers' markets to transnational supply networks selling to an international customer base. Let's look at the commodity chain of tea.

Tea production employs millions of people worldwide, most of them living in remote poverty-stricken rural communities. The tea supply chain is very intricate and involves many players. Tea leaves are grown either on large estates with their own processing factories or by thousands of small farmers who send their tea leaves to a local factory. From there, the tea moves to a broker, who auctions it off to an international trader. The international trader sells the tea to various tea companies, who then sell the product to retailing and catering companies and the consumer finally gets the box of tea bags. In this long and detailed commodity chain, only a few powerful multinational companies control the buying and retailing of tea. Most of the profits are made at the retail end of tea's commodity chain and the oversupply of tea (combined with the poverty of the producers) is a matter of great concern to international aid groups.

Natural Resources

Natural resource production can be divided into two pairs of linked sectors based on their renewability and prices:

Mining and **energy extraction** can be valuable depending on the global commodity prices. Oil (petroleum), for instance, became highly valuable in 2008 and was traded for over $120 per barrel in mid-summer, only to fall below $50 per barrel by the year's end. Oil export-based economies like Saudi Arabia and Venezuela can rise and crash with the radical price changes. Such price volatility is difficult for both producers and consumers.

Likewise, copper-mining countries like Zambia are doing well now that metal prices are rising. However, this **resource-dependent country** was economically devastated in the early 1980s when one of the largest consumers of copper, the U.S. Mint, decided to switch to cheaper zinc cores for pennies—a move that caused a global crash in the price of copper.

Fisheries and **timber markets** are not as volatile, but have increased in price and value over the years due to reduced supply. However, in these heavily regulated and increasingly protected natural resources, companies must use more technology and larger processing facilities to remain profitable and meet growing consumer demand, especially from large and growing newly industrialized markets like China and India.

Renewability

We can also classify resources by their renewability. Minerals and fossil fuel energy are **nonrenewable products**. Once they are extracted, the Earth cannot reproduce them. Some mineral products like metals and glass can be recycled. For some products like steel and aluminum, it's far cheaper to buy scrap metal to recycle than to mine new mineral ores. That's why you can sometimes get rebates for turning in your soda cans and bottles. Energy sources that do not run on fossil fuels are generally **renewable** if managed properly. With the exception of hydroelectricity, **alternative energy** sources such as solar, wind, nuclear, tidal, and geothermal power tend to be more expensive to harness than fossil fuels and are thus less common. Despite this history, technological advances continue to bring down the cost of renewable energy to bring it closer to parity with nonrenewable energy.

Alternative forms of energy are being developed and used to shift energy usage away from nonrenewable resources such as coal and oil. Wind power, solar energy, and nuclear power are alternate energy sources that work with differing degrees of utility to power industries and generate electricity. France relies heavily on nuclear power and certain coastal regions of Spain have enough constant, steady wind to power wind energy parks. California continues progress toward developing alternative energy sources; its Ivanpah Solar Electric Generating System is currently the largest solar power installation in the world.

Sustainability

Products drawn from living resources like fisheries and forestry are renewable. Here, our ability to continuously rely on a resource depends on the **sustainable use** of the resource. This means that fish cannot be taken from the sea at rates greater than those at which they can replace themselves (with or without the help of hatcheries). Likewise, forest replanting is necessary for trees to be available perpetually.

How trees are cut and how fish are caught makes a difference in terms of overall **ecosystem** survival and sustainability. Using two-mile-long microfilament gill nets to catch fish is considered an unsustainable practice that harms the ocean ecosystem. These massive nets can easily tear and then float free in the ocean, trapping and killing other sea life. Likewise, clear cutting of virgin forests destroys not only the trees, but also the delicate habitats of the many other species in the forest community. Tree farms with one species of tree are, by comparison, much less diverse and are not considered natural. Most animals and plants that are found in natural forests are rarely seen on tree farms.

Manufacturing

Manufacturing remains the hallmark of economic development, and factory-made products far out-value those of agricultural and natural resource-based economies. Why? Manufactured goods are farm products and natural resources that have been taken through **value-added processing.** The more complex and technology-driven the manufacturing is, the higher the value applied to the finished product. The utility of a product and the demand for it can also influence its value.

Manufacturing can be divided into groups in a couple of different ways. One system, **durable goods** and **non-durable goods**, divides production based on the amount of time the product is going to be used. Goods that are intended for use of more than a year are classified as durable goods. Those intended for use of less than a year are classified as non-durable. Durable goods tend to have greater value and represent a more lucrative form of production.

Another categorization can be made by product type. Here is a list of manufacturing sectors based on product category:

- **Resource processing:** oil refineries, metals, plastics, chemicals, lumber, paper, food and beverage, concrete and cement, glass
- **Textiles:** clothing, shoes and leather products, artificial fibers and thread
- **Furniture:** home, office, bedding
- **Appliances:** home appliances, commercial equipment, power tools, lighting
- **Transport:** automotive, rail, aerospace, shipbuilding, recreational vehicles
- **Health:** pharmaceuticals, medical devices, personal care products
- **Technology:** home computers, business computing and servers, industrial control devices, phones, television and audio entertainment

Services

Services are intangible products, as opposed to manufactured goods, which are physically tangible or touchable. As a group, services are the most valuable form of economic production. However, not all services are as valuable as others.

One way to classify services is by the level of pay and benefits they provide employees. **Low-benefit services** are sectors in which the labor force tends to be hourly employees who receive few, if any, additional benefits, like paid vacation or health insurance (not an issue in Canada or Europe where there is free public health care). Examples of low-benefit service jobs include hotel and food services, retail, customer services, contract agricultural labor, and construction.

Conversely, **high-benefit services** are sectors in which pay tends to be salaried and includes considerable fringe benefits like health, dental, and vision insurance; vacation; sick days; and retirement reimbursements. Note that the benefits are provided by other high-benefit service industries such as insurance companies. High-benefit positions include the areas of business services, health care, government, and education.

The more common way to classify **service firms** is by the type of activity performed as part of the service:

Retailing	Media and entertainment
Labor and workforce services	Advertising and marketing
Food, travel, and tourism (hospitality services)	Medical, health, and personal care
Government	Finance and banking
Education	Insurance
Transportation and delivery services	Real estate
Environmental and waste management services	Accounting and business consulting
	Legal services
Construction and engineering	Software, data, and computer consulting
Energy utilities	Research and development
Communications utilities	

Remember that these are all tertiary services and represent the most valuable areas of economic production worldwide.

Deindustrialization: Why America Is Not a Manufacturing-Based Economy

CED 7.7

Changes as a Result of the World Economy

When we analyze the overall economic productivity of First-World countries like the United States and Canada, it soon becomes clear that services produce the majority of the countries' economic value and employment. In recent history, the United States and Canada, like other service-based economies, have **deindustrialized**, shifting away from manufacturing as the main source of economic production. Roughly 80 percent of these economies' value is drawn from services, only 19 percent from manufacturing and resources, and a mere 1 percent from agriculture (despite the massive amount of land dedicated to farming and ranching). In employment figures, the labor force percentages are similar, with 83 percent in services, 16 percent in manufacturing, and 1 percent in agriculture.

The downside is that in the 1970s and 1980s when deindustrialization was widespread in Anglo-America and Western Europe, millions of factory workers lost jobs and many old industrial cities suffered from the economic downturn. The workforce had to adjust to new service sector employment that paid less and had fewer benefits compared to unionized factory jobs. Manufacturing businesses also had to focus on highly priced manufactured goods like vehicles, heavy equipment, and computing devices to keep profits and investment up amid **foreign competition** and keep the remaining First-World manufacturing labor force paid and employed.

See the discussion on the Old Asian Tigers beginning on page 372 for more on foreign competition, and see Chapter 8 for the effects of deindustrialization.

Understanding Why Services Are Important in America

Why are the United States and Canadian economies based on services instead of manufacturing? Sure, there are cheaper **off-shore locations** overseas to build factories. But deindustrialization really has to do with the **investment value** of each sector. Investors in new businesses are looking to maximize their **returns on investment,** and services are the most valuable investments out there.

To illustrate this, consider the following thought experiment. If you could fill your classroom with corn, that corn might be worth $1,000 or so depending on the size of the room. Fill the room with coal, and you might have $3,000. Now, imagine that there are three dump trucks filling most of the room, instead of corn or coal. The combined price of those trucks would be about $270,000. You can see that moving from natural resources to manufactured products adds a massive amount of value.

Now imagine the room empty, and you're standing there with a manila folder in hand. This folder represents a service product. Inside that folder is a corporate insurance policy, or maybe a stock portfolio. It could be a software license or a patent on a new drug therapy. Whatever it is, imagine that it is worth $5 million. Now fill the room with folders. The billions of dollars in this one room is why investors see services as the best potential investment in the United States and Canada, and it's why they are far less interested in manufacturing and agriculture.

The Importance of High Technology for Services

In addition to the fill-the-room analogy, another way to better understand services is to think historically about how technology has affected economies. When we look at agriculture's long history, the development of the **plow** is the technical advancement that revolutionized farming and radically increased the amount of land that could be cultivated. During the industrial era, the product that made all manufacturing possible was **steel**. Everything from railroad locomotives to skyscrapers and automobiles is made possible by steel alloys, as iron alone is too brittle and heavy.

In the service economy era, the **computer** makes all sectors of the service economy more efficient and capable of handling large numbers of consumers and data. Even more specific is the impact of the **microchip,** as these miniature processor circuits have made desktop computers possible as well as smaller handheld and wireless devices. Without computers and micro-devices, the services industries in the First World today would not exist without a much larger administrative labor force and the labor costs would make many of the services too expensive to afford.

Levels of Development

We can categorize countries in terms of their levels of economic development. We use the following terms to compare development level verbally and to acknowledge the patterns of **uneven development** in the world economy. Some categories are better descriptors than others and some countries aren't categorized as easily as others. Make sure to use terms appropriately.

First World: Industrialized and **service-based economies** that have free markets, a high level of productivity value per person and, thus, a high quality of life. In addition to the United States and Canada, there are the European Union countries, Norway, Switzerland, Iceland, Israel, Australia, New Zealand, Japan, South Korea, Singapore, Taiwan, and Middle-Eastern oil states Saudi Arabia, Kuwait, United Arab Emirates, Oman, and Bahrain.

Borderline First-World economies might include Argentina, Chile, South Africa, and some island nations like Trinidad and the Seychelles. These have productivity statistics that are higher than the Third World, but not quite at First-World levels yet. You might be tempted to call them Second World, but that term has a very different meaning.

Second World: Describes the **communist** countries of which only two "hard line" communist states remain today: Cuba and North Korea. These states still have centrally planned economies. The term is occasionally used to designate "former communist" states that are still **restructuring** their economy to free-market systems like the former Soviet Union and Eastern European states, although many have joined the EU. It can also describe China and Vietnam, which are newly industrialized countries still controlled by communist parties but that have adapted **free-market reforms** to their economies.

Third World: Countries with mainly **agricultural** and **resource-based economies** that have low levels of per-person productivity and a low quality of life. These **underdeveloped states** are found across Latin America, the Caribbean, Africa, and the Asian countries not listed above. Some Third-World states have made a distinct economic shift toward industrialization and urbanization (see newly industrialized countries or NICs, below), while others remain firmly in a rural, agricultural category. Examples of the poorest Third-World states are Haiti, Niger, Malawi, Tanzania, Madagascar, Nepal, and the former USSR countries Kyrgyzstan and Tajikistan.

> Though you will encounter the terms First World, Second World, and Third World throughout this course and this book, these terms are slowly disappearing from popular usage. They were invented to describe a geopolitical world order dominated by the Cold War, which ended over thirty years ago. For now, accept these terms for what they are: outdated words that will be eventually replaced by more accurate ones.

Countries That Are More Developed or Less Developed…

More developed countries (MDCs) and **less developed countries (LDCs)** are terms used to describe the relative economic differences between states. First- and Second-World countries generally tend to fit in the MDC category, while Third, Fourth, and Fifth Worlds are LDCs—even if they are NICs (newly industrialized countries, which are discussed below).

Where the dividing line is between the two categories is up to debate. If you are asked to assign MDC or LDC status to a country based on gross national product *per capita* or GNI PPP, use the following basic rule: $10,000 GNP per capita, above it are MDCs, below it, LDCs. You can argue against this dollar value on a number of technical points. It's just a simple dividing line to help you analyze data that you may be presented with on the exam.

Newly Industrialized Countries

Newly industrialized countries (**NICs**) are Third-World states with economies that have made a distinct shift away from agriculture and toward manufacturing as the focus of economic development and production. Industrialization is a long-term process that can last decades in larger countries. NICs are in a constant process of building **infrastructure** (roads, ports, power plants, water systems, railways), which facilitate the construction and operation of factories.

Two characteristics of NICs link back to your knowledge of population and migration. First, NICs have **rapid population growth** and are usually on the border of stage two and stage three of the demographic transition model. Several of the more advanced NICs like Brazil, Mexico, and India are well into early stage three. China, due to its One-Child Policy, appears to be the most advanced in terms of demographic transition, but in fact it should be economically categorized with the other NICs. Secondly, NICs experience **rapid rural-to-urban migration** as their economies industrialize and, as a result, urbanize.

Here is a list of NICs (with their important sectors):

Mexico (manufacturing, oil, tourism)*

Brazil (manufacturing, heavy industry, services)*

Dominican Republic (manufacturing, tourism)

Nigeria (oil, chemicals)

Gabon (oil)

Indonesia (manufacturing, oil, tourism)

Vietnam (manufacturing)

China (manufacturing, high tech, heavy industry, finance, transport)*

India (manufacturing, pharmaceuticals, high tech, computing services)*

Thailand (manufacturing, medical services)*

Malaysia (manufacturing, high tech)*

Philippines (manufacturing)

*Industrialization started in these countries earlier than others, so they are further along in the manufacturing development process.

NIC Development Funding

Funds to develop infrastructure and factories can come from internal sources, from **foreign aid,** or from **foreign direct investment (FDI). Development loans** are also sought by NICs to help pay for new large-scale infrastructure projects. Foreign development aid is money provided by **donor state** governments in the First World that is not expected to be given back.

Rarely does foreign aid go to building for-profit private businesses. Instead it often provides public funding for schools, nutrition, health programs, and other government spending. Military aid is one of the largest areas and plays the practical purpose of providing security for the state, which reassures foreign firms and investors doing business in the NIC. A less expensive but important source of foreign aid comes in the form of **technology transfer**, where technical knowledge, training, and industrial equipment is provided to NIC governments to increase business efficiency and capacity.

How Foreign Direct Investment Works

FDI is money from international **private investors** or **investment firms** in other countries who are looking to earn a profit. These investors put up money to start a new business or build a new factory in an NIC. As the business grows or the factory operates over time, investors are paid back plus a portion of the profits. If the venture is unprofitable, then investors may get less back, or in the case of business failure, they could get nothing—the accepted risk of investing. When there is high demand for cheaply made products in the world, factory investment in NICs can have high returns on investment of 10 to 15 percent within a few years of factories opening.

Development Loans

To help develop the necessary infrastructure to attract FDI, some NICs seek international development loans from organizations like the **World Bank**. These loans are most often given to help build major infrastructure projects such as electric power systems, dams, water purification and waste treatment centers, pipelines, highways, and national rail systems. The expectation is that these new services can charge fees that will be used to pay back the loans to the donor agency.

In many cases worldwide, NICs and other Third-World states have defaulted on loans due to the inability of LDC economic systems to pay the full principal and interest payments. Criticism has also been made that some development loans don't make the positive impact on the economy that was intended, or cause costly and significant environmental problems, but they still have to be paid back.

Empowering Women Is Smart Economics

In developing nations, female empowerment is tied closely to economic development. Multiple studies have demonstrated that when women are given an education, they contribute to forming capital, which lifts their communities, and their nations experience economic growth.

India's Jump to Services

Indian export development had been centered on manufacturing areas like cotton, textiles, and steel for many years until the 1990s, when an important change occurred in investment patterns. High-tech markets in software development and computing services began to open up in India due to certain **comparative advantages** it has over other NICs.

The English-language heritage of India's colonial past with Britain has two distinctly positive effects: access to the American technology markets via language and a large number of educated workers who speak the language. Not everyone in India speaks English, but it is common among highly educated workers. There are many English speakers due to the colonial legacy of British-style high schools and universities—many of which were begun during the colonial period that ended in 1948.

American tech firms like Dell have opened several customer-service and technical-assistance phone centers in India. Likewise, Microsoft has partnered with a number of Indian sub-contracting firms to write software for existing products like word processing and spreadsheet programs that need upgrading. Both of these are examples of the **off-shoring** of computing services from the United States to NICs in recent years.

Comparative Advantage

The term *comparative advantage* means that a country has the ability or resources to produce a good or service at less cost and more efficiently than other countries. As such, these advantageous goods and services are selected for industrial production over other possible alternatives.

China's Demand for Energy

Industrial development in China and the newly earned wealth of the Chinese people have combined to create a large demand for energy in industry and transportation. Coal has been the primary source for electrical production and is plentiful in the country. Oil demand is also high, as industry and Chinese citizens have more use for trucks and personal cars. China is not oil-rich and has invested heavily in oil exploration and production in the Third World, including in politically sensitive countries like Sudan and Myanmar. Other problems facing the Chinese are pollution in the form of urban smog, acid rain, and an increasingly large portion of the world's greenhouse gas emissions.

During the 2008 Beijing Olympics, news commentators remarked that the skies over the city appeared clean during the games. Why? Factories in the region were closed for a week beforehand and thousands of cars were restricted from use until after the games ended.

Not Such a Good Idea

Sometimes terms are used to describe levels of development that don't work well. An example is the **North versus South analogy** that some economists use in describing the developed world (North) and less developed countries (South). It's problematic geographically in two ways. First, Australia and New Zealand are First-World countries that lie in the southern hemisphere, south of many LDCs. Furthermore, most of the world's less developed economies sit at or north of the equator.

Another thing to avoid, especially when writing free responses, is referring to less developed economies or countries as "backward" or to their people in negative or racial terms. This is a sign to the FRQ-readers who score your test that you may not deserve additional points for discussion of examples. Don't risk it.

State of Respect

Never insult or demean a population on the AP Human Geography Exam (or anyplace else). It's just not a good idea.

Asian Tigers: Old and New

The **Asian Tigers** is a term used to describe the industrial economies of Asia that have been aggressive in terms of economic growth rates and their ability to compete for consumers. There are two classes of Asian Tigers depending on the age of the manufacturing economy and a few other important factors:

Old Asian Tigers	Source of Development Funding	Manufacturing Redevelopment Period
Japan	Foreign aid programs such as the Macarthur Plan	1950s–1970s
South Korea		
Taiwan		
Hong Kong		
Singapore		

The building of a large manufacturing capacity in the Old Asian Tigers was the result of Cold War realities in the region. These states were seen as free-market bastions against the spread of Communism. The United States and Britain had no choice but to pour in foreign aid money to support development and democracy in the region. These funds were not loans and were not paid back. U.S. money was critical to the rebuilding of war-torn Japan and South Korea. Likewise, the fledgling refugee state of Taiwan, following the Chinese Civil War, was desperate for American funding to aid in development. The British rebuilt industry in their two colonial possessions as they had both suffered damage in World War II.

The irony of postwar development aid in the region is that, by the 1970s, these countries had become competitive with the United States and the United Kingdom for global markets in manufactured goods. By the 1980s, highly efficient factories and a focus on product quality in both Japan and Korea had created significant **market share** in the American automobile and electronics markets. This **foreign competition** along with the **oil shocks of the 1970s** triggered deindustrialization in the United States, Canada, and Western Europe.

New Asian Tigers	Source of Development Funding	Manufacturing Development Period
China	Foreign direct investment (FDI)	1980s–1990s (until the 1997 Asian Economic Crisis)
India		
Indonesia		
Malaysia		
Thailand		
Vietnam		

Manufacturing development in the New Asian Tigers was mainly funded through FDI that came from firms in New York, London, and Tokyo, as well as from companies in South Korea and Taiwan that constructed and operated the factories in the New Tigers. These new locations proved to be profitable investments for all involved, including foreign investors and the newly industrialized countries.

Demand for Off-Shoring Locations

Growth in these countries was made possible by the global demand for low-cost consumer products. The New Asian Tigers offered **cheap labor** and **low-cost land and resources**, as well as **few labor and environmental regulations** that had become costly for businesses in the First World. For some low-end product lines, like clothing and shoes, these countries proved to be the only profitable manufacturing locations. China had the lowest costs of all and a large available labor force. Therefore, companies flocked to the special economic zones to open factories and, in turn, helped fund China's free-market reform movement.

The Asian Economic Crisis

Growth in all of Asia came to an abrupt halt in 1997. A banking crisis in Thailand rippled through the region, affecting South Korea and Japan disproportionately, and resulting in a **credit crisis**. This is sometimes referred to as a "credit crunch" and results from banks and investors holding back on industrial loans and investments. As a result, money to develop new factories and infrastructure projects in the New Asian Tigers dried up. After a short rebound, the 2008 credit crisis in the United States has similarly slowed investment and development in the region.

The 1997 Asian economic crisis also was the trigger for **deindustrialization** in the Old Asian Tigers. Many large firms, like Japan's Toyota and the Korean Hyundai conglomerate, had employed extra workers and their adult children under an old, traditional benefits system of **guaranteed family employment**. Likewise, corporate cartels (*kiretsu* in Japan and *chaebol* in South Korea), headed by major automakers and electronics firms, propped up money-losing partner companies such as steel manufacturers.

The whole system had to change. Payrolls were cut and workers laid off by the hundreds of thousands. Several unprofitable companies shut down as they could no longer get loans from banks or their corporate cartels. Like Western First-World economies in the 1970s and 1980s, the Old Asian Tigers now focus much of their new investment on service sectors and only in the most valuable and high-priced forms of manufacturing such as cars, electronics, and medical devices.

THE INDUSTRIAL REVOLUTION

CED 7.1

The Industrial Revolution

There are few events that have carried a greater impact on human development than the Industrial Revolution. Despite the dramatic name, the Industrial Revolution wasn't a sudden change so much as a hastening of the technological advancement that had already been occurring gradually for centuries. That said, industrialization rapidly transformed the global economic landscape and the way that people lived.

Great Britain: The OG NIC

The process of industrialization began in the second half of the 18th century in Great Britain. There are a variety of factors that may have helped put Britain at the forefront of technological development, from its relative political and economic stability to the presence of existing manufacturing industries that would eventually become mechanized. However, there were two driving forces that undoubtedly contributed to Britain's shift to an industrialized society: the first was a significant shift in the size and distribution of the population. Thanks largely to improved diets and living conditions, the population of Great Britain had nearly doubled during the 18th century, creating an expanded pool of potential laborers as well as a fresh base of consumers. In addition, many small-scale farmers at this time were being forced from the rural land they worked into urban areas, where they sought employment in factories.

In addition to an increased supply of workers and consumers, the availability of coal and iron ore allowed British industry to rapidly mechanize. Coal became a widely used source of power and was used to smelt iron, which was in turn used to create larger, more productive machines. These two essential resources were ultimately the key combination behind one of the Industrial Revolution's most important inventions: the railroad. With the advent of the railroad, Britain had the means to efficiently move people and goods around the country, as well as a robust new employment sector centered around building the extensive rail infrastructure and providing transportation services.

Effects of Industrialization

The impacts of industrialization have been wide-ranging and deeply felt to this day. As the Industrial Revolution spread from Britain to surrounding European nations and to the United States by the mid-19th century, they too saw major shifts in the size and distribution of their populations. The technological advancements in manufacturing enabled concurrent innovations in agriculture, spawning the Second Agricultural Revolution. The mechanization and scientific developments that occurred in agriculture boosted food production, which in turn allowed populations to grow and death rates to fall partly due to improved diets.

With industrialization came a major push toward urbanization. The use of new mechanical devices in agriculture also reduced the need for farm labor, just as the proliferation of factories in centralized areas called for a much larger workforce in cities. For the first time, urban populations in Britain and other industrializing nations outpaced those of rural areas. In many cases, the explosive growth in these cities meant that they were overcrowded and unsanitary, and mortality rates for urban residents were substantially higher than those for their rural counterparts as diseases such as cholera ran rampant. Over time, living conditions would improve as infrastructure, services, and labor and environmental regulations caught up with the population boom.

In addition to changes in population density, the Industrial Revolution caused major shifts in family and class structures. As you know from our study of the demographic transition model in Chapter 4, families in agricultural societies work together to manage farms, and children are a critical source of labor. At first, industrialization by no means meant an end to child labor—it simply meant that children were sent to work in factories rather than alongside their parents on the family farm. In fact, women and children often worked for lower pay and in environments even worse than the deplorable conditions that the men faced. After it was discovered that children were being beaten in the factories, the British government passed legislation restricting the number of hours that children were permitted to work (the United States would see a similar series of reforms after its own industrialization). As this reduction in child labor brought an attendant reduction in the wages they brought home, children contributed less to the family income and instead increasingly became an economic burden. Without the need for families to have multiple children, birth rates in urban industrial areas declined.

The working-class life in the Industrial Revolution was initially a very bleak existence. This was true not only for the urban working poor, who faced terrible living and working conditions and low wages, but also for those who had become economically displaced when their traditional professions were mechanized, such as weavers and farm laborers. Workers began to organize into cooperative societies and trade unions, which provided benefits and services to their members and began to advocate for higher wages and better working conditions. Over time, the standard of living for workers improved as well with (marginally) better sanitation and health care, educational opportunities, and—for the first time—the time and money to enjoy entertainment such as dance halls and sports leagues.

The latter part of the 19th century also saw a burgeoning middle class of professionals such as merchants, engineers, factory owners, doctors, and lawyers. For these individuals, who were often, in fact, rather wealthy, the standard of living was comparatively luxurious. Any family considered middle class employed at least one servant and enjoyed new innovations such as indoor plumbing and heat. For them, the home became a haven from the workplace. This economic shift brought along a marked shift in gender roles. Since middle-class families had the financial security to survive on a single income, women were increasingly discouraged from joining the workforce and instead were expected to focus on raising children and maintaining a comfortable home. While the middle class had the means to send children to school, higher education and professional opportunities largely excluded women. Instead, middle-class women were expected to become well-versed in home economics and domesticity. (It should be noted that such standards did not extend to working-class women, who continued to work just as hard as the men and often in multiple jobs.)

> **CED 7.4**
> Women and Economic Development

Global Impact

For the countries that followed Great Britain's path toward industrialization, the results were largely similar: technological innovation, urbanization, and an eventual improvement in the overall standard of living. Productivity increased exponentially due to mechanization, helping turn these countries into economic powerhouses. However, industrialization has its drawbacks as well. For one, economies that industrialize typically begin a roller coaster ride of boom-and-bust. Periods of explosive growth are followed by periods of economic crises, as regular as the rain. Furthermore, not all parts of the world experience the same benefits. The Industrial Revolution was relatively limited in its scope, and we know that there are countries even today, such as Mexico and Malaysia, that are only recently industrialized. The current patterns in population growth and living standards in these places are much like those of Great Britain in the early 1800s.

Furthermore, the productivity boom in industrialized European countries left them hungry for both raw materials and new markets for their finished goods. They set their sights on Africa and Asia. Although European nations had been colonizing other parts of the world for centuries, the speed and scope of this "new imperialism" was unprecedented. While there were also numerous social and cultural factors in Europe's desire for expansion, the need for resources was one of the most important. The British textile industry was the first to mechanize and required cotton imports from other parts of the world to meet its production capabilities. This was one of the primary reasons for Britain's expansion into areas like India and Egypt. Africa held numerous other natural resources such as precious metals, diamonds, and palm oil. Many colonialists viewed these areas as sources of untold wealth, though—with the major exception of India—it often turned out to be more difficult to extract economic value from them than was worthwhile.

Not only did industrialization create a need for European nations to conquer new parts of the world, it made it much easier for them to do so. Technological advancements allowed Europeans greater mobility and faster communication to these colonies, not to mention the development of weaponry that no unindustrialized country could compete with. Europeans were therefore able to easily invade and control vast areas of Africa and Asia; additionally, innovations in medicine led to vaccines and treatments for dreaded tropical diseases, thus allowing Europeans to more easily survive in these areas.

Colonialism did bring some benefits to certain parts of the world: improved infrastructure, educational opportunities, and standards of living. For many, however, the results of imperialism were less positive, as they were stripped of whatever natural resources they had, culturally oppressed, and often thrown into political turmoil. (For more on the effects of colonization, see Chapter 6.)

KNOW THE MATH

Measures of Development

CED 7.3
Measures of Development

We use **economic indicators** to help understand the variable levels of development and measure the degrees of uneven development between states. In these figures, we can see the country-level economic differences created by gaps in development, technology gaps, and the poor standards of living created by the effects of colonialism, war, and disasters.

Gross Domestic Product

Gross domestic product (GDP) is the dollar value of all goods and services produced in a country in one year. It measures the **total volume** of a country's economy. This is done without adjusting for international trade; therefore, it measures only the domestic economy:

$$GDP = GOODS + SERVICES$$

In addition, GDP is often reported in the news as "…quarterly GDP increasing by 3.5 percent…." This means that GDP for the most-recent three-month quarter of the year grew by 3.5 percent over the previous three months (sometimes it's compared to the same quarter in the previous year).

Gross National Income

Gross national income (GNI) is the dollar value of all goods and services produced in a country, plus the dollar value of **exports minus imports** in the same year. It also measures economic volume. However, it adjusts for the "national" wealth lost when imported goods are purchased from abroad. And GNI includes wealth gained when money comes from other countries for exports:

$$GNI = GOODS + SERVICES + (EXPORTS - IMPORTS)$$

Many economists argue that GNI is a much more accurate measure of economic volume compared to GDP. In most countries, there is a foreign trade imbalance represented by either a positive or negative impact on the volume of the economy. In countries where export value exceeds import value, there is a **trade surplus**, which adds value to the economy. Conversely, in countries where import value exceeds export value, there is a **trade deficit**, which removes value from the economy. Mathematically, this is what can happen:

Trade Surplus: (EXPORTS > IMPORTS)
This is a positive number, and adds value to the economy.

Trade Deficit: (EXPORTS < IMPORTS)
This is a negative number, and removes value from the economy.

In the United States, there was a trade deficit of over $1 trillion in 2021 caused by one significant imported good: oil. The large volume of petroleum needed to fuel the U.S. economy and car culture requires the import of such a large dollar amount of oil that it erases the value of American exports to other parts of the world.

Per Capita Calculations

To compare the level of development between countries, we have to use a *per capita* average. *Per capita* means "for every head" in Latin, meaning for each person. Gross national income (GNI) *per capita* is the estimated income of a person converted to U.S. dollars at currency exchange rates. It is a modified form of GDP *per capita*. These **level of development comparisons** are done by dividing the volume of the economy by the population, like so:

GDP *per capita* =   (GOODS + SERVICES) ÷ POPULATION

GNI *per capita* =   [(GOODS + SERVICES) + (EXPORTS − IMPORTS)]
                       ÷ POPULATION

This data is converted to U.S. dollars for comparison purposes. However, it's important to understand that these numbers are not indicators of personal income or the average salary of each worker. Instead, they are basically a measure of the country's collective wealth or productivity. It indicates a relative **standard of living** measured by the services that such productivity provides for the population.

Purchasing Power Estimates

Economists have refined these comparative indicators further as relative indicators of income and purchasing power between countries. These are complicated estimated indicators that do not have simple formulaic definitions.

Gross National Income Purchasing Power Parity

Gross national income purchasing power parity (GNI PPP) is an estimate that takes into account differences in prices between countries. By comparison, gross national income *per capita* can make a First-World country appear more prosperous than other states and can make larger Third-World countries appear less prosperous, but it doesn't factor in the cost of living in each country. The purchasing power parity correction theoretically makes a basic good, like a loaf of bread, the same price in all countries.

Here's an example to illustrate the difference between the two indicators. In the United States, a loaf of bread costs $2.20, but in China it costs the equivalent of $1.63. In China, the GNI *per capita* is about $5,740, but this does not represent that money's true value. China's GNI PPP is $9,210, which reflects the estimated actual value of an individual's purchasing power, using the same ratio as the bread example.

Alternative: Human Development Index

The **Human Development Index (HDI)** was designed by the United Nations to measure the level of development of states based on a number of social indicators in addition to economic production. An indexed score from 0.00 to 1.00 is calculated for countries by combining GDP *per capita*, the adult literacy rate, average level of education, and total life expectancy. The intent is to provide a more balanced measure of development and indicate some of the factors that illustrate the negative impact of poverty on economic potential in Third-World countries.

Economic Indicator Data for Selected Countries

Here is a comparison of the different major indicators for nine countries. Know at least three countries' GNI PPP and HDI for the exam. At minimum, pick one MDC, one NIC, and one LDC.

State	GNI per capita	GNI PPP	HDI	Categories
United States	56,810	53,245	0.920	First World, MDC
Canada	43,680	42,582	0.920	First World, MDC
United Kingdom	42,360	37,931	0.909	First World, MDC
Russia	9,720	23,286	0.804	Second World, MDC
China	8,250	13,345	0.738	Second World, NIC
India	1,670	5,663	0.624	Third World, NIC
Kenya	1,380	2,881	0.555	Third World, LDC
Haiti	780	1,657	0.493	Third World, LDC
Nepal	730	2,337	0.558	Third World, LDC

Other Alternatives

Here's a brief summary of two other alternative development indicators:

The **Gini coefficient** measures the level of **income disparity** between the country's richest and poorest population groups on a scale of 0 to 100. Higher numbers indicate a wide gap between the rich and poor and suggest major issues with poverty and the distribution of wealth in the country. Lower numbers indicate the existence of a large middle-class population where the nation's wealth is more equitably distributed.

The **Gender-Related Development Index (GDI)** takes the same indicators used to calculate HDI but replaces GDP *per capita* with income. Then the data between men and women is mathematically compared by dividing the female score by the male score. The closer the score is to 1.00, the higher women's roles are in society. The closer the score is to 0.00, the more subjugated women are and the fewer rights women have in the country. Comparing **gender equality** can be an effective indicator of social development, and this measure considers labor-market participation as well as reproductive health.

Likewise, the **sectoral structure** can be considered in the evaluation of an economy. If a national economy is centered too much upon services, for example, and not enough upon manufacturing, then the overall health of that economy is made weaker owing to the excessive imports necessary to sustain the economy. Other ways to measure an economy include measuring the size of the black market, income distribution, use of fossil fuels, and even "soft" indicators such as infant mortality rates and literacy rates.

KNOW THE THEORIES

Development Theories

The Demographic Transition Link

To help remember the path of development that countries generally follow, you can relate development theory to the demographic transition model from Chapter 4. Remember that each of the stages represents a type of economic context, and that the economy directly impacts the patterns of birth rates, death rates, and population. Here is the composite model again.

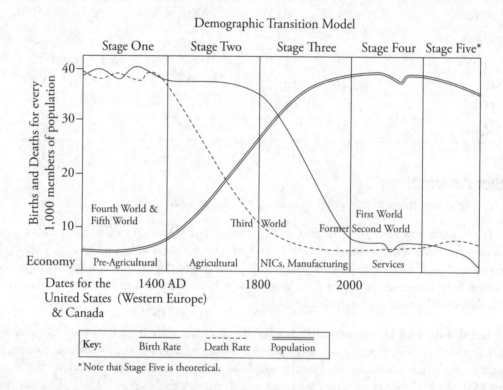

Demographic Transition Model

* Note that Stage Five is theoretical.

Rostow's Stages of Growth

CED 7.5

Theories of Development

Another approach to understanding the development process was developed in the 1950s by theorist Walt Rostow, who later became national security adviser to President Lyndon Johnson. Rostow proposed that countries went through five stages of growth between agricultural and service-based economies. One of Rostow's assumptions was that each country had at least some form of **comparative advantage** that could be utilized in international trade and thus fund the country's economic development over time.

The five stages progressed in the following pattern of growth:

1. **Traditional society:** The economy is focused on primary production such as agriculture and fishing. The country's limited wealth is spent internally on things that do not promote economic development. Technical knowledge is low.

2. **Preconditions for takeoff:** The country's leadership begins to invest the country's wealth in infrastructure such as roads, ports, electrification, and school systems that promote economic development and trade relations with other nations. More technical knowledge is learned that stimulates the economy.

3. **Takeoff:** The economy begins to shift focus onto a limited number of industrial exports. Much of the country still participates in traditional agriculture, but the labor force begins to shift to factory work. Technical experience is gained in industrial production and business management.

4. **Drive to maturity:** Technical (or technological) advancements diffuse throughout the country. Advancements in industrial production are seen in many sectors of the economy, which grow rapidly. Workers become increasingly skilled and educated, and fewer people are engaged in traditional activities like agriculture.

5. **Age of mass consumption:** An industrial trade economy develops in which highly specialized production such as vehicles, energy, and consumer products dominate the economy. Technical knowledge and education levels are high. Agriculture is mechanized (no longer traditional) and employs a small labor force.

Criticism of Rostow's Stages of Growth

Rostow's model is based on the historical development patterns of the United States and other industrialized countries. Although the model provides a framework for the economic development of nations, not all countries have had the capacity to utilize potential comparative advantages for international trade. For example, colonial powers extracted many of the valuable natural resources in the Third World. When these colonies gained independence, they had limited or zero access to the wealth that had been extracted from their countries during the colonial era. And many of the resources that existed within their borders were technically owned by multinational corporations.

The **colonial legacy** and other barriers to development such as **government corruption** or capital flight (see the dependency theory, below) are not accounted for in Rostow's theory. He assumed that all countries could progress smoothly through the stages if their investment focused on trade and technology development. Realistically, the world economy tends to leave many countries far behind, as the large sums of international investment needed to develop an industrial economy tend to be focused only on the most capable and stable newly industrialized countries (NICs).

Dependency Theory

Dependency theory holds that most LDCs (including all NICs) are highly dependent on foreign-owned factories, foreign direct investment, and technology from MDCs to provide employment opportunities and infrastructure. The main problem arises when Third-World countries get stuck in a continuous **cycle of dependency** on First-World loans to pay for additional economic development needs.

These concerns were first raised in Argentina in 1950 by economist Raul Prebisch. The **Prebisch thesis** detailed the dependency of Third-World economies on First-World loans and investments to pay for the building of new industries and infrastructure. Money made by LDCs from the sale of manufactured goods and natural resources is then used to pay off loans and investments and to buy manufactured products from the First World such as vehicles, heavy equipment, and consumer goods.

In the end, LDCs are left with little money to show for their productivity, while MDCs grow richer. Thus, Third-World countries have few funds in their banking systems to invest in their own new business and investment opportunities. Their only choice is to seek First-World funding to keep people working and expand productivity, therefore continuing the cycle of dependency.

At the heart of Prebisch's theory stands a claim about the dominant role of First World-based **transnational corporations (TNCs)** and investors in a postcolonial exploitation of the Third World in which MDCs have economically and politically subordinated LDC populations. Some describe this as **economic imperialism** in a modern reference to the European empires of the colonial era.

Dependency creates additional **economic risks**, as Third-World economies are also subject to the level of demand for LDC-made products and the overall global economic climate. If demand and investment decline, as in the recent economic crisis, then LDCs suffer job layoffs, and international loan payments are unable to be made. This risk is magnified if an LDC's trade economy is based solely on the export of one or two agricultural or mineral resources. **Market stagnation** in an LDC product can be catastrophic to its economy and harm the quality of life of its citizens.

Breaking the Cycle of Dependency

As dependency theory was expanded over the years, theorists and politicians have suggested approaches in which Third-World governments incorporate policies to break the cycle of dependency. Many of these efforts were focused on keeping the money made from industrial production in the country, to be used later for **internal investment** in local development projects.

Here are some LDC policies and programs that attempted to increase **capital accumulation** within Third-World national economies:

- **Internalization of economic capital:** Requires companies to deposit profits from factories in LDC banks and reinvest locally. This is to prevent **capital flight**, which occurs when factory earnings are sent to banks back in the First World where they cannot be used to further local development in the LDC. Wealthier citizens can also be required to keep their money in national banks instead of hiding their money "off-shore."

- **Import substitution:** Instead of buying simple First World-made consumer products like laundry soap, this approach calls for building laundry soap factories and producing it within the LDC. The manufacturing profits can then be sent to LDC banks and reinvested locally.

- **Nationalization of natural resource-based industries:** Foreign corporate ownership of oil fields and mines robs the national government and local companies of potential earnings. If these resources are "nationalized," kicking out the foreign companies but keeping their infrastructure, the money made from the production of publicly owned resources can then be used for local economic development.

- **Profit-sharing agreements:** In China, Vietnam, and a few local cases elsewhere, foreign companies are given permission to build new factories on land leased to them by the government. In exchange, the foreign companies agree to share a portion of the factory's profits with the government, which are then used for further internal investment by government-owned companies.

- **Technology development programs:** Some countries have used their limited public funds to invest in high-technology equipment and worker training for locally owned manufacturers. These companies can then compete globally for contracts to produce goods as sub-contractors to First-World corporations. The factory profits then stay with locally owned companies.

In sum, the point of these programs is to accumulate a pool of national wealth that is recycled into the country's economy to help local businesses and improve the overall quality of life through funding for public services and utility infrastructure. Doing this without financial help from the First World is a positive sign of development.

Additional Development Approaches

There are a number of other factors that can give a country a distinct advantage in trade or development. Here are three important areas to know for the exam:

Tourism

By attracting international tourists, countries can gain large inputs of cash from foreign countries without having to export manufactured goods. There are tradeoffs, though, because the countries must provide a large, low-benefit service workforce for the hospitality industry and must be perceived as safe from crime, warfare, and terrorism. To attract tourists, the country must have some degree of historical value, natural beauty, sport recreation locations, or combinations thereof. Beach resorts, golf, skiing, wine regions, historical districts, and cultural attractions like festivals and archaeological sites can all create **tourist draw**.

In the past 30 years, **ecotourism** has become very popular. Rainforest, marine reef, savannah grassland, and polar habitats have all become destinations for paying tourists. These were once the travel sites of hunters, fishermen, and adventurers, but today there are well-established and accessible ecotourism resorts or cruise ships.

Countries that once had little international tourist draw such as Ecuador, Honduras, Belize, Costa Rica, Tanzania, Botswana, and Chile have become valuable ecotourism destinations.

CED 7.8
Sustainable Development

Free-Trade Agreements

Regional free-trade agreements between states have become a common way to improve international trade. Supranational **free-trade zones** like the European Union (EU) and North American Free Trade Agreement (NAFTA) have made regional economies of multiple states much stronger and have opened the doors of development for less-developed neighbors. In the case of the EU, new member states that were once part of the Soviet Union or former communist states in Eastern Europe have been able to develop their free-market economies more quickly.

CED 7.6
Trade and the World Economy

Mexico has benefited significantly from its free-trade relationship with the United States and Canada. The NAFTA treaty, signed in 1991, went into full effect in 2001 with the full removal of all **tariffs** (taxes on goods that cross international borders) between the three members. Mexico had already become a location for some U.S. and Canadian firms seeking a low-cost manufacturing location. NAFTA, however, opened the floodgates and allowed several hundred firms to build facilities and contract with local firms in Mexico to produce goods. As of 2020, NAFTA is set to be replaced by USMCA (United States-Mexico-Canada Agreement), which modifies its predecessor.

This shift in production location moved the manufacturing of everything from boots to light pickup trucks to northern Mexican border communities. ***Maquiladoras***, foreign-run factories operating under favorable tariff policies such as NAFTA, have become a major economic force in northern cities like Tijuana and Ciudad Juarez. As a result, both population and manufacturing output have boomed in these cities. Better-paying jobs, especially for women, and increased services have improved the quality of life for many residents. However, growth has been so rapid that many employed people still lack permanent housing and access to services such as clean water. Furthermore, pollution from the *maquiladoras* has contributed to a number of health problems for residents of these factory cities. Fortunately, a push by the Mexican government toward stricter environmental policies has helped improve conditions in recent years.

Free-Market Reforms

In the 1980s, communist states like China and Vietnam began to reform the old Soviet-style **command economy** in which all economic production was managed and planned by the central government. These reforms included allowing farmers to sell surplus agricultural goods in local and regional markets for profit. In cities, the reforms allowed people to open privately owned businesses like restaurants, repair services, and transportation companies. Other reforms such as the free movement of labor and the ability to purchase private real estate have also been introduced.

The most significant reform is allowing foreign companies to open factories and retail services in these countries. China established the first **special economic zones (SEZs)** in 1980, in which foreign firms were allowed to build facilities in coastal port cities. SEZs are a type of **export processing zone,** defined as port locations where foreign firms are given special tax privileges to incentivize trade.

China's SEZs were such a success that by the late 1990s, all of the coastal provinces in China and Vietnam had been opened to foreign manufacturing firms. Low-cost labor, land, and utilities provided by provincial governments were in large demand by transnational corporations seeking to maximize factory profits, which are shared with the Chinese and Vietnamese governments.

Economic productivity has more than tripled in China and Vietnam since the introduction of the reforms. Due to its large size, China has been able to integrate itself into the global economy through their state-owned corporations that have purchased Western brand-name product lines, like Whirlpool®. Chinese state-owned banking and finance firms also play a significant role in trade integration with export markets, especially in the United States, which sells many of its treasury bonds to China. Free-market reforms have enabled China to become an important player in the global economy—so important that the United States has become dependent on China for low-priced manufactured goods and to support the U.S. government's finances.

Wallerstein's World Systems Theory

In the 1970s, Immanuel Wallerstein developed a **world systems theory** that also sought to explain uneven development around the world. According to Wallerstein, capitalism was an unintentional result of the collapse of the feudal system. The modern nation-state, he argued, was birthed in Europe as a way of protecting capitalist interests, which were based on the same highly unequal division of labor as feudalism. Europeans were able to gain control over much of the world economy, engulfing smaller economic systems and spreading capitalism worldwide.

Rather than each country on Earth having its own economy, Wallerstein argued that there is one world economy with a strongly distorted balance of power among its various markets.

He divided the world into three interdependent realms:

1. **Core** nations are the most developed and economically influential in the world. They generally have strong, centralized governments and powerful militaries, and their populations are largely bourgeois or working class. Their economies are highly industrialized with emphasis on manufacturing or, increasingly, services. Core nations hold significant cultural, military, and especially economic dominance over the rest of the world. They import goods from periphery nations, taking advantage of those countries' cheap labor, raw materials, and agriculture.

2. **Periphery** nations are the least developed. They tend to have relatively weak governments and institutions. Social inequality tends to be high with large numbers of poor and uneducated citizens. Their economies are the least diversified, usually dependent on one or two forms of economic activity. More often than not, that activity is primary such as agriculture or extraction of natural resources for export. Periphery nations are heavily influenced and exploited by core countries.

3. **Semi-periphery** nations fall in between the core and periphery in terms of development and influence. They are frequently moving toward industrialization and tend to have somewhat developed and diversified economies, but are not dominant in the world system. Semi-periphery countries may have strongly protectionist policies, as they are constantly striving to keep themselves out of the periphery and join the core. They tend to send exports to the periphery and import goods from the core. Because of their middle ground, the semi-periphery nations can play both peripheral and core-like roles. They're able to assert some dominance over the periphery, but they can also be influenced and to some extent exploited by the core.

Below is a world map according to Wallerstein's theory:

Core, Semi-Periphery, and Periphery Countries

World systems theory is heavily influenced by dependency theory, but the two differ on the point of the First World's exploitation of the Third World. World systems theory, while recognizing the potential of core countries to exploit other nations, focused more heavily on a division of labor in the world economy. Also, Wallerstein argued that capitalism is capable of exploiting workers in all realms, not only the periphery.

Location Theory

Industrial Location Theory

The location of factories has been the focus of much economic and geographic study. Going back to the work of **Alfred Weber**, whose 1909 *Theory of Industrial Location* is still influential, the selection of optimal factory locations has much to do with the minimization of land, labor, resource, and transportation costs. By their nature, manufactured goods have a variable-cost framework that affects the potential location of factory sites. Weber states that, in terms of location, manufactured goods can be classified into two categories based on the amount of input in relation to product output:

> Weber's Theory is a favorite topic for both multiple-choice and free-response questions on the AP Human Geography Exam.

Weight-losing, or **bulk-reducing, manufacturing** involves a large amount of input that is reduced to a final product that weighs less or has less volume or bulk than the input. These factories tend to be located near the inputs that lose the most bulk in the manufacturing process, like trees or metal ore.

Weight-gaining, or **bulk-gaining, manufacturing** involves a number of inputs that are combined to make a final product that gains bulk, volume, or weight in the production process. These factories tend to be located closer to consumers because the cost of transporting the finished product is more than the cost of transporting the inputs; one example is refrigerators.

Weight-Losing Industries

In weight-losing processing in which there is only one major input, such as seafood packaging, lumber mills, and metal ore-processing or smelting, the industrial location is in very close proximity to the resource location. By comparison, when there are a number of major inputs to the production process, location must be balanced given the variable transportation costs of each input. The inputs that lose the most bulk in the production process are relatively more expensive to transport than those inputs that could represent a more significant portion of the finished product.

Example: Steel

The industrial location of steel factories is dependent on four major inputs: iron ore, coal, limestone, and water. Of these, iron ore has the lowest loss of volume of the finished product. Limestone is used to refine the steel and give it comparative lightness and strength. However, limestone makes up only a small proportion of the final product, and much of its bulk is lost in the manufacturing process. Coal, refined into coke to burn hotter, is completely lost during production, as is water, which is required in large amounts to cool steel products so that they retain their form. Condensers often capture steam produced and recycle it into liquid.

Therefore, iron ore is most **distance elastic**, meaning it can be transported over short or long distances to the steel plant, whereas coal, limestone, and water need to be in **close proximity,** as shown in the following table and example locations.

Industrial Location and Steel Production		
Resources	**Production Loss**	**Location**
Iron Ore	Low Loss	Distance Elastic
Limestone	High Loss	Close Proximity
Coal	High Loss	Close Proximity
Water	High Loss	Close Proximity

Using Pittsburgh and the cities of Essen and Dortmund in the Ruhr valley of Germany as examples, you can describe weight-losing industrial locations in relation to multiple natural resources:

In Pittsburgh	From
Iron Ore	Mesabi and Iron Ranges (Northern Michigan, Wisconsin, and Minnesota)
Limestone	Ohio Valley
Coal	Monongahela Valley
Water	The "Three Rivers" (Ohio, Monongahela, and Allegheny Rivers)
In the Ruhr Valley	**From**
Iron Ore	Harz (Eastern Germany) and Jura (Alps) Mountains
Limestone	Ruhr Valley
Coal	Ruhr Valley
Water	Ruhr and Rhine Rivers

In the United States, steel production around Pittsburgh had consolidated in the 1870s using small local sources of iron. As production later expanded, the iron fields near Lake Superior became the main supplier of iron ore (taconite) to large firms like United States Steel. At this time, the steel industry expanded to port locations on the Great Lakes like Cleveland, Toledo, Detroit, and Gary. In the case of U.S. Steel's plant in Gary, just outside Chicago, the company found that by not having to transport ore from Lake Erie to Pittsburgh by rail, they were able to cut **transportation costs**. Elbert Gary first made this proposal to Andrew Carnegie, president of U.S. Steel, who named the new city for his company's vice president in 1906.

Today, new steel plants tend to be much smaller operations that focus on specialized steel products. Steel **mini-mills** run by companies such as NUCOR or ArcelorMittal have a number of building materials, vehicle parts, and high-tech steel alloys for medical and aerospace sectors. Some of these mills are located in old steel-producing cities, but others have been constructed in Southern states where land and labor are less expensive and there are fewer regulations.

Weight-Gaining Industries

Weight-gaining manufacturing generally involves the assembly of several inputs into a finished product. As this finished product is more bulky and thus more costly to transport, the factory location should be relatively close to consumers to minimize delivery costs.

A basic example is bread. Flour from wheat grown in regions like the Great Plains is combined with water, sugar, and yeast to make dough that rises from the yeast's CO_2 production. Once baking is complete, the loaf of bread has gained significant volume compared to its inputs. An added issue for food products like bread is the limited **shelf life** that also affects industrial location. Bread, milk, and other **perishable products** tend to be manufactured in many individual plants that serve the local regions. This **decentralized network** approach keeps fresh products in stores longer by reducing transportation time. Bread production is so decentralized that bakeries are found in all cities and are an example of **ubiquitous industries**.

Conversely, when shelf life is not an issue for weight-gaining manufacturing, production tends to be **centralized** within larger consumer market areas. Frozen foods, for example, are made in large centralized facilities, which then ship to stores and grocery warehouses across the country. When Luigino's Inc., maker of Michelina's brand frozen dinners, first selected a plant location, they chose the small town of Jackson, Ohio, a central location in the eastern half of the United States. From this low-cost rural location, delivery trucks could easily access a number of nearby interstate highways. Within 24 hours, trucks leaving Jackson could reach 60 percent of their consumers in the United States and Canada.

The Geography of Supply Chains

A **supply chain** exists when parts are assembled into components that are then joined together to create larger finished products. Automobiles are an example of heavy industry that requires a large supply chain network to support the assembly of a final product. As price and corporate profit requirements have increased over time, the size of supply chain regions has expanded. In 1903, when Henry Ford opened his River Rouge plant in Detroit, every part of the car was made in one large factory complex, with the exception of tires, which were a highly specialized product made for Ford by Firestone in Akron, Ohio. **Fordist production** (**Fordism**) relied on a single company owning all aspects of production, from steel manufacture to advertising.

In the **Post-Fordist era**, car companies changed and became dependent on large networks of regional supply chains that, in the case of Detroit-area assembly plants, stretch throughout the Midwestern United States, with some specialized electronic parts coming from overseas suppliers. **Outsourcing** is common in auto parts, and car companies rely on several other companies to provide vehicle components such as brakes, electronics, glass, and specialized plastics. Car companies must still oversee the quality of supplier products.

To minimize inventory costs and keep factories efficient, car companies today also utilize **just-in-time production** methods, in which suppliers send parts to assembly plants on an as-needed basis. These practices minimize potential cost-overruns due to over-supply and save space and money by not requiring warehouse and handling facilities for parts. In addition, car models change design more frequently now, sometimes even annually. If you get too many parts for a model that goes out of style, they will go unused and become a wasted production cost.

Retail Location Theory

The market area of a city is defined by two factors: **threshold** and **range.** As is described in the section on central place theory in Chapter 8, the threshold of a service is the minimum number of people required to support a business. The range is the maximum distance people are willing to travel to gain access to a service.

However, the precise location of **retail services** is spatially dependent on the relationship between variable cost and revenue surfaces based on local geography. Business owners look to find locations where they can maximize profits. In economic geography, we use the concept of the **spatial margin of profitability** to define these areas of maximization. The spatial margin of profitability is the area where local demand for a service creates revenue higher than the local costs of doing business, as shown in the diagram on the following page.

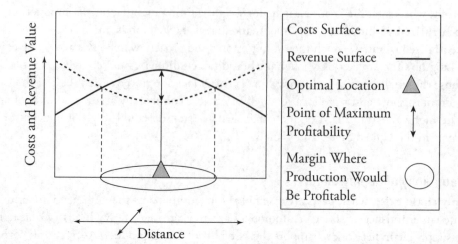

The diagram shows a theoretical location where revenues would exceed costs. The spot where revenues are furthest above costs is the point of maximum profit, or the optimal location for this theoretical retail location. Not all businesses will be able to locate exactly on this point due to the availability of commercial real estate. However, business owners will want to be as close to this point as possible to assure profitability. Other factors such as the consumers' ability to access the optimal location have to be considered before a location choice can be finalized. You could find the perfect spot to put your bakery, but if it's down a flood-prone dirt road, no one will be able to get to it.

Service Location Theory

The location of businesses in the service economy era (since the 1990s) has become a new area of research in economic geography. Compared to the older retail location theory, much of this recent work has focused on the location of **high-benefit services.** The term **footloose industry** has come to describe businesses whose locations are not tied to resources, transportation, or consumer locations. In high-benefit services, a number of different activities are technically footloose and can be located anywhere executives desire.

Here are a few examples:

- Corporate headquarters and regional offices
- Customer-service call centers
- Bill, claim, and records processing centers
- Research and development centers
- Software development centers
- Accounting and insurance service centers
- Business consulting service centers
- Architecture and engineering service centers

However, research has shown that there is not really such a thing as a completely footloose industry. As with manufacturers, there are a number of factors to consider before selecting a location to house a service-industry office. Often corporate executives are interested in a location for a number of particular qualities that compose a "best fit" for their **corporate culture**.

Economist Richard Florida has proposed that there is a **creative class** of high-benefit service-industry firms and workers. **Local economic development** programs have become focused on the attraction of "creative" firms and laborers. Localities, states, and provinces in the United States and Canada are all competing to attract these creative-class employers. However, they also have to compete with other countries, especially English-language states like Ireland, Australia, and New Zealand.

Some of the local attributes that are in demand by high-benefit and creative service industries are as follows:

- Language of the workforce
- Availability of the workforce
- Education level of the workforce
- Climate and natural environment
- Recreation opportunities
- Entertainment venues
- Tolerant community
- "Cool" factor

Communities like Austin, Seattle, Portland, Vancouver, Toronto, Memphis, Atlanta, Boston, and San Francisco have all gained creative-class employment due to their amenable combination of local qualities. Internationally, city governments in Dublin, Glasgow, Auckland, Sydney, Melbourne, Brisbane, and Cape Town are in the business of attracting top service firms and young, cool, well-educated workers to their cities. These cities fall within the "cool" category. Unfortunately, coolness is something most social scientists have great difficulty defining, as so few of us have any idea what it is!

Can a city become too cool for its own good? Turn to page 350 to learn about the drawbacks of gentrification and rapid economic growth.

Additional Theoretical Principles and Examples

In addition to the theories presented here, there are a few other theoretical and spatial principles of economic geography that you should know for the exam:

Agglomeration

In its most basic form, agglomeration refers to the concentration of human activities in a cluster or around a central place. **Agglomeration economies** exist where firms with related or similar products locate together in clusters or regions. Together, the firms enjoy the advantages of a shared skilled-labor pool, specialized suppliers, and service providers and can share (or steal) technical knowledge on production or marketing. Normally, when one firm finds a cost-minimizing advantage of a location, other firms will move to that location to achieve the same savings. Likewise, when a location is known for a particular product, such as Detroit for automakers, related suppliers and competing firms will attempt to locate there as well.

Deglomeration occurs when a location is overloaded with similar firms and services. If local resources or the labor pool are fully utilized or over-utilized, some firms may seek alternate locations to expand to or may move all operations completely. Again, in the case of automobile production, in the early 1980s Japanese firms looked to open factories in the United States to reduce transportation costs of moving new cars across the Pacific. The first company, Honda, looked at Detroit but found the labor force and land there too expensive. Instead, they went 165 miles south to rural Marysville, Ohio. Still close to many parts suppliers in Ohio, Marysville has proven to be an effective and inexpensive location.

The Foreign Auto Firms Move South

As Japanese firms looked into American production sites, they found further reduced-cost advantages as they moved south from Michigan and Ohio. These northern **unionized-labor states** had higher payroll and benefit costs which were ingrained into state workforce regulations. Southern locations were **right-to-work states** where regulation does not favor unions and did not impact pay benefit costs.

The next Japanese plant opened during 1982 in Smyrna, Tennessee, for the Nissan Motor Company. This was followed in 1986 with the Toyota assembly facility in Georgetown, Kentucky. As these firms expanded operations at these sites, auto parts supply firms located in the surrounding region. In effect, this expanded the American auto parts manufacturing region from Ontario to the Gulf Coast states of Mississippi and Alabama.

In the 1990s, European automakers looked for similar locations to build affordable luxury-brand cars (an oxymoron). BMW opened its 3-series production plant in the Greenville-Spartanburg area of South Carolina in 1996. Tire supplier Michelin had moved its North American headquarters and several facilities to the area in the late 1980s. Mercedes, likewise, selected Vance, Alabama, to manufacture its E-class cars, which began production in 1997.

KNOW THE MAPS

Industrial Regions

In addition to understanding why agglomeration occurs, make sure to know the location and composition of the major industrial regions around the world:

North America
- American Industrial Belt or "Rust Belt" following deindustrialization
- Canadian Industrial Heartland or Canada's "Main Street"
- Piedmont Industrial Region

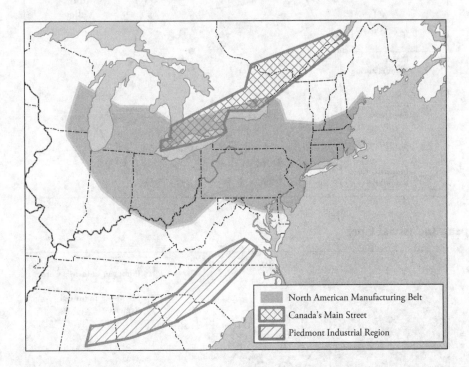

Legend:
- North American Manufacturing Belt
- Canada's Main Street
- Piedmont Industrial Region

Europe

- British Midlands
- Ruhr Valley
- Northern Italy or the "Third Italy"

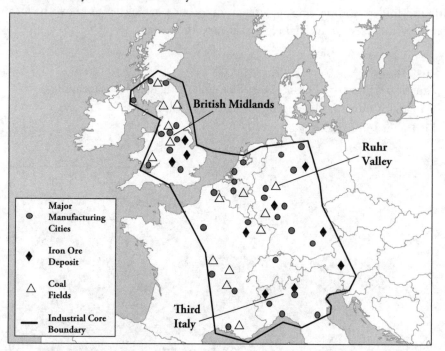

European Industrial Core

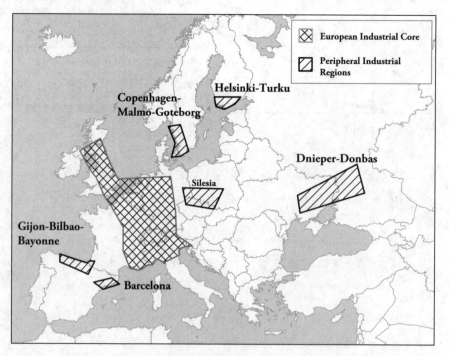

Asia

- Japan
- Korea
- Taiwan
- China

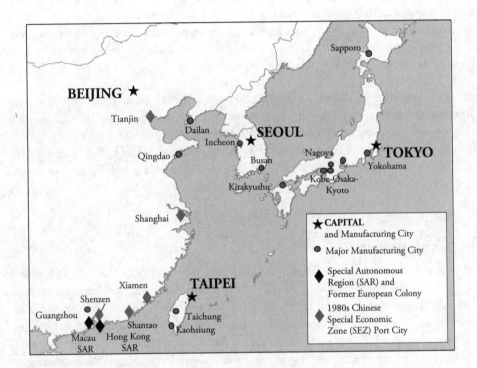

Maps often appear in the free-response section of the exam, so familiarize yourself with these examples.

Other World Industrial Regions

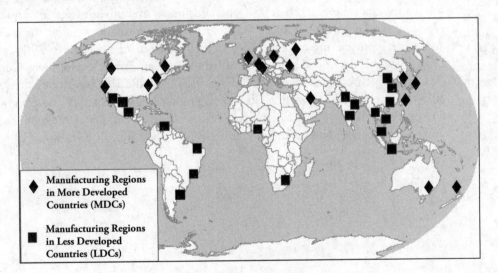

Economies of Scale

By definition, **economies of scale** are achieved when producers expand their operations but incur lower per-unit costs in the process. When a company increases output of a single product, it can save money by purchasing supplies in bulk, managing more workers with the same staff, financing larger sums of credit at lower interest rates, and negotiating discounts for per-mile transportation costs in larger bulk amounts. In addition, more goods are sold without increasing advertising, accounting, research, or other fixed service costs. Companies that achieve large size are said to receive "return from scale" as they reap the long-term profit benefits from expanded production. For example, Walmart has leveraged economies of scale for decades to offer low prices and become the ubiquitous retail outlet we know today.

This is related to **economies of scope,** in which companies benefit from the increase in the number of different products under a larger brand name. For instance, several product lines can be marketed by a single sales staff, and produced in the same factories. Larger economies of scope are especially useful when one product at the end of its useful life, or **product cycle,** is replaced by a new model or alternative device. Apple's iPhone, iPod, and iMac products fall under economies of scope.

Women in Development

For more resources on economic geography, check out *Economic Geography: A Contemporary Introduction* by Neil M. Coe, Philip F. Kelly, and Henry W. C. Yeung.

Women work more hours per day (in paid and unpaid labor) than men in every country in the world *except* in Anglo America and Australia. Women in the paid workforce are also growing in numbers across the world in both developed and developing countries and regions. Their role in society is changing and improving as opportunities for education, childcare, and maternity benefits open up. However, women in many places still have not achieved equity in pay and employment opportunities. Some programs are working to close this gap. Improved access to microcredit, such as the Grameen Bank microcredit loans in Bangladesh, give women the chance to start their own small businesses and provide for their families. Practices similar to the Grameen Bank loans have spread throughout the world and are responsible for helping move participants out of poverty. In 2000, the United Nations developed a mandate called the **Millennium Development Goals (MDGs),** which was designed with the intention of eradicating poverty by the year 2015. These eight development goals seek to promote gender equality and empower women through provision of better women's health care, hunger eradication, basic universal education, and an end to abject poverty. They are still working on it.

CHAPTER 9 KEY TERMS

sectors

primary production

secondary production

manufacturing

tertiary production

services

quaternary production (business service)

quinary production (consumer service)

commodity chains

mining

energy extraction

resource-dependent country

fisheries

timber markets

nonrenewable products

renewable products

alternative energy

sustainable use

ecosystem

value-added processing

durable goods

non-durable goods

low-benefit services

high-benefit services

service firms

deindustrialized

foreign competition

off-shore locations

investment value

returns on investment

plow

steel

computer

microchip

uneven development

industrialized economies

service-based economies

communist

restructuring

free-market reforms

agricultural economies

resource-based economies

underdeveloped states

more developed countries (MDCs)

less developed countries (LDCs)

newly industrialized countries (NICs)

infrastructure

rapid population growth

rapid rural-to-urban migration

foreign aid

foreign direct investment (FDI)

development loans

donor state

technology transfer

private investors

investment firms

World Bank

comparative advantages

off-shoring

North versus South analogy

Asian Tigers

market share

foreign competition

oil shocks of the 1970s

cheap labor

low-cost land and resources

few labor and environmental regulations

credit crisis

deindustrialization

guaranteed family employment

kiretsu

chaebol

economic indicators

gross domestic product (GDP)

total volume

gross national income (GNI)

exports minus imports

trade surplus

trade deficit

level of development comparisons

standard of living

gross national income purchasing power parity (GNI PPP)

Human Development Index (HDI)

Gini coefficient

income disparity

Gender-Related Development Index (GDI)

gender equality

comparative advantage

colonial legacy

government corruption

capital flight

dependency theory

cycle of dependency

Prebisch thesis

transnational corporations (TNCs)

economic imperialism

economic risks

market stagnation

internal investment

capital accumulation

capital flight

import substitution

nationalization of natural resource-
based industries

profit-sharing agreements

technology development programs

tourist draw

ecotourism

free-trade zones

tariffs

maquiladoras

command economy

special economic zones (SEZs)

export processing zone

Alfred Weber

Theory of Industrial Location

World Systems Theory

weight-losing (bulk-reducing) manufacturing

weight-gaining (bulk-gaining) manufacturing

distance elastic

close proximity

transportation costs

mini-mills

shelf life

perishable products

decentralized network

ubiquitous industries

centralized production

supply chain

Fordist production (Fordism)

Post-Fordist era

outsourcing

just-in-time production

threshold

range

retail services

special margin of profitability

high-benefit services

footloose industry

corporate culture

creative class

local economic development

agglomeration economies

deglomeration

unionized-labor states

right-to-work states

economies of scale

economies of scope

product cycle

Millennium Development Goals (MDGs)

CHAPTER 9 DRILL

See the end of this chapter for answers and explanations.

1. Which stage of production is concerned with activities such as finance and banking?

    (A) Primary
    (B) Secondary
    (C) Tertiary
    (D) Quarternary
    (E) Quinary

2. According to Wallerstein's world systems theory, which of the following would be true?

    (A) Core countries primarily export raw materials to other countries.
    (B) Semi-peripheral countries are located between the core and periphery.
    (C) Peripheral countries have mostly service-based economies.
    (D) Core countries are the most economically developed and powerful.
    (E) Semi-peripheral countries primarily export goods to core countries and import goods from peripheral countries.

3. All of the following are Old Asian Tigers EXCEPT

    (A) Japan
    (B) Taiwan
    (C) China
    (D) South Korea
    (E) Singapore

4. Which of the following includes only aspects of tertiary production?

    (A) Finance, mining, transportation
    (B) Transportation, wholesaling, retailing
    (C) Agriculture, energy, fisheries
    (D) Forestry, processing, fabrication
    (E) Tourism, entertainment, communications

5. The links between producers and consumers in the production and distribution of goods are known as

    (A) value-added processing
    (B) sustainable economies
    (C) commodity chains
    (D) low-benefit services
    (E) high-benefit services

6. One of the problems with using the terms First World, Second World, and Third World to describe countries is that

    (A) First-World countries are sometimes lacking free markets and a high level of productivity value per person
    (B) the terms are slightly misleading, since Second-World countries are not necessarily between First- and Third-World countries, but instead are communist centrally planned economies
    (C) Third-World countries have agricultural or resourced-based economies but a high quality of life
    (D) some First-World countries, such as Argentina, actually resemble Second-World countries
    (E) some countries, such as Japan, can't be categorized in this schema

7. Rostow's theory of stages of growth fails to take into account all of the following EXCEPT

    (A) a set of preconditions needed to transition from an agricultural to a manufacturing economy
    (B) the historical patterns of non-industrialized countries
    (C) industrialized nations' forcible extraction of valuable natural resources in the Third World
    (D) the role of governmental corruption in the development of a country
    (E) the Third-World countries' dependence upon international loans to transnational corporations

8. Software development, customer-service call centers, and corporate headquarters are all examples of

    (A) outsourced services
    (B) weight-losing manufacturing
    (C) activities located at the end of the supply chain
    (D) activities that have struck a balance between threshold and range
    (E) activities that aren't tied to any specific location

9. Which of the following is NOT a characteristic of the modern service economy?

(A) A labor force composed of hourly employees who receive few benefits

(B) A labor force composed of salaried employees who receive many benefits

(C) A draw for investors

(D) The creation of both durable and non-durable goods

(E) Heavily dependent upon computer technology

10. The difference between GDP (gross domestic product) and GNI (gross national income) is

(A) GDP measures collective wealth or productivity, but GNI measures general well-being

(B) GDP considers goods and services, but GNI also considers exports and imports

(C) GDP absorbs only data from the service economy, but GNI takes into account data from both service and manufacturing economies

(D) GDP is a measure of inflation, but GNI indicates a standard of living

(E) GDP measures the personal income of an average worker, while GNI measures the purchasing power of that worker

11. All of the following are complaints about First-World transnational corporations EXCEPT

(A) their tendency to create economic dependency of LDCs (lesser developed countries) on MDCs (more developed countries)

(B) their postcolonial exploitation of the populations of LDCs for lower wages

(C) their desire to invest in modern technological equipment and worker training

(D) the sudden loss of jobs in LDCs if demand and investment decline, particularly when the trade is based on one or two resources

(E) their lack of profit-sharing agreements with local governments and populations

CHAPTER 9 DRILL: ANSWERS AND EXPLANATIONS

1. **D**   Quarternary production, (D), is the only choice to focus on finance, banking, and other business services. Primary production, (A), is concerned with industries like mining and energy, and secondary production, (B), is concerned with manufacturing. Tertiary production, (C), deals with transportation and wholesaling. Finally, quinary production, (E), concerns itself with consumer services.

2. **D**   Core countries are the most developed and hold political and economic power over other countries. Peripheral countries have the least diversified economies and tend to engage in primary economic activities like agriculture and natural resource extraction. The reverse of (E) is true.

3. **C**   If you're not sure of the answer, try to eliminate as many incorrect choices as possible. The Old Asian Tigers, who funded their manufacturing development period with foreign aid during the 1950s–1970s, are Japan, Taiwan, South Korea, and Singapore. Accordingly, (A), (B), (D), and (E) can be eliminated. China is an example of a New Asian Tiger and, therefore, (C) is the correct answer.

4. **B**   Tertiary production, or third-stage production, largely includes everything that follows the production of goods. This includes moving the goods, selling the goods to wholesalers, or selling the goods directly to consumers. Primary production is resource extraction; secondary production is processing and manufacturing. Choose (B).

5. **C**   A commodity chain is a process used by firms to gather resources, transform them into goods or commodities, and finally, distribute them to consumers. It is a series of links connecting the many places of production and distribution, and resulting in a commodity that is then exchanged on the world market. The correct answer is (C).

6. **B**   Second-World countries are technically all communist, centrally planned economies. Since the fall of the Soviet Union, there are only two left, Cuba and North Korea, and nobody knows how much longer they'll continue. Many economists prefer the terms MDCs (more developed countries) and LDCs (less developed countries). Choice (B) is correct.

7. **A**   Rostow examined only First-World countries when formulating his theory of how civilizations grow. This means that the theory has a massive blind spot regarding Third-World countries, including their colonial legacy, capital flight, government corruption, and radically different histories. Choose (A).

8. **E**   Any business that can easily pick up and move is considered a part of the so-called footloose industry. These creative-class executives can choose the location of their companies based on whatever qualities have a best fit for their culture. Many cities bend over backwards trying to attract these corporations because of the injection of money that they represent to the local economy. The correct answer is (E).

9. **D** The creation of any goods, whether durable or non-durable, is part of a manufacturing economy. Choices (A) and (B), while seemingly opposites, are actually both present in service economies. Uber drivers and graphic designers provide services, are paid hourly, and receive no benefits; meanwhile, a systems administrator for a major corporation provides a service for a salary and benefits.

10. **B** Gross domestic product (GDP) per capita is defined as the sum of goods and services divided by population. Gross national income (GNI) per capita is defined as the sum of goods and services plus the difference between exports and imports, divided by population.

11. **C** Investing transnational corporate money in technology and worker training is an excellent acknowledgment by transnational companies of the importance of the local population that their business depends upon. How often this occurs is up to interpretation.

Summary

o There are five sectors of production in the world economy: primary (agriculture and extraction of natural resources), secondary (manufacturing), tertiary (transportation and sale of manufactured goods), quaternary (business services), and quinary (consumer services).

o Many First-World countries like the United States and Canada have deindustrialized, moving toward service-based economies.

o There are several key measures of development:
   • Gross domestic product (GDP) measures the value of all the goods and services a country produces in a year: *GDP = Goods + Services*.
   • Gross national income (GNI) is the GDP, plus the difference in the value of exports and imports:
     GNI = Goods + Services + (Exports – Imports).
   • The Human Development Index (HDI) was designed by the United Nations to measure social as well as economic development.

o Rostow's Stages of Growth tracks a country's development through five stages:
   1. Traditional society
   2. Preconditions for takeoff
   3. Takeoff
   4. Drive to maturity
   5. Age of mass consumption

o Dependency theory holds that most LDCs (Less Developed Countries) become trapped in a cycle of depending on loans, direct investment, and technology from MDCs (More Developed Countries) to stimulate their economies.

o   In the era of globalization, international free-trade agreements like NAFTA and that of the EU have become extremely important.

o   Wallerstein's world systems theory divides nations into three categories: core nations, semi-periphery nations, and periphery nations.

o   Weber's Theory of Industrial Location states that factory location should be based on minimizing resource and transportation costs: weight-losing manufacturing should be located near its bulky inputs, while weight-gaining manufacturing should be located nearer to consumers.

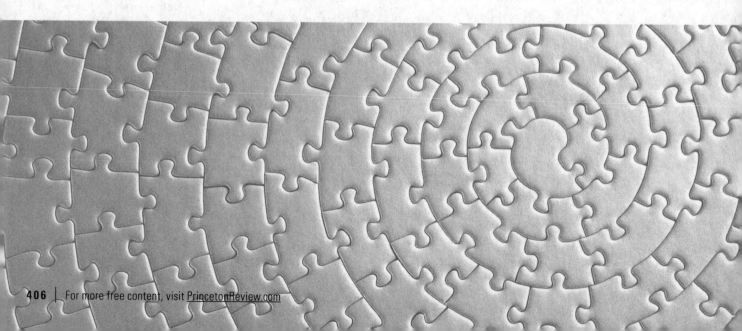

Part VI
Additional
Practice Tests

Practice Test 2

AP® Human Geography Exam

SECTION I: Multiple-Choice Questions

DO NOT OPEN THIS BOOKLET UNTIL YOU ARE TOLD TO DO SO.

At a Glance

Total Time
60 minutes
Number of Questions
60
Percent of Total Grade
50%
Writing Instrument
Pencil required

Instructions

Section I of this exam contains 60 multiple-choice questions. Fill in only the ovals for numbers 1 through 60 on your answer sheet.

Indicate all of your answers to the multiple-choice questions on the answer sheet. No credit will be given for anything written in this exam booklet, but you may use the booklet for notes or scratch work. After you have decided which of the suggested answers is best, completely fill in the corresponding oval on the answer sheet. Give only one answer to each question. If you change an answer, be sure that the previous mark is erased completely. Here is a sample question and answer.

Sample Questions   Sample Answers

The first president of the United States was   Ⓐ ● Ⓒ Ⓓ Ⓔ
(A) Millard Fillmore
(B) George Washington
(C) Benjamin Franklin
(D) Andrew Jackson
(E) Harry Truman

Use your time effectively, working as quickly as you can without losing accuracy. Do not spend too much time on any one question. Go on to other questions and come back to the ones you have not answered if you have time. It is not expected that everyone will know the answers to all the multiple-choice questions.

About Guessing

Many candidates wonder whether or not to guess the answers to questions about which they are not certain. Multiple-choice scores are based on the number of questions answered correctly. Points are not deducted for incorrect answers, and no points are awarded for unanswered questions. Because points are not deducted for incorrect answers, you are encouraged to answer all multiple-choice questions. On any questions you do not know the answer to, you should eliminate as many choices as you can, and then select the best answer among the remaining choices.

GO ON TO THE NEXT PAGE.

This page intentionally left blank.

HUMAN GEOGRAPHY
SECTION I
Time—60 minutes
60 Questions

Directions: Each of the questions or incomplete statements below is followed by five suggested answers or completions. Select the one that best answers the question or completes the statement.

1. The demographic transition model states that stage 3 societies differ from stage 2 societies primarily in that

   (A) a stage 3 economy is agricultural, not manufacturing
   (B) a stage 3 birth rate is decreasing, not increasing
   (C) a stage 3 death rate is increasing, not decreasing
   (D) a stage 3 total population has leveled off
   (E) a stage 3 gender imbalance has rebalanced itself

2. Countries that are near or below zero population growth will often

   (A) eliminate guest worker programs
   (B) elect nativist or authoritarian leaders
   (C) experience reduced levels of manufacturing
   (D) offer incentives to citizens to have more children
   (E) exhibit an increased death rate

3. The primary reason that humanity has been able to escape the Malthusian trap is

   (A) changing weather patterns
   (B) improvements in human digestion
   (C) increased government intervention
   (D) reduced open-border policies
   (E) improved agricultural technology

GO ON TO THE NEXT PAGE.

Question 4 refers to the following graph from 2014.

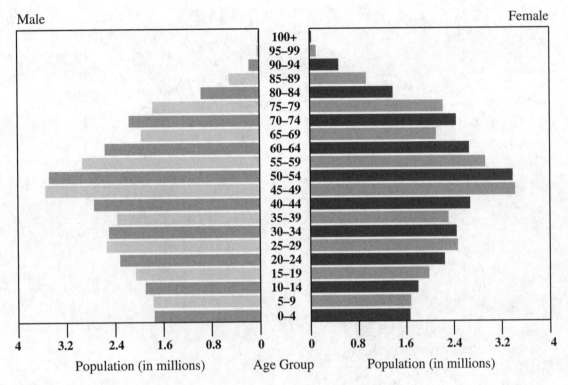

Male   Female

Population (in millions)   Age Group   Population (in millions)

Source: U.S. Census Bureau, International Data Base

4. The 2014 population pyramid depicted above most likely describes a nation in

(A) sub-Saharan Africa
(B) western Europe
(C) central Asia
(D) South America
(E) the Middle East

5. An example of cyclic movement is

(A) a Polish woman working as a housekeeper in Ireland each summer
(B) a Chinese software entrepreneur opening a branch of his business in Ethiopia
(C) a French woman with dual citizenship retiring to her parents' homeland of Tunisia
(D) a Syrian refugee seeking refuge with his family in Germany
(E) a young Colombian moving from the countryside to Bogotá to attend university

6. An example of an officially multilingual society is

(A) Canada
(B) the United States
(C) Bolivia
(D) France
(E) South Korea

7. A Bangladeshi immigrant to France, who has limited grammar and few vocabulary words in French, speaks a

(A) *lingua franca*
(B) pidgin
(C) creole
(D) patois
(E) dialect

GO ON TO THE NEXT PAGE.

Questions 8–10 refer to the map below.

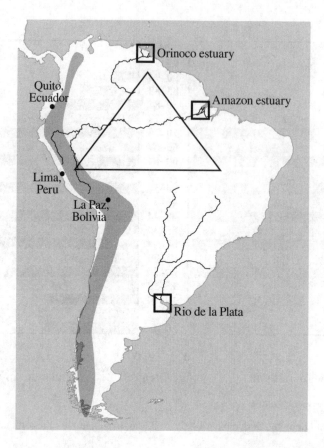

8. The cities noted on the map all share which of the following characteristics?

   (A) All share a history of agricultural wealth.
   (B) All have sizable indigenous populations.
   (C) All have seen population decline in recent years.
   (D) All are located in former Portuguese states.
   (E) All are majority Protestant populations.

9. The regions inside the squares on the map all share which of the following characteristics?

   (A) Cultural hearths
   (B) Regions of monoculture
   (C) Value-added agriculture
   (D) Linguistic dialect regions
   (E) Estuaries

10. The triangular region on the map has been facing which of the following challenges in recent years?

   (A) Religious fundamentalism
   (B) Loss of native architectural forms
   (C) Multilingualism
   (D) Transnational migration
   (E) Ecological degradation

GO ON TO THE NEXT PAGE.

11. The influence of German music upon the *norteño,*
ranchera, and *banda* forms of music in northern Mexico
is an example of

    (A) contagious diffusion
    (B) stimulus diffusion
    (C) hierarchical diffusion
    (D) expansion diffusion
    (E) relocation diffusion

12. All of the following are differences between monotheistic
and polytheistic traditions EXCEPT

    (A) monotheistic traditions emerged in what is now
        the Middle East, while polytheistic traditions
        emerged in the Far East
    (B) monotheistic traditions grew out of the visions of a
        single founder, while polytheistic traditions grew
        out of collective culture
    (C) monotheistic traditions believe in one divine being,
        while polytheistic traditions believe in many
        divine beings
    (D) monotheistic traditions maintain an egalitarian
        structure, while polytheistic traditions maintain a
        hierarchical structure
    (E) monotheistic traditions practice moral absolutism,
        while polytheistic traditions practice moral
        relativism

13. The difference between a *site* and a *situation* is defined as
the difference between

    (A) the physical characteristics of a place versus the
        interconnectedness of that place with other places
    (B) the investment in historical renovation versus the
        investment in new construction
    (C) the fixed characteristics of a place versus the
        changing characteristics of a place
    (D) the tendency for a place to retain its own unique
        characteristics over time versus the tendency for
        a place to lose those unique characteristics over
        time
    (E) the power of a group effort versus the strength of
        individual effort

GO ON TO THE NEXT PAGE.

Questions 14–16 refer to the following diagrams.

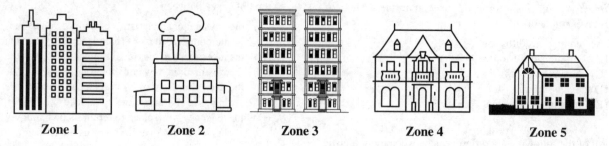

Zone 1   Zone 2   Zone 3   Zone 4   Zone 5

Baltimore, 1920

14. In 1920, what was the primary obstacle preventing working-class people living in Zone 3 from moving to Zone 4?

    (A) Racist housing policies
    (B) Prejudice against immigrants
    (C) Cost of transportation
    (D) Fervent religiosity
    (E) Lack of employment

15. If this urban model of Baltimore in 1920 were placed next to an urban model of Baltimore in 2020, which of the following changes would be evident during those one hundred years?

    (A) Zone 1 would have remained unchanged.
    (B) Zone 2 would have remained unchanged.
    (C) Zone 3 would have increased in population density.
    (D) Zone 4 would have declined in population density.
    (E) Zone 5 would have grown in real population.

16. Unlike the concentric zone model above, the sector model of urban structure takes into account which of the following factors?

    (A) Ethnicity
    (B) Gender
    (C) Socioeconomic class
    (D) Transportation
    (E) Religion

17. The scientific idea that a culture's physical traits are decided by the physical geography of its hearth region is known as

    (A) external identity
    (B) environmental determinism
    (C) ethnic cleansing
    (D) syncretism
    (E) appellations

18. The concept of sequent occupance is best illustrated by which of the following situations?

    (A) The arrival of a Somali family into a white Minnesota neighborhood
    (B) The discovery by construction workers in Rome of previously unknown ancient ruins
    (C) A young girl who is sharing an apartment with her parents and two sets of grandparents
    (D) The laws that allow squatters legal rights to a property after a set period of time has elapsed
    (E) The construction of Las Vegas on flat, untouched desert

19. The perception of Mexicans as wearing large sombreros and eating tacos is an example of Mexico as a(n)

    (A) political region
    (B) environmental region
    (C) absolute location
    (D) relative location
    (E) vernacular region

GO ON TO THE NEXT PAGE.

Questions 20–22 refer to the following graph.

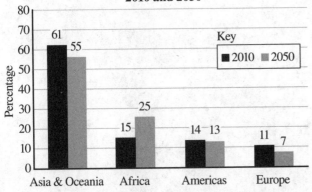

Regional Distribution of the Global Population, 2010 and 2050

20. According to the bar graph, total population is projected to increase the most in which region?

    (A) Asia & Oceania
    (B) Africa
    (C) Americas
    (D) Europe
    (E) There is not enough information to determine.

21. Instead of a bar graph, what type of graphic would more accurately describe the demographic makeup of these regions?

    (A) Mercator projections
    (B) population pyramids
    (C) demographic transition models
    (D) concentric zone models
    (E) sector models

22. Given the fact that 55% of the global population now lives in cities, which of the following statements can be safely assumed?

    (A) It's not likely that the concentric zone model is being adopted in regions such as Africa or Asia & Oceania.
    (B) The future of the human species is entirely urban.
    (C) The most typical human profile is a person who lives in a city in Asia or Oceania.
    (D) Europe features greater urban density than any other region.
    (E) Africa's population density is projected to grow faster than that of any other region.

23. In the United States in the 1830s, the change in land survey patterns from a traditional system of metes and bounds to a rectilinear township and range system was the result of

    (A) new territory obtained via the Louisiana Purchase
    (B) new waves of Southern and Eastern European immigrants
    (C) new incentives for redistricting state apportionments
    (D) new surveying tools derived from seafaring technology
    (E) new methods of calculating population density

GO ON TO THE NEXT PAGE.

Questions 24 and 25 refer to the following map.

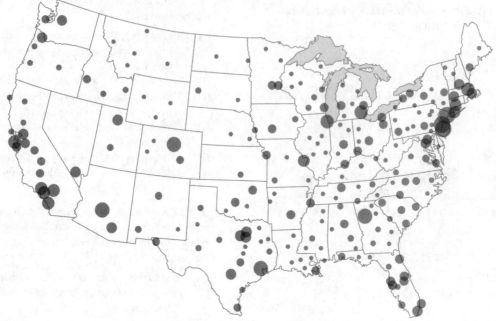

H1N1 Influenza Pandemic Map, 2009

24. The above is an example of a
    (A) cartogram
    (B) flow-line map
    (C) graduated symbol map
    (D) isoline map
    (E) choropleth map

25. The spread of the influenza is most analogous to
    (A) absolute location
    (B) contagious diffusion
    (C) relocation diffusion
    (D) orthomorphic projection
    (E) choropleth

26. Two neighboring villages with populations of 300 and 400 are separated by 10 miles. What is their gravity model?
    (A) 12
    (B) 24
    (C) 120
    (D) 240
    (E) 1,200

27. GIS (Geographic Information Systems) would be LEAST useful in which of the following situations?
    (A) Plotting the effects of an economic crash on immigration
    (B) Dialing 911 from a landline
    (C) Using in-car navigational systems
    (D) Assessing crop damage after a flood
    (E) Planning the construction of roads and bridges

28. The racist method of real estate agents encouraging white homeowners to sell their homes at a loss by implying that minorities were moving in is known as
    (A) gentrification
    (B) blockbusting
    (C) functional zonation
    (D) redlining
    (E) new urbanism

29. In the United States, the process of suburbanization that has occurred since the 1950s has resulted in all of the following EXCEPT
    (A) increased automobile ownership
    (B) diminished economic power of urban cores
    (C) loss of agricultural land
    (D) increased environmental degradation
    (E) a greater sense of community

GO ON TO THE NEXT PAGE.

30. The heartland theory holds that

    (A) the American Midwest is the center of the United States because of its agricultural bounty
    (B) Eurasia is the core of global influence owing to its size, population, and resources
    (C) all national cultural identity can be traced to a central region in that nation
    (D) far more important than the geographic expression of culture is the internal possession of that culture's norms
    (E) the Middle East, and Jerusalem in particular, is the center of the world's monotheistic religions

31. The type of world order in which one state is dominant over the others, issuing orders for allies to follow instead of pursuing a joint decision-making process, is known as

    (A) unilateralism
    (B) absolute monarchy
    (C) totalitarianism
    (D) First World
    (E) neo-multilateralism

32. Which of the following has NOT been a challenge to pastoral nomadic herders?

    (A) Changes in economic relationships within regional contexts
    (B) Domination of political relationships by central states
    (C) Climatic change resulting in loss of resources for animals, such as food
    (D) Reduced numbers of livestock
    (E) Erosion of resource base

33. The "tragedy of the commons" is best exemplified by which of the following situations?

    (A) Deteriorating language because of poor formal instruction
    (B) The Malthusian idea of population limited by its food production
    (C) Neighboring ethnic groups that have coexisted peacefully devolving into warfare
    (D) Degrading land as a result of too many individuals grazing their livestock on publicly held pasture
    (E) Declining resistance to viruses as a result of more densely packed populations

34. One consequence of the Soviet collectivization of farmland was

    (A) a wider variety of food
    (B) a lack of surplus food
    (C) a greater profit margin for farmers
    (D) a more effective system of distribution
    (E) a greater resistance to disease

35. In history, the rice farmers of Southeast Asia and the farmers of the Andes both increased crop yield by utilizing

    (A) terrace farming
    (B) wetland draining
    (C) deforestation
    (D) chemical farming
    (E) pesticides

36. When the World Bank or the International Monetary Fund make "structural adjustment loans" to a country, those loans are often accompanied by requests

    (A) to separate religion from politics
    (B) to adopt a set of collectivist policies
    (C) to open that country to outside trade and investment
    (D) to restrict immigration to and emigration from that country
    (E) to hold democratic elections

37. The primary economic difference between urban and rural areas is that

    (A) urban areas feature higher levels of education, while rural areas feature higher levels of experience
    (B) urban areas offer more entertainment options, while rural areas offer more outdoor activities
    (C) urban areas are built upon services, while rural areas are built upon resources
    (D) urban areas promote free-market policies, while rural areas promote big-government policies
    (E) urban areas contain elite residential neighborhoods, while rural areas contain housing for the poor

GO ON TO THE NEXT PAGE.

38. The spinning jenny, power loom, and steam engine were inventions of

    (A) the Italians
    (B) the Chinese
    (C) the United States
    (D) the First Industrial Revolution
    (E) the Second Industrial Revolution

39. The primary reason that "First World/Second World/Third World" terminology is being replaced by "developing country/developed country" terminology is that

    (A) the former describes a world defined by the Cold War
    (B) many developing countries objected strongly to being ranked last
    (C) a public awareness campaign forced intellectuals to redefine their language
    (D) the former implies that some societies are unable to improve themselves
    (E) the latter implies that all societies are in a state of constant improvement

40. One common characteristic of FTZs (free-trade zones) is that they are

    (A) responsible for a marked increase in theft
    (B) organized around seaports, airports, and national frontiers
    (C) found primarily in developed countries
    (D) a new innovation in world trade
    (E) subject to the same laws regarding immigration

41. In places like Kenya and Ethiopia, all of the following accelerate the process of desertification EXCEPT

    (A) continuous cultivation without adding supplements
    (B) overgrazing
    (C) lack of soil and water conservation
    (D) the planting of trees
    (E) random bushfires

42. Groups such as Doctors Without Borders, the World Wildlife Fund, and Heifer International provide relief and policy advocacy in foreign countries, often using funds raised from private philanthropy. These groups are examples of

    (A) policy think tanks
    (B) international non-governmental organizations
    (C) microcredit programs
    (D) transnational migration
    (E) political action committees

43. Investors in the United States and Canada view which of the following as the best potential investments?

    (A) Durable goods
    (B) Non-durable goods
    (C) Service products
    (D) Raw agricultural products
    (E) Stocks

44. In the field of high-tech services, the primary advantage that India enjoys over other nations is

    (A) its population of nearly one billion
    (B) its tradition of hosting many diverse religions
    (C) its traditional caste system
    (D) its inability to manufacture textiles and other goods
    (E) its English language heritage owing to its colonial past

45. The economic indicator GNI (Gross National Income) attempts to correct GDP (Gross Domestic Product) by

    (A) adjusting for inflation
    (B) taking into account the dollar value of exports minus imports
    (C) considering inheritances as earned income
    (D) counting multiple currencies within the same country
    (E) including petroleum imports

46. The least cost theory, which tries to explain the location of manufacturing establishments, takes into account which of the following three factors?

    (A) Labor, transportation, agglomeration
    (B) Labor, agglomeration, climate
    (C) Agglomeration, climate, investment
    (D) Investment, transportation, labor
    (E) Transportation, climate, supply chain

47. A rural feed and farm supply store often draws customers from up to 100 miles away. This indicates that the business has a very high

    (A) agglomeration
    (B) threshold
    (C) range
    (D) margin
    (E) point of maximum profitability

GO ON TO THE NEXT PAGE.

48. The difference between buying a single hot dog at the corner convenience store, a pack of six hot dogs at the nearest grocery store, and a case of forty-eight hot dogs at a faraway big-box retail outlet is the difference in

    (A) comparative advantage
    (B) distance elastic
    (C) supply chain
    (D) peak land value intersection
    (E) urban hierarchy

49. The difference between the close clustering of rural communities in New England and the wide dispersal of rural communities in the Great Plains is best explained by

    (A) the difference between the climates of the two regions
    (B) the different level of ethnic and family ties that existed in each region prior to settlement
    (C) the different level of religiosity of the two populations
    (D) the need for trade in New England versus the need for privacy in the Great Plains
    (E) the pre-existing housing stock in each region

50. A diamond-cutting company that employs four different workers, and whose only physical need is four machines on a table, can be regarded as part of

    (A) a special economic zone
    (B) a decentralized network
    (C) a supply chain
    (D) a footloose industry
    (E) a high-benefit service

51. Unlike other models of urban structure, the multiple-nuclei model

    (A) analyzes the different areas of a city from a scientific standpoint
    (B) can be applied to all urban environments around the world
    (C) explains the growth at the periphery of cities
    (D) admits that there is often more than one commercial center in a city
    (E) defines zones more loosely than other theories do

52. The set of Spanish colonial codes that specifically required all towns to be centered around a plaza was

    (A) the Laws of Burgos
    (B) the Laws of the Indies
    (C) the Napoleonic Code
    (D) the Spanish Requirement of 1513
    (E) the Fueros of Navarre

53. One important difference between real estate laws in Latin America and real estate laws in the United States is that in Latin America

    (A) trade agreements such as NAFTA have made it easier to purchase real estate
    (B) the rights of landowners are stronger than in the U.S.
    (C) real estate laws discourage English-speaking foreigners from buying property
    (D) only the middle and upper classes are legally allowed to purchase land
    (E) idle land can be legally squatted upon if residents use it

GO ON TO THE NEXT PAGE.

Questions 54 and 55 refer to the following images.

Source A: Sint-Laurenskerk, Rotterdam, The Netherlands

Source B: Pauluskerk, Rotterdam, The Netherlands

GO ON TO THE NEXT PAGE.

54. The difference between the two religious structures is the difference between

    (A) the Christian and Judaic traditions
    (B) high and low budgets
    (C) reverent and irreverent attitudes towards religion
    (D) medieval and modern design
    (E) Eastern Orthodox and Western Christianity

55. These religious structures do NOT share which of the following characteristics?

    (A) An effective use of natural interior light
    (B) A floor plan with centralized seating
    (C) A tall, nearly flat facade
    (D) Lack of a dome
    (E) Symmetry and perpendicularity

56. Megacities in the developing world, such as São Paulo, Brazil, share all of the following characteristics EXCEPT

    (A) a thriving and modern center of commerce
    (B) an immigrant population from rural areas
    (C) a military presence in the central business district
    (D) a rapidly growing rate of natural increase
    (E) squatter settlements that lack basic amenities

57. In 2004, General Motors relocated its world headquarters from suburban Detroit to downtown Detroit. In 2018, McDonald's relocated its world headquarters from suburban Chicago to downtown Chicago. These decisions can best be seen to signify

    (A) the way that large global corporations are leading the way in urban renewal
    (B) a precursor to wide-scale rejection of suburbanization
    (C) the inevitability of the gentrification movement
    (D) a renewed interest from American companies in the central business district
    (E) the debatable intentions of leaders of industry

58. Taking a cruise to the Galapagos Islands for the purpose of seeing its exotic wildlife during limited shore excursions can be classified as

    (A) relocation diffusion
    (B) globalization
    (C) offshore production
    (D) ecotourism
    (E) distance decay

59. A person who takes a bus to a subway to an airport for a flight has experienced several

    (A) examples of rapid transit
    (B) convergence zones
    (C) vertical integrations
    (D) intermodal connections
    (E) spatial fixes

60. Which of the following lists includes Chinese innovations that were brought to Europe?

    (A) Compass, paper, gunpowder, spinning jenny
    (B) Paper, gunpowder, printing press, porcelain
    (C) Porcelain, compass, paper, gunpowder
    (D) Compass, paper, spinning jenny, porcelain
    (E) Printing press, compass, porcelain, gunpowder

END OF SECTION I

HUMAN GEOGRAPHY

SECTION II

Time—1 hour and 15 minutes

3 Questions

Directions: You have <u>1 hour and 15 minutes</u> to answer all three of the following questions. It is recommended that you spend approximately one-third of your time (25 minutes) on each question. It is suggested that you take up to 5 minutes of this time to plan and outline each answer. You may use the unlined space below each question for notes. For this practice test, write your answers on lined notebook paper..

Question 1

1. A wave of cultural globalization has swept across the world during the twentieth and twenty-first centuries.

   A. Describe ONE reason for this wave of globalization.

   B. Describe ONE example of an ADVANTAGE of cultural globalization.

   C. Describe ONE example of a DISADVANTAGE of cultural globalization.

   D. Discuss ONE way that a specific society has ACCEPTED cultural globalization.

   E. Discuss ONE way that a specific society has REJECTED cultural globalization.

   F. Discuss ONE way that an indigenous culture has been harmed by globalization.

   G. Discuss ONE way that an indigenous culture has benefited from globalization.

GO ON TO THE NEXT PAGE.

Question 2

MULTIPLE-NUCLEI MODEL 1945

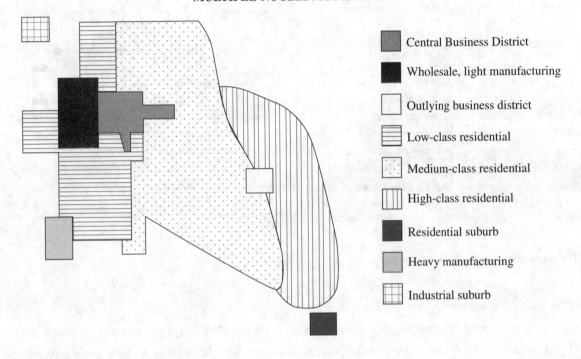

2. The multiple-nuclei model is an urban model created in 1945 by Chauncey Harris and Edward Ullman. In the decades since its debut, it has gained popularity for many different reasons.

   A. Define the multiple-nuclei model.

   B. Explain ONE advantage that the multiple-nuclei model presents over earlier urban models, such as the concentric zone model.

   C. Describe ONE disadvantage that the multiple-nuclei model offers.

   D. List ONE reason why the multiple-nuclei model became so popular in the United States when other urban models did not.

   E. Describe TWO advantages that businesses hold in a city built upon a multiple-nuclei model.

   F. Using a specific example, describe ONE city that has fully evolved under the multiple-nuclei model.

   G. Describe ONE contemporary challenge to the multiple-nuclei model.

GO ON TO THE NEXT PAGE.

Question 3

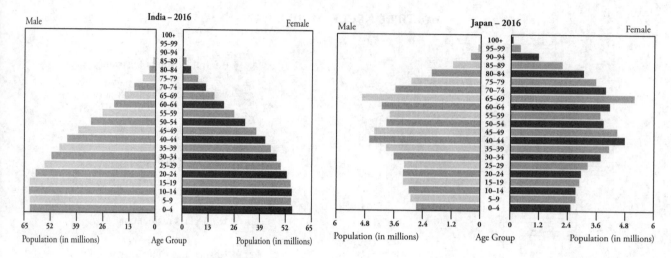

Source: U.S. Census Bureau, International Data Base

3. Use the diagrams to answer the following questions.

   A. Using specific evidence or speculation, discuss the reasons for ONE baby boom revealed by either graph.

   B. Using specific evidence or speculation, discuss the reasons for ONE baby bust revealed by either graph.

   C. Describe a general ADVANTAGE of using a population pyramid.

   D. Describe a general DISADVANTAGE of using a population pyramid.

   E. Using specific evidence or speculation, discuss what the sex ratios of each pyramid reveal about each society.

   F. Describe at least ONE demographic problem facing India in the future.

   G. Describe at least ONE demographic problem facing Japan in the future.

STOP

END OF EXAM

Practice Test 2: Answers and Explanations

PRACTICE TEST 2 ANSWER KEY

1. B	21. B	41. D
2. D	22. C	42. B
3. E	23. D	43. C
4. B	24. C	44. E
5. A	25. B	45. B
6. C	26. E	46. A
7. B	27. A	47. C
8. B	28. B	48. E
9. E	29. E	49. B
10. E	30. B	50. D
11. E	31. A	51. D
12. D	32. D	52. B
13. A	33. D	53. E
14. C	34. B	54. D
15. E	35. A	55. E
16. A	36. C	56. C
17. B	37. C	57. D
18. B	38. D	58. D
19. E	39. A	59. D
20. E	40. B	60. C

PRACTICE TEST 2 EXPLANATIONS

Multiple-Choice Questions

1. **B** Stage two societies are marked by high birth rates, high death rates, and agricultural economy. As they enter stage three, those societies experience decreasing birth rates, decreasing death rates, and a transition to a manufacturing economy. Their overall population also continues to increase, but levels off by stage four.

2. **D** Guest worker programs become more popular in countries with low population growth, so eliminate (A). There is no evidence to support (B) and (C), so eliminate those. While an increased death rate may sound like a logical reason for zero population growth, the demographic transition model shows us that zero population growth usually occurs with a decreased death rate. Eliminate (E). Zero population growth generally results from lowered birth rates and greater longevity. Governments often provide incentives, usually in the form of tax breaks.

3. **E** The Malthusian trap refers to the crisis point at which population growth exceeds the population's ability to feed itself. The population then drops to sustainable levels, at which point it starts growing again, until it reaches another crisis point. Malthus didn't foresee humanity ever escaping this trap, but new 20th-century technological advances such as artificial fertilizers, pesticides, irrigation pumps, and the internal combustion engine did exactly that.

4. **B** A population pyramid in a pentagon shape describes a country with a shrinking population, since the number of youth is less than the number of middle-aged people. Of all the regions in the world, the one with the most obvious decreasing population is Western Europe. The other regions listed are all either increasing or stable.

5. **A** Cyclic movement is defined as any human movement that has a closed route and is repeated annually or seasonally. The Polish housekeeper working in Ireland for the summer is a good example of this. There is no repeated action described or implied in the other answer choices.

6. **C** Note that the question asked for an *officially* multilingual country. Many nations do not designate any official language, such as the United States, (B). Others, such as France, (D), and South Korea, (E), are officially monolingual countries. Canada, (A), is an officially bilingual country (English and French). Using POE, therefore, you can arrive at Bolivia, (C)—a country that has officially recognized 36 different official languages!

7. **B** *Lingua franca*, (A), refers to a bridge language. Patois, (D), is commonly a mixture of French with a native colonial language, though one form of it has been popularly associated with Jamaica. Creole, (C), is a fully formed language that was created by the meeting of two different pidgin languages. And a dialect, (E), is a distinct strain of a particular language with unusual pronunciation and vocabulary words.

8. **B** The cities of La Paz, Lima, and Quito are the capitals of Bolivia, Peru, and Ecuador, respectively. Those three countries, which all rest on the spine of the Andes, have the most indigenous populations in South America. Bolivia has 55% indigenous population. By contrast, Argentina has almost none—it is nearly 90% white European. One other region, not noted on the map, is the area just south of Santiago, Chile, in the Biobio region. None of the cities are Protestant, Portuguese, or agricultural.

9. **E**   Estuaries are transition zones between rivers and ocean environments. They're partly enclosed bodies of water that are often too wide to be rivers, but yet are clearly not oceans. They're defined mostly by their salinity—they contain an inconsistent mixture of freshwater and saltwater, depending on many factors, particularly the tide. The three regions indicated on the map are the Rio de la Plata estuary between Argentina and Uruguay, the Amazon River estuary in Brazil, and the Orinoco River estuary in Venezuela.

10. **E**   The triangular region denotes the Amazon jungle, often referred to as "the lungs of the earth." The deforestation that has occurred there in the last twenty years is astonishing in its scale. While the rate has been rising and falling, private industry (mostly cattle companies) is projected to cut down nearly 30% of the entire Amazon forest by 2030. While it's true that some areas are regrowing, this is still seen as an ecological disaster by most environmentalists.

11. **E**   The five types of diffusion can be applied to the ways that various phenomenon spread across the globe. In this case, German immigrants brought their music to northern Mexico, so we can eliminate hierarchical diffusion, (C), and stimulus diffusion, (B). Contagious diffusion, (A), is used to describe the spread of diseases and news, usually along transport lines, so it cannot be applied to artistic forms. Expansion diffusion, (D), refers to the spread of ideas in many different directions from a central point, so eliminate that. In relocation diffusion, the pattern crosses a physical barrier to relocate itself.

12. **D**   Choice (D) has it exactly reversed. Monotheistic traditions, such as the Catholic Church, are strongly hierarchical with several levels of bureaucracy. Polytheistic traditions, on the other hand, such as Buddhism, have no such defining structure.

13. **A**   A *site* is a place that has a specific set of physical characteristics, including elevation, topography, climate, and more. A *situation* is that place's relationship to other nearby places—the degree to which it is integrated (or not integrated) with other places. The trap answer is (C), but *fixed* versus *changing* doesn't fit the above definition.

14. **C**   While things like racist housing policies and prejudice against immigrants certainly existed in 1920, the primary thing keeping working-class people out of the suburban areas was the cost of transportation. To get to a job in the central business district from the suburbs, one needed to use public transportation or drive an automobile. However, not all suburbs were served by public transportation, and automobiles were still (to a degree) a wealthier person's toy. So, the working classes were stymied and remained in Zone 3 until the 1950s, when the rapid construction of Zone 4 suburban housing—and widespread adoption of the automobile—allowed millions of them to escape the density of the urban zone.

15. **E**   One of the biggest stories of the last forty years has been the growth in the exurban landscape—those large tracts of land outside the city that function either as small farms or as *de facto* farms. They were less common in the early and mid-twentieth century, but with the accessibility of transportation and paved roads, many people have chosen to leave the regular suburbs and head for more distant pastures. The growth of this sector has resulted in reduced biodiversity and greater environmental damage via aquifer depletion—not to mention more damage owing to wildfires.

16. **A**   The sector model of urban structure is quite similar to the concentric zone model, but with an important addition—it considers ethnicity in its calculations. However, since it was theorized in 1939, it does not take into account the idea of private ownership of automobiles, which has come to define the American

landscape. It also does not allow for the existence of "edge cities," and cannot explain the migration of jobs from the central business district into the suburbs.

17. **B** *Environmental determinism* is the simple idea that "nature shapes culture." It was promoted in the 19th and early 20th century and unfortunately became associated with a lot of hateful political ideologies at that time. However, the concept itself is quite neutral—and it does explain why some cultures' forms of art developed in certain ways and why mountain cultures often adopt unique verbal structures.

18. **B** *Sequent occupance* is the way that the current cultural landscape of a region is defined as the sum total of all the marks that previous civilizations have left on the region. The construction workers' discovery of previous civilization's ruins beneath the streets of Rome is a perfect example of this. (And it's true—the extension of new subway lines in Rome continues to result in the discovery of ancient artifacts, even as recently as 2018.) The other answers are all red herrings and can be eliminated as either out-of-scope or unrelated.

19. **E** A vernacular region is based upon the perception, or collective mental map, of the habits and customs of a region's residents. It's true that there is a considerable overlap between this term and the idea of stereotypes, but *vernacular region* is an academic term devoid of all judgment, either positive or negative. However, the accuracy of such perceptions can be called into question—for example, those wide sombreros are typically found only in one or two states in northern Mexico. The rest of the nation sells them as jokes, the same way that few people outside the American South wear cowboy hats. (Tacos, however, are popular everywhere!)

20. **E** The bar graph describes the regions' percentages of world population. In order to determine the growth in real population, we would need to be given a total global population, or the population of at least one of the sectors. Without that data, it's impossible to calculate.

21. **B** The population pyramid easily and visually describes the population of a society by age and gender, which makes it the obvious answer to the question—if you are able to eliminate the other choices. A *Mercator projection* is a type of geographic map that doesn't consider population. The *demographic transition model* doesn't consider demographics, but it does consider birth and death. The *concentric zone model* and *sector model* are urban models that don't measure population size or demographics.

22. **C** Since Asia and Oceania have the greatest percentage of the global population, and since a majority of humans now live in cities, it's fair to assume that the most typical human is a person living in a city in Asia or Oceania. We cannot assume that the future of the species is entirely urban, even if the trends are moving in that direction. We don't know anything about population density from the bar graph, and so cannot assume anything about either Europe or Africa.

23. **D** The system of metes and bounds was based on a medieval European method of dividing land. It depended almost solely upon natural features—rivers, forests, etc.—and therefore featured irregular property lines. After the 1830s, new surveying techniques borrowed from sea navigation changed the boundaries of those plots of land into straight lines, because they'd been drawn by tools and not by nature. The Louisiana Purchase, (A), did double the size of the United States but had been done nearly thirty years earlier and didn't affect these particular changes in mapping. The new waves of Southern and Eastern European immigrants, (B), wouldn't arrive for another fifty years. The other choices, (C) and (E), are out-of-scope. (Pro tip: When in doubt, assume that advances in technology drive human change—that answer will often be right!)

24. **C**   Graduated symbol maps are used to show relative quantitative values by varying the size of symbols, which can indicate the volume or density of something. They're perfect for displaying outbreaks of communicable disease, as well as many other types of information. Cartograms, (A), use geometric shapes to represent real-world places. Flow-line maps, (B), use lines of varying thickness to indicate movement of humans. Isoline maps, (D), calculate data values between points across a variable surface. Choropleth maps, (E), use colors to express geographic variability.

25. **B**   If you recognized that the word *contagious* can be applied to both disease and ideas, then you probably got this question correct. *Contagious diffusion* refers to the spread of ideas through a population—and they move the same way as disease. *Relocation diffusion*, (C), occurs when a person migrates from his or her home and shares his or her culture with a new culture. *Orthomorphic projection*, (D), is a type of map projection in which an area is rendered in its true shape. A *choropleth* map, (E), uses shades to indicate differences in degree of the characteristic being rendered, such as population density. *Absolute location*, (A), is the exact site on an objective coordinate system, such as latitude and longitude.

26. **E**   The gravity model of geography is a mathematical model that is used to analyze the strength of a relationship between two places. It's measured by the equation Location$_1$ Population $\times$ Location$_2$ Population, then divided by the square of the distance between them. Mathematically, that would mean 300 $\times$ 400, in the numerator, which equals 120,000. In the denominator, 10 squared is 100. So 120,000 divided by 100 = 1,200. The answer is (E).

27. **A**   Geographic Information Systems are already used extensively in satellite technology as it relates to transportation, (C), in agriculture, (D), and in civil engineering, (E). It is also used extensively by the 911 emergency response network, whether from a cell phone or a landline, so eliminate (B). *Plotting the effects of an economic crash on immigration* would most likely require market data and longitudinal economic trends, not the up-to-the-minute geographic data that GIS provides.

28. **B**   *Blockbusting* was the name given to this illegal and discriminatory practice, which was undertaken by real estate agents particularly in the 1960s and 1970s. It often relied upon false scare tactics because the reality in many instances was that there were no minorities arriving—the real estate agents would simply turn a higher profit by buying low and reselling high. Gentrification, (A), is the phenomenon of a poorer, often older city neighborhood attracting wealthier people. Functional zonation, (C), is the division of cities into residential and commercial zones. Redlining, (D), is the closest to the right answer—but it refers precisely to the racist exclusion of Black people and minorities from using the services of banks, insurance companies, and even supermarkets. Choice (E), the new urbanism, indicates the trend towards walkable neighborhoods.

29. **E**   Suburbanization started in the late 1800s, but it wasn't until the 1950s that the middle classes were able to afford to get out of the city, and that's when the movement took off. (This was reflected on television—*The Honeymooners*, a sitcom set in a city apartment, versus *Leave it to Beaver*, a sitcom set in a suburban single-family detached house.) As a result, people began buying more automobiles to commute into the city, (A). Over time, many companies that had been based in the city found cheaper and more attractive quarters in the suburbs, (B). As the subdivisions sprang up across what had formerly been agricultural land, (C), environmental degradation occurred as wildlife was displaced, and air and water pollution worsened, (D). Finally, suburbanization was supposed to help people become happier, but most studies from the 1970s onwards have discovered an increased level of isolation among suburban residents, particularly among teenagers and the elderly—the two groups that cannot hold driver's licenses and feel marooned in their homes.

30. **B**   British geographer Halford Mackinder stated at the beginning of the 20th century that any political power that could get established in Eurasia would necessarily dominate the world, since its location, population, and resources would make it unstoppable. This idea informed part of the German military strategy during World War II—to attack Eastern Europe—since controlling those states would allow for an all-out attack on the Soviet Union. The other choices are incorrect, though (E) is the right answer to a different question.

31. **A**   Unilateralism occurs in a "first among equals" type of scenario—a group of equal allies transforms into a hierarchical group with an obvious leader. For example, the United States' foreign policy in the second half of the 20th century was mostly unilateral, owing to its power. Absolute monarchy, (B), is an 18th-century term, while totalitarianism, (C), is a domestic power structure, not an international one.

32. **D**   Reduced numbers of livestock are an effect of challenges to nomadism, not one of the challenges itself. Unfortunately, traditional nomadic herders around the world have seen changes in politics, economics, climate, and resources that have led to a reduction in the numbers of their animals. In Mongolia, for example, as a result of bad winters and lowered market prices, many traditional nomadic herders have reduced the size of their herds. This ensures that the remaining ones have enough food to last through the winter.

33. **D**   The *tragedy of the commons* refers to a situation in a shared-resource system whereby commonly held land, water, air, or other resources are exploited by individuals acting in their own best interests, leading to degradation of those resources such that nobody can use them anymore. (Think of a parent scolding a group of children who've just ruined a sandbox: *See, this is why we can't have nice things!*) The term was first coined in the late 19th century and popularized in the late 20th century. It's quite common (ba-DUM) in questions of sustainable development, climate change, anthropology, social science, and economics.

34. **B**   The Soviets instituted a system of collectivized farms. This meant that all private farmland was turned over to the state. In return, large farms were established that were state-owned but run by several large families. These were called *communes*. (Hence, communism.) The communes had to meet quotas for food production, but they had no incentive to go past that amount. This led to a Soviet culture of do-enough-to-get-by. It also led to no surplus food, and there were frequent shortages during droughts. Long lines became normal.

35. **A**   Terrace farming is the practice of cutting flat areas out of hilly or mountainous areas in order to grow crops. It decreases erosion and surface runoff and is typically used to grow crops that need irrigation. People in both Southeast Asia and the Andes have been using this technique for hundreds and even thousands of years. The totalitarian Kim regime of North Korea apparently forgot this principle and, in the 1990s, tried planting crops directly onto the slopes of mountains only to watch in horror as rainstorms washed the entire sides of mountains, crops, and soil down into the valleys.

36. **C**   This is the reason that many Latin American countries view the World Bank with suspicion, and even outright hostility. The World Bank and the IMF demand certain economic and political reforms in exchange for their relief loans. In other words, strings are always attached, and those strings usually reflect a globalist view of trade. Of the wrong answers, (E) may be tempting, but even though free elections are Western and globalist, neither body regularly makes them prerequisites for loans.

37. **C**   Use POE on this one. Two of the wrong answers, such as (B) and (E), are the right answers to the wrong question. Choice (D) has it backwards—typically people in cities prefer big-government policies because they are the ones running that very government. Choice (A) is gobbledygook. If you chose (C),

congratulations—resource extraction is a primary characteristic of rural economies, such as mining and agriculture, while service industries such as medicine, law, and finance are more typical of urban areas.

38. **D** James Hargreaves invented the spinning jenny in 1764, James Watt invented the steam engine in 1775, and Edmund Cartwright invented the power loom in 1785. These were all invented well before the start of the Second Industrial Revolution in the 1820s–1830s, so eliminate (E). The inventors were all Englishmen as well, so eliminate (C). The Chinese did invent many things such as dynamite and noodles, but not the three items listed—eliminate (B). The same goes for Italy, so eliminate (A).

39. **A** The First World/Second World/Third World terminology was originally invented by a French political critic in 1952 to define the world according to Cold War standards. The First World corresponded to the Western countries bonded through NATO and capitalism, while the Second World corresponded to Soviet bloc countries bound together through the Warsaw Pact and communism. So-called Third-World countries had no political alignment either way. Since the fall of the Soviet Empire, this no longer represents the state of the world, and has been falling out of favor. Choices (D) and (E), while possibly correct interpretations of the change in terminology, are not the *primary* reason for the change.

40. **B** Free-trade zones are geographic areas where goods may be received, sent, manufactured, or reconfigured, usually under customs regulation and—most importantly—without having to pay any customs duty. Choice (A) is unsupported by any data; eliminate it. Choice (C) is the opposite; most free-trade zones are found in developing countries in South America, Africa, and Southeast Asia. Choice (D) is incorrect because free-trade zones have been in existence for at least two thousand years; the ancient Greeks ran one on the island of Delos. And often the people who work in these zones are not subject to the nation's immigration laws, so eliminate (E).

41. **D** Use POE to work your way down. The other four answers are poverty-related agricultural practices that are also pursued in other areas of the world. However, Africa is in dire straits because it suffers from low soil fertility owing to the low amount of clay in the soil, which allows the soil to erode more easily; it could get worse. In fact, 70 percent of Ethiopia and 80 percent of Kenya are prone to desertification. One idea to combat this problem is the Great Green Wall of Africa, an initiative that aims to stop the Sahara from creeping any further across the continent. The initiative's proponents would like to plant 8,000 kilometers of trees across the edge of the Sahara, creating a new "world wonder" and transforming the lives of millions.

42. **B** NGOs (non-governmental organizations) are independent groups that are usually funded by private donations, though sometimes governments contribute, too. They are active in issues relating to humanitarianism, education, health care, environment, and many other areas—their goal is to either provide relief or change policy. An INGO (*international* non-governmental organization) is exactly the same, except it provides these services in foreign nations.

43. **C** While the manufacturing sector of an economy is usually instrumental in bringing an economy like that of the U.S. or Canada to greatness, it ultimately disappears due to lower returns on investment. Eliminate (A) and (B). In its place arises a service economy, based on intellectual innovations, which have the potential to provide a much larger return on investment. Which would you rather have—a basket full of cotton still on the stem, or the printed rights to a machine that will separate that cotton from the stem? The latter is worth exponentially more. That's the difference between a manufacturing economy and a service economy.

44. **E** India was first an economic partner of English trading firms such as the British East India Company, and then gradually became a political possession of the British government. It was regarded as the "jewel in the crown" of the British Empire. In the 20th century, people such as Mahatma Gandhi led an Indian movement for independence, which was finally achieved in 1947. Nonetheless, the educated portion of the nation all still speak English, which has given them a leg up in landing lucrative international contracts with tech firms such as Dell and Microsoft. India's population, religion, and caste system offer no advantages in a high-tech market, so eliminate (A), (B), and (C). Also, India had quite a thriving textile manufacturing economy until the 1980s, so eliminate (D).

45. **B** Gross National Product (GNP) is defined as goods + services. Gross National Income (GNI) is defined as goods + services + (exports – imports). In other words, GNI recognizes the value of trade deficits and trade surpluses when calculating the wealth of a nation. In cases of trade deficits, the difference between the exports and imports is a negative number, which decreases the GNI. In cases of trade surpluses, the difference between the exports and imports is a positive number, which increases the GNI.

46. **A** The least cost theory was created by Alfred Weber in his 1909 book, *The Theory of Industrial Location*. In it, he postulates that manufacturing sites are best determined by looking at the site's available transportation, labor, and agglomeration. The third term, *agglomeration*, refers to how concentrated human activity is around a central place. Recently, this theory made national headlines as Amazon.com made a very long and tantalizing public decision about where it would base its second headquarters.

47. **C** The range of a business is defined as the maximum distance that people are willing to travel to gain access to a service. In rural areas, that range tends to be quite a bit higher than it would be in a densely packed urban area. The agglomeration is the density of the clustering around a central node, and the threshold is defined as the minimum number of people required to support a business. Eliminate (A) and (B). Both margin and point of maximum profitability depend on revenues and costs, but no data is offered on those. Eliminate (D) and (E).

48. **E** Urban hierarchy is a theory promoted by Walter Christaller, a German theorist, in the 1920s. It shows several layers of places across the human landscape that follow regular patterns. One of those is the overlapping areas between villages (small), towns (medium), and cities (large). Consumers will go to the village market for small items, the town market for medium items, and the city market for large items. While the other four answer choices are somewhat related to this central place theory, none describe it as precisely as urban hierarchy.

49. **B** In New England settlements, immigrants from the same region of Europe—and sometimes even the same village—sought one another out. They set up densely packed villages because they had pre-existing trust based on ethnic and even family ties. By contrast, in the Great Plains, the South, and other regions, immigrants arrived alone, and were greeted by unfamiliar immigrants from other countries in Europe and elsewhere. Without any pre-existing trust based on nationality or family—and also because of the massive stretches of land out West that they were given to farm by the federal government—these settlers dispersed themselves.

50. **D** A footloose industry is one that can be placed at any location because it is not affected by factors such as transportation or resources. It has spatially fixed costs, which means that the costs of the products do not change no matter where the products are made. It also generally makes items in small quantities, such as computer chips, and employs very few workers. The diamond company fits the description well. This industry is also able to react well to recessions or bad political changes because it can quickly pick up and move.

51. **D** You can figure this one out from its name. The multiple-nuclei theory refers to the concept that, in the 21st century, not all urban business is concentrated in a single central node. Newer cities such as Phoenix, Arizona, don't have a proper business center—they're decentralized, with smaller clusters of business scattered across the entire urban region.

52. **B** The Laws of the Indies were a set of laws that governed most aspects of settlement in the New World. In particular, one of the 1680 additions set forth was that all Spanish settlements in the New World be modelled after Madrid, which was (and is) centered around a massive plaza. The Laws of Burgos (1512) did set restrictions on the behavior of Spaniards in the New World—but only with regard to treatment of the indigenous people, not with urban planning. The Spanish Requirement of 1513, on the other hand, declared that Spain had the divine right to take territories in the New World and exploit the native inhabitants.

53. **E** Squatters are people who settle on land that they don't own. The legal system of the United States frowns on squatters, affording them almost no rights—mostly because the United States has a long tradition of building affordable housing for the working classes and poor in urban areas. However, in most Latin American countries, there is no such tradition of affordable housing in urban areas, and as a result squatters have far more legal rights. A team of squatters can arrive on an unoccupied piece of land outside of a city, set up makeshift houses in a day or two, and claim that land for their own.

54. **D** The Sint-Laurenskerk (translation: "St. Lawrence Church") is a classic example of medieval northern European religious architecture. It wasn't Gothic—the walls are too thick and there are no buttresses—but it is the only remaining piece of medieval architecture left in Rotterdam. It was damaged by Nazi bombs in World War II and has been extensively repaired. The Pauluskerk, meanwhile, features an irregular exterior cladding that almost screams modern design.

55. **E** No matter what era, religious structures often have common characteristics—it's the nature of religion, after all. The interior of both of these structures feature interesting use of natural light, (A)—the stained glass of the Laurenskerk, and the triangular windows of the Pauluskerk. Both feature chairs arranged around a center, (B), as well as a tall, flat (or nearly flat) façade, (C). And both structures lack a dome, (D); among societies in snowy climates, steeples and spires are more practical and common. However, whereas the Laurenskerk is symmetrical and composed of a series of ninety-degree angles, the Pauluskerk is neither—its exterior consists of a series of irregular triangles.

56. **C** A military presence is not a defining characteristic of the modern developing megacity, and certainly not in the central business district. True, the national military may occasionally make appearances in these cities. For example, the Brazilian military has occasionally been dispatched to fight gang violence in Rio de Janeiro's slums—picture armed soldiers and even tanks patrolling the narrow streets of the slums. Still, this is not necessarily common in the developing world.

57. **D** Careful on this one: don't choose an answer that goes too far in its assumptions. There's no reason to believe that these global corporations are *leading the way in urban renewal*—they could very well be following the pack. Likewise, we don't know that the future holds a *wide-scale rejection of suburbanization* or an inevitable *gentrification movement* (which applies mostly to residential neighborhoods anyway). The *intentions of leaders of industry* are also unknown.

58. **D** Ecotourism is defined as the responsible travel to natural areas in such a way that it conserves the environment, sustains the local communities, and educates the public. The money generated by ecotourism improves the standard of living for the local people. Many tours to the Galapagos Islands satisfy these criteria; as there are almost no hotels on the islands, most tourists sleep onboard their vessels and interrupt the ecosystem very briefly on short daily excursions ashore.

59. **D** An intermodal connection is defined as any place in which two different forms of transportation meet. The intersection of the bus with the subway, and the intersection of the subway with the airport, are both intermodal connections. The trap answer, *examples of rapid transit*, is incorrect because rapid transit is defined as fast urban transportation, particularly subways or elevated heavy rail. Neither a bus nor an airplane qualifies as such.

60. **C** The four correct innovations—porcelain, compass, paper, gunpowder—were brought to Europe either by sea or via the Silk Road. The wrong answers all feature either the printing press or the spinning jenny. The printing press was invented by Johann Gutenberg in Germany in 1440, while the spinning jenny was invented by William Hargreaves in England in 1764.

Free-Response Questions

Don't look at the following section until you've completed the free-response questions in Practice Test 2.

For each of the questions, we have provided a rubric that will give you a decent sense of what information your responses should have mentioned. Each of the questions comprises seven parts (A–G), each of which is worth one point. That point is awarded for addressing any of the possible ideas listed under that part.

Keep in mind that these rubrics are by no means exhaustive. We recommend asking your AP Human Geography teacher to check your responses, particularly if they mention other details not listed here.

Scoring Rubrics for Free-Response Questions

1. A wave of cultural globalization has swept across the world during the twentieth and twenty-first centuries.

   A. Describe ONE reason for this wave of globalization.

   B. Describe ONE example of an ADVANTAGE of cultural globalization.

   C. Describe ONE example of a DISADVANTAGE of cultural globalization.

   D. Discuss ONE way that a specific society has ACCEPTED cultural globalization.

   E. Discuss ONE way that a specific society has REJECTED cultural globalization.

   F. Discuss ONE way that an indigenous culture has been harmed by globalization.

   G. Discuss ONE way that an indigenous culture has benefited from globalization.

Rubric—1 + 1 + 1 + 1 + 1 + 1 + 1 = 7 pts

A. Reasons for this wave of cultural globalization
   a. Improved transportation, such as air travel and shipping containers
   b. Growth of global trading blocks, such as NAFTA and European Union
   c. New globalized media, such as CNN, YouTube, Facebook, etc.
   d. Increased mobility of capital and labor—people are more willing to move to a foreign country for work

B. Advantages of cultural globalization
   a. Greater opportunity to understand other cultures, which reduces distrust and reduces potential conflict
   b. Creates economic growth in emerging markets
      i. New jobs
      ii. More efficiency
      iii. More affordable goods

C. Disadvantages of cultural globalization
   a. Disconnection from heritage leads to depression or psychological problems
   b. Loss of linguistic traditions
   c. Loss of culinary traditions
   d. Loss of local economic advantage
      i. Reduced production of traditional, local artistic products
      ii. Increased dependence on foreign science and technology

D. Ways that societies accept cultural globalization
   a. Indigenous populations
      i. In Australia, the U.S., and elsewhere, native people have accepted Coca-Cola, liquor, fast food, jeans and sneakers, etc.
   b. Mandatory English instruction
      ii. Germany, Holland, and Portugal all mandate years of English instruction
   c. Tax breaks to foreign companies
      iii. India offers very generous tax breaks and other incentives to multinational corporations, including no tax on long-term capital gains

E. Ways that societies reject cultural globalization
   a. Attempts to restrict use of English words
      i. France has restricted use of English vocabulary in the workplace
      ii. Spain dubs all foreign entertainment so that its people only hear Spanish spoken
      iii. Basque Country has no signs in English or Spanish, only the local language, Euskadi
   b. Promotion of local language programming
      i. Wales, for example, promotes a Welsh television channel that ensures continued fluency in the ancient Welsh language
   c. Limits on entrance visas for foreigners
      i. Bhutan charges $150 per day
      ii. Fernando do Noronha, a Brazilian island, doubles its visitors' fee every week

F. Indigenous culture that has been harmed by globalization
   a. Aboriginal cultures in Australia and indigenous villages in Mexico both struggle with public health crises as their populations turn away from a traditional diet to a modern diet filled with liters of Coca-Cola
   b. Exploitation of forests in the Amazon
   c. Drilling for oil wells without permission

G. Indigenous culture that has benefited from globalization
   a. E-learning brings education to distant reservations that might have trouble attracting teachers otherwise. Experiments with this are being done with aboriginal people in Australia.
   b. Native cultures can advertise their cultures on modern media
      i. The Aboriginal People's Television Network in Canada
      ii. The Inuit have their own website
      iii. Novels written about the modern indigenous experience, such as *Ceremony* by Leslie Marmon Silko

2. The multiple-nuclei model is an urban model created in 1945 by Chauncey Harris and Edward Ullman. In the decades since its debut, it has gained popularity for many different reasons.

    A. Define the multiple-nuclei model.

    B. Explain ONE advantage that the multiple-nuclei model presents over earlier urban models, such as the concentric zone model.

    C. Describe ONE disadvantage that the multiple-nuclei model offers.

    D. List ONE reason why the multiple-nuclei model became popular in the United States when other models did not.

    E. Describe TWO advantages that businesses hold in a city built upon a multiple-nuclei model.

    F. Using a specific example, describe ONE city that has fully evolved under the multiple-nuclei model.

    G. Describe ONE contemporary challenge to the multiple-nuclei model.

Rubric—1 + 1 + 1 + 1 + 1 + 1 + 1 = 7 pts

A. Define multiple-nuclei model
    a. It's a model of urban development that views the business district not as a single central entity, but as scattered in various nuclei across the city. Other activities and areas are grouped together out of convenience (e.g., university town and bookstores).

B. Advantages over the concentric zone model
    a. In two words: automobile ownership. The multiple-nuclei model took into account the effect of autos and trucks on private business, which freed cities from the rigid CBDs determined by railroads. It's a looser, modern view of city design.
    b. It more accurately describes modern American cities than do other models, especially the concentric zone model.

C. Disadvantages
    a. Housing gets more expensive the further it gets from the CBD, and since there are CBDs across the city, there's no easily discernible pattern to the settlement.
    b. Negative externalities such as noise and air pollution develop around airports and industrial areas, which lie adjacent to wealthy residential areas.
    c. It assumes even distribution of resources and transportation costs.
    d. It doesn't consider the physical geography of the city or the effect of government policies.

D. Reasons for its adoption in the U.S.
    a. U.S. business culture has always emphasized speed, adaptability, and repurposing older cities for the automobile
    b. It allowed planners to take suburbs into account

E. Business advantages
   a. In a multiple-nuclei model, transportation hubs outside the CBDs are constructed on locations that provide the lowest possible transportation costs.
   b. Profit maximization: a business will establish itself in the location where the greatest possible profit can be made, and the multiple-nuclei model acknowledges that this happens
   c. Relocation of industrial pollution far from residential areas

F. Cities that evolved
   a. Detroit is an example of a city that was originally designed in a concentric zone model. With the arrival of the automobile, it began to rearrange itself into a multiple-nuclei form, the businesses and population spreading out ever deeper into the suburbs.
   b. Phoenix, Arizona, is an example of a city that grew during the age of the automobile. Therefore, it never had a traditional 19th century CBD, but was a decentralized conglomerate of multiple nuclei from the very start.

G. Contemporary challenge
   a. Gentrification of the cities has presented a new challenge to the model's viability. Young adults and older retirees—in other words, those without dependent children—have been flocking into the urban hearts of the cities, making them denser, and driving an urban gentrification boom. The multiple-nuclei model doesn't describe this happening—ever.
   b. Retail apocalypse. The big box stores that grew so popular in the 1980s, 1990s, and the 2000s have been going out of business in record numbers, leaving entire suburban shopping malls empty. The multiple-nuclei model doesn't describe this happening either.

3. Use the diagrams to answer the following questions.

A. Using specific evidence or speculation, discuss the reasons for ONE baby boom revealed by either graph.

B. Using specific evidence or speculation, discuss the reasons for ONE baby bust revealed by either graph.

C. Describe a general ADVANTAGE of using a population pyramid.

D. Describe a general DISADVANTAGE of using a population pyramid.

E. Using specific evidence or speculation, discuss what the sex ratios of each pyramid reveal about each society.

F. Describe at least ONE demographic problem facing India in the future.

G. Describe at least ONE demographic problem facing Japan in the future.

Rubric—1 + 1 + 1 + 1 + 1 + 1 + 1 = 7 pts

A. Reasons for baby boom
   a. India has a very obviously wide base on its population pyramid, which means that it's been undergoing a sustained baby boom. This can be pinned to a couple of different causes.
      i. The system of early marriage prolongs child-bearing age
      ii. Poverty: many poor families believe that more children equals more income
   b. Japan also has a couple of mini baby booms.
      i. The 65–69 cohort has a large spike compared with other groups. Do the math and you'll see that this corresponds to birth years in the late 1940s. This means that there was a baby boom shortly after World War II—same as in the United States.
      ii. The 40–44 cohort has a spike as well. This corresponds to birth years in the early 1970s. The reasons are unclear, but it might be due to the first baby boom having their own children.

B. Baby bust
   a. There is no baby bust in India, but Japan shows a very clear baby bust that began about 40 years ago and has accelerated to the present. Reasons include low fertility rates and a high life expectancy.

C. Advantages of using a population pyramid
   a. Shows population by gender
   b. Shows population by age
   c. Able to distinguish between young dependents, working-age people, and old dependents—and draw a ratio between them
   d. Visual nature allows for quick comparisons between pyramids

D. Disadvantages of using a population pyramid
    a. Doesn't allow means or medians
    b. Figures are age cohorts, so some data get lost in the details

E. Sex ratios
    a. India
        i. The sex ratio is skewed heavily towards men from birth—roughly, 62 million boys for 54 million girls. This can be explained by family planning policies. In India, boys are seen as more reliable future sources of income than girls, so parents often abort female fetuses.
    b. Japan
        i. The biggest difference is at the end of life: there are many more elderly women than men in Japan. This can be connected perhaps to the loss of males during World War II, to the Japanese culture of intense work, or to better nutrition and self-care among women in their later years.

F. Demographic problems in the future of India
    a. Overpopulation, which leads to
        i. Congestion
        ii. Inflation
        iii. Unemployment
        iv. Pollution

G. Demographic problems in the future of Japan
    a. Underpopulation, which leads to
        i. Lack of workers
            1. Greater burden on younger workers to care for the old, particularly in the health care system and retirement system
        i. Lack of taxpayers
        ii. Weakened economy
            1. Fewer producers
            2. Fewer consumers

HOW TO SCORE PRACTICE TEST 2

Section I: Multiple Choice

_____   × 1.25 =   _____
Number Correct   Weighted
(out of 60)   Section I Score
                                (Do not round)

Section II: Free Response

Question 1:   _____   × 3.5714 =   _____
               (out of 7)   (Do not round)

Question 2:   _____   × 3.5714 =   _____
               (out of 7)   (Do not round)

Question 3:   _____   × 3.5714 =   _____
               (out of 7)   (Do not round)

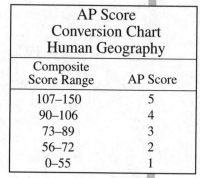

AP Score Conversion Chart Human Geography	
Composite Score Range	AP Score
107–150	5
90–106	4
73–89	3
56–72	2
0–55	1

Sum =   _____
          Weighted
          Section II Score
          (Do not round)

Composite Score

_____   +   _____   =   _____
Weighted   Weighted   Composite Score
Section I Score   Section II Score   (Round to nearest
                                                    whole number)

Practice Test 3

AP® Human Geography Exam

SECTION I: Multiple-Choice Questions

DO NOT OPEN THIS BOOKLET UNTIL YOU ARE TOLD TO DO SO.

At a Glance

Total Time
60 minutes
Number of Questions
60
Percent of Total Grade
50%
Writing Instrument
Pencil required

Instructions

Section I of this exam contains 60 multiple-choice questions. Fill in only the ovals for numbers 1 through 60 on your answer sheet.

Indicate all of your answers to the multiple-choice questions on the answer sheet. No credit will be given for anything written in this exam booklet, but you may use the booklet for notes or scratch work. After you have decided which of the suggested answers is best, completely fill in the corresponding oval on the answer sheet. Give only one answer to each question. If you change an answer, be sure that the previous mark is erased completely. Here is a sample question and answer.

Sample Question

The first president of the United States was
(A) Millard Fillmore
(B) George Washington
(C) Benjamin Franklin
(D) Andrew Jackson
(E) Harry Truman

Sample Answer

Use your time effectively, working as quickly as you can without losing accuracy. Do not spend too much time on any one question. Go on to other questions and come back to the ones you have not answered if you have time. It is not expected that everyone will know the answers to all the multiple-choice questions.

About Guessing

Many candidates wonder whether or not to guess the answers to questions about which they are not certain. Multiple-choice scores are based on the number of questions answered correctly. Points are not deducted for incorrect answers, and no points are awarded for unanswered questions. Because points are not deducted for incorrect answers, you are encouraged to answer all multiple-choice questions. On any questions you do not know the answer to, you should eliminate as many choices as you can, and then select the best answer among the remaining choices.

GO ON TO THE NEXT PAGE.

This page intentionally left blank.

HUMAN GEOGRAPHY
SECTION I
Time—60 minutes
60 Questions

Directions: Each of the questions or incomplete statements below is followed by five suggested answers or completions. Select the one that best answers the question or completes the statement.

1. An "ecotone" can best be described as

   (A) an area in which everyone speaks the same language
   (B) the environmental transition zone between two biomes
   (C) a functional region that has a central node that serves a practical purpose
   (D) the fuzzy borders that combine one or more cultural regions
   (E) the collective mental map of the region's residents

2. All of the following countries are examples of constitutional monarchies EXCEPT

   (A) Bahrain
   (B) Cambodia
   (C) Kuwait
   (D) Monaco
   (E) Portugal

3. The practice of planting two crops consecutively on a single plot each year is referred to as

   (A) conservation agriculture
   (B) crop rotation
   (C) double cropping
   (D) inter-planting
   (E) swidden

4. Which of the following is NOT a weight-gaining industry?

   (A) Automobile manufacturing
   (B) Beverage production
   (C) Clothing production
   (D) Steel manufacturing
   (E) Bread production

5. A place on the map that is defined by coordinates of longitude or latitude is a(n)

   (A) absolute location
   (B) formal region
   (C) prime area
   (D) relative location
   (E) functional region

GO ON TO THE NEXT PAGE.

Questions 6–8 refer to the graph below.

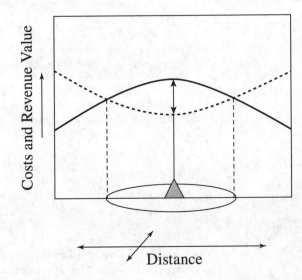

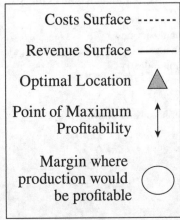

6. The precise location of retail services is spatially dependent on the relationship between

 (A) potential cost-overruns and projected revenue
 (B) consumer demand and local supply
 (C) variable cost and revenue surfaces
 (D) infrastructure costs and recaptured revenue
 (E) local consumer demand and geographic viability

7. The market area of a city is defined by both

 (A) profit margin and product cost
 (B) accessibility and necessity
 (C) threshold and range
 (D) economy and population
 (E) proximity and production

8. This diagram best models

 (A) the cost-to-distance relationship in agricultural land use
 (B) elastic distance proximity
 (C) supply chain management
 (D) a cycle of dependency based on capital accumulation
 (E) the spatial margin of profitability

9. The Human Development Index was designed to

 (A) measure the level of development of states based on social indicators and economic production
 (B) take into account differences in prices between countries
 (C) measure the level of income disparity between the country's richest and poorest population groups
 (D) compare gender equality amongst different countries
 (E) calculate the dollar value of all goods and services produced in a country annually

GO ON TO THE NEXT PAGE.

10. Furniture requires parts to be assembled into components that are then assembled together to create a larger finished product. In this regard, furniture is an example of a

    (A) footloose industry
    (B) high-benefit service
    (C) supply chain
    (D) bulk-losing industry
    (E) deglomeration

Questions 11–13 refer to the following map.

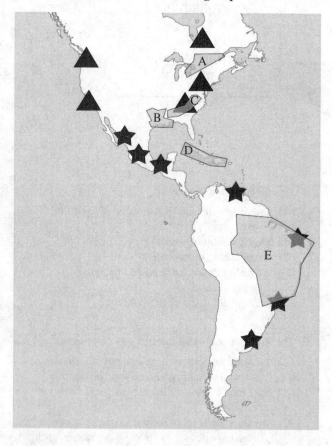

11. Which of the regions on the map would contain the Piedmont Industrial Region?

    (A) A
    (B) B
    (C) C
    (D) D
    (E) E

12. Locations on the map that are marked with a ▲ are

    (A) service regions in less-developed countries
    (B) regions that practice subsistence agriculture
    (C) megacities
    (D) manufacturing regions in more-developed countries
    (E) regions that specialize in plantation agriculture

13. Which of the regions on the map contain areas that would be a cultural hub of Cajun and Zydeco influences?

    (A) A
    (B) B
    (C) C
    (D) D
    (E) E

14. Tibet, Nepal, and Bhutan share commonalities in cultural landscape features such as architecture due to the influence of

    (A) Buddhism
    (B) Judaism
    (C) Hinduism
    (D) Jainism
    (E) Christianity

15. Which of the following is true of the United States and Australia?

    (A) They are in the same environmental region.
    (B) Their cultural regions overlap significantly.
    (C) Their political boundaries are fuzzy.
    (D) Their vernacular regions are identical.
    (E) They are in the same linguistic region.

GO ON TO THE NEXT PAGE.

16. All of the following statements are true of Mexico and Malaysia EXCEPT that both

    (A) have birth rates that exceed their death rates
    (B) are newly industrialized countries
    (C) have positive rates of natural increase
    (D) are in stage 4 of the demographic transition model
    (E) have experienced increases in quality of life in recent decades

17. The diplomatic meeting between European colonial powers to set the internal political boundaries in Africa

    (A) led to the Oregon Treaty
    (B) is referred to as the Conference of Berlin
    (C) resulted in the Antarctic Treaty
    (D) established the Organization of the African Union
    (E) is known as the Paracel consortium

18. Which of the following is NOT associated with the quaternary stage of production of goods and services?

    (A) Wholesaling
    (B) Financing
    (C) Manufacturing
    (D) Advertising
    (E) Marketing

19. Nonrenewable resources include

    (A) uranium and wind power
    (B) biofuel and coal
    (C) solar energy and tidal power
    (D) petroleum and natural gas
    (E) hydropower and nuclear energy

20. A port location where foreign firms are given special tax privileges to incentivize trade is known as a(n)

    (A) free-trade zone
    (B) transport node
    (C) export processing zone
    (D) resource node
    (E) agglomeration

21. Which of the following models best represents the post-industrial city with its several, dispersed business districts?

    (A) Galactic city
    (B) Latin American city
    (C) Multiple-nuclei
    (D) Sector
    (E) Concentric zone

22. The Total Fertility Rate is the estimated average number of children born to each female aged

    (A) 10–40
    (B) 10–45
    (C) 15–40
    (D) 15–45
    (E) 18–50

23. If the Rate of Natural Increase (RNI) for the United States is 4.25, approximately how many years would it take for the United States to double its population?

    (A) 4.25
    (B) 8.25
    (C) 16.5
    (D) 23.5
    (E) 33

24. _____ diffusion occurs when an innovation occurs in a central place and then expands outwards in all directions to other locations.

    (A) Relocation
    (B) Stimulus
    (C) Contagious
    (D) Hierarchical
    (E) Expansion

25. All of the following underwent balkanization EXCEPT

    (A) Yugoslavia
    (B) Mongolia
    (C) the Austro-Hungarian Empire
    (D) Czechoslovakia
    (E) the USSR

GO ON TO THE NEXT PAGE.

Questions 26–28 refer to the following diagrams.

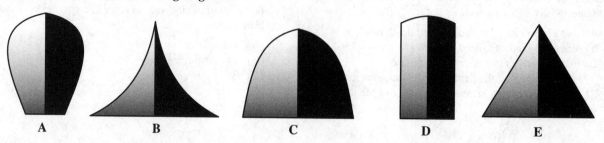

A   B   C   D   E

26. The provided images would best be described as

    (A) life expectancy curves
    (B) migration models
    (C) population pyramids
    (D) demographic transition models
    (E) total fertility rate curves

27. Diagram E represents a country that is experiencing

    (A) fast growth
    (B) moderate growth
    (C) slow growth
    (D) zero growth
    (E) negative growth

28. Which diagram would best exemplify a country that is in stage 1 of the demographic transition model?

    (A) A
    (B) B
    (C) C
    (D) D
    (E) E

29. The concept that the living space for each distinct nation is based upon the optimal physical geography of a culture group is known as

    (A) sequent occupance
    (B) environmental determinism
    (C) acculturation
    (D) possibilism
    (E) *lebensraum*

30. The curved strip of arable land that connects Mesopotamia and Egypt through to the Levant is known as

    (A) a Sunbelt State
    (B) the Etruscan environment
    (C) a Special Economic Zone
    (D) the Fertile Crescent
    (E) the Tiberian Trench

31. All of the following countries are considered New Asian Tigers and received development funding through Foreign Direct Investment EXCEPT

    (A) China
    (B) Japan
    (C) Indonesia
    (D) Thailand
    (E) Vietnam

GO ON TO THE NEXT PAGE.

32. A population under a single government is best defined as a

    (A) country
    (B) nation
    (C) state
    (D) nation state
    (E) stateless nation

33. Which of the following is NOT considered a plantation crop?

    (A) Cane Sugar
    (B) Palm Oil
    (C) Tea
    (D) Rubber
    (E) Pistachios

34. An operational border dispute occurs when

    (A) borders are agreed to, but passage across the border is a problem
    (B) border treaties are interpreted two different ways by states
    (C) a resource lies on two sides of a border
    (D) the border moves, like when a river changes course
    (E) borders do not match cultural boundaries

35. What percent of the world's freshwater is used in irrigation agriculture worldwide?

    (A) 10%
    (B) 25%
    (C) 50%
    (D) 75%
    (E) 95%

36. Which of the following is NOT a potential consequence of gerrymandering?

    (A) Minority representation is decreased.
    (B) Election outcomes are predictable.
    (C) Both minority and majority parties are equally represented.
    (D) Incumbents are protected in their positions.
    (E) Election outcomes favor the majority party which minimizes the power of the minority party.

37. Primary production, which includes agriculture, mining, and forestry, consists of

    (A) activities that include the extraction of natural resources from the earth
    (B) the transportation, wholesaling, and retailing of finished goods to consumers
    (C) activities that include the fabrication of components
    (D) the processing of raw materials
    (E) activities that include the assembly of finished goods

38. The number of immigrants minus the number of emigrants for every thousand members of the population is known as the

    (A) population growth rate
    (B) net migration rate
    (C) rate of natural increase
    (D) demographic equation
    (E) gross immigration rate

39. Specific things about the rural agricultural landscape and livelihood that force people off the farm are known as

    (A) life-course changes
    (B) pull factors
    (C) shift factors
    (D) push factors
    (E) migration opportunities

GO ON TO THE NEXT PAGE.

40. Which of the following is NOT a characteristic of newly industrialized countries (NICs)?

   (A) They experience rapid internal rural-to-urban migration.
   (B) NICs have high birth rates and high death rates.
   (C) They are transitioning their focus away from agriculture to manufacturing as the primary form of economic production.
   (D) NICs experience rapid population growth.
   (E) They have high rates of natural increase.

41. According to the United Nations Conference on the Law of the Seas (UNCLOS), sovereign territory that includes the area of the sea from the shore out to the 12-nautical-mile limit is referred to as

   (A) an exclusive economic zone
   (B) admiralty law
   (C) a special economic zone
   (D) the high seas
   (E) the territorial sea

Questions 42 and 43 refer to the following diagram.

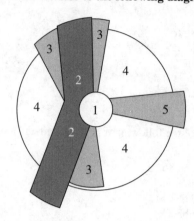

42. This model of urban structure is known as the

   (A) concentric zone model
   (B) Latin American city model
   (C) peripheral model
   (D) multiple-nuclei model
   (E) sector model

43. In which region does middle-class housing exist?

   (A) 1
   (B) 2
   (C) 3
   (D) 4
   (E) 5

GO ON TO THE NEXT PAGE.

44. In the United States, crops and animals that must not be grown using genetic engineering, must be free of pesticides, antibiotics, and synthetic hormones, and must feed on completely organic crops are classified as

    (A) appellation products
    (B) cottage industry yields
    (C) heirloom
    (D) natural food products
    (E) organic

45. Which of the following is a list of microstates?

    (A) Antigua and Barbuda, Bahrain, and Hong Kong
    (B) Denmark, Dominica, and Mexico
    (C) Andorra, Liechtenstein, and St. Lucia
    (D) Malta, Nigeria, and Palau
    (E) Brazil, Luxembourg, and Singapore

46. Which of the following can be stated about the Green Revolution?

    (A) It led to the domestication of New World crops throughout Europe and Asia during the 16th century.
    (B) It occurred in the 1950s and 1960s when plant and animal hybrids and chemical fertilizers began to be used in Third World agriculture.
    (C) It was spurred on by parallel innovations in both agricultural technology and manufacturing in post-industrialized countries.
    (D) It occurred due to disastrous global food shortages post-World War II and the necessity of adopting environmentally sustainable practices.
    (E) It led to the adoption of vegetative planting techniques, in which the shoots, stems, and roots of existing wild plants are collected and grown together.

47. The North Atlantic Treaty Organization is a supranational organization that is primarily concerned with

    (A) military cooperation
    (B) governmental loans
    (C) regional diplomacy
    (D) petroleum pricing regulation
    (E) free-trade zones

48. In Ernest Burgess' concentric zone model, the outermost ring would best be described as

    (A) the suburbs
    (B) the central business district
    (C) inner-city housing
    (D) the industrial zone
    (E) the exurbs

49. Since the first census was conducted in 1790, the population center of the United States has

    (A) moved north each decade
    (B) moved east each decade
    (C) remained stationary
    (D) moved south each decade
    (E) moved west each decade

GO ON TO THE NEXT PAGE.

Questions 50 and 51 refer to the following images.

50. The two photos above most clearly display the difference between

    (A) developed and developing world agriculture
    (B) Old World and New World agricultural techniques
    (C) wheat and corn
    (D) fallow fields and crop rotation
    (E) monoculture and biodiversity

51. The type of agriculture seen in the second photo is LEAST likely to be associated with which of the following?

    (A) Plantation agriculture
    (B) Subsistence farming
    (C) Better nutrition
    (D) Sustainability
    (E) Multi-cropping

52. Which of the following is NOT a pillar of Islam?

    (A) Six Daily Prayers
    (B) Islamic Creed
    (C) Alms to the Poor
    (D) Observance of Ramadan
    (E) The Hajj

53. The bluegrass music tradition, in which the fiddle and the banjo are the primary interests, is most prevalent in

    (A) Texas
    (B) the Ozarks
    (C) Louisiana
    (D) the Caribbean
    (E) Appalachia

54. Underdeveloped countries with primarily agricultural and resource-based economies that have no formal national government are best described as

    (A) Fifth World countries
    (B) Fourth World countries
    (C) Third World countries
    (D) Second World countries
    (E) First World countries

GO ON TO THE NEXT PAGE.

55. All of the following statements regarding women are true EXCEPT

(A) the percentage of female-headed households in urban areas has increased significantly in recent decades

(B) women surpass men in terms of average pay in the service sectors of health care and education

(C) female heads of household are less likely to rely on public transportation than male heads of household

(D) the 19th Amendment to the U.S. Constitution granted American women the right to vote in 1920

(E) on average, women live approximately 5 years longer than men

56. Gateway cities are best characterized as

(A) centers of colonial trade or administration, originally

(B) places where immigrants make their way into a country

(C) port cities where goods are shipped in at one price and shipped to other port cities at a higher price

(D) urban centers that predate the European Renaissance

(E) metropolitan areas that are global centers for finance, trade, and commerce

57. The primary purpose of the European Court of Justice is to

(A) ensure that no taxes or tariffs are charged on goods and services that cross the internal borders of the European Union

(B) provide a legal venue for cases between litigants in separate European Union member states

(C) set the European Union's annual policy agenda

(D) propose and approve laws within the European Union

(E) act as the executive branch of the European Union to enact programs and enforce regulations set by the European Union Parliament and Council

Questions 58 and 59 refer to the following graph.

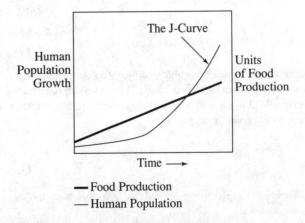

— Food Production
— Human Population

58. The graph provided best illustrates

(A) Mendel's theory

(B) von Thünen's model

(C) Malthusian theory

(D) Magnuson's model

(E) population-consumption theory

59. The point at which the lines of food production and human population cross would best be described as the point at which

(A) rapid migration to North America leads to a decline in the world economy

(B) a former communist economy completes the transition from a Second World country to a Third World country

(C) technological innovations will eliminate global food shortages

(D) a former agrarian economy completes the transition into an industrialized economy

(E) the population exceeds its ability to feed itself

60. Which of the following crops did NOT diffuse to the Old World from the New World as part of the Columbian exchange?

(A) Maize

(B) Potatoes

(C) Tobacco

(D) Chickens

(E) Turkeys

END OF SECTION I

HUMAN GEOGRAPHY

SECTION II

Time—1 hour and 15 minutes

3 Questions

Directions: You have <u>1 hour and 15 minutes</u> to answer all three of the following questions. It is recommended that you spend approximately one-third of your time (25 minutes) on each question. It is suggested that you take up to 5 minutes of this time to plan and outline each answer. You may use the unlined space below each question for notes. For this practice test, write your answers on lined notebook paper.

Question 1

1. Theorist Walt Rostow proposed that countries went through a series of stages of economic development over time.

   A. Define the five stages of Rostow's stages of economic growth.

   B. Examine the second stage proposed by Rostow and describe the social and economic characteristics of that stage.

   C. Examine the fourth stage proposed by Rostow and describe the social and economic characteristics of that stage.

   D. List a different nation or society that is currently found in each of the five stages. Briefly describe a characteristic to support your example.

   E. Define *comparative advantage* and explain Rostow's assumption of comparative advantage.

   F. Explain ONE criticism of Rostow's model.

   G. Describe ONE factor *not* described by Rostow's model that can affect the economic future of a society.

GO ON TO THE NEXT PAGE.

Question 2

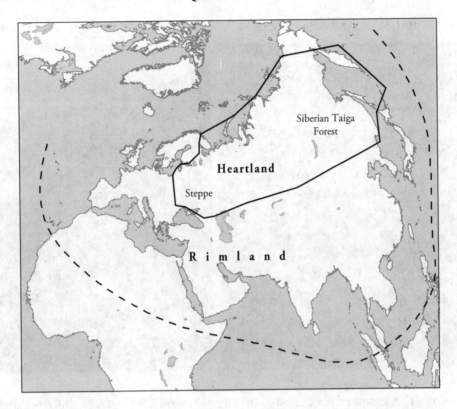

2. The following questions are based on Halford Mackinder's Heartland-Rimland model (shown above).

    A. Explain the purpose of the Heartland-Rimland model, defining both the Heartland and the Rimland.

    B. Discuss the predictive power of the Heartland-Rimland model.

    C. Describe the Shatterbelt theory and explain how it modified Mackinder's Heartland-Rimland theory.

    D. Define the difference between political power and territoriality.

    E. Explain the Heartland theory's effect on post-World War II U.S. foreign policy.

    F. Describe ONE military or diplomatic action of the last century that reflects the importance of the Heartland-Rimland model.

    G. Explain ONE national security problem faced by countries in the Rimland.

GO ON TO THE NEXT PAGE.

Question 3

CLUSTERED RURAL SETTLEMENT PATTERN

DISPERSED RURAL SETTLEMENT PATTERN

3. The patterns of rural land settlement have defined much of the geographic history of the world, especially in Europe and the United States. The way in which rural land was plotted, divided up, settled, and farmed carries significance even to the modern day.

    A. Explain the difference between a clustered and a dispersed rural settlement.

    B. Define TWO types of clustered settlements.

    C. Describe how the English political system led to early settlement patterns in the U.S.

    D. Describe the effect of sea navigation upon settlement patterns in the U.S.

    E. Explain how New England's settlement patterns contributed to the development of distinctive dialects of English in the region.

    F. Describe how the enclosure movement led to the contemporary European pattern of rural settlement.

    G. Explain the rectangular survey system.

STOP

END OF EXAM

Practice Test 3:
Answers and
Explanations

PRACTICE TEST 3 ANSWER KEY

1.	B	21.	A	41.	E
2.	E	22.	D	42.	E
3.	C	23.	C	43.	D
4.	D	24.	E	44.	E
5.	A	25.	B	45.	C
6.	C	26.	C	46.	B
7.	C	27.	A	47.	A
8.	E	28.	B	48.	E
9.	A	29.	E	49.	E
10.	C	30.	D	50.	E
11.	C	31.	B	51.	A
12.	D	32.	C	52.	A
13.	B	33.	E	53.	E
14.	A	34.	A	54.	A
15.	E	35.	D	55.	C
16.	D	36.	C	56.	B
17.	B	37.	A	57.	B
18.	C	38.	B	58.	C
19.	D	39.	D	59.	E
20.	C	40.	B	60.	D

PRACTICE TEST 3 EXPLANATIONS

Multiple-Choice Questions

1. **B**   The environmental transition zone between two bioregions, or biomes, is known as an ecotone. Choice (A) is incorrect because an area in which everyone speaks the same language is known as a linguistic region and (C) is incorrect because a functional region is an area that has a central place as the focus that expresses some practical purpose. Eliminate (D) because cultural regions are those that tend to have fuzzy borders. Finally, eliminate (E) because a vernacular region is that which is based upon the perception or collective mental map of the region's residents.

2. **E**   The kingdom of Portugal was a constitutional monarchy until the Republican Revolution of 1910. Bahrain, Cambodia, Kuwait, and Monaco are all examples of constitutional monarchies, so eliminate (A), (B), (C), and (D).

3. **C**   The practice of planting two crops consecutively on a single plot each year is referred to as double cropping. Conservation agriculture refers to the agricultural practices that provide sustainable farming without sacrificing crop production; eliminate (A). Choice (B) can be eliminated since crop rotation is the process of planting a crop on one plot of land and then switching to another plot in subsequent years. Inter-planting is the process of planting fast-growing crops alongside slow-growing crops, allowing the farmer to double the yield of the land; eliminate (D). Eliminate (E) as swidden is the practice of slash-and-burn agriculture.

4. **D**   A weight-gaining industry is one in which the finished product is more bulky and more costly to transport than the original inputs of the product. Eliminate (A), (B), (C), and (E) because automobile, beverage, clothing, and bread production all weigh more than the original individual inputs and are made through a decentralized network of industries. Conversely, steel manufacturing is a weight-losing process that has only one major input and a centralized network of production.

5. **A**   A place on the map that is defined by coordinates of longitude or latitude is an absolute location. A formal region is bounded space that possesses some uniformity; eliminate (B). There is no definition for a prime area; eliminate (C) for being pure nonsense. A relative location refers to the location of a place compared to a known place or geographic feature; eliminate (D). Finally, a functional region is an area that has a central place that is a focus that expresses some practical purpose; eliminate (E).

6. **C**   The precise location of retail services is spatially dependent on the relationship between variable cost and revenue surfaces based on local geography.

7. **C**   The market area of a city is defined by both threshold, the minimum number of people required to support a business, and range, the maximum distance people are willing to travel to gain access to a service.

8. **E**   This diagram best models the spatial margin of profitability, or the area where local demand for a service creates revenue higher than the local costs of doing business.

9. **A**   The Human Development Index was designed to measure the level of development of states based on social indicators and economic production. Choice (B) can be eliminated because gross national income purchasing power parity takes into account differences in prices between countries. The Gini coefficient measures the level of income disparity between the country's richest and poorest population groups; eliminate (C). Eliminate (D) because the Gender-Related Development Index compares gender equality amongst different countries. Gross Domestic Product is used to calculate the dollar value of all goods and services produced in a country annually; eliminate (E).

10. **C**   Furniture is an example of a supply chain because it requires parts to be assembled into components that are then assembled together to create a larger finished product. Eliminate (A) because a footloose industry describes a business whose location is not tied to resources, transportation, or consumer locations. Choice (B) can be eliminated because a high-benefit service is one that has multiple footloose activities and can be located anywhere geographically. A bulk-losing industry has only one major input and a centralized network of production; eliminate (D). Choice (E) can be eliminated because a deglomeration is the process of multiple firms expanding operations to locations wherein the market is not oversaturated with a service.

11. **C**   The Piedmont Industrial Region is an industrial region in the southeastern United States. This area is represented on the map in the shaded area marked C.

12. **D**   Locations on the map that are marked with a ▲ are manufacturing regions in more-developed countries.

13. **B**   The area surrounding present-day Louisiana is a cultural hub of Cajun and Zydeco influences. Thus, the correct region on the map is that marked B.

14. **A**   Tibet, Nepal, and Bhutan share commonalities in cultural landscape features such as architecture due to the influence of Buddhism.

15. **E**   Since the English language is the most commonly spoken language in both the United States and Australia, these countries are in the same linguistic region.

16. **D**   Mexico and Malaysia are both Newly Industrialized Countries (NICs) that are in late stage two and early stage three of the demographic transition model. NICs are characterized by economies that are transitioning from an agricultural-based economy to a manufacturing economy. NICs, such as Malaysia and Mexico, have birth rates that exceed their death rates, have positive rates of natural increase, and have experienced increases in quality of life in recent decades. Thus, Mexico and Malaysia are not in stage four of the demographic transition model and the correct answer is (D).

17. **B**   The diplomatic meeting between European colonial powers to set the internal political boundaries in Africa is known as the Conference of Berlin. Eliminate (A), as the Oregon Treaty set the western border between Canada and the United States. Choice (C) can be eliminated because the Antarctic Treaty sets aside the continent for scientific research and prohibits military or mining activities. The Organization of African Union is a supranational organization that is focused on regional diplomacy within the continent; eliminate (D). There is no meeting known as the Paracel consortium, so (E) can be eliminated.

18. **C**   The economy can be divided into categories known as sectors, which can further be categorized by the types of products or services they create. Quaternary production includes "business services," such as wholesaling, finance, banking, insurance, real estate, advertising, and marketing. Thus, eliminate (A), (B), (D), and (E). All forms of manufacturing occur in the secondary stage of production.

19. **D**   Nonrenewable resources include petroleum, coal, natural gas, and uranium, while renewable resources include solar energy, wind power, tidal power, hydroelectric power, geothermal energy, and biofuel. Thus, the correct answer is (D).

20. **C**   A port location where foreign firms are given special tax privileges to incentivize trade is known as an export processing zone. Choice (A) can be eliminated because a free-trade zone is an economic zone where goods can be stored, displayed, manufactured, or processed without customs fees. A transport node is a town or city that was established due to its intersection with multiple lines of transportation, while a resource node is a town or city that was established due to its proximity to natural resources; (B) and (D) can be eliminated. An agglomeration occurs when similar business activities are found in a local cluster; eliminate (E).

21. **A**   The galactic city model best represents the post-industrial city with its several, dispersed business districts. Eliminate (B) since the Latin American city model describes the planning and layout of colonial cities. The multiple-nuclei model recognizes the formation of multiple suburban business districts forming on the urban periphery; eliminate (C). Choice (D) can be eliminated because the sector model of urban structure combines the concepts of the industrial corridor and the neighborhood to provide a realistic representation of an urban area. Finally, the concentric zone model represents the commercial business district, industrial zone, inner city housing, suburbs, and exurbs as five concentric, non-overlapping zones; (E) can be eliminated.

22. **D**   The Total Fertility Rate is the estimated average number of children born to each female of birthing age, which is considered to be ages 15–45.

23. **C**   In order to answer this question, you need to know the formula used to estimate the length of time necessary for a country to double its population: $Doubling\,Time = \dfrac{70}{Rate\,of\,Natural\,Increase}$. In this scenario, if the RNI for the United States is 4.25, then the $Doubling\,Time = \dfrac{70}{4.25} = 16.47 \approx 16.5\,years$.

24. **E**   Expansion diffusion occurs when an innovation occurs in a central place and then expands outwards in all directions to other locations. Relocation diffusion occurs when an innovation begins at a point of origin and then crosses significant physical barriers to relocate on the opposite side; eliminate (A). Choice (B) can be eliminated because stimulus diffusion occurs when an innovation stimulates the creation of new products or ideas. Contagious diffusion occurs when an innovation occurs at a point of origin before moving outward to nearby locations, especially those on adjoining transportation lines; eliminate (C). Choice (D) can be eliminated because hierarchical diffusion occurs when an innovation occurs in a first-order location before moving to a second-order location and onwards to increasingly local locations.

25. **B**   Balkanization is when the political landscape goes from a larger state to several smaller states. Yugoslavia, Czechoslovakia, the Austro-Hungarian Empire, and the USSR were all large states that broke into multiple smaller states; thus, they underwent balkanization. Mongolia, however, did not undergo balkanization.

26. **C**   The provided images would best be described as population pyramids, which are graphical means of visualizing the population structure of a country or place.

27. **A**   Diagram E represents a country that is experiencing fast growth. In this situation the number of births is greatly outpacing the number of deaths.

28. **B**   The diagram that would best exemplify a country in stage one of the demographic transition model would be diagram B. There are currently no countries in the world that have stage one populations, which are characterized by high birth rates, high death rates, low life expectancies, and a low to moderate rate of natural increase.

29. **E**   The concept that the living space for each distinct nation is based upon the optimal physical geography of a culture group is known as *lebensraum*. Sequent occupance is the idea that for a single place, different dominant cultures replace each other over time; eliminate (A). Choice (B) can be eliminated because environmental determinism is the scientific ideology that states that a culture's traits are defined by the physical geography of its cultural region. Acculturation is the process of adapting to a new culture while still keeping some of one's original culture; eliminate (C). Choice (D) can be eliminated because possibilism states that cultures are to a partial degree shaped by their environment and the resources available.

30. **D**   The curved strip of arable land that connects Mesopotamia and Egypt through to the Levant is known as the Fertile Crescent. Eliminate (B) and (E) because there are no areas referred to as either the Etruscan Environment or the Tiberian Trench. Choice (A) can be eliminated because Sunbelt States are located in the southern tier of the United States of America. Special Economic Zones, first established in the 1980s, are areas in which foreign firms are allowed to build facilities in coastal port cities; eliminate (C).

31. **B**   New Asian Tigers are countries that received development funding through Foreign Direct Investment during the 1980s and 1990s. China, India, Indonesia, Malaysia, Thailand, and Vietnam are all countries that are considered New Asian Tigers. Conversely, Old Asian Tigers received development funding through foreign aid programs, such as the Macarthur Plan, during the 1950s, 1960s, and 1970s. Japan, South Korea, Taiwan, Hong Kong, and Singapore are all considered Old Asian Tigers.

32. **C**   A population under a single government is best defined as a state. A country refers to an identifiable land area, while a nation refers to a population with a single culture; eliminate both (A) and (B). A nation state is defined as a single culture under a single government, while a stateless nation is a culture group that is not included or allowed to share in the state political process; eliminate (D) and (E).

33. **E**   Plantations tend to be vast monoculture farms that are reliant upon low-wage labor and plantation crops produce exporting value from large-scale monoculture practices. Plantation crops include bananas, cane sugar, coffee, tea, rubber, cacao, and palm oil. Pistachios, however, are specialized crops that are associated with Mediterranean agricultural practices; the correct answer is (E).

34. **A**   An operational border dispute occurs when borders are agreed to, but passage across the border is a problem. A definitional border dispute occurs when border treaties are interpreted two different ways by states; eliminate (B). An allocational border dispute occurs when a resource lies on two sides of a border; eliminate (C). A locational border dispute occurs when the border moves, like when a river changes course; eliminate (D). Choice (E) does not define any type of border dispute and, therefore, can be eliminated.

35. **D**   Irrigation agriculture is responsible for close to 75% of freshwater use worldwide and 90% of freshwater use in the most poverty-stricken countries of the world.

36. **C**   Gerrymandering is the purposeful manipulation of political boundaries in order to favor a particular party or class. The consequences of gerrymandering are vast and include the protection of incumbent politicians that lead to predictable election outcomes for a favored political party and unequal representation for minority populations.

37. **A**   Primary production, which includes agriculture, mining, and forestry, consists of activities that include the extraction of natural resources from the earth. Secondary production includes activities that include the fabrication of components, the assembly of finished goods, and the processing of raw materials; eliminate (C), (D), and (E). Tertiary production includes the transportation, wholesaling, and retailing of finished goods to consumers; eliminate (B).

38. **B**   The number of immigrants minus the number of emigrants for every thousand members of the population is known as the net migration rate.

39. **D**   Specific things about the rural agricultural landscape and livelihood that force people off the farm are known as push factors. Life-course changes occur when people move because of major changes during the course of their lives; eliminate (A). Pull factors are specific things about cities than draw people to the urban landscape; eliminate (B). Eliminate (C) and (E) because there are no specific AP Human Geography definitions for "shift factors" or "migration opportunities."

40. **B**   Newly industrialized countries experience both rapid internal rural-to-urban migration and population growth. Furthermore, NICs have high rates of natural increase and are transitioning their focus away from agriculture to manufacturing as the primary form of economic production. However, high birth and death rates are characteristic of countries in stage one of the demographic transition model; NICs have decreasing birth rates and decreasing death rates.

41. **E**   According to the United Nations Conference on the Law of the Seas (UNCLOS), sovereign territory that includes the area of the sea from the shore out to the 12-nautical-mile limit is referred to as the territorial sea. An exclusive economic zone includes the region from shore out to the 200-nautical-mile limit; eliminate (A). Admiralty law is a part of international law that dictates legal procedures on the high seas, or those outside the 12-nautical-mile limit; eliminate both (B) and (D). A special economic zone is a type of export processing zone, defined as port locations where foreign firms are given special tax privileges to incentivize trade; eliminate (C).

42. **E**   This model of urban structure is known as the sector model.

43. **D**   In the given Sector Model, middle-class housing exists in the region marked 4.

44. **E** In the United States, crops and animals that must not be grown using genetic engineering, must be free of pesticides, antibiotics, and synthetic hormones, and must feed on completely organic crops are classified as organic. A product's appellation is the local or regional geographic name for a product; eliminate (A). A cottage industry refers to a small-scale business that focuses on labor-intensive goods and is often run out of a personal, rather than factory, setting; eliminate (B). Heirloom crops are produced from unadulterated, non-hybridized plants; eliminate (C). Specialized crops are non-traditional crops that only grow in a specific geographical region and, therefore, are in high demand; eliminate (D).

45. **C** A microstate is a sovereign state that despite their very small size still holds the same position of much larger states like the United States and Canada. The following are all considered microstates: Andorra, Antigua and Barbuda, Bahrain, Barbados, Comoros, Djibouti, Dominica, Grenada, Liechtenstein, Luxembourg, Malta, Monaco, Nauru, Palau, St. Kitts and Nevis, St. Lucia, Samoa, San Marino, Singapore, and the Vatican City.

46. **B** The Green Revolution occurred in the 1950s and 1960s when plant and animal hybrids and chemical fertilizers and pesticides began to be used in Third World agriculture.

47. **A** The North Atlantic Treaty Organization (NATO) is a supranational organization that is primarily concerned with military cooperation. The World Bank, International Monetary Fund (IMF), and Organization of African Union (OAU) are organizations concerned with governmental loans and regional diplomacy; eliminate both (B) and (C). The Organization of Petroleum Exporting Countries (OPEC) and the North American Free Trade Agreement (NAFTA) are organizations concerned with petroleum pricing regulation and free-trade zones, respectively; eliminate (D) and (E).

48. **E** In Ernest Burgess' Concentric Zone Model, the concentric rings from innermost to outermost are the central business district, the industrial zone, inner-city housing, the suburbs, and the exurbs.

49. **E** Since the first census was conducted in 1790, the population center of the United States has continuously moved west each decade. Originally, land in the eastern United States was owned and had high population numbers. However, those wanting their own land and immigrants moving to the United States moved westward to find available land.

50. **E** Monoculture is the cultivation of a single crop in a given area. This technique, together with pesticides and cross-breeding, has been the method by which the developed world has achieved enormous gains in agricultural production. In places such as India, monoculture has allowed humans to break free of the Malthusian trap, sustaining ever-larger numbers of population.

51. **A** The second photo, which is an example of biodiverse agriculture, is not associated with plantation agriculture. Plantation agriculture has traditionally been most common in tropical areas of Latin America, and it is defined as a form of commercial farming in which crops are grown for profit. Monoculture is typical on plantation agriculture, examples of which can be seen in single-crop banana plantations, sugar plantations, coffee plantations, etc.

52. **A** The five pillars of Islam, which are the moral principles emphasized in the Koran, include Five Daily Prayers, Islamic Creed, Alms to the Poor, Observance of Ramadan, and the Hajj. Thus, choose (A), as Six Daily Prayers is not a pillar of Islam.

53. **E** The bluegrass music tradition, in which the fiddle and the banjo are the primary interests, is most prevalent in Appalachia, a region that stretches from Mississippi to the Maritime provinces.

54. **A** Underdeveloped countries with primarily agricultural and resource-based economies that have no formal national government are best described as Fifth World countries.

55. **C** Female heads of household are *more* likely to rely on public transportation than male heads of household because women heads of household must access food shopping, health care, and other services; thus, female heads of household choose their home locations accordingly. It is true, however, that the percentage of female-headed households in urban areas has increased significantly in recent decades, women surpass men in terms of average pay in the service sectors of health care and education, the 19th Amendment to the U.S. Constitution granted American women the right to vote in 1920, and, on average, women live approximately 5 years longer than men.

56. **B** Gateway cities are places where immigrants make their way into a country. Colonial cities have origins as centers of colonial trade or administration and entrepôts are port cities where goods are shipped in at one price and shipped to other port cities at a higher price; eliminate (A) and (C). Medieval cities are urban centers that predate the European Renaissance, while world cities have metropolitan areas that are global centers for finance, trade, and commerce; eliminate (D) and (E).

57. **B** The European Court of Justice provides a legal venue for cases between litigants in separate European Union member states. The European Union ensures that no taxes or tariffs are charged on goods and services that cross its internal borders; eliminate (A). Choices (C) and (E) can be eliminated, as the European Commission sets the European Union's annual policy agenda and acts as the executive branch of the European Union to enact programs and enforce regulations set by the European Union Parliament and Council. The 785-seat European Union Parliament proposes and approves laws within the European Union; eliminate (D).

58. **C** The graph provided best illustrates Malthusian Theory. In his *An Essay on the Principle of Population* in 1798, Thomas Malthus predicted that the global population would one day expand to the point where it could not produce enough food to feed everyone. While the Malthusian catastrophe has yet to happen, neo-Malthusians think it could in the future.

59. **E** Based on Malthusian Theory, the point at which the lines of food production and human population cross would best be described as the point at which the population exceeds its ability to feed itself.

60. **D** The Columbian exchange refers to the diffusion of crops and livestock between the Old World and the New World that occurred after the conquest of mainland Central and South America in the 1500s. Maize, potatoes, tobacco, and turkeys were all crops and livestock that diffused to the Old World from the New World. Chickens, however, diffused from the Old World to the New World.

Free-Response Questions

Don't look at the following section until you've completed the free-response questions in Practice Test 3.

For each of the questions, we have provided a rubric that will give you a decent sense of what information your responses should have mentioned. Each of the questions comprises seven parts (A–G), each of which is worth one point. That point is awarded for addressing any of the possible ideas listed under that part.

Keep in mind that these rubrics are by no means exhaustive. We recommend asking your AP Human Geography teacher to check your responses, particularly if they mention other details not listed here.

Scoring Rubrics for Free-Response Questions

1. Theorist Walt Rostow proposed that countries went through a series of stages of economic development over time.

   A. Define the five stages of Rostow's stages of economic growth.

   B. Examine the second stage proposed by Rostow and describe the social and economic characteristics of that stage.

   C. Examine the fourth stage proposed by Rostow and describe the social and economic characteristics of that stage.

   D. List a different nation or society that is currently found in each of the five stages. Briefly describe a characteristic to support your example.

   E. Define *comparative advantage* and explain Rostow's assumption of comparative advantage.

   F. Explain ONE criticism of Rostow's model.

   G. Describe ONE factor *not* described by Rostow's model that can affect the economic future of a society.

Rubric—1 + 1 + 1 + 1 + 1 + 1 + 1 = 7 pts

A. Five stages
   a. Stage 1: Traditional societies
   b. Stage 2: Preconditions for takeoff
   c. Stage 3: Takeoff
   d. Stage 4: Drive to maturity
   e. Stage 5: Age of high mass consumption

B. Second stage: closer examination
   a. Preconditions for takeoff
      i. There is an external demand for raw materials from that country
      ii. More commercial agriculture, some of which is exported
      iii. Infrastructure is improved to expedite this new international trade (irrigation, canals, access roads, ports, etc.)
      iv. Increased use of technology; more advanced technologies arrive
      v. Individual social mobility

C. Fourth stage: closer examination
   a. Drive to maturity
      i. Diversification of industrial base
      ii. Manufacturing changes to consumer durables and domestic consumption
      iii. Infrastructure grows rapidly
      iv. Social institutions are funded and built

D. An example for each stage
  a. Stage 1: Amazonian tribes. Traditional hunter-gatherer societies are rare nowadays, but they can still be found in the deepest parts of the Brazilian jungle.
  b. Stage 2: Mozambique, Uganda, and most of sub-Saharan Africa. These societies are still socially traditional, even while they are slowly making the transition from agriculture to small manufacturing by using profits from surplus agriculture to support factory growth.
  c. Stage 3: Vietnam. It has become a major electronics exporter in recent years, and with that sector charging out ahead, the rest of the nation is benefitting. Its entrepreneurial middle class is growing.
  d. Stage 4: China. It has been busy applying the whole range of modern technology to the whole range of its resources. Output far outstrips the population. Strong position in international market. Domestic production of formerly imported goods. Reduction in poverty rate, increase in standard of living.
  e. Stage 5: USA, Canada, UK, France, Germany, etc. Zero subsistence concerns, consumer durable goods are produced, slow transition beginning to a service economy as goods have saturated the market. Society has the luxury of promoting arts, music, equality, general welfare, etc.

E. Comparative advantage
  a. The term *comparative advantage* means that a country has the ability or resources to produce a good or service at less cost and more efficiently than other states. As such these advantageous goods and services are selected for industrial production over other possible alternatives.
  b. Rostow's assumption of comparative advantage was that each country had at least some form of comparative advantage that could be utilized in international trade and thus fund the country's economic development over time.

F. Criticism of Rostow's model
  a. Rostow's model is only based on the historical development patterns of the United States and other industrialized countries, and not all countries have had the capacity to utilize potential comparative advantages for international trade. He assumed that all countries could progress smoothly through the stages if their investment focused on trade and technology development.
  b. Colonial legacy and other barriers to development, such as government corruption and capital flight, are ignored in his theory.
  c. He assumes neoliberal trade policies that allow manufacturing to leave to cheaper, still-developing nations.
  d. Model does not apply to very small nations with no desirable natural resources available, such as Liberia.

G. Factors not described by Rostow's model that can affect the economic future of a nation

    a. International aid. Many developing countries, instead of relying on a single sector of the economy, are receiving foreign aid from the World Bank or International Monetary Fund. These are controversial loans, but they can be used to bring a stage 2 nation into stage 3.

    b. International development. Chinese corporations, for example, are busy building infrastructure in African nations for the purpose of extracting resources found there. If not given any access to its own extracted wealth, the stage 2 society cannot escape its own cycle of dependency. This can result in a de facto colonization of a stage 2 society, and it is not described by Rostow.

    c. WiFi. This single development, quite recent, has enabled people in stage 2 societies, for example, to work remotely for corporations in stage 4 or 5 societies. (Think personal assistants in India helping people organize their day in California.) This cuts out the need for the nation-state completely.

2. The following questions are based on Halford Mackinder's Heartland-Rimland model (shown above).

   A. Explain the purpose of the Heartland-Rimland model, defining both the Heartland and the Rimland.

   B. Discuss the predictive power of the Heartland-Rimland model.

   C. Describe the Shatterbelt theory and explain how it modified Mackinder's Heartland-Rimland theory.

   D. Define the difference between political power and territoriality.

   E. Explain the Heartland theory's effect on post-World War II U.S. foreign policy.

   F. Describe ONE military or diplomatic action of the last century that reflects the importance of the Heartland-Rimland model.

   G. Explain ONE national security problem faced by countries in the Rimland.

Rubric—1 + 1 + 1 + 1 + 1 + 1 + 1 = 7 pts

A. Explain the purpose of the Heartland-Rimland model, defining both the Heartland and the Rimland.

   a. The Heartland-Rimland model was proposed by Halford Mackinder at the beginning of the 20th century in an effort to define the global geopolitical landscape and determine areas of potential future conflict. He identified agricultural land as the primary commodity that states were interested in, and the largest of these was the Eastern European steppe, a very productive area of grain cultivation mostly controlled by the Russian Empire at the time. This, combined with the mineral and timber-rich region across the Urals into Siberia, he called the Pivot, or later, the Heartland.

   b. The Rimland theory, proposed by Nicholas Spykman sixty years later, took exception. It stated that the domination of the coastal fringes of Eurasia would provide the base for world conquest—not its internal resources. Thus he placed importance on naval powers at the edge of the Eurasian continent, such as Great Britain and Japan, who had already used navies to leverage geopolitical power. Naval power, he argued, kept the Heartland power in check.

B. Discuss the predictive power of the Heartland-Rimland model.

   a. Mackinder accurately predicted the battle lines of the Eastern Front during World War I. In 1921, he revised the model, expanding the Heartland further into Central Europe. In essence, Mackinder stated that the same geopolitical situation remained, with land still being the primary commodity of conflict: the thing that countries were willing to fight over. From 1904 onward, Mackinder points out that the areas of future conflict are the borderlines between the Heartland and Rimland. This prediction comes true again with the 1931 invasion of Manchuria by the Japanese, which some Asian scholars identify as the actual start of World War II. The European border conflict areas in the model are also realized with the 1939 German invasion of Poland, a country within the redrawn Heartland.

C. Describe the Shatterbelt theory and explain how it modified Mackinder's Heartland-Rimland theory.

    a. American geographer Saul Cohen proposed the Shatterbelt theory. He modified Mackinder's Heartland into the Pivot Area and Rimland into the Inner Crescent. The rest of the world became the Outer Crescent, including the United States. His land-based concept was that Cold War conflicts would likely occur within the Inner Crescent. Noting that most of the world's population lived in the Inner Crescent, he pointed out several Inner Crescent areas of geopolitical weakness that he called Shatterbelts. Like Mackinder's earlier predictions, Cohen's Shatterbelts accurately identified numerous areas where wars emerged between 1950 and the end of the Cold War in 1991.

D. Define the difference between political power and territoriality.

    a. Political power is expressed geographically as control over people, land, and resources.

    b. Territoriality is the connection of people, their culture, and their economic systems to the land.

E. Explain the Heartland theory's effect on post-World War II U.S. foreign policy.

    a. U.S. foreign policy was dominated from 1945 to 1990 by the Cold War and specifically by its policy of containment. This referred to the attempt by the U.S. to restrict the expansion of the Soviet Union. This fits neatly with the Heartland theory; the U.S. was in essence attempting to stop the USSR from occupying all of the Heartland, which constitutes a majority of the world resources.

F. Describe ONE military or diplomatic action of the last century that reflects the importance of the Heartland-Rimland model.

    a. Hitler's invasion of both Poland and the Soviet Union. As dictator of the Rimland power of Germany, he desired the Heartland resources found in Polish and Soviet territory.

    b. The founding of NATO. It was established by Rimland powers to keep the Heartland power in check.

    c. Vladimir Putin's invasion of Crimea in 2014. This peninsula into the Black Sea would give Russia an all-important port from which to transport its resources. Putin's more general claim on the Ukraine fits as well; that country has long been called "the breadbasket of Russia."

G. Explain ONE national security problem faced by countries in the Rimland.

    a. The so-called "buffer states" along the Rimland are the ones who've suffered waves of invasions both from land and sea over the centuries. These include, famously, Afghanistan, Iran, Arabia, Malaysia, China, and others. These countries often have to defend themselves from both land and sea. China, for example, has defended against the Mongols attacking from the Heartland to the north (land), and Europeans attacking from the east and south (ocean).

3. The patterns of rural land settlement have defined much of the geographic history of the world, especially in Europe and the United States. The way in which rural land was plotted, divided up, settled, and farmed carries significance even to the modern day.

   A. Explain the difference between a clustered and a dispersed rural settlement.

   B. Define TWO types of clustered settlements.

   C. Describe how the English political system led to early settlement patterns in the U.S.

   D. Describe the effect of sea navigation upon settlement patterns in the U.S.

   E. Explain how New England's settlement patterns contributed to the development of distinctive dialects of English in the region.

   F. Describe how the enclosure movement led to the contemporary European pattern of rural settlement.

   G. Explain the rectangular survey system.

Rubric—1+ 1 + 1 + 1 + 1 + 1 + 1 = 7 pts

A. Explain the difference between a clustered and a dispersed rural settlement.
   a. Clustered
      i. Rural settlements in which the houses and farm buildings of each family are situated close to one another, with fields surrounding the hamlet. Common in New England.
   b. Dispersed
      i. Rural settlements characterized by isolated farms rather than tight villages. Very common in Midwest and Great Plains.
B. Two types of clustered settlements
   a. Circular
      i. A rural settlement pattern with a central open space surrounded by low structures. Found in sub-Saharan Africa.
   b. Linear
      i. A rural settlement pattern in which buildings are clustered along a line (initially rivers, now roads). The French did this exclusively, making sure that everyone got a small access to a river, since trading was the reason for their arrival in the U.S. This is known as the French long-lot system.
   c. New England
      i. There are many reasons the early New England settlers stuck closely together—common religious ideology, protection from attacks by indigenous people, importance of school and church structures to daily life.

C. English system led to early U.S. settlement patterns

    a. The short answer: metes and bounds. The practice of using the natural landscape to inform the ownership pattern was quite common in England for centuries before the U.S. These decisions simply followed creeks, rivers, edges of forests, rock walls, and many other physical obstacles. It was brought to the original 13 English colonies in the U.S. Private ownership was extremely important.

D. Sea navigation effect on settlement patterns

    a. The tools used by sea navigators—lines of latitude and longitude—were brought and used on land. So the older technique of metes and bounds, which relied on natural features and which had been used in Europe for centuries, fell away in favor of land surveying, which used rectilinear lines.

E. New England's development of dialects

    a. Over centuries, the clustered rural settlement pattern seen in New England resulted in the development of small linguistic pockets. This accounts for the unique accents in New England (and Southern towns).

F. The enclosure movement

    a. In England, prior to 1750, peasants often farmed small bits of land individually, land that they rented or even used for free—it was called the commons. However, from 1750 to 1850, these small landholdings were consolidated into a number of larger farms, and the peasants lost the right to work on them. This enclosure movement displaced many peasants, who found themselves unattached to any land, leaving them free to move into the cities and work in factories. This meant that the small clustered villages they had lived in emptied out. The rural settlement changed to a dispersed pattern, with each large tract of land controlled by one aristocratic family.

G. Rectangular survey system

    a. This is the only totally American system put into practice by the Land Ordinance of 1785. It was designed for rapid settlement of large amounts of land, especially useful after the Louisiana Purchase. Works well on flat, uninhabited land. It uses no physical features—only abstract lines known as baselines and principle meridians. It's essentially a system of large squares subdivided into small squares (townships).

HOW TO SCORE PRACTICE TEST 3

Section I: Multiple Choice

_____ × 1.25 = _____
Number Correct   Weighted
(out of 60)   Section I Score
                        (Do not round)

Section II: Free Response

Question 1:
_____ × 3.5714 = _____
(out of 7)   (Do not round)

Question 2:
_____ × 3.5714 = _____
(out of 7)   (Do not round)

Question 3:
_____ × 3.5714 = _____
(out of 7)   (Do not round)

AP Score Conversion Chart Human Geography	
Composite Score Range	AP Score
107–150	5
90–106	4
73–89	3
56–72	2
0–55	1

Sum = _____
Weighted
Section II Score
(Do not round)

Composite Score

_____ + _____ = _____
Weighted   Weighted   Composite Score
Section I Score   Section II Score (Round to nearest
                                    whole number)

1

YOUR NAME: _____
(Print)   Last   First   M.I.

SIGNATURE: _____ DATE: ___/___/___

HOME ADDRESS: _____
(Print)   Number and Street

_____
City   State   Zip Code

PHONE No.: _____
(Print)

IMPORTANT: Please fill in these boxes exactly as shown on the back cover of your test book.

2. TEST FORM

_____

3. TEST CODE

⊂0⊃	⊂A⊃	⊂0⊃	⊂0⊃	⊂0⊃	⊂0⊃	⊂0⊃	⊂0⊃	⊂0⊃	⊂0⊃
⊂1⊃	⊂B⊃	⊂1⊃	⊂1⊃	⊂1⊃	⊂1⊃	⊂1⊃	⊂1⊃	⊂1⊃	⊂1⊃
⊂2⊃	⊂C⊃	⊂2⊃	⊂2⊃	⊂2⊃	⊂2⊃	⊂2⊃	⊂2⊃	⊂2⊃	⊂2⊃
⊂3⊃	⊂D⊃	⊂3⊃	⊂3⊃	⊂3⊃	⊂3⊃	⊂3⊃	⊂3⊃	⊂3⊃	⊂3⊃
⊂4⊃	⊂E⊃	⊂4⊃	⊂4⊃	⊂4⊃	⊂4⊃	⊂4⊃	⊂4⊃	⊂4⊃	⊂4⊃
⊂5⊃	⊂F⊃	⊂5⊃	⊂5⊃	⊂5⊃	⊂5⊃	⊂5⊃	⊂5⊃	⊂5⊃	⊂5⊃
⊂6⊃	⊂G⊃	⊂6⊃	⊂6⊃	⊂6⊃	⊂6⊃	⊂6⊃	⊂6⊃	⊂6⊃	⊂6⊃
⊂7⊃		⊂7⊃	⊂7⊃	⊂7⊃	⊂7⊃	⊂7⊃	⊂7⊃	⊂7⊃	⊂7⊃
⊂8⊃		⊂8⊃	⊂8⊃	⊂8⊃	⊂8⊃	⊂8⊃	⊂8⊃	⊂8⊃	⊂8⊃
⊂9⊃		⊂9⊃	⊂9⊃	⊂9⊃	⊂9⊃	⊂9⊃	⊂9⊃	⊂9⊃	⊂9⊃

4. REGISTRATION NUMBER

6. DATE OF BIRTH

Month		Day		Year		
⊂ ⊃ JAN						
⊂ ⊃ FEB						
⊂ ⊃ MAR	⊂0⊃	⊂0⊃	⊂0⊃	⊂0⊃		
⊂ ⊃ APR	⊂1⊃	⊂1⊃	⊂1⊃	⊂1⊃		
⊂ ⊃ MAY	⊂2⊃	⊂2⊃	⊂2⊃	⊂2⊃		
⊂ ⊃ JUN	⊂3⊃	⊂3⊃	⊂3⊃	⊂3⊃		
⊂ ⊃ JUL		⊂4⊃	⊂4⊃	⊂4⊃		
⊂ ⊃ AUG		⊂5⊃	⊂5⊃	⊂5⊃		
⊂ ⊃ SEP		⊂6⊃	⊂6⊃	⊂6⊃		
⊂ ⊃ OCT		⊂7⊃	⊂7⊃	⊂7⊃		
⊂ ⊃ NOV		⊂8⊃	⊂8⊃	⊂8⊃		
⊂ ⊃ DEC		⊂9⊃	⊂9⊃	⊂9⊃		

7. SEX

⊂ ⊃ MALE
⊂ ⊃ FEMALE

5. YOUR NAME

First 4 letters of last name				FIRST INIT	MID INIT
⊂A⊃	⊂A⊃	⊂A⊃	⊂A⊃	⊂A⊃	⊂A⊃
⊂B⊃	⊂B⊃	⊂B⊃	⊂B⊃	⊂B⊃	⊂B⊃
⊂C⊃	⊂C⊃	⊂C⊃	⊂C⊃	⊂C⊃	⊂C⊃
⊂D⊃	⊂D⊃	⊂D⊃	⊂D⊃	⊂D⊃	⊂D⊃
⊂E⊃	⊂E⊃	⊂E⊃	⊂E⊃	⊂E⊃	⊂E⊃
⊂F⊃	⊂F⊃	⊂F⊃	⊂F⊃	⊂F⊃	⊂F⊃
⊂G⊃	⊂G⊃	⊂G⊃	⊂G⊃	⊂G⊃	⊂G⊃
⊂H⊃	⊂H⊃	⊂H⊃	⊂H⊃	⊂H⊃	⊂H⊃
⊂I⊃	⊂I⊃	⊂I⊃	⊂I⊃	⊂I⊃	⊂I⊃
⊂J⊃	⊂J⊃	⊂J⊃	⊂J⊃	⊂J⊃	⊂J⊃
⊂K⊃	⊂K⊃	⊂K⊃	⊂K⊃	⊂K⊃	⊂K⊃
⊂L⊃	⊂L⊃	⊂L⊃	⊂L⊃	⊂L⊃	⊂L⊃
⊂M⊃	⊂M⊃	⊂M⊃	⊂M⊃	⊂M⊃	⊂M⊃
⊂N⊃	⊂N⊃	⊂N⊃	⊂N⊃	⊂N⊃	⊂N⊃
⊂O⊃	⊂O⊃	⊂O⊃	⊂O⊃	⊂O⊃	⊂O⊃
⊂P⊃	⊂P⊃	⊂P⊃	⊂P⊃	⊂P⊃	⊂P⊃
⊂Q⊃	⊂Q⊃	⊂Q⊃	⊂Q⊃	⊂Q⊃	⊂Q⊃
⊂R⊃	⊂R⊃	⊂R⊃	⊂R⊃	⊂R⊃	⊂R⊃
⊂S⊃	⊂S⊃	⊂S⊃	⊂S⊃	⊂S⊃	⊂S⊃
⊂T⊃	⊂T⊃	⊂T⊃	⊂T⊃	⊂T⊃	⊂T⊃
⊂U⊃	⊂U⊃	⊂U⊃	⊂U⊃	⊂U⊃	⊂U⊃
⊂V⊃	⊂V⊃	⊂V⊃	⊂V⊃	⊂V⊃	⊂V⊃
⊂W⊃	⊂W⊃	⊂W⊃	⊂W⊃	⊂W⊃	⊂W⊃
⊂X⊃	⊂X⊃	⊂X⊃	⊂X⊃	⊂X⊃	⊂X⊃
⊂Y⊃	⊂Y⊃	⊂Y⊃	⊂Y⊃	⊂Y⊃	⊂Y⊃
⊂Z⊃	⊂Z⊃	⊂Z⊃	⊂Z⊃	⊂Z⊃	⊂Z⊃

Start with number 1 for each new section. If a section has fewer questions than answer spaces, leave the extra answer spaces blank.

1 ⊂A⊃ ⊂B⊃ ⊂C⊃ ⊂D⊃ ⊂E⊃
2 ⊂A⊃ ⊂B⊃ ⊂C⊃ ⊂D⊃ ⊂E⊃
3 ⊂A⊃ ⊂B⊃ ⊂C⊃ ⊂D⊃ ⊂E⊃
4 ⊂A⊃ ⊂B⊃ ⊂C⊃ ⊂D⊃ ⊂E⊃
5 ⊂A⊃ ⊂B⊃ ⊂C⊃ ⊂D⊃ ⊂E⊃
6 ⊂A⊃ ⊂B⊃ ⊂C⊃ ⊂D⊃ ⊂E⊃
7 ⊂A⊃ ⊂B⊃ ⊂C⊃ ⊂D⊃ ⊂E⊃
8 ⊂A⊃ ⊂B⊃ ⊂C⊃ ⊂D⊃ ⊂E⊃
9 ⊂A⊃ ⊂B⊃ ⊂C⊃ ⊂D⊃ ⊂E⊃
10 ⊂A⊃ ⊂B⊃ ⊂C⊃ ⊂D⊃ ⊂E⊃
11 ⊂A⊃ ⊂B⊃ ⊂C⊃ ⊂D⊃ ⊂E⊃
12 ⊂A⊃ ⊂B⊃ ⊂C⊃ ⊂D⊃ ⊂E⊃
13 ⊂A⊃ ⊂B⊃ ⊂C⊃ ⊂D⊃ ⊂E⊃
14 ⊂A⊃ ⊂B⊃ ⊂C⊃ ⊂D⊃ ⊂E⊃
15 ⊂A⊃ ⊂B⊃ ⊂C⊃ ⊂D⊃ ⊂E⊃
16 ⊂A⊃ ⊂B⊃ ⊂C⊃ ⊂D⊃ ⊂E⊃
17 ⊂A⊃ ⊂B⊃ ⊂C⊃ ⊂D⊃ ⊂E⊃
18 ⊂A⊃ ⊂B⊃ ⊂C⊃ ⊂D⊃ ⊂E⊃
19 ⊂A⊃ ⊂B⊃ ⊂C⊃ ⊂D⊃ ⊂E⊃
20 ⊂A⊃ ⊂B⊃ ⊂C⊃ ⊂D⊃ ⊂E⊃

21 ⊂A⊃ ⊂B⊃ ⊂C⊃ ⊂D⊃ ⊂E⊃
22 ⊂A⊃ ⊂B⊃ ⊂C⊃ ⊂D⊃ ⊂E⊃
23 ⊂A⊃ ⊂B⊃ ⊂C⊃ ⊂D⊃ ⊂E⊃
24 ⊂A⊃ ⊂B⊃ ⊂C⊃ ⊂D⊃ ⊂E⊃
25 ⊂A⊃ ⊂B⊃ ⊂C⊃ ⊂D⊃ ⊂E⊃
26 ⊂A⊃ ⊂B⊃ ⊂C⊃ ⊂D⊃ ⊂E⊃
27 ⊂A⊃ ⊂B⊃ ⊂C⊃ ⊂D⊃ ⊂E⊃
28 ⊂A⊃ ⊂B⊃ ⊂C⊃ ⊂D⊃ ⊂E⊃
29 ⊂A⊃ ⊂B⊃ ⊂C⊃ ⊂D⊃ ⊂E⊃
30 ⊂A⊃ ⊂B⊃ ⊂C⊃ ⊂D⊃ ⊂E⊃
31 ⊂A⊃ ⊂B⊃ ⊂C⊃ ⊂D⊃ ⊂E⊃
32 ⊂A⊃ ⊂B⊃ ⊂C⊃ ⊂D⊃ ⊂E⊃
33 ⊂A⊃ ⊂B⊃ ⊂C⊃ ⊂D⊃ ⊂E⊃
34 ⊂A⊃ ⊂B⊃ ⊂C⊃ ⊂D⊃ ⊂E⊃
35 ⊂A⊃ ⊂B⊃ ⊂C⊃ ⊂D⊃ ⊂E⊃
36 ⊂A⊃ ⊂B⊃ ⊂C⊃ ⊂D⊃ ⊂E⊃
37 ⊂A⊃ ⊂B⊃ ⊂C⊃ ⊂D⊃ ⊂E⊃
38 ⊂A⊃ ⊂B⊃ ⊂C⊃ ⊂D⊃ ⊂E⊃
39 ⊂A⊃ ⊂B⊃ ⊂C⊃ ⊂D⊃ ⊂E⊃
40 ⊂A⊃ ⊂B⊃ ⊂C⊃ ⊂D⊃ ⊂E⊃

41 ⊂A⊃ ⊂B⊃ ⊂C⊃ ⊂D⊃ ⊂E⊃
42 ⊂A⊃ ⊂B⊃ ⊂C⊃ ⊂D⊃ ⊂E⊃
43 ⊂A⊃ ⊂B⊃ ⊂C⊃ ⊂D⊃ ⊂E⊃
44 ⊂A⊃ ⊂B⊃ ⊂C⊃ ⊂D⊃ ⊂E⊃
45 ⊂A⊃ ⊂B⊃ ⊂C⊃ ⊂D⊃ ⊂E⊃
46 ⊂A⊃ ⊂B⊃ ⊂C⊃ ⊂D⊃ ⊂E⊃
47 ⊂A⊃ ⊂B⊃ ⊂C⊃ ⊂D⊃ ⊂E⊃
48 ⊂A⊃ ⊂B⊃ ⊂C⊃ ⊂D⊃ ⊂E⊃
49 ⊂A⊃ ⊂B⊃ ⊂C⊃ ⊂D⊃ ⊂E⊃
50 ⊂A⊃ ⊂B⊃ ⊂C⊃ ⊂D⊃ ⊂E⊃
51 ⊂A⊃ ⊂B⊃ ⊂C⊃ ⊂D⊃ ⊂E⊃
52 ⊂A⊃ ⊂B⊃ ⊂C⊃ ⊂D⊃ ⊂E⊃
53 ⊂A⊃ ⊂B⊃ ⊂C⊃ ⊂D⊃ ⊂E⊃
54 ⊂A⊃ ⊂B⊃ ⊂C⊃ ⊂D⊃ ⊂E⊃
55 ⊂A⊃ ⊂B⊃ ⊂C⊃ ⊂D⊃ ⊂E⊃
56 ⊂A⊃ ⊂B⊃ ⊂C⊃ ⊂D⊃ ⊂E⊃
57 ⊂A⊃ ⊂B⊃ ⊂C⊃ ⊂D⊃ ⊂E⊃
58 ⊂A⊃ ⊂B⊃ ⊂C⊃ ⊂D⊃ ⊂E⊃
59 ⊂A⊃ ⊂B⊃ ⊂C⊃ ⊂D⊃ ⊂E⊃
60 ⊂A⊃ ⊂B⊃ ⊂C⊃ ⊂D⊃ ⊂E⊃

DO NOT MARK IN THIS AREA

⊂ ⊃ ⊂ ⊃ ⊂ ⊃ ⊂ ⊃ ⊂ ⊃ ⊂ ⊃ ⊂ ⊃ ⊂ ⊃ ⊂ ⊃ ⊂ ⊃ ⊂ ⊃ ⊂ ⊃

The Princeton Review®

1

YOUR NAME: (Print) _____ Last _____ First _____ M.I.

SIGNATURE: _____ DATE: ___/___/___

HOME ADDRESS: (Print) _____ Number and Street

_____ City _____ State _____ Zip Code

PHONE No.: (Print) _____

IMPORTANT: Please fill in these boxes exactly as shown on the back cover of your test book.

2. TEST FORM

6. DATE OF BIRTH

Month	Day	Year
⊂ ⊃ JAN		
⊂ ⊃ FEB		
⊂ ⊃ MAR	⊂0⊃ ⊂0⊃	⊂0⊃ ⊂0⊃
⊂ ⊃ APR	⊂1⊃ ⊂1⊃	⊂1⊃ ⊂1⊃
⊂ ⊃ MAY	⊂2⊃ ⊂2⊃	⊂2⊃ ⊂2⊃
⊂ ⊃ JUN	⊂3⊃ ⊂3⊃	⊂3⊃ ⊂3⊃
⊂ ⊃ JUL	⊂4⊃	⊂4⊃ ⊂4⊃
⊂ ⊃ AUG	⊂5⊃ ⊂5⊃	⊂5⊃
⊂ ⊃ SEP	⊂6⊃ ⊂6⊃	⊂6⊃
⊂ ⊃ OCT	⊂7⊃ ⊂7⊃	⊂7⊃
⊂ ⊃ NOV	⊂8⊃ ⊂8⊃	⊂8⊃
⊂ ⊃ DEC	⊂9⊃ ⊂9⊃	⊂9⊃

3. TEST CODE   4. REGISTRATION NUMBER

⊂0⊃	⊂A⊃	⊂0⊃	⊂0⊃	⊂0⊃	⊂0⊃	⊂0⊃	⊂0⊃	⊂0⊃	⊂0⊃	⊂0⊃
⊂1⊃	⊂B⊃	⊂1⊃	⊂1⊃	⊂1⊃	⊂1⊃	⊂1⊃	⊂1⊃	⊂1⊃	⊂1⊃	⊂1⊃
⊂2⊃	⊂C⊃	⊂2⊃	⊂2⊃	⊂2⊃	⊂2⊃	⊂2⊃	⊂2⊃	⊂2⊃	⊂2⊃	⊂2⊃
⊂3⊃	⊂D⊃	⊂3⊃	⊂3⊃	⊂3⊃	⊂3⊃	⊂3⊃	⊂3⊃	⊂3⊃	⊂3⊃	⊂3⊃
⊂4⊃	⊂E⊃	⊂4⊃	⊂4⊃	⊂4⊃	⊂4⊃	⊂4⊃	⊂4⊃	⊂4⊃	⊂4⊃	⊂4⊃
⊂5⊃	⊂F⊃	⊂5⊃	⊂5⊃	⊂5⊃	⊂5⊃	⊂5⊃	⊂5⊃	⊂5⊃	⊂5⊃	⊂5⊃
⊂6⊃	⊂G⊃	⊂6⊃	⊂6⊃	⊂6⊃	⊂6⊃	⊂6⊃	⊂6⊃	⊂6⊃	⊂6⊃	⊂6⊃
⊂7⊃		⊂7⊃	⊂7⊃	⊂7⊃	⊂7⊃	⊂7⊃	⊂7⊃	⊂7⊃	⊂7⊃	⊂7⊃
⊂8⊃		⊂8⊃	⊂8⊃	⊂8⊃	⊂8⊃	⊂8⊃	⊂8⊃	⊂8⊃	⊂8⊃	⊂8⊃
⊂9⊃		⊂9⊃	⊂9⊃	⊂9⊃	⊂9⊃	⊂9⊃	⊂9⊃	⊂9⊃	⊂9⊃	⊂9⊃

7. SEX
⊂ ⊃ MALE
⊂ ⊃ FEMALE

The Princeton Review®
© 2016 TPR Education IP Holdings, LLC.
FORM NO. 00001-PR

5. YOUR NAME

First 4 letters of last name				FIRST INIT	MID INIT
⊂A⊃	⊂A⊃	⊂A⊃	⊂A⊃	⊂A⊃	⊂A⊃
⊂B⊃	⊂B⊃	⊂B⊃	⊂B⊃	⊂B⊃	⊂B⊃
⊂C⊃	⊂C⊃	⊂C⊃	⊂C⊃	⊂C⊃	⊂C⊃
⊂D⊃	⊂D⊃	⊂D⊃	⊂D⊃	⊂D⊃	⊂D⊃
⊂E⊃	⊂E⊃	⊂E⊃	⊂E⊃	⊂E⊃	⊂E⊃
⊂F⊃	⊂F⊃	⊂F⊃	⊂F⊃	⊂F⊃	⊂F⊃
⊂G⊃	⊂G⊃	⊂G⊃	⊂G⊃	⊂G⊃	⊂G⊃
⊂H⊃	⊂H⊃	⊂H⊃	⊂H⊃	⊂H⊃	⊂H⊃
⊂I⊃	⊂I⊃	⊂I⊃	⊂I⊃	⊂I⊃	⊂I⊃
⊂J⊃	⊂J⊃	⊂J⊃	⊂J⊃	⊂J⊃	⊂J⊃
⊂K⊃	⊂K⊃	⊂K⊃	⊂K⊃	⊂K⊃	⊂K⊃
⊂L⊃	⊂L⊃	⊂L⊃	⊂L⊃	⊂L⊃	⊂L⊃
⊂M⊃	⊂M⊃	⊂M⊃	⊂M⊃	⊂M⊃	⊂M⊃
⊂N⊃	⊂N⊃	⊂N⊃	⊂N⊃	⊂N⊃	⊂N⊃
⊂O⊃	⊂O⊃	⊂O⊃	⊂O⊃	⊂O⊃	⊂O⊃
⊂P⊃	⊂P⊃	⊂P⊃	⊂P⊃	⊂P⊃	⊂P⊃
⊂Q⊃	⊂Q⊃	⊂Q⊃	⊂Q⊃	⊂Q⊃	⊂Q⊃
⊂R⊃	⊂R⊃	⊂R⊃	⊂R⊃	⊂R⊃	⊂R⊃
⊂S⊃	⊂S⊃	⊂S⊃	⊂S⊃	⊂S⊃	⊂S⊃
⊂T⊃	⊂T⊃	⊂T⊃	⊂T⊃	⊂T⊃	⊂T⊃
⊂U⊃	⊂U⊃	⊂U⊃	⊂U⊃	⊂U⊃	⊂U⊃
⊂V⊃	⊂V⊃	⊂V⊃	⊂V⊃	⊂V⊃	⊂V⊃
⊂W⊃	⊂W⊃	⊂W⊃	⊂W⊃	⊂W⊃	⊂W⊃
⊂X⊃	⊂X⊃	⊂X⊃	⊂X⊃	⊂X⊃	⊂X⊃
⊂Y⊃	⊂Y⊃	⊂Y⊃	⊂Y⊃	⊂Y⊃	⊂Y⊃
⊂Z⊃	⊂Z⊃	⊂Z⊃	⊂Z⊃	⊂Z⊃	⊂Z⊃

Start with number 1 for each new section. If a section has fewer questions than answer spaces, leave the extra answer spaces blank.

1 ⊂A⊃ ⊂B⊃ ⊂C⊃ ⊂D⊃ ⊂E⊃   21 ⊂A⊃ ⊂B⊃ ⊂C⊃ ⊂D⊃ ⊂E⊃   41 ⊂A⊃ ⊂B⊃ ⊂C⊃ ⊂D⊃ ⊂E⊃
2 ⊂A⊃ ⊂B⊃ ⊂C⊃ ⊂D⊃ ⊂E⊃   22 ⊂A⊃ ⊂B⊃ ⊂C⊃ ⊂D⊃ ⊂E⊃   42 ⊂A⊃ ⊂B⊃ ⊂C⊃ ⊂D⊃ ⊂E⊃
3 ⊂A⊃ ⊂B⊃ ⊂C⊃ ⊂D⊃ ⊂E⊃   23 ⊂A⊃ ⊂B⊃ ⊂C⊃ ⊂D⊃ ⊂E⊃   43 ⊂A⊃ ⊂B⊃ ⊂C⊃ ⊂D⊃ ⊂E⊃
4 ⊂A⊃ ⊂B⊃ ⊂C⊃ ⊂D⊃ ⊂E⊃   24 ⊂A⊃ ⊂B⊃ ⊂C⊃ ⊂D⊃ ⊂E⊃   44 ⊂A⊃ ⊂B⊃ ⊂C⊃ ⊂D⊃ ⊂E⊃
5 ⊂A⊃ ⊂B⊃ ⊂C⊃ ⊂D⊃ ⊂E⊃   25 ⊂A⊃ ⊂B⊃ ⊂C⊃ ⊂D⊃ ⊂E⊃   45 ⊂A⊃ ⊂B⊃ ⊂C⊃ ⊂D⊃ ⊂E⊃
6 ⊂A⊃ ⊂B⊃ ⊂C⊃ ⊂D⊃ ⊂E⊃   26 ⊂A⊃ ⊂B⊃ ⊂C⊃ ⊂D⊃ ⊂E⊃   46 ⊂A⊃ ⊂B⊃ ⊂C⊃ ⊂D⊃ ⊂E⊃
7 ⊂A⊃ ⊂B⊃ ⊂C⊃ ⊂D⊃ ⊂E⊃   27 ⊂A⊃ ⊂B⊃ ⊂C⊃ ⊂D⊃ ⊂E⊃   47 ⊂A⊃ ⊂B⊃ ⊂C⊃ ⊂D⊃ ⊂E⊃
8 ⊂A⊃ ⊂B⊃ ⊂C⊃ ⊂D⊃ ⊂E⊃   28 ⊂A⊃ ⊂B⊃ ⊂C⊃ ⊂D⊃ ⊂E⊃   48 ⊂A⊃ ⊂B⊃ ⊂C⊃ ⊂D⊃ ⊂E⊃
9 ⊂A⊃ ⊂B⊃ ⊂C⊃ ⊂D⊃ ⊂E⊃   29 ⊂A⊃ ⊂B⊃ ⊂C⊃ ⊂D⊃ ⊂E⊃   49 ⊂A⊃ ⊂B⊃ ⊂C⊃ ⊂D⊃ ⊂E⊃
10 ⊂A⊃ ⊂B⊃ ⊂C⊃ ⊂D⊃ ⊂E⊃   30 ⊂A⊃ ⊂B⊃ ⊂C⊃ ⊂D⊃ ⊂E⊃   50 ⊂A⊃ ⊂B⊃ ⊂C⊃ ⊂D⊃ ⊂E⊃
11 ⊂A⊃ ⊂B⊃ ⊂C⊃ ⊂D⊃ ⊂E⊃   31 ⊂A⊃ ⊂B⊃ ⊂C⊃ ⊂D⊃ ⊂E⊃   51 ⊂A⊃ ⊂B⊃ ⊂C⊃ ⊂D⊃ ⊂E⊃
12 ⊂A⊃ ⊂B⊃ ⊂C⊃ ⊂D⊃ ⊂E⊃   32 ⊂A⊃ ⊂B⊃ ⊂C⊃ ⊂D⊃ ⊂E⊃   52 ⊂A⊃ ⊂B⊃ ⊂C⊃ ⊂D⊃ ⊂E⊃
13 ⊂A⊃ ⊂B⊃ ⊂C⊃ ⊂D⊃ ⊂E⊃   33 ⊂A⊃ ⊂B⊃ ⊂C⊃ ⊂D⊃ ⊂E⊃   53 ⊂A⊃ ⊂B⊃ ⊂C⊃ ⊂D⊃ ⊂E⊃
14 ⊂A⊃ ⊂B⊃ ⊂C⊃ ⊂D⊃ ⊂E⊃   34 ⊂A⊃ ⊂B⊃ ⊂C⊃ ⊂D⊃ ⊂E⊃   54 ⊂A⊃ ⊂B⊃ ⊂C⊃ ⊂D⊃ ⊂E⊃
15 ⊂A⊃ ⊂B⊃ ⊂C⊃ ⊂D⊃ ⊂E⊃   35 ⊂A⊃ ⊂B⊃ ⊂C⊃ ⊂D⊃ ⊂E⊃   55 ⊂A⊃ ⊂B⊃ ⊂C⊃ ⊂D⊃ ⊂E⊃
16 ⊂A⊃ ⊂B⊃ ⊂C⊃ ⊂D⊃ ⊂E⊃   36 ⊂A⊃ ⊂B⊃ ⊂C⊃ ⊂D⊃ ⊂E⊃   56 ⊂A⊃ ⊂B⊃ ⊂C⊃ ⊂D⊃ ⊂E⊃
17 ⊂A⊃ ⊂B⊃ ⊂C⊃ ⊂D⊃ ⊂E⊃   37 ⊂A⊃ ⊂B⊃ ⊂C⊃ ⊂D⊃ ⊂E⊃   57 ⊂A⊃ ⊂B⊃ ⊂C⊃ ⊂D⊃ ⊂E⊃
18 ⊂A⊃ ⊂B⊃ ⊂C⊃ ⊂D⊃ ⊂E⊃   38 ⊂A⊃ ⊂B⊃ ⊂C⊃ ⊂D⊃ ⊂E⊃   58 ⊂A⊃ ⊂B⊃ ⊂C⊃ ⊂D⊃ ⊂E⊃
19 ⊂A⊃ ⊂B⊃ ⊂C⊃ ⊂D⊃ ⊂E⊃   39 ⊂A⊃ ⊂B⊃ ⊂C⊃ ⊂D⊃ ⊂E⊃   59 ⊂A⊃ ⊂B⊃ ⊂C⊃ ⊂D⊃ ⊂E⊃
20 ⊂A⊃ ⊂B⊃ ⊂C⊃ ⊂D⊃ ⊂E⊃   40 ⊂A⊃ ⊂B⊃ ⊂C⊃ ⊂D⊃ ⊂E⊃   60 ⊂A⊃ ⊂B⊃ ⊂C⊃ ⊂D⊃ ⊂E⊃

DO NOT MARK IN THIS AREA
⊂ ⊃ ⊂ ⊃ ⊂ ⊃ ⊂ ⊃ ⊂ ⊃ ⊂ ⊃ ⊂ ⊃ ⊂ ⊃ ⊂ ⊃ ⊂ ⊃ ⊂ ⊃

1

YOUR NAME: _____
(Print)   Last   First   M.I.

SIGNATURE: _____ DATE: ___ / ___ / ___

HOME ADDRESS: _____
(Print)   Number and Street

_____
City   State   Zip Code

PHONE No.: _____
(Print)

IMPORTANT: Please fill in these boxes exactly as shown on the back cover of your test book.

2. TEST FORM

_____

6. DATE OF BIRTH

Month	Day	Year
⊂ ⊃ JAN		
⊂ ⊃ FEB		
⊂ ⊃ MAR	⊂0⊃ ⊂0⊃	⊂0⊃ ⊂0⊃
⊂ ⊃ APR	⊂1⊃ ⊂1⊃	⊂1⊃ ⊂1⊃
⊂ ⊃ MAY	⊂2⊃ ⊂2⊃	⊂2⊃ ⊂2⊃
⊂ ⊃ JUN	⊂3⊃ ⊂3⊃	⊂3⊃ ⊂3⊃
⊂ ⊃ JUL	⊂4⊃	⊂4⊃ ⊂4⊃
⊂ ⊃ AUG	⊂5⊃	⊂5⊃ ⊂5⊃
⊂ ⊃ SEP	⊂6⊃	⊂6⊃ ⊂6⊃
⊂ ⊃ OCT	⊂7⊃	⊂7⊃ ⊂7⊃
⊂ ⊃ NOV	⊂8⊃	⊂8⊃ ⊂8⊃
⊂ ⊃ DEC	⊂9⊃	⊂9⊃ ⊂9⊃

3. TEST CODE   **4. REGISTRATION NUMBER**

⊂0⊃	⊂A⊃	⊂0⊃	⊂0⊃	⊂0⊃	⊂0⊃	⊂0⊃	⊂0⊃	⊂0⊃	⊂0⊃	⊂0⊃
⊂1⊃	⊂B⊃	⊂1⊃	⊂1⊃	⊂1⊃	⊂1⊃	⊂1⊃	⊂1⊃	⊂1⊃	⊂1⊃	⊂1⊃
⊂2⊃	⊂C⊃	⊂2⊃	⊂2⊃	⊂2⊃	⊂2⊃	⊂2⊃	⊂2⊃	⊂2⊃	⊂2⊃	⊂2⊃
⊂3⊃	⊂D⊃	⊂3⊃	⊂3⊃	⊂3⊃	⊂3⊃	⊂3⊃	⊂3⊃	⊂3⊃	⊂3⊃	⊂3⊃
⊂4⊃	⊂E⊃	⊂4⊃	⊂4⊃	⊂4⊃	⊂4⊃	⊂4⊃	⊂4⊃	⊂4⊃	⊂4⊃	⊂4⊃
⊂5⊃	⊂F⊃	⊂5⊃	⊂5⊃	⊂5⊃	⊂5⊃	⊂5⊃	⊂5⊃	⊂5⊃	⊂5⊃	⊂5⊃
⊂6⊃	⊂G⊃	⊂6⊃	⊂6⊃	⊂6⊃	⊂6⊃	⊂6⊃	⊂6⊃	⊂6⊃	⊂6⊃	⊂6⊃
⊂7⊃		⊂7⊃	⊂7⊃	⊂7⊃	⊂7⊃	⊂7⊃	⊂7⊃	⊂7⊃	⊂7⊃	⊂7⊃
⊂8⊃		⊂8⊃	⊂8⊃	⊂8⊃	⊂8⊃	⊂8⊃	⊂8⊃	⊂8⊃	⊂8⊃	⊂8⊃
⊂9⊃		⊂9⊃	⊂9⊃	⊂9⊃	⊂9⊃	⊂9⊃	⊂9⊃	⊂9⊃	⊂9⊃	⊂9⊃

7. SEX
⊂ ⊃ MALE
⊂ ⊃ FEMALE

© 2016 TPR Education IP Holdings, LLC.
FORM NO. 00001-PR

5. YOUR NAME

First 4 letters of last name				FIRST INIT	MID INIT
⊂A⊃	⊂A⊃	⊂A⊃	⊂A⊃	⊂A⊃	⊂A⊃
⊂B⊃	⊂B⊃	⊂B⊃	⊂B⊃	⊂B⊃	⊂B⊃
⊂C⊃	⊂C⊃	⊂C⊃	⊂C⊃	⊂C⊃	⊂C⊃
⊂D⊃	⊂D⊃	⊂D⊃	⊂D⊃	⊂D⊃	⊂D⊃
⊂E⊃	⊂E⊃	⊂E⊃	⊂E⊃	⊂E⊃	⊂E⊃
⊂F⊃	⊂F⊃	⊂F⊃	⊂F⊃	⊂F⊃	⊂F⊃
⊂G⊃	⊂G⊃	⊂G⊃	⊂G⊃	⊂G⊃	⊂G⊃
⊂H⊃	⊂H⊃	⊂H⊃	⊂H⊃	⊂H⊃	⊂H⊃
⊂I⊃	⊂I⊃	⊂I⊃	⊂I⊃	⊂I⊃	⊂I⊃
⊂J⊃	⊂J⊃	⊂J⊃	⊂J⊃	⊂J⊃	⊂J⊃
⊂K⊃	⊂K⊃	⊂K⊃	⊂K⊃	⊂K⊃	⊂K⊃
⊂L⊃	⊂L⊃	⊂L⊃	⊂L⊃	⊂L⊃	⊂L⊃
⊂M⊃	⊂M⊃	⊂M⊃	⊂M⊃	⊂M⊃	⊂M⊃
⊂N⊃	⊂N⊃	⊂N⊃	⊂N⊃	⊂N⊃	⊂N⊃
⊂O⊃	⊂O⊃	⊂O⊃	⊂O⊃	⊂O⊃	⊂O⊃
⊂P⊃	⊂P⊃	⊂P⊃	⊂P⊃	⊂P⊃	⊂P⊃
⊂Q⊃	⊂Q⊃	⊂Q⊃	⊂Q⊃	⊂Q⊃	⊂Q⊃
⊂R⊃	⊂R⊃	⊂R⊃	⊂R⊃	⊂R⊃	⊂R⊃
⊂S⊃	⊂S⊃	⊂S⊃	⊂S⊃	⊂S⊃	⊂S⊃
⊂T⊃	⊂T⊃	⊂T⊃	⊂T⊃	⊂T⊃	⊂T⊃
⊂U⊃	⊂U⊃	⊂U⊃	⊂U⊃	⊂U⊃	⊂U⊃
⊂V⊃	⊂V⊃	⊂V⊃	⊂V⊃	⊂V⊃	⊂V⊃
⊂W⊃	⊂W⊃	⊂W⊃	⊂W⊃	⊂W⊃	⊂W⊃
⊂X⊃	⊂X⊃	⊂X⊃	⊂X⊃	⊂X⊃	⊂X⊃
⊂Y⊃	⊂Y⊃	⊂Y⊃	⊂Y⊃	⊂Y⊃	⊂Y⊃
⊂Z⊃	⊂Z⊃	⊂Z⊃	⊂Z⊃	⊂Z⊃	⊂Z⊃

Start with number 1 for each new section. If a section has fewer questions than answer spaces, leave the extra answer spaces blank.

1 ⊂A⊃ ⊂B⊃ ⊂C⊃ ⊂D⊃ ⊂E⊃   21 ⊂A⊃ ⊂B⊃ ⊂C⊃ ⊂D⊃ ⊂E⊃   41 ⊂A⊃ ⊂B⊃ ⊂C⊃ ⊂D⊃ ⊂E⊃
2 ⊂A⊃ ⊂B⊃ ⊂C⊃ ⊂D⊃ ⊂E⊃   22 ⊂A⊃ ⊂B⊃ ⊂C⊃ ⊂D⊃ ⊂E⊃   42 ⊂A⊃ ⊂B⊃ ⊂C⊃ ⊂D⊃ ⊂E⊃
3 ⊂A⊃ ⊂B⊃ ⊂C⊃ ⊂D⊃ ⊂E⊃   23 ⊂A⊃ ⊂B⊃ ⊂C⊃ ⊂D⊃ ⊂E⊃   43 ⊂A⊃ ⊂B⊃ ⊂C⊃ ⊂D⊃ ⊂E⊃
4 ⊂A⊃ ⊂B⊃ ⊂C⊃ ⊂D⊃ ⊂E⊃   24 ⊂A⊃ ⊂B⊃ ⊂C⊃ ⊂D⊃ ⊂E⊃   44 ⊂A⊃ ⊂B⊃ ⊂C⊃ ⊂D⊃ ⊂E⊃
5 ⊂A⊃ ⊂B⊃ ⊂C⊃ ⊂D⊃ ⊂E⊃   25 ⊂A⊃ ⊂B⊃ ⊂C⊃ ⊂D⊃ ⊂E⊃   45 ⊂A⊃ ⊂B⊃ ⊂C⊃ ⊂D⊃ ⊂E⊃
6 ⊂A⊃ ⊂B⊃ ⊂C⊃ ⊂D⊃ ⊂E⊃   26 ⊂A⊃ ⊂B⊃ ⊂C⊃ ⊂D⊃ ⊂E⊃   46 ⊂A⊃ ⊂B⊃ ⊂C⊃ ⊂D⊃ ⊂E⊃
7 ⊂A⊃ ⊂B⊃ ⊂C⊃ ⊂D⊃ ⊂E⊃   27 ⊂A⊃ ⊂B⊃ ⊂C⊃ ⊂D⊃ ⊂E⊃   47 ⊂A⊃ ⊂B⊃ ⊂C⊃ ⊂D⊃ ⊂E⊃
8 ⊂A⊃ ⊂B⊃ ⊂C⊃ ⊂D⊃ ⊂E⊃   28 ⊂A⊃ ⊂B⊃ ⊂C⊃ ⊂D⊃ ⊂E⊃   48 ⊂A⊃ ⊂B⊃ ⊂C⊃ ⊂D⊃ ⊂E⊃
9 ⊂A⊃ ⊂B⊃ ⊂C⊃ ⊂D⊃ ⊂E⊃   29 ⊂A⊃ ⊂B⊃ ⊂C⊃ ⊂D⊃ ⊂E⊃   49 ⊂A⊃ ⊂B⊃ ⊂C⊃ ⊂D⊃ ⊂E⊃
10 ⊂A⊃ ⊂B⊃ ⊂C⊃ ⊂D⊃ ⊂E⊃   30 ⊂A⊃ ⊂B⊃ ⊂C⊃ ⊂D⊃ ⊂E⊃   50 ⊂A⊃ ⊂B⊃ ⊂C⊃ ⊂D⊃ ⊂E⊃
11 ⊂A⊃ ⊂B⊃ ⊂C⊃ ⊂D⊃ ⊂E⊃   31 ⊂A⊃ ⊂B⊃ ⊂C⊃ ⊂D⊃ ⊂E⊃   51 ⊂A⊃ ⊂B⊃ ⊂C⊃ ⊂D⊃ ⊂E⊃
12 ⊂A⊃ ⊂B⊃ ⊂C⊃ ⊂D⊃ ⊂E⊃   32 ⊂A⊃ ⊂B⊃ ⊂C⊃ ⊂D⊃ ⊂E⊃   52 ⊂A⊃ ⊂B⊃ ⊂C⊃ ⊂D⊃ ⊂E⊃
13 ⊂A⊃ ⊂B⊃ ⊂C⊃ ⊂D⊃ ⊂E⊃   33 ⊂A⊃ ⊂B⊃ ⊂C⊃ ⊂D⊃ ⊂E⊃   53 ⊂A⊃ ⊂B⊃ ⊂C⊃ ⊂D⊃ ⊂E⊃
14 ⊂A⊃ ⊂B⊃ ⊂C⊃ ⊂D⊃ ⊂E⊃   34 ⊂A⊃ ⊂B⊃ ⊂C⊃ ⊂D⊃ ⊂E⊃   54 ⊂A⊃ ⊂B⊃ ⊂C⊃ ⊂D⊃ ⊂E⊃
15 ⊂A⊃ ⊂B⊃ ⊂C⊃ ⊂D⊃ ⊂E⊃   35 ⊂A⊃ ⊂B⊃ ⊂C⊃ ⊂D⊃ ⊂E⊃   55 ⊂A⊃ ⊂B⊃ ⊂C⊃ ⊂D⊃ ⊂E⊃
16 ⊂A⊃ ⊂B⊃ ⊂C⊃ ⊂D⊃ ⊂E⊃   36 ⊂A⊃ ⊂B⊃ ⊂C⊃ ⊂D⊃ ⊂E⊃   56 ⊂A⊃ ⊂B⊃ ⊂C⊃ ⊂D⊃ ⊂E⊃
17 ⊂A⊃ ⊂B⊃ ⊂C⊃ ⊂D⊃ ⊂E⊃   37 ⊂A⊃ ⊂B⊃ ⊂C⊃ ⊂D⊃ ⊂E⊃   57 ⊂A⊃ ⊂B⊃ ⊂C⊃ ⊂D⊃ ⊂E⊃
18 ⊂A⊃ ⊂B⊃ ⊂C⊃ ⊂D⊃ ⊂E⊃   38 ⊂A⊃ ⊂B⊃ ⊂C⊃ ⊂D⊃ ⊂E⊃   58 ⊂A⊃ ⊂B⊃ ⊂C⊃ ⊂D⊃ ⊂E⊃
19 ⊂A⊃ ⊂B⊃ ⊂C⊃ ⊂D⊃ ⊂E⊃   39 ⊂A⊃ ⊂B⊃ ⊂C⊃ ⊂D⊃ ⊂E⊃   59 ⊂A⊃ ⊂B⊃ ⊂C⊃ ⊂D⊃ ⊂E⊃
20 ⊂A⊃ ⊂B⊃ ⊂C⊃ ⊂D⊃ ⊂E⊃   40 ⊂A⊃ ⊂B⊃ ⊂C⊃ ⊂D⊃ ⊂E⊃   60 ⊂A⊃ ⊂B⊃ ⊂C⊃ ⊂D⊃ ⊂E⊃

NOTES

NOTES

NOTES